A PLUME BOOK

WHAT EVERY AMERICAN SHOULD KNOW ABOUT EUROPE

MELISSA ROSSI is an award-winning journalist who has written articles for *Newsweek*, *National Geographic Traveler*, *Newsday*, *Esquire*, *George*, MSNBC, the *New York Observer*, and the *London Times*. She has written extensively about Europe, Asia, and the Middle East, and has lived abroad for many years.

ALSO BY MELISSA ROSSI

*What Every American Should Know
About the Rest of the World*

*What Every American Should Know
About Who's Really Running the World*

WHAT EVERY AMERICAN SHOULD KNOW ABOUT EUROPE

The Hot Spots, Hotshots, Political Muck-ups, Cross-Border
Sniping, and Cultural Chaos of Our Transatlantic Cousins

Melissa Rossi

A PLUME BOOK

PLUME
Published by Penguin Group
Penguin Group (USA) Inc., 375 Hudson Street, New York, New York 10014, U.S.A.
Penguin Group (Canada), 90 Eglinton Avenue East, Suite 700, Toronto, Ontario,
Canada M4P 2Y3 (a division of Pearson Penguin Canada Inc.)
Penguin Books Ltd., 80 Strand, London WC2R 0RL, England
Penguin Ireland, 25 St. Stephen's Green, Dublin 2, Ireland (a division of Penguin Books Ltd.)
Penguin Group (Australia), 250 Camberwell Road, Camberwell, Victoria 3124, Australia
(a division of Pearson Australia Group Pty. Ltd.)
Penguin Books India Pvt. Ltd., 11 Community Centre, Panchsheel Park,
New Delhi – 110 017, India
Penguin Books (NZ), cnr Airborne and Rosedale Roads, Albany, Auckland 1310, New Zealand
(a division of Pearson New Zealand Ltd.)
Penguin Books (South Africa) (Pty.) Ltd., 24 Sturdee Avenue, Rosebank, Johannesburg 2196,
South Africa

Penguin Books Ltd., Registered Offices: 80 Strand, London WC2R 0RL, England

Published by Plume, a member of Penguin Group (USA) Inc. Originally published in Great
Britain by Penguin Books Ltd. in different form as *The Armchair Diplomat on Europe*.

First American Printing, December 2006
10 9 8 7 6 5 4 3 2 1

Map design, pp. 7–390, by Karl Abramovich. Template: CIA's *World Factbook*.

℗ REGISTERED TRADEMARK—MARCA REGISTRADA

LIBRARY OF CONGRESS CATALOGING-IN-PUBLICATION DATA

Rossi, M. L. (Melissa L.), 1965–

   What every American should know about Europe : the hot spots, hotshots, political muck-
ups, cross-border sniping, and cultural chaos of our transatlantic cousins / by Melissa Rossi.

   p. cm.

Includes bibliographical references and index.

ISBN 0-452-28776-6

1. Europe—Civilization.   2. Europe—History.   3. Europe—Description and travel.
I. Title.

D1055.R59 2006

940—dc22

                                                                    2006024070

Printed in the United States of America
Set in Helvetica and Grotesque Black

To all those who long to see life on the other side
of the Atlantic, with the hopes that their
dreams are realized

Acknowledgments

This book was made possible due to the kindness of thousands of Europeans who took me out, put me up, put up with me, and rarely let me down in assorted corners of the continent. Whether they were offering their guest rooms, inviting me to dinners, teaching me languages, hauling my camel caravan's worth of luggage, helping me find lodging, telling me jokes, or offering insights on living in their countries, so many total strangers enlightened me and made my life so sweet that Europe feels like a second home. Particularly, I will be eternally grateful to Miss Laura Milan of Milan for diligent research; Roxanne Rowles for scathing insights; Sophie Cotter for digging up info and photos; Katherine Dunn for being the most gracious person on the planet; Melik "The Research God" Boudemagh for all-purpose brilliance; Anne Pramaggiore and the Pramaggiore clan for fab vacations; Karl Abramovic for his fine maps; Sarah Jane Kincaid and Enrique García Lozano for rushing my coffee-drenched laptop to the computer doctor; Erin and Marcello for Florentine nights on the Duomo-hugging terrace; Sarah and Nancy Jenkins for amazing dinners in the Tuscan countryside; my husband from another life, Stefano Bemer, who always hit the nail on the head (while crafting his world-famous shoes); Eva, Max, Marina, Sofia, and Bill for opening the doors to foreign lands; Latvian president Vaira Vike-Freiberga and her assistant Aiva Rozenberga for welcoming me to the presidential castle; Estonian prime minister Juhan Parts and his assistants for meeting with me in Tallinn; fashion designer Asnate Smeltere and artists Ritums Ivanovs and Andris Vitolins for showing me Riga; Lee Anthony Courchesne for opening up Barcelona's multicultural magnet Andu; Anne Millereau for (amazingly) making Brussels fun; *National Geographic Traveler* for sending me across all corners of Europe; *Newsweek* for eye-opening assignments; Catherine and Sam Couplan for Monday night dance-a-thons; Krasny, the sexiest DJ at "The Nest"; Philippe Herzog and Gypsy for all-night Parisian tours; Ricky Burdett, Christina Roosen, Luis Afonso, master musician "Don G," puppeteer PJ and Mifalda of Portugal for astute insights; Davil for showing me Denmark despite my shared nationality with Danny Kaye; Peter Lemeer in Maastricht, who helped put together the pieces of the puzzle; the particularly helpful tourism boards of Spain, the Netherlands, Hungary, and Belgium, and all European tourism boards (except for those in Britain and France) who kindly donated pictures;

the thousands of Europeans whom I interviewed on planes, trains, and in bars and cafés; the many politicians and academic sorts who provided invaluable info; Plume production editor Lavina Lee for overseeing a million important details and, with production queen Norina Frabotta, transforming this from a mountain of words to a physical book; Eve Kirch for her brilliant layout design; Melissa Jacoby for the great cover; Lily Kosner for organizing a mass of photos; Plume's visionary leader Trena Keating and my inspirational editor Emily Haynes for bringing this out in the U.S.; and, as always, a deep thanks to my agent Bill Gladstone (and his accountant Maureen Maloney) for perpetual optimism and his modern-day Marshall Plan.

Contents

WHAT EVERY AMERICAN SHOULD KNOW ABOUT EUROPE

0   200   400 miles
0   200   400 kilometres

RUSSIA

FINLAND

Helsinki

★Tallinn
ESTONIA

★Moscow

LATVIA
Riga★

LITHUANIA
Vilnius★   Minsk★

KALININGRAD
RUSSIA

BELARUS

KAZAKHSTAN

Warsaw
★

★Kiev

ND

UKRAINE

OVAKIA

★Budapest

MOLDOVA
Kishinev★

ARY

ROMANIA

Belgrade
★

Bucharest
★

Caspian Sea

Black Sea

GEORGIA
AZERBAIJAN

SERBIA &
ONTENEGRO

★Sofia

ARMENIA

BULGARIA

MAC.

TURKEY

ALBANIA

TURKEY

GREECE

IRAN

Athens★

SYRIA

CYPRUS

CRETE

LEBANON

IRAQ

Map design: Karl Abramovich

Introduction

I was born in Dayton, Ohio. When people asked what I wanted to do when I grew up, the answer was always the same: "Move!" My answer invariably provoked the same response from Daytonians: "Why move? Life's the same everywhere."

After spending the better part of two decades hopscotching across the planet, I can say with great confidence in the direction of that capital of suburban ennui: "You're wrong!" Life amid the olive trees and vineyards of Tuscany is not the same as life in windmill-happy Holland, where the masses still bicycle to work. Life in party town Barcelona is not the same as life in Budapest, where depression seems to hover like a permanent cloud. The oh-so-polite Brits are not the same as the charmingly gruff French; thoughtful Swedes are not the same as shy Portuguese; Germans are just not the same as, well, anybody else. Europe is entirely different from the United States, where culture is more or less homogenous from state to state. Europe is different not only from country to country but from region to region. In Europe, you need only move thirty miles to have a dialect change and a totally different take on cuisine.

And, as you are about to discover, Europe is at the most curious moment of her history. Certainly there have been more violent times, when emperors, kings, and knights launched battles and wars that left the ground blood-soaked and scorched. There have been more volatile eras, when ideas and ideals brewed up revolutions that had heads rolling in the streets. And there have been more repressed periods, as when half the continent was forced into Communism and the other half turned its back and tried to forget. But at least for most of European history, you could point at what was Europe and what wasn't.

> *Eight of the ten countries that came into the European Union in 2004 were Communist for over four decades after the Second World War; seven of those were Soviet republics or satellites.*

Now, thanks to recent political changes, the image of "The Continent" has been revamped: Europe now stretches to Cyprus, which dangles forty miles from Syria, but somehow currently skips Turkey, which lies along the way; Romania and Bulgaria are part of it geographically at least, but it often excludes

Russia, Moldova, and the Ukraine. It apparently extends nearly to Africa since it now includes Malta, but Britons debate whether the western-flung United Kingdom is really even part of Europe anymore, or if she ever was.

What's changed is there's now a strong push to shove Europe into one entity: the European Union, a "supranational umbrella government" that in some ways treats its twenty-five member countries like states. The EU can make laws, which member countries are supposed to adopt, but the biggest draws to EU membership—and the reasons it expanded from fourteen members in 1994 to twenty-five members a decade later—are the economic lures and the fact that the EU can increase profitability for all member nations. For one thing, the EU (with 455 million residents) can act as a powerful bloc that can at least try to rival the U.S. Member countries pay dues according to their GDP and redistribute the wealth; poorer countries can access many billions of dollars' worth of funding to bring them closer to the EU norm. Despite their language differences, historical grudges, and divergent personalities, EU countries trade without tariffs, limit production of competing goods, and engage in multicountry economic ventures, such as the hugely successful Airbus (a joint production of France, Germany, the UK, and Spain). The EU also introduced a common currency in 2002: the euro, now stronger than the dollar. Currently used by twelve EU countries, and in the future (theoretically) to be adopted by all, the euro has negated the need for trading in Italian lira for French francs, or Dutch guilders for Spanish pesetas every time you cross a border. In fact, traveling in Europe is a bizarrely different experience since the EU lifted most border guards. Where you once spent hours being stopped by passport control, you now just zip across the boundaries with little to notify you that the language and country just changed except for small "Welcome" signs. And EU residents (at least those in Western Europe) can resettle and take jobs in other EU countries without hassle. Londoners can easily work in Madrid, Romans can set up in Paris, and Danes can move to Berlin without going through mountains of paperwork.

> *Not all of Europe is in the EU. In Western Europe, Norway and Switzerland decline membership, and only eight countries from Eastern Europe are now in. This book covers only those countries that are in the EU as of June 2006.*

So much has changed so quickly in Europe that most Europeans, be they Lithuanians or Luxembourgers, can't keep up. Many Europeans can't tell you which countries are among those in the EU. They have an image of the European Union as little more than a money machine in Brussels that dumps a mountain of euros out of a slot. And they still seem somewhat perplexed at the EU's ongoing enlargement, which saw ten new countries enter in 2004—and has countries such as Romania, Bulgaria, and Turkey preparing to someday join up. The Europeans' confusion about the current status of Europe is what prompted me to write this book in the first place as *The Armchair Diplomat on Europe* (Penguin UK, 2005).

> *Until recently, most people in EU member countries regarded the European Union as a topic more boring than taxes, the understanding of which was as daunting as unraveling a DNA molecule. "The EU doesn't affect me," Europeans said with a shrug, while the EU was passing laws about everything: the types of food that Europeans eat, how it is cultivated, and how much Europeans pay for it; what power source fuels European electricity; the airlines, ships, and lorries that enter European countries; property sales to foreigners; and how minorities are treated.*

My American editors at Plume surprised me when they wanted a version of *The Armchair Diplomat* for the U.S. This book is updated, shortened, and Americanized, though it's still thick with European history and culture that we rarely learn in school. Although Americans tend to view Europe as little more than an oversize Disneyland, brimming with wine, cheese, and handsome devils with exotic accents, Europe is more than simply a vacation destination full of castles, kings, and antiquities. Europe as a whole is a huge trading partner with the U.S.—we swap over $1 billion in goods and services every day with France alone—and her stable, democratic, industrialized countries are the ones most similar to ours on the planet. Europe is where most of our ancestors came from, and it was the birthplace of many of the ideals we hold dear, including democracy, inalienable rights to all, and freedom of religion.

There are differences, of course. Having pummeled itself nearly to death during two world wars, Europe is often more reluctant to engage in armed battle—although many European countries still require one year of military service for males. Western Europeans tend to have more "socialized" economies, with health care and low-cost drugs as part of the package—although many Europeans pay higher taxes than we do. Europeans have abolished the death penalty, and many look askance at the U.S. for continuing it. European cities tend to be pedestrian friendly and offer great public transport, lessening the need for cars, and Europeans, particularly the French and Italians, are obsessed with food, a topic they can talk about for hours. After centuries of religious wars—that at times killed a third of their populations—Europeans tend to be less religious than Americans, and they like to get into political debates. And even though their views toward the U.S. government have generally changed since George W. Bush rode in, they still are curious about us.

In short, Europe is anything but a snooze these days, and the next few years will either see Europe rise as a unified superpower or see it collapse and implode. In the pages that follow, you can glean insight into the players, the histories, the issues, and the dynamics involved in what is called "the greatest peacemaking project in history."[1]

Melissa Rossi

PART I

OLD EUROPE

INTRODUCTION

You can call it "Old Europe," you can call it "Western Europe and Greece," you can call it "the Europe Americans think of when they think of Europe." But whatever you call it, this is the energetic power center of Europe, the industrial heartland, and the population core of what is now the European Union.

OLD EUROPE

France:	Most land, most pushy, biggest food producer
Germany:	Most people, biggest economy, most anxious
United Kingdom:	Most aligned with U.S., least likely to use euro
Italy:	Most embarrassing ex-prime minister, best political soap opera
Belgium:	Most eurocratic: headquarters of EU and "capital of Europe"
Ireland:	Best example of how EU can turn a place around
Spain:	Most fun, highest unemployment rate
Portugal:	Most behind, highest illiteracy rate
The Netherlands:	Most tired of being ignored
Austria:	Most vehemently antinuclear, first to start immigration debate
Greece:	Most easterly, most tied up with Cyprus
Denmark:	Most surprising: anti-immigration, antieuro
Sweden:	Most likely to suffer mysterious political assassinations
Finland:	Most gung ho of Scandinavian countries about EU
Luxembourg:	Most joked about, also smallest and richest

EU-15 *is Eurocratese for the fifteen Western European countries that were part of the European Union prior to the 2004 enlargement to the east.*

A dense assemblage of diverse cultures, ethnicities, and languages, these are the nations that laid the foundations—roads, maps, religions, language, and sociopolitical ideas and governmental frameworks—for what Europe is today. These are the countries that kept alive the concept of an organized landmass for millennia, as the Roman Empire, Holy Roman Empire, Napoleonic Empire, Third Reich, or European Union.

> *Of all the EU-15 countries, only three don't use the euro: Britain, Denmark, and Sweden.*

And outside of occasional alliances, for most of history these nations have been sniping, taunting, clobbering, and slaughtering each other—doing it so well, in fact, that it took years and sometimes decades to put everything together again after military run-ins that sometimes lasted over a century. The Second World War took it to a new extreme: were the EU-15 to go through a more advanced version of that again, they might as well commit collective suicide.

These are now the richest, most developed countries of Europe—and they are among the most affluent in the world—for three reasons. They had a multibillion dollar loan from the United States in the form of the Marshall Plan to rebuild themselves after World War II, and they had sixty years to heal from the devastation—both physical and emotional—of that war. And in the course of re-creating themselves they devised a novel method to lessen the likelihood of so thoroughly destroying themselves again. Sharing resources, dividing power, creating an expanding trade market, and redistributing income, they cobbled together what would evolve into the EU.

> *Another factor that kept cohesion: shared military. While NATO served the purpose of militarily uniting most of these countries since the Second World War, new European military alliances are being created. The EU has its own forces, but some members are aligning separately.*

Even with most of Old Europe joined as a loose union that abides by the same trade rules and laws and (mostly) shares the same currency, these countries still occasionally bicker and snarl at each other, and there is plenty of discontent within the union. With growing skepticism within most EU member countries, who knows? The EU could unravel if certain countries decide to back out. Without EU membership, however, countries risk being a lone weak voice against a united whole.

In 2004, with most of Western Europe linked together as part of the EU, the EU opened the door to the East for a number of reasons. But while it welcomes the new states, the EU hasn't yet welcomed its workers. Citizens of the ten new EU countries cannot legally work in most EU-15 countries until 2012.

WHY WESTERN EUROPE OPENED THE DOOR TO THE EAST

- Create a political-socioeconomic power that can rival the U.S.
- Take advantage of cheap labor
- Increase available resources
- Expand market and foreign-investment opportunities
- Stabilize Europe and keep it from warring
- Minimize risk of Russia again moving west
- Expand strategic influence
- Guilt

The hesitation among EU-15 countries to allow the new EU countries' workers to enter hints at the most looming problem for all of Western Europe at the moment: immigration. While new workers are indeed needed, increasingly powerful groups have risen in many countries, questioning the social impact of foreigners living in their lands. And while many countries are now shutting the door, they will not be able to do so forever.

In the meantime, Old Europe finds itself at the most interesting, complicated, and intense moment of its history: never before has there been such a massive, voluntary union of this sort across Europe. U.S. Secretary of Defense Donald Rumsfeld used the term "Old Europe" to signify a rusty, decaying Europe, but the poor man was misguided. For all the stresses involved in stitching together most of Europe in an "ever-closer union," the end result is a reinvigoration of both old and new.

1. FRANCE
(La République Française)
The Trendsetter

FAST FACTS

Country:	French Republic; La République Française
Capital:	Paris
Government:	Republic
Independence:	486 (unified by Clovis)
Population:	60,657,000 (July 2005 estimate)
Head of State:	President Jacques Chirac (1995)
Head of Government:	Prime Minister Dominique de Villepin (2005)
Elections:	President elected by universal suffrage for five-year term; prime minister nominated by House of Representatives
Name of Parliament:	Assemblée Nationale
Ethnicity:	Exact percentages not known: government not allowed to ask ethnicity

Religion:	83% Roman Catholic; 10% Muslim; 2% Protestant; 1% Jewish (estimated)
Language:	French (but of course)
Literacy:	99% (estimated)
Famous Exports:	Christian Dior, Coco Chanel, L'Oréal
Economic Big Boy:	Total (oil and gas); 2004 total sales: $131.64 billion[1]
Per Capita GDP:	$29,900 purchasing power parity (2005 estimate)
Unemployment:	9.2% (January 2006 Eurostat figure)
Percentage in Poverty:	6.5% (2000 estimate)
EU Status:	Founding member (EEC member since 1957)
Currency:	Euro

Quick Tour

Synonymous with silky wines, glossy chocolates, and thick, buttery accents, France is all wrapped up with food. Whether it's cheese bursting out of the rind, a chewy baguette spread with pâté, or duck-rich cassoulet, the art-on-the-plate that's made to consume is as integral to La République Française as fashion and perfume.

THE FRENCH PARADOX

Is it the flaky croissant, the stone houses amid lavender fields, the location nudged against an ocean, two seas, or the Alps that draws 75 million foreigners to France every year? Is it the history of the cliff-perched castles, glittering Versailles, the marble-tabled cafés where creators once tipped back absinthe, or the lure of haute cuisine and haute couture and the perfume houses that beckon with scents pressed from flowers? Is it the romance that bubbles from the ground, the stylish culture that surrounds or the happy sounds of the lilting *bonjour* and *merci*? The symbols of France are well stamped in the mind, but who really knows what France really is, except an ephemeral, sometimes playful, sometimes grumpy geographical state of mind that is perhaps best defined with a smug shrug? From the palm tree–lined Riviera to snow-dusted Mont Blanc, France is a contradiction, a moody artist of a nation that creates vibrant masterpieces, then dwells in dark conspiracy theories; a popular bon vivant who rarely appears to have fun; a thinker who triggers ideological revolutions but never fathoms contentment; a country that swells with nationalistic pride but whose people identify most with their regions, plenty of which want to secede. The country that penned Europe's first declaration of human rights was one of the world's most brutal colonizers; the nation that loudly demands responsible international action is tainted by shady backroom deals; the people who dish out criticism of everyone else are secretly sensitive and easily wounded. Even while complaining that their country is declining, the French so adore France and her lifestyle that they rebel every time any privilege is whittled away, even if it's for the nation's own good. But like a distant lover whose mannerisms and smells are alluring, but whose true thoughts are rarely revealed, the appeal of France is her moody mystique and inimitable style, which, along with the omnipresent culture and history that seep in from every corner, keep the romance with France alive, and the tourists coming back for yet another fling.

One thing you can count on in France: the chitchat soon turns to cuisine. Little wonder the French are obsessed: fishing villages strung along rocky shores, oyster beds along an inland sea, blossoming fruit orchards, silvery olive groves, lush vineyards, and swaying fields of grain assure mouth-watering variety in France's open-air markets and megagrocery stores. More edibles push up and plump out in France than in any other country outside the U.S. With over half of French land devoted to farming, agriculture yields over $31 billion per year, and nearly a quarter of European Union food originates here. And French fare—whether savored in swanky restaurants or in black-and-white tiled bistros, whether the glazed confections in patisseries or the dusted loaves in *boulangeries*, or whether found in these tiny stores that reek of pungent cheese—is but one reason why France is the world's number one tourist magnet.

Fromage fiends: The average French person consumes over fifty pounds of cheese annually.

FRENCH STANDOUTS

- Biggest food producer in Europe, second in the world (behind U.S.)
- World's top travel destination (75 million visitors a year)
- Largest European Union country by area on the Continent
- Most EU agricultural subsidies ($10 billion+ annually)[2]
- Launched EU (inadvertently) with Germany
- Most nuclear power in Europe (56 plants)
- One of the two EU countries with nuclear arms (other is Britain)
- Second-biggest European economy (after Germany)
- Largest Muslim population in Europe (about 5 million)
- Stood up most brashly to U.S. over Iraq
- Language most suited to love (makes "ticket, please" sound sexy)

The geographical giant of Western Europe, with towering leaders to match, France is the mightiest European country alongside former foe Germany, the other head chef in Europe's kitchen, with whom France inadvertently hatched the EU when Europe rose again from the ashes of World War II. (See "History Review," page 17). For much of the past three centuries, France dominated culture across the Continent, cooking up the latest and greatest in fashion, thought, art, and political trends. Eighteenth-century French peasants launched the revolution that whipped up a continental frenzy, and French patriots wrote the world's first declaration of universal human rights, beating out even the Americans. French thinkers served up Enlightenment ideals to the masses, including encyclopedias and essays that flavor our outlook even today. Napoleon apportioned more European land than Hitler, and the laws he penned are still used from Paris to Peru. French artists and writers—and foreigners drawn like moths to the City of Light—stirred the creative world with waves of movements, from impressionism to cubism, symbolism to existentialism. French poets (Rimbaud and Verlaine among them) were the world's most drunken and bawdy. The French have been fashion plates since the days of the three Louis, and French chefs have been melting our hearts for at least two hundred years. Long a creative hotbed of intellectuals, providing endless food for thought, France was so edgy and arty that she led the avant-garde even before the term had been cooked up. For centuries upon centuries, so important was France and so crucial was knowledge of Français, the language of *les beaux arts* and international diplomacy (and the language that peppered intellectual writings), that for ages powerful Americans and Brits actually bothered to learn it.

English is shoving French aside as the EU's lingua franca—and the French are appalled. Jacques Chirac stormed out of a 2006 EU meeting when an influential French business leader shockingly addressed the attendees in the language of business, i.e., Anglais.

NOTABLE MOMENTS IN FRANCO-AMERICAN RELATIONS

The Franco-American relationship was founded on friendship, but it's been rocky lately. A few highlights:

1770s: France gives and loans so much money to American revolutionaries fighting British rule that she nearly goes broke, a factor leading to the French Revolution.

1860s: France's vineyards devastated by grape blight phylloxera; U.S. ships over disease-resistant grape stalks that save the wine industry.

1884: France sends Statue of Liberty to New York, a symbol of their mutual love of *liberté, égalité, et fraternité*.

1917: France hammered in First World War; U.S. enters the war and evens the score.

1941: U.S. and British leaders loathe French resistance leader Charles de Gaulle; U.S. refuses to recognize him as legit.

1944: Allied forces liberate France from Nazi occupation; de Gaulle leads liberation parade through Paris; Roosevelt and Churchill don't invite de Gaulle to Yalta Conference where Germany's fate is decided and acquired lands are divided.

1947: U.S. offers Marshall Plan funding to rebuild after Second World War.

1956: France (with Britain and Israel) invades Egypt during Suez Crisis; U.S. forces them to retreat.

1966: President Charles de Gaulle gives NATO marching orders out of France.

1984: French and U.S. scientists battle over who isolated the AIDS virus first.

1986: President François Mitterrand refuses use of French air bases for refueling when U.S. fighters fly over to attack Libya; U.S. aircraft "accidentally" drops a bomb over France.

1991: France fights alongside U.S. against Iraq in Persian Gulf War.

2003: President Jacques Chirac opposes war in Iraq, threatens veto on any UN Security Council resolution approving an invasion; U.S. promises economic reprisals and tries to delete "French" from vocabulary and wine cellars.

2004: Bush bashes France during presidential campaign:"The use of troops to defend America must never be subject to a veto by countries like France." Chirac calls to congratulate Bush on victory, suggests France and U.S. strengthen ties.

2005: Secretary of State Condi Rice wows in Paris, speaks of new chapter in "Franco-American relations."

2006: U.S. and France agree to take matter of Iran's uranium enrichment program to the UN Security Council. President Jacques Chirac and President George Bush meet in Russia for G-8 meeting and smile for the cameras, pretending that everything is *très fantastique*.

Despite the recent feuding, France and the U.S. are economically married. Each business day "over $1 billion in commercial transactions take place" between France and the U.S.[3]

But something has changed. Once the idea muscle of Europe, France has grown flabby and is now painfully examining her lumpy form in the mirror. Creativity is stymied, the government sector is bloated—providing a quarter of French jobs—and the formerly state-dominated economy is bilious, with un-employment hovering near an unappetizing 10 percent. French chefs are los-ing their hats to Spaniards and Belgians, tourism recently shrank by 2 million visitors a year, wine sales are sagging, and in a recent show of cross-Atlantic passive aggressiveness, the U.S. (still steamed about Iraq) banned imports of French foie gras, mumbling something about facilities being unclean. The cor-ruption, once as acceptable as Burgundy with lunch, is no longer palatable, and courts keep throwing the book at unsavory politicians and corporate heads for cooking theirs. The government's attempts at economic belt-tightening measures don't suit French tastes: workers have a simmering dislike of any-thing that may threaten their thirty-five-hour workweek and paid five-week va-cations.

THE FRENCH MODEL

French society re-created itself after World War II, this time guaranteeing every citizen the rights to the sweet life. The "French model" embraced a num-ber of practices and ideals, including:

- Free high-quality education, including advanced university degrees
- Free/low-cost health care (80 percent to 100 percent reimbursed) with free (reimbursed) pharmaceutical drugs
- Universal medical coverage even to the poorest
- Labor laws that protect workers and discourage dismissal except for economic necessities and misbehavior
- Outstanding railway linking the country at affordable prices
- Industry and utilities that were largely state-owned until recently
- Heavy government regulation and high taxes (near 50 percent)

Some say the French model is no longer sustainable—stalling business growth, making France uncompetitive, and creating a top-heavy bureaucracy while sidelining minorities who complain it does not fully extend to them. But whenever the French see their rights being chipped away, they flip out.

Although nowhere near as common as in the United States, crime and vio-lence are rising—murder rates alone jumped 26 percent in 2001[4]—and politi-cians, including President Jacques Chirac (target of a neo-Nazi gunman) and Paris mayor Bertrand Delanoë (stabbed in 2002) are dodging knives and duck-ing bullets, sometimes unsuccessfully—as in Nanterre, where an activist sprayed bullets across a city council meeting, killing eight. Frequent anti-Semitic acts are a growing source of international concern—and the 2006 kidnapping of twenty-three-year-old Jew Ilan Halimi, who was burned and tortured (allegedly by the young "Gang of Barbarians") when his family couldn't turn over $500,000 in ransom—horrified the world. And lately, roving gangs of second-generation North African and other immigrant youths—who roam cities vandalizing, pickpocketing, painting swastikas on Jewish graves, torching cars, and gang-raping for fun—symbolize encroaching danger and an unhappy second-generation immigrant population impossible to ignore.

In November 2005, thousands of young French restless youth and ghetto gangs ravaged the country. Furious over the deaths of two French African youth who were electrocuted while climbing the fences of a power station—rioters said they had been chased there by police—their anger boiled over in fiery mayhem. During three weeks of rioting, they torched 9,000 cars, attacked the weak and elderly (killing at least one old man, and setting one woman on fire), and wrecked $230 million of property. The government declared a state of emergency and enforced curfews in banlieues, *and three thousand were arrested. Even after the massive fires went out, the problem didn't stop smoldering.*

ANGRY YOUNG MEN: *LA RACAILLE*

The 2005 riots were just another dramatic show of a social ill that has been simmering for years—the problem of angry, unemployed minority youth, most of them second-generation offspring of Algerians and Moroccans who arrived in the 1960s. (See "Algerian War of Independence," page 28.) They typically don't speak Arabic and are not practicing Muslims, but they come from *les banlieues*—seedy suburbs filled with low-income housing, which were the center of most of the 2005 riots. It's a tricky issue—one that twists together historical misdeeds, the inequality of the lauded French lifestyle, cultural clashes, violent tempers, and a fascination with fire. *La Racaille* (the rascals or riffraff), as they are derogatorily known, began making news about five years ago for violent rumbles in parking lots, where they torched cars for fun, and for street mugging, pickpocketing, and robbing tourists. In 2002, their violence again grabbed headlines: seventeen-year-old Sohane Benziane died when a *banlieue* thug made her drink lighter fluid, then doused her with it and set her on fire. Reports of violent attacks on *banlieue* women skyrocketed: one thirteen-year-old girl was sexually assaulted by eighty-eight boys.[5] Gang rape is a rite of membership, and hard-hitting books and movies documenting the common phenomenon (reports of which are said to increase 20 percent a year[6]) have rattled the country. Certainly not all young men in the *banlieues* are of their ilk, but *La Racaille* pose a problem that nobody is quite sure how to solve.

Strained relations with French Africans have roots in the brutal Algerian War of Independence that ended in 1962, but recent events have escalated fear levels. In 1994, Algerian Islamists hijacked an Air France flight, intending to plow it into the Eiffel Tower; in 1995, French Algerian radicals bombed the Paris Métro, killing eight and injuring hundreds. In 2004, the French government passed a law banning obvious shows of religion in school—Muslim headscarves, skullcaps, and large crosses among them; Muslim radicals retaliated with threats of attack. The fact that Zacarias "The Twentieth Hijacker" Moussaoui is a French Moroccan national, and that failed "shoe bomber" Richard Reid boarded his flight in Paris haven't helped matters. However, some French Arabs have soared to hero status, including French Algerian soccer star Zinedine Zidane, who scored France's two winning goals in the 1998 World Cup Final, making him the country's most popular man. And banlieue hip-hop music, including that of girl rapper Diam's and MC Solaar, is making French minority youth famous worldwide. Talented filmmakers, writers, and comedians are also rising out of the banlieue, helping to link that long-obscured culture to the mainstream.

In April 2006, France was rocked again: this time a million French students flooded the streets, closing down subways, trains, and entire cities as they protested proposed changes in labor laws. La Racaille showed up for that event too, turning what were largely peaceful demonstrations turbulent by attacking protesters and police.

TAKING IT TO THE STREETS

Here in the republic born of mass rebellion, protests are an often-exercised national right. Rising fuel prices, pension cuts, and duties on cheese are a few issues that prompt fishermen to block ports, truck drivers to jam highways, and farmers to let bulls charge through government buildings, leaving steaming "calling cards" in front of photocopy machines. In June 2004, protests amped up: when the government announced plans to partially privatize state-owned electricity utilities, factory workers—worried about job loss—cut off power to the Eiffel Tower, government buildings, train lines, and the homes of the president and prime minister to show how bright an idea they thought any utility sell-off was. Almost every time the government attempts to tweak the system, the French head to the streets as though ready to storm the Bastille. The French may "over-protest," but they make their points—few contested changes in France actually get through.

The recent fireworks are taking their toll: France is gripped by uneasiness that the media calls *l'insécurité*. The pervasive feeling that French society is curdling catapulted two dissimilar characters to the forefront. Popular interior minister Nicolas Sarkozy, a second-generation immigrant himself, was shoved in front of the cameras as the Chirac administration's tough guy. Sarkozy unveiled a crime bill that increased police forces, broadened search rights, banned youth loitering, and cracked down on prostitution—and he formed an official government board to discuss issues with Muslims. To appeal to the right, he's also pushing "selective immigration," which would make it easier for skilled foreign workers to move to France, and more difficult for the poor to gain citizenship. He was also blamed by some for triggering the 2005 riot by promising to clean up the *banlieue* even if it took a sandblaster to do it.

The turbulent times also brought radical right-winger Jean-Marie Le Pen (of the National Front Party) into the action. In the first round of voting in the 2002 parliamentary elections, Le Pen grabbed 17 percent of the vote, pitting him against Chirac in the final runoff—the first time since World War II that a hard-core nationalist made it so close to the Élysée Palace. France's problem, said Le Pen (as he has said for three decades), was simple: Africans and other immigrants had overrun the place. He pledged "an immediate end to all immigration and to send three million immigrants home!"[7] (See "Hotshots," page 35.)

Courtesy of French government

But if France is faltering on the home front, on the global stage she's flexing muscle not seen from Europe in decades. First she pushed (with Germany) to enlarge the EU to make it a major economic force and rising superpower. Along with Germany, Britain, and Spain, she launched Airbus, whose commercial planes are so cutting into Boeing's biz that the U.S. filed a WTO complaint. And France squarely stood up to the U.S., which nobody's had the nerve to so loudly defy since the Vietnam War.

Slick Sarko:
Eye on the presidency

*   *   *

The Bush government was stunned in 2003 when Chirac (and German chancellor Gerhard Schröder) questioned the need for stomping into Iraq, clearly annoyed that the European duo challenged the pyramidal power structure that casts the United States as world dominator. The Bush administration was also unhappy when the pair linked arms with Belgium and Luxembourg to form an independent military alliance that the U.S. fears might challenge NATO. It would be nothing but an army of "chocolate makers," the U.S. State Department snorted in response.[8]

TRANSATLANTIC HOSTILITIES

Never mind that President Chirac was entirely justified in not backing President Bush's attack on Iraq, or that his actions may have been motivated as much by France's oil investments as by his prescient knowledge of the political instability and violence that the invasion would unleash. When he condemned the U.S.-led Iraq war in 2003, Chirac's disapproval let loose a fierce anti-France movement in the United States that still reverberates on both sides. Retirees felt particularly betrayed by Chirac's chastisement: half a million American troops had died when the U.S. fought for France in the world's two biggest wars—how dare France not help take down the twenty-first-century face of evil who (President Bush falsely warned) was probably about to attack them with biological and nuclear weapons? Millions of bottles of champagne and French wine were poured out; Americans boycotted French restaurants, French water, French cheese; one senator even proposed that U.S. troops who had died during the world wars be freed from French cemeteries and sent home. The furious Americans renamed French fries and French toast—calling them "freedom fries" and "freedom toast"—while the *Wall Street Journal*'s editorial page hurled insults, calling Chirac "a rat"[9], and pundits chastised the French as "cheese-eating surrender monkeys," an epithet tellingly taken from *The Simpsons*. In the following year, U.S. imports of French wines dropped 20 percent, American tourists to France declined by nearly 2 million, and Americans continually growled about crippling the French economy. Meanwhile, anti-American sentiment swelled up again in France (and across Europe), where boycotts of American products were launched and conspiracy theories flourished, helped along by a best-selling French book that stated the 9/11 attack on the Pentagon was a hoax.

Despite moves toward *rapprochement*—the frosty smile for the camera and the lukewarm words about the long Franco-American mutual friendship—the Bush administration is still ticked off at France. The bigger issue, however, is that France is leading Europe in restructuring the global power dynamic. The world's only superpower doesn't like it a bit.

*Warming up: French nuclear group Areva is moving into the U.S. big-time,
snagging billions' worth of nuclear projects.*

History Review

In the beginning was France. No country shaped the current state of modern
Europe more than France, where prevailing thoughts sweep through as forcefully as the remorseless mistral wind. Clovis, king of the Franks, first lassoed
the northwestern land together as a kingdom in AD 486, but another Frankish
king, Charlemagne, took it much further. In the year 800, with the pope's
blessing, he roped together most of western Europe, forcibly creating the
Holy Roman Empire, which lasted in one form or another for the next thousand years.

HISTORICAL HOTSHOTS: THE CATHARS

The French aren't the fervent Catholics they once were. Historically, their
beliefs fueled battles and massacres, among them the sixteenth-century Wars
of Religion that drove Protestant Huguenots out of France. Catholicism also
spelled doomsday to Cathars, a liberal Christian sect that lived in southwest
France (Languedoc), where chestnut forests, limestone caves, and cliff-top
castles hold clues to their past. Arriving in seventh-century France from eastern
Europe, the vegetarian Cathars worshipped outdoors, and believed in reincar-
nation, equality between the sexes, and vegetarianism, while shunning serfdom and taxes. Sex was a devilish temptation, but marriage was worse, giving
the illusion of God-approved copulation; thus Cathars had liberal attitudes
about the romping of singles, and some say the concept of romantic love grew
out of here. Regarding the church's riches as evil and the pope as corrupt, they
refused to tithe to the Catholic Church; they also preached that Jesus didn't die
on the cross, but had been hanging out with their ancestors, to whom he
passed such mementos as the holy grail—notions that didn't play well in Rome.
In 1209, Pope Innocent III sent out armed mercenaries to permanently silence
the heretical sect. Nobles in Languedoc honored Cathars, opening castles to
them, and knights battled in their name. Most of the area's castles were destroyed in the anti-Cathar crusade and nearly all 20,000 Cathars were burned
at the stake or driven off cliffs within the first year. Cathar relics—coins, pliers,
and jewelry—are still found today, and pilgrims now travel to Albi and Carcas-
sonne to search out treasures that some say still lie hidden there.

Since then there's rarely been a dull moment, although plenty have been violent. From the earliest years, the French and English didn't hit it off, and their mutual dislike heated up in 1066 after French William the Conqueror sailed over and lived up to his moniker on English soil. French-Anglo battling and sniping continued for eight centuries, including during the Hundred Years War, which, stretching from 1337 to 1453, actually lasted 116.

The defining moments of the French monarchy took place during the era of the three Louis. Simply put, Louis "I am the State" XIV (1638–1715), aka the "Sun King," built up France as Europe's most powerful and most cultured country, expanded the French Empire, built glittering Versailles, and made French the Western world's most important language. His grandson, flirtatious philanderer Louis XV (b. 1710, ruled 1715–1774) lost the French Empire to Brits, and *his* grandson Louis XVI (lived 1754–1793, ruled 1774–1791), aka "Louis the Last," lost the rest of the country's riches and ultimately his head.

> *Arriving in Paris in 1776 as ambassador from the colonies, Benjamin Franklin lobbied Louis XVI, who ultimately heavily contributed to the American Revolutionary War effort, donating arms, fighters, and millions of dollars—and loaning millions more—without which the rebels would probably have lost the War of Independence. Crucial to the victory: Marquis de Lafayette and Count Rochambeau, who led decisive battles. Also helpful to the American Revolution: powerful Parisian aristocrat Jacques-Donatien Le Ray, who befriended Franklin, pressured the king to help out, and gave vast amounts of money to the cause. The American, who had explained the nature of electricity and invented the lightning rod, library, and Franklin stove, was so popular in Parisian society that paintings and sculptures of Franklin often adorned aristocratic homes.[10]*

While the Renaissance was Italy's apex and Brits dominated the Scientific Revolution, the French were stars (along with British) of the eighteenth-century Enlightenment, when such concepts as original sin were questioned, the pursuit of the rational was idealized, and corrupt clergy were loudly condemned. As critical encyclopedias rumbled off the printing presses, along with essays calling for liberty for one and all, they fell into the hands of the growing middle class, and these ideas charged the air. Inspired by the idea that all humans are created equal, and quoting Jean-Jacques Rousseau—"Man is born free, yet he is everywhere in chains"—commoners rose up and demanded change.

A FEW INFLUENTIAL FRENCH IDEA PEDDLERS

René Descartes (1596–1650): The mathematician launched modern philosophy with three words: *Cogito, ergo sum*—"I think, therefore I am."

Denis Diderot (1713–1784): His twenty-eight-volume encyclopedia raised blood pressures of the church (which condemned it) and the state (which burned it). The critical encyclopedia hinted at the ascent of man from ape and questioned slavery, church corruption, and absolute monarchies.

Charles Louis de Secondat Montesquieu (1689–1755): Abolitionist and advocate of prying church from state, Montesquieu wrote *The Persian Letters* mocking France's religious obsession; his 1748 *Spirit of Laws* drew the blueprint for separation of government's powers.

Voltaire (1694–1778): Adored for satirical novel *Candide* about the hazards of naive optimism, playwright, essayist, and political activist Voltaire decried corrupt clerics and championed human rights, outrageously asserting that Protestants had some.

Jean-Jacques Rousseau (1712–1778): Believing that mankind was inherently good, the Swiss-born dreamer presented a radical idea in his "social contract": government should serve the people, and not vice versa.

Poverty, hunger, unfair taxes, lack of representation, and the novel idea that every human had rights all led to Europe's most memorable, far-reaching, and monumental revolution. King Louis XVI, strapped for cash and losing power in 1789, opened the door by calling for a revival of the Estates General, a pseudo-parliament that hadn't met since 1614, because he needed help raising taxes. Representing three classes—the clergy (First Estate), who were tax exempt; nobility (Second Estate), who were also tax exempt; and the bourgeoisie, peasants, and all the rest (Third Estate), most of whom weren't tax exempt—the meeting was hijacked by the Third Estate, representing 98 percent of the population (about 25 million people). The bourgeoisie-led Third Estate wanted more voting clout and formed the Assemblée Nationale, inviting the other two estates to join; Louis tried to block their meeting. Instead they gathered in an indoor tennis court and issued the Tennis Court Oath, vowing to write a constitution that would address such issues as liberty, equality, and freedom for all. Louis was livid, and rumors swirled that his army would steamroll the Assemblée Nationale. Angry mobs stormed the Bastille, the prison that stood as a symbol of monarchical oppression. From there, chaos broke loose as "the people" battled over who should rule. The Assemblée Nationale passed the Declaration of the Rights of Man—guaranteeing liberty, freedom of expression, and equality—on August 17, 1789, but it apparently didn't apply to royals or the rich, who were soon marched to the guillotine. Finally penned in 1791, the constitution initially allowed a limited monarchy, but a later version declared France a republic. Louis XVI, caught trying to sneak out, was ultimately shoved under the National Razor too. In 1792, France formed her first republic; instead of a king, chaos reigned for the next decade.

> *A republic is the opposite of a monarchy—it's a government that is headed*
> *by an elected ruler, not a royal. Like France, the United States is a republic.*

Political clubs and zealous leaders, including the Jacobins headed by maniacal Robespierre, wrestled over power, and the newly liberated streets were thick with blood. France declared war on much of Europe (and vice versa) in the continuing power struggle, during which 450,000 died in uprisings, counterrevolutions, massacres, and meetings with the executioner. Anarchy continued until 1799, when General Napoleon Bonaparte galloped back into Paris to seize the reins and clean up the revolutionary mess. Appointing himself leader to slap the country back into shape, the former commander in chief took the title First Consul, and in 1804 declared himself emperor.

NAPOLEON (1769–1821)

Short, balding, and suffering from hemorrhoids—a factor, some say, in his final battlefield performance—Napoleon Bonaparte, a young general from Corsica who'd skillfully maneuvered battles in Italy and Egypt, ravaged Europe. Nearly 6 million died during his military campaigns, and most who dared oppose him were imprisoned or snuffed out by secret police.[11] However, he exerted a benevolent touch in many areas. Extending the French Empire across almost all of Europe save the British Isles, he established governments (usually led by his kin) that showed his more humane side: he abolished serfdom, cleaved church from state, and guaranteed freedom of religion and equality for all—offering Jews, among others, rights never before known in Europe. Just as important: his policy of universal education that extended to women and the poor. His legacies are varied: He made it legally possible for commoners to own land, he popularized central banking, formalized the draft, and widely introduced city sewer systems. He provided the key to decipher hieroglyphics in 1799, when his troops in Egypt uncovered the Rosetta Stone, and he inadvertently triggered independence in Latin America by invading Spain (which called her military home). (See "Spain," page 132.) He physically shaped the United States when, in 1803, he sold a vast territory of North America stretching from Louisiana to Wyoming (nearly one-quarter of the United States) to President Thomas Jefferson for $15 million. And he made male birth control difficult even into the twenty-first century; his legal code is still used in France, where his law on mutilation is read as a ban on vasectomies. Thanks to Napoleon, French men wanting "Le Snip" have to head out of the country.

Napoleon's little brother, nineteen-year-old Jerome, snuck off and married Baltimore beauty Betsy Patterson, whom he'd met on a yachting trip, in 1803. Napoleon did not approve, and annulled the two-year marriage, shuttling Jerome off to reign as King of Westphalia in Germany. Jerome and Betsy's offspring, Jerome Napoleon, grew up in Baltimore, and his son, the witty Charles Joseph Bonaparte, became a popular magazine writer—and U.S. Attorney General under President Theodore Roosevelt. Besides being the first royal in U.S. government, Napoleon's great-nephew stood out for assembling the first federal "G-Men"—better known as the FBI.[12]

After thirteen years of unbridled successes, Napoleon slipped in the Russian snow. Ignoring advice, he marched over 300,000 soldiers toward Moscow, in a brutal war made crueler by the wretched Russian winter. He briefly took Moscow, but couldn't rule her, and quickly retreated. Barely a fifth of his soldiers limped back with him, and many deserted. Following another defeat at Leipzig the next year, he abdicated in 1814, and was exiled to the Mediterranean island of Elba. That "vacation" didn't last long. While European leaders assembled in Vienna, toasting Napoleon's downfall and dividing up his empire, Napoleon slipped back and ruled France for another 100 days. That reign ended with the 1815 Battle of Waterloo, where he arrived late and fought poorly. British general Wellington's army easily walloped Napoleon's, defeating it in twelve hours. The ex-emperor was packed off to British-run St. Helena—far out in the Atlantic—where he dictated his memoirs and complained about British food, saying Brits were poisoning him. When he died six years later in 1821—probably from stomach cancer—arsenic was found in his hair, although the toxin was also used to treat syphilis, which Napoleon may have contracted.

France's fallen leader had requested burial in Paris, but was denied that honor until 1840, when his remains were shipped from St. Helena. A formal procession to Les Invalides, where he is entombed, passed under the Arc de Triomphe that he'd ordered built in 1805.

The French Revolution still wasn't over—at least not ideologically. The search for fair and balanced government continued throughout the tumultuous nineteenth century. Monarchs returned and were toppled, the power of the commoner was ripped away and restored, the Church regained tremendous power and lost it, and France was in such upheaval that in the 1800s she called a second, then a third republic. France also continued her colonization kick, claiming new territories in Africa, Asia, and the Americas, and battling with Brits around every bend.

ALGERIA AND THE SWAT THAT LED
TO COLONIZATION

Until that day in 1827, Algeria, the Mediterranean-edged African land of sinewy mountains and sweeping Saharan dunes, was, for the French, simply a place to buy wheat. Decades after huge shipments of grain had been delivered to feed Napoleon's soldiers, France still hadn't paid off the multimillion-dollar bill. The debt led to a showdown: in 1827, after being brushed off by French king Charles X, the enraged Algerian leader Hussein Dey beckoned the French ambassador in Algiers to a meeting; Dey called the diplomat a number of unflattering names, then slapped him with a flyswatter and booted him from the palace.[13] King Charles soon settled the dispute: he sent in the military and declared Algeria a French colony. Given the clash of cultures—Algeria was Arab-Berber, Muslim, and tribal—it would never have been a happy cohabitation, but it began on an excessively violent note. Claiming to be on a "civilizing mission," French soldiers raped the women, robbed the treasury, pillaged villages, defaced cemeteries, and looted mosques[14]—and then grabbed the prime agricultural lands. France shipped in farmers—*pied-noirs*—and turned Algeria into an agricultural annex. Many *pied-noirs* fell in love with the exotic land, but few Algerians were in love with the French, and it all led to an ugly blow-out when Algeria tried to shake off France 130 years later and France wouldn't let go.

Outside Napoleon, France's most remarkable nineteenth-century ruler was his nephew, Louis Napoleon, who in 1848 was elected to the presidential chair in Élysée Palace, where by law he could sit for only one term. Stupid law, thought Louis, who changed the law (with a military coup in 1851), his name (to Napoleon III), and his title (to emperor). Napoleon III modernized Paris, hiring Baron Haussmann to redesign the city, creating the wide boulevards and Mansard buildings that are her trademarks today. Beyond that, he was a nightmare.

VICTOR HUGO (1802–1885)

The 1800s are often described as "The Century of Victor Hugo," reflecting the immense power of the man of letters who ran one of the era's most raucous salons (attendees flounced about in medieval costumes while puffing cigars) and whose best-known works are *Les Misérables* (the dense novel about a convict and a jailer in postrevolutionary France, begun in the 1840s, finished 1862) and *The Hunchback of Notre-Dame* (which he'd signed a contract to deliver in 1828 and finally began writing two years after the deadline). Elected to the Assemblée Nationale in 1848, he fled France under threat of being jailed for treason in 1851, but returned and served as parliamentarian again twenty years later. The poet, painter, and playwright had a libido as big as his impact. Into his seventies, Hugo insisted on taking on a lover a day for his insatiable "lyre"; he's said to have blown through dozens of new paramours a month.[15]

Generally well-meaning, Napoleon III was a dilettante and dabbler in international affairs. His worst error: declaring war on German state Prussia in July 1870. Otto von Bismarck's Prussian forces quickly captured the emperor and pounded Paris for four months; with food supplies cut off, Parisians ate cats and rats, and Leon Gambetta, the emperor's fill-in, floated out of town in a hot air balloon.[16] Napoleon III's foolish move lost France's strategic and resource-rich region Alsace-Lorraine, and once released, he threw down his crown and fled Paris, leaving France financially crippled after Prussia hit her with a $1 billion war reparations bill.

The constant clash of political forces, the occasional bloody revolt, and the ideas batted around at salons and literary cafés launched an era of decadence, made blurrier by absinthe, opium, and laudanum. The creative crowd (painters Toulouse-Lautrec, Van Gogh, Monet, and Manet, and poets Rimbaud and Verlaine among them) found new edges to fall over, and plenty frolicked in brothels, many contracting syphilis, the AIDS of that day.

By the early twentieth century, France had a new reason to twitch. Newly unified Germany was turning into a military and industrial powerhouse, invading in 1914. World War I devastated France, killing or injuring 11 percent of the population.[17]

Stagnant trench warfare led to huge losses, as shown in 1916 at Verdun, where Marshal Philippe Pétain stupidly directed French soldiers to protect the strategically worthless fortress. The French and Germans dug in, and 600,000 died within the year.

Once that dark war was over, France exploded in *Les Années Folles* (The Crazy Years), a creatively frenzied era of debauchery, dance halls, and disposable spouses, when cultures and classes mixed in the cafés of St. Germain and the bars of Montmartre, and new art forms emerged—gypsy jazz, journalizing, and automatic writing among them. Intellectuals, iconoclasts, and outcasts from all corners (Marc Chagall, René Magritte, Salvador Dalí, and George Orwell were a few) flapped toward the creative flame of postwar Paris and the renowned École des Beaux-Arts. "Lost Generation" Americans (including Gertrude Stein, Ernest Hemingway, F. Scott Fitzgerald, and T. S. Eliot) arrived en masse after 1920, when Prohibition dried up their alcohol-guzzling muses. Josephine Baker can-canned in the buff save for a belt of bananas; Picasso designed sets for experimental Jean Cocteau ballets, set to Erik Satie's music of typewriters and sirens that kept audiences hissing; Surrealists rioted during plays, brandishing guns and swinging from chandeliers. Travelers such as André Malraux brought the Orient to literature, Colette penned tales of bedroom romps with foppish lads, Anäis Nin captured steamy escapades with Henry Miller (and his wife, June) in her diaries, Céline depressed the hell out of everyone with the monsters unleashed in his books, and the status of mail pilots soared when Antoine de Saint-Exupéry wrote *Night Flight*, made into a Clark Gable flick. The Great Depression of the 1930s drained wallets and bank accounts, but not the vitality of the Crazy Years.

MARCEL PROUST (1871–1922)

For a man who spent most of his life in bed—suffering from asthma and hypochondria—Proust made up for lost time when he ventured out, charming Guy de Maupassant, Émile Zola, Edgar Degas, and Sarah Bernhardt at the literary salons and dinner parties of Parisian high society, gallivanting through the Ritz with fashionable friends in tow, and paying butlers to detail the soirées that he had missed. His first two novels flopped, but the notebooks he filled with his detailed observations of the elite held his masterpiece. Eating little but ice cream and beer in a soundproof room lined with cork, he painstakingly reworked the notes into a staggering 3,000-page, thirteen-volume novel considered by many to be the most brilliant of the twentieth century. Called *À la Recherche du Temps Perdu* (*In Remembrance of Things Past*), the first volume appeared in 1913; the second volume, published in 1914, was such a rage that it garnered the prestigious Prix Goncourt and prompted him to write five more volumes. Six more came out after his death. In fact, the obsessive scribe hadn't finished editing the final chapters when he died, leaving it to his publisher to sort out what the man known to edit at the printing press had actually intended.

Were they too snockered or simply in denial? France snoozed right through all the warning signals that Germany was gearing up for another war. French leaders slept peacefully, assured that any attack from Germans would be stopped by the Maginot Line, underground fortifications designed for trench warfare. At least one person knew that France was facing big trouble: Colonel Charles de Gaulle. But he couldn't wake anyone up.

CHARLES DE GAULLE (1890–1970)

With a huge, bulbous nose and sad brown eyes that seemed to reflect the battlefield misery he had witnessed, towering Charles de Gaulle was Nostradamus and Napoleon rolled into one. Like the sixteenth-century mystic, de Gaulle was a seer, although his predictions, many uncannily accurate, were derived through military strategy and Machiavellian logic. As early as 1905—long before World War I—he was obsessed with Germany's impending rise, writing term papers about a future Franco-German war, and even short stories in which the fifteen-year-old cast himself as General Charles de Gaulle fighting back Germans. Like Napoleon—to whom he was derogatorily likened by his professors at military school—he was arrogant, autocratic, and a skilled military strategist—and (later) a profoundly powerful leader. After fighting in the trenches, he foresaw how wars would move away from stagnant fighting fronts. Future military clashes, he reasoned, would be multifront blitzkriegs using modern vehicles—tanks and fighter planes—that would bombard from land and sky. France needed to modernize her armed forces and update her war thinking, he warned in the 1920s. Germany, he predicted shortly after World War I ended, would be back.

As military instructor and assistant to Marshal Pétain, de Gaulle feverishly campaigned right up until 1940. He wrote books demanding that France update her army and anticipate attacks from multiple sources; he gave lectures, he dashed off memos, and he bent the ears of the powerful, gaining only a reputation of being a doomsayer. In 1940, when Nazi Germany rolled in with tanks, using the exact methods and routes that he had foreseen, Colonel de Gaulle was promoted to brigadier general and helped to draw up battle plans. Even then the French military was slow to employ coordinated attacks using armored vehicles. On one occasion, however, de Gaulle led a battle and demonstrated how to aggressively use tanks, forcing Nazis to retreat. It marked the only military victory for France in the war.

Lacking a modernized military, France couldn't hold her territory. Some generals advocated continuing attacks from Algeria; others suggested running the war from Britain. "Non," said Marshal Philippe Pétain, who was wheeled out to conduct the war. He instead negotiated an armistice.

PÉTAIN AND VICHY

Elegant Marshal Philippe Pétain was a grandfatherly sort, whose questionable valor in directing millions of World War I soldiers to fight at the same battle line for a year led to his nickname "the hero of Verdun." Twenty-two years later, Grandpapa Pétain, then eighty-four, was half-batty. But a mighty symbol he was, so they whisked him out as leader in May 1940, when France was under Nazi attack. Pétain engineered France's quick surrender, handing over the north and west for Nazi occupation and setting up his government in the southern resort town of Vichy; he was cheered as a hero for saving France. Unbidden by Nazis, the man who personified kindliness, and whose beaming likeness hung from store windows above the slogan "Work, Family, Motherland," hastily wrote up anti-Semitic laws that banned Jews from cinemas and public pools, and forbade them from holding high posts or even owning radios or bicycles. He unleashed a vicious secret police, the Milice, and, starting in 1942, deported 75,000 Jews, rounding up 13,000 on one day that June. While his people (subjected to strict food rationing) went to bed hungry, Pétain lived a luxurious life, feasting in grand Burgundian style. By August 1944, when the Allies and de Gaulle's Free French forces liberated France, 150,000 political hostages had been shot, 750,000 were forced laborers in German factories, and 270,000 had been deported due to their political conviction, religion, or race. Tried and convicted of treason in 1945, Pétain's sentence read "The death penalty and national disgrace."[18] President Charles de Gaulle spared him execution and commuted the punishment to life imprisonment. Pétain spent the next six years looking out over the Bay of Biscay from his cell. Upon his death in 1951, his death certificate was supposed to have said "Philippe Pétain, without profession." A last-minute change allowed it to read as he would have preferred: "Philippe Pétain, Marshal of France."[19]

The news that France had so easily surrendered came as a shock, particularly to de Gaulle, who had just negotiated continuing the war from Britain, only to discover that Pétain was signing an armistice. De Gaulle turned on his heel and ran back to London, where he appointed himself savior of France and set up the Free France resistance. He encountered several problems. First, he had few troops to command, and second, the Allied leaders couldn't stand him. Prime Minister Winston Churchill considered de Gaulle arrogant and dictatorial and often ignored him; President Franklin D. Roosevelt found the pushy man distasteful, instead recognizing Pétain as legitimate leader of France. Frustrated, de Gaulle finally bolted to Algeria in 1943, where he set up the French Committee of National Liberation; Churchill and Roosevelt refused to recognize it. They didn't even let de Gaulle in on "Operation Overlord" and the D-day landing in Normandy until hours before it was launched.

Anglo-American snubs continued after the war: de Gaulle was not invited to attend the 1945 Yalta Conference, where the fate of Germany was decided.

De Gaulle's moment finally arrived in 1944. On August 26, he led the liberation march down the Champs-Elysées to wild cheers. Appointed provisional president in 1945, and voted in the following year, the general created the Fourth Republic and set about penning a new constitution. De Gaulle envisioned a government with a much weaker parliament and a well-muscled president. When his constitutional plan was shot down, de Gaulle stormed out after a mere six months in office. He had to wait nearly fourteen years before being called back.

In the meantime, Europe began pulling herself back together. Jean Monnet, a behind-the-scenes diplomat, put forth an idea for preventing Europe from self-destructing again. Instead of competing, European countries should pool their resources—particularly the two most instrumental to war: coal and steel. By becoming more united economically—merging their assets, sharing their profits, and jointly overseeing production—Europe's disparate countries, Monnet believed, would be less likely to knock themselves out in war.

HERO: JEAN MONNET (1888–1979)

Economist, thinker, and diplomat Monnet—a one-time cognac salesman with a high school education—profoundly affected France and Europe. The deputy secretary general of the League of Nations (precursor to the United Nations), Monnet later convinced the United States to sell arms to the Allies; his actions shaved at least a year off the Second World War. He helped Romania and Poland stabilize their postwar economies, aided China in revamping her ailing railway system, and helped kick-start postwar France. Most important, he realized that France and Germany would function more harmoniously through joint economic ventures and drew up plans for the Coal and Steel Agreement that ultimately led to the European Union. "There is no future for the people of Europe other than in union," Monnet pronounced, and his vision brought the disparate European countries more closely together than before dreamt possible.[20]

France and Germany signed the Coal and Steel Agreement in 1951—along with Italy, Belgium, Luxembourg, and the Netherlands. Over the next five decades, the economy-merging concept snowballed into free-trade agreements, atomic energy agreements, agricultural subsidies, open borders, common military, umbrella policies, and a shared currency, with France and Germany mostly running the EU show.

His resignation spared de Gaulle one heartbreak: after the war, France lost most of her colonies, including Morocco, Tunisia, and Guinea. However, the French fought to regain their hold in Indochina (today's Vietnam), taken by

Japan during the war. Despite superior equipment and financing from the U.S. (which did not want to see Indochina under Communist rule), 58,000 Frenchmen died in the eight-year war (1946–1954). After the Viet Minh thrashed French fighters at Dien Bien Phu in 1954, the French granted independence and hurried home.

The military was soon deployed again—this time to Algeria, Africa's second largest country, a substantial provider of France's food and a symbol of French colonial greatness. Her ego battered by pathetic battle performance in World War II and Indochina, France wouldn't let go of this last vestige of her superiority without a fight. And a fight she got—one that dragged out for seven ugly years.

ALGERIAN WAR OF INDEPENDENCE

Minutes after midnight on November 1, 1954, loud explosions shattered the calm of the Algerian night, as dozens of bombs ripped apart police stations, knocked out communication towers and electrical utilities, and blew up French stores and businesses. Fires soon blazed across the land, and a message crackled over the radio calling for independence from the French and "the restoration of the Algerian state . . . within the framework of the principles of Islam." French interior minister François Mitterrand responded from Paris the next day: "The only possible negotiation is war." And so began one of the most savage episodes in postwar history. Initiated by the militant group FLN—many members were Algerian officers in the French army—the calls for independence were not at first supported by most Algerians, even though many had lost their land, were living in poverty, and were working as slaves. But as French forces rounded up innocent civilians from villages, and as stories began to circulate about torture—the electrodes attached to testicles and eyes, the suffocations and the drownings—many Algerians did indeed want to eject the French. Most pied-noir farmers—French, Spanish, and Italians who worked on French farms—opposed independence. Whenever Algerians raided a pied-noir village or left another pied-noir *colon* hanging in the street with the trademark "Kabyle smile"—a slit throat—vigilantes launched another *ratonnade* (rat hunt) and massacred Algerians, sometimes a thousand a night. By 1955, some 500,000 French troops were erecting electric fences along borders with Tunisia and Morocco, slaughtering villagers believed to hide rebels, and pushing mountain farmers into concentration camps; by 1957, 2 million Algerians lived in squalid camps, where many starved to death. Algerian guerrillas were no better. They raided colonial villages, exploded bombs in restaurants, and blew up buses—averaging thirty attacks every day. FLN took their fight to France, to battle another Algerian independence group; in France, 5,000 died in bombings and machine-gun attacks during the vicious Café Wars.

In 1958, the French armed forces in Algeria took over government buildings, threatening a full-fledged coup d'état unless the government brought General Charles de Gaulle in as leader of France. Believing the powerful general could resolve the Algerian conflict, they also thought he would back them in keeping Algeria a French colony.[21] They were wrong.

INTELLECTUAL EXERCISES

Algeria's right to independence was an issue heatedly debated by writer-philosophers Albert Camus, Jean-Paul Sartre, and Simone de Beauvoir, the era's intellectual heavyweights and fixtures at Café de Flore. Camus, author of *The Stranger*, and 1957 winner of the Nobel Prize for Literature, grew up in Algeria. During the war, he tried to negotiate peace between the two factions, but had mixed feelings about cutting Algeria entirely free. Jean-Paul Sartre, author of the existentialist masterpiece *Nausea* (and who declined the Nobel Prize in 1964), and Simone de Beauvoir, author of *The Second Sex* (the bible of feminism), supported Algerian independence, greatly swaying French left-wing public opinion. Algeria was only one issue in the writers' furious arguments: Camus and Sartre dramatically ended their friendship (and nearly came to blows) over the Soviets' post–World War II aggressions, which Sartre and de Beauvoir supported. Camus pointed out Stalin was slaughtering millions; Sartre and de Beauvoir dismissed it as necessary for Communism to take hold.

Summoned by the president, de Gaulle was appointed prime minister in 1958. Elected president that November, he wrote a new constitution, creating a top-heavy power pyramid with a greatly bolstered presidency and weakened parliament, and called for a new republic—the Fifth. He strengthened France's role in the European Economic Community (precursor to the EU), obtaining huge agricultural subsidies for France (currently $12 billion annually),[22] and he nationalized French industry and utilities, creating powerful oil giant Elf (and authorizing a multimillion-dollar "black box" for bribes). He established an elite college to educate future politicians, which formed the backbone of the French political elite. Internationally, he forged a new identity for France, as a country that would not bow down to any other, be it the U.S., Britain, or Soviet Union—and he controversially made France a nuclear power, unleashing the "Force de Frappe" as a show of her independent strength. Previous slights from Churchill and Roosevelt weren't forgotten: de Gaulle yanked France's gold out of the U.S. Federal Reserve Bank and converted France's dollar holdings to gold, effectively forcing the U.S. to later drop the gold standard for backing the dollar. He kicked NATO out of France, and twice vetoed Britain's entry into the European Economic Community.

But for many Frenchmen, de Gaulle is remembered most for what he did in Algeria: he gave it away.

De Gaulle granted independence to Algeria in July 1962. France erupted in riots. In between dodging assassination attempts, he fought to keep France from breaking into civil war. For his bravery in setting Algeria free, Time hailed him as the 1958 Man of the Year.

NUCLEAR MATTERS

In February 1960, France announced she was a nuclear power—the world's third—backing up the statement by testing a nuclear bomb in Algeria. The international community, particularly Japan and the U.S., was outraged. A nuclear test ban was in effect, and the United States had discouraged France from developing nuclear capabilities. France also heavily developed nuclear energy, and now has fifty-nine reactors—second only to the U.S.—which produce 78 percent of French electricity. In 1985, she opened the much-touted Superphénix, the world's largest fast breeder reactor; plagued by leaks and technical problems, it's now the world's largest decommissioned breeder reactor. Unlike most Europeans, the French are huge fans of nuclear energy, and remain relatively unconcerned about any hazards posed by nuclear plants.

After surviving numerous assassination attempts, de Gaulle was at least symbolically taken down by rowdy youth. Millions of students and workers protested overcrowded colleges and low minimum wages in the riots of 1968, which closed the country down for three days. De Gaulle looked like a wimp when he fled Paris, while Prime Minister Georges Pompidou stayed on and toughed it out. De Gaulle negotiated the end of the protest, but never fully regained his confidence or clout. The following year, when a referendum he initiated about senate and regional reforms failed, the man who had made France an international heavyweight dejectedly resigned—not knowing that in 2005, the French would vote de Gaulle the greatest French person in history.

"De Gaulle was a magician. He made us believe we were great again."
—Sorbonne history professor André Kaspi[23]

Pompidou succeeded de Gaulle; his only lasting contribution was the Pompidou Center—an impressive cultural hub boasting a modern art museum and library—encased in a postmodern architectural monstrosity. But the person who most shaped contemporary France was François Mitterrand, who became president in 1981.

FRANÇOIS MITTERRAND (1916–1996)

With his extramarital affairs, political changes of heart, and hidden health problems, Mitterrand led a double life, and there are two takes on his two-term presidency as well. On the one hand, Mitterrand—who'd switched from right wing to left in the 1970s—brought fresh hope to France. The first Socialist president since before the war, Mitterrand abolished the death penalty, nationalized ailing businesses, and revved up the economy with his *Grands Projets* (Great Projects), a $3 billion-plus program that put tens of thousands to work building a new library, opera house, and more, in the city's most dramatic face-lift since the days of Baron Haussmann. Among the standouts: I. M. Pei's pyramid blocking the front of the Louvre. On the downside, Mitterrand's government was involved in shady deals in Africa, many involving national oil company Elf, accused of bribery and arms running. During his reign, France was slapped with two of its biggest scandals ever. In 1985, the *Rainbow Warrior*—flagship of Greenpeace—sank off the coast of New Zealand, after two bombs exploded. The French government admitted it was behind the bombing. That same year, thousands in France were exposed to HIV through tainted blood supplies; the French government had opted not to use an American test for the virus, waiting for a French lab to develop one. While his presidency started out as gangbusters, Mitterrand slipped in his final years, probably because he was dying of prostate cancer—another issue kept from the public. After fourteen years in the power spot—making him France's longest-lasting twentieth-century leader—Mitterrand was succeeded by Jacques Chirac. He died six months after he stepped down from the presidency.

France's best-known icons these days aren't intellectual heavyweights who sniff at Nobel Prizes, but graceful athletes who butt heads on the field and DJs who spin lounge music and peddle $40 CDs. The artiste lost in swirls of Gauloise smoke at the sidewalk café gazes out not just at the light dancing upon elegant Parisian domes, but at the cold, glassy angles of La Défense looming over the city, and that milky coffee in a bowl now competes with Starbucks' paper-cup café au lait to go. And to keep France French and not overly distracted by Hollywood, these days the French ensure that their films and songs are heard across the country through "the cultural exception": a high percentage of movies shown and music broadcast must be "made in France."

This isn't France's finest hour, and in a recent flurry of books intellectuals now lament that she is falling. But the economy is still soaring, tourists are still flapping in, and, internationally, France hasn't been more prominent since the days of de Gaulle. The hand-wringing and whining is just part of a national process of transformation, pointing out the need to address problems long shoved to the suburbs. Like Napoleon himself, fetching France never appears content with what she is or possesses—she is forever pulled in a struggle between joie de vivre and ennui, self-aggrandizement and self-loathing. But that chronic discontent is what powers France, unleashing a flood of novel ideas through the centuries. How she plans to address burning issues remains to be seen, but don't rule out the old standby wheeled out whenever the country undergoes major change. Perhaps it's time to call a new French republic—the Sixth.

Hot Spots

Paris: With her Arc de Triomphe, la Tour Eiffel, and ubiquitous wicker-chaired, marble-tabled sidewalk cafés, the world's most visited city still somehow lives up to the hype. Whether you're winding up the twisting rues of Montmartre, past street artists capturing Sacré Coeur's dome in watercolor, or washing down garlicky escargot with crisp sauvignon in a zinc-wrapped bistro; whether peeling hard-boiled eggs at a smoky bar where Serge Gainsbourg rasps from the jukebox, or gazing into a cloudy pastis in an ivy-shrouded garden; whether inching toward *Mona Lisa* at the Louvre, or tossing back vodka at new ice bar Kube, the city along the Seine marries his-

Paris: A showy marriage of old and new, as seen at the Louvre

Photo by Neil Vilanueva

tory with style, and still intoxicates, despite her distant moodiness. Days filled with perfume sniffing, museum hopping, and boutique shopping slip into nights of boozy laughter with jazz musicians in basement discos, and easily roll into mornings over café au laits and golden croissants that never taste better than they do here. Still trendy—all the more with her new floating bars, designer hotels, and beachfront bars on the Seine—Paris frustrates too. Her artistic and intellectual past was so rich that one fears that, here or elsewhere, it may never be repeated—although sometimes, like a ghost, you can glimpse it.

Eiffel Tower: Built to showcase modern engineering marvels, the Eiffel Tower was to be a temporary display in the 1889 Universal Exhibition in Paris. Initially hated by the city's artistic community—300 French VIPs signed a petition against it in 1887—it was scheduled to come down around 1914. It instead served as a World War I radio tower, intercepting enemy messages. The 984-foot-tall Eiffel Tower is now the symbol of Paris, and has been a target in assorted planned terrorist attacks. The tower caught fire in 2003, and nearly 400 have taken suicidal plunges from there. One attempt was foiled when a woman landed on top of a car; legend has it that she married the car's owner.[24]

Père Lachaise Cemetery: Almost everybody who was anybody in Paris lies here: Gertrude Stein, Edith Piaf, Molière, Sarah Bernhardt, Colette, Bizet, Georges Seurat, Oscar Wilde, and Chopin (minus his heart) are a few of the 100,000 dead whose lives are immortalized with elaborate vaults, sculptures, and tombs. The grave of Jim Morrison, whose fire flickered out in 1971 in Paris, is a huge draw. Multitudes of Doors fans heap love letters, albums, and booze bottles upon his tomb, trampling and trashing the plots of dead neighbors en route. After complaints from the neighbors' kin, cemetery officials considered moving Jim elsewhere when his thirty-year lease ran out, but opted to let sleeping Doors lie.

Corsica: The lovely island of lavender and wind-battered cliffs is Napoleon's birthplace and France's hottest spot of dissent. Separatists are only one-fifth of the islanders, but they're furious about land development, taxes, and France's mismanagement, and claim to have been behind three thousand bombings in the past three decades.

Eurosatory: Every spring, Paris puts on the world's biggest international exhibition of land armaments, showcasing the latest and greatest ways for humans to kill and mutilate each other. Well attended, of course.

COGEMA La Hague: Perched atop the cliffs of Normandy, this ticking time bomb reprocesses nuclear waste, producing weapons-grade plutonium and uranium, and plenty of "enriched" effluent that radioactivates the English Channel. Since 2001, an antiaircraft missile system protects this national hazard. The French are now selling the U.S. this iffy technology.

> *Scientists report that children who go to the beach near COGEMA even twice a month are three times more likely to develop leukemia.*[25]

Marseille: Some adore this predominantly Arab port city for open-air markets, sea urchins, bouillabaisse, and exotic flair; others find it seedy. The wealthy pull up in yachts, and smugglers pull in with drugs in this underworld haven.

Grasse: Since the sixteenth century, this perfume capital outside Cannes has been pressing essential oils from jasmine, violets, roses, cedar, and spices. The scent of flowers from the farms—Chanel owns one—wafts in the air, making it hard to imagine this was once a stinking town of leather tanneries. When people took to scenting leather gloves during Louis XVI's reign, the French perfume industry was born.

Alsace-Lorraine: Snuggling up against Belgium, Luxembourg, Switzerland, and Germany, this northeastern region is actually two: Alsace spreads along the River Rhine, and Lorraine tumbles down from mountains to meet her. Important for industry, resources, and trade links to the Rhine, the region is adored for natural beauty that is likened to a continuous garden. When the Germans ran off with her in 1871 (and again during World Wars I and II), it was a French national tragedy. The French got her back after a few more rounds of tug-of-war, but German speakers still dominate Alsace; French speakers are the majority in Lorraine.

Provence: Overhyped by writer Peter Mayle and his Provence series, the southern region of olive groves and tiny towns does have charms: Roman ruins, open-air markets, vineyards, charming villages, and delightful restaurants are a few. Van Gogh went loopy here and cut off his ear; he really would have gone nuts if he could see how prices for houses have shot through the roof since Mayle began cooing.

Chunnel (aka le tunnel sous la Manche): A dream since 1802, the thirty-mile Chunnel connecting Folkestone, England, to Calais, France, finally opened in May 1994. The rail tunnel that shoots under the English Channel cost $21 billion and took three years to dig.

Brittany (Breizh): Settled by Welsh and Irish missionaries, this region of medieval stone villages and renaissance châteaux rises from the boulder-strewn northwest coast and may be the only place you can find Frenchmen playing bagpipes. Legends are as thick as fog; sprites and gnomes frolic amid the heather, fairies live in caves, and mermaids beguile from the shores, they say.

Bureaucrat school: It's tough to get into l'École Nationale d'Administration, where students learn how to be bureaucrats, but those who get through are virtually guaranteed top positions in government.

Hotshots

Jacques Chirac: President, 1995–present, Union for a Popular Majority. So what if he's allegedly corrupt, wears a hearing aid, and can't seem to get through EU summits without knocking back a bottle of wine? The man who started out his presidency by controversially testing nuclear bombs in French Polynesia will go down in history for being right about Iraq.

Nicolas Sarkozy: Minister of the Interior, head of Union for a Popular Majority, former finance minister, former friend of Chirac. Political mover Sarkozy, who loves the media and vice versa, steals the show. He's gunning for the presidential chair, and to many French, the second-generation Hungarian Frenchman law-and-order enthusiast smells sweet in a system that stinks more by the day. Head of the party that Chirac created, the conservative who dated Chirac's daughter is no longer chummy with the Chiracs; once Jacques's protégé, Sarkozy didn't back him in the 1995 elections. Chirac's daughter, whom he dumped, belittles Sarkozy as being too short to lead France—apparently forgetting about Napoleon.

Dominique de Villepin: Prime Minister, 2005–present. Debonair Villepin, a diplomat and poet, was once said to be able to seduce with his words. Few jumped in bed with him when he introduced his youth labor law, which was ultimately deleted from the law books. Along with rumors of scandals that keep popping up like mushrooms in a moist cowfield, that law spelled doomsday for his presidential plans.

Ségolène Royal (aka the Princess): President, Poitou-Charentes; previous parliamentarian. With most of the competition besmirched in scandals, personable Royal stands a chance of representing Socialists in the 2007 presidential run-off and could be France's first woman president. One problem: her common-law husband, François Hollande, who heads France's Socialist Party, is also a contender.

MAD JEAN-MARIE LE PEN

Given his doughy face, glass eye, and tightly drawn snake of a mouth, seventy-nine-year-old Jean-Marie Le Pen, who grew rich selling recordings of Nazi marching tunes and calls the Holocaust "a detail of history," hasn't soared in popularity from looks alone. Le Pen, the obscure leader of the National Front, which he started in 1972, is now the bête noire of French politics. His success is due to his contagious rage, much of it concerning Algerians, whom he says milk welfare and are the cause of France's unemployment and crime—an idea endorsed by neo-Nazis who flock to his rallies. His speeches are so rabid that violence often breaks out. In 1995, a group of skinheads left his rally and promptly killed a Moroccan, pushing him over a bridge; one of his campaigners murdered a black youth—a move that Le Pen defended. Le Pen himself is no pacifist. He temporarily lost his European Parliament in 1998, after assaulting a female Socialist, and he lost his eye in a brawl with a Communist. Now Le Pen, who likens himself to Joan of Arc, official patron saint of his party, is protected by his own 300-strong paramilitary force, at least some of whom are neo-Nazis.[26]

Marine Le Pen: Nicknamed "The Clone," she's taking over for Pops.

Bertrand Delanoë: Mayor of Paris, 2001–present. At his request, the right bank of the River Seine is covered in over 2,000 tons of sand and planted with palm trees in summer, and millions enjoy outdoor concerts. On Valentine's Day, he beckons the city's residents to gather in front of the Hôtel de Ville for a collective reenactment of Robert Doisneau's famous photo "The Kiss." In 2002, he threw an all-night party for Parisians, with art shows, concerts, and bashes all over town, but paid for it with more than a hangover: a French Algerian stabbed him in the midst of the merrymaking at City Hall; Delanoë quickly recovered. Parisians adore their first liberal mayor in 130 years, except for one thing. He wants them to stoop so low as to pick up their dogs' doo; dog owners barked loud protests.

> *In canine-friendly Paris, the pavements are covered in some sixteen tons of dog dirt every day.*

Médecins Sans Frontières (Doctors without Borders): Founded by French physicians in 1971, this independent emergency relief agency is the world's largest, swooping in to give free medical care during emergencies, disasters, and epidemics, and entering war zones that few others dare touch. It won the Nobel Peace Prize in 1999 and is now headquartered in Brussels.

News you can understand: *Le Monde Diplomatique* is decidedly left, but you can find articles here that nobody else will touch. Some articles free: www .Mondediplo.com

2. GERMANY
(Deutschland)
Reinventing Herself

FAST FACTS

Country: Federal Republic of Germany; Bundesrepublik Deutschland

Capital: Berlin

Government: Federal republic

Independence: 1871 formation of united Germany (Second German Reich); 1990 East and West reunified

Population: 82,423,000 (2006 estimate)

Head of State: President Horst Köhler (2004)

Head of Government: Chancellor Angela Merkel (2005)

Elections: President elected by Federal Convention (parliament and state delegates) for five-year term; chancellor elected by absolute majority in parliament for four-year term

Name of Parliament:	Federal Assembly; Bundestag
Ethnicity:	91.5% German; 2.4% Turkish; 6.1% Serb, Croat, Greek, Italian, Polish, Russian
Religion:	34% Protestant; 34% Roman Catholic; 3.7% Muslim; 28.3% other or none
Language:	German
Literacy:	99% (1997 estimate)
Famous Exports:	Cinderella, the Easter bunny, Faustian dilemmas
Economic Big Boy:	DaimlerChrysler (Mercedes-Benz, etc.); 2004 total sales: $192.75 billion[1]
Per Capita GDP:	$29,800 (2005 estimate)
Unemployment:	9.1% (January 2006 Eurostat figure)
EU Status:	Founding member (EEC member since 1957)
Currency:	Euro

Quick Tour

The majestic land pushed against the Alps is awash with spectacular cities and tiny wine towns, folded with steep hills and deep forests, and home to numerous spas with water believed to have great restorative powers, which come in handy after days of museum-hopping and nights of oompah-pahing in beer halls.

> *Each region of Germany has her own special beers, all made according to particular legal requirements called* Reinheitsgebot. *Regulations call for purity; water, hops, yeast and malt are the only acceptable ingredients.*

From artist haven Berlin and bustling banking center Frankfurt to the somber cathedrals of Cologne and the castled-crowned cliffs along the "fairy-tale route" where the Brothers Grimm collected their tales, Germany's calling the masses. Surging in popularity, she was the world's ninth most visited country in 2004, when over 20 million visitors dropped in. Locals speculate that tourists often love Deutschland because they have such low expectations when they arrive.

That Germany—as of 2006 the world's largest exporter and the major cog in the industrial economic motor of Europe—has a festive and glamorous side is indeed news to much of the world. After all, world famous Germans appear deep, dark, and gloomy. The land of brooding thinkers including Kant, Hegel, and Nietzsche may be the heaviest country on the planet, and there's little

Schwarzwald: One of Germany's tucked-away treasures

question that any other country has rearranged the world more. Gutenberg revolutionized communications when he turned a wine press into a printing press in 1455, and reformer Martin Luther shattered sixteenth-century Catholic Europe by nailing his ninety-five theses to a church door. Johannes Kepler rearranged our view of the universe, proving that planets circle the sun, and Karl Marx, with his utopian delusion that mankind could selflessly toil together as one, planted ideas for a societal makeover, never knowing that his nineteenth-century dreams would cleave the twentieth-century world. Albert Einstein and Max Planck decoded the keys to the universe, and Rudolf Peierles and Otto Frisch worked with Einstein's equations to produce the world's first atomic bomb, supervised by Robert Oppenheimer, a German American. And no single person has triggered a more extensive restructuring of the globe than Hitler did when he launched his war—the single event that most defines the twentieth century, with effects still shaping the planet today. Among those effects: Germany has been sitting in the corner ever since.

WORLD WAR II: EXPENSIVE IN EVERY WAY

When someone mentions Germany, perhaps Mercedes-Benz, Boris Becker, and Becks beer come to mind. But three other things often still associated with Germany are Hitler, concentration camps, and the violent rise of the Aryan nation. The ugliest chapter in human history closed six decades ago, but the loss of life, the devastation, and the Nazis' genocidal atrocities were so painful that Europe is still feeling the psychological effects. Of all of Europe's military showdowns, World War II most rattled the long-running assumption that humankind is basically good. With 60 million dead and Europe in ruins, the destruction that resulted from Hitler's attempt to take over the planet was so vast that it required trillions of dollars and decades of labor to fix Europe back up; the emotional scars still remain. What is often overlooked, however, is that Germany suffered too—and not only because not all Germans supported Hitler or shared his maniacal plan. Most of Germany was flattened during the last months of the war; when the Allied forces tried out new weapons that sucked off roofs and torched entire cities, residents suffocated and charred in giant fireballs that dropped from the sky. Twelve million Germans were shoved out of Eastern European lands in forced repatriations after the war; 2 million died in violent reprisals along the way. Germany lost a quarter of her original territory when Allies redrew the map, and the remaining land was politically divided, with a third of Germany becoming a Soviet satellite for the next forty-five years. Germany paid out billions in war reparations, and sixty years later Germany is still paying—for Holocaust victims, for slave labor, for damages, and for looted riches and art. But perhaps the heaviest debt is the guilt that still weighs upon Germans, most of whom were born after the war.

Germany paid over $69 billion to victims of the Second World War, including to families of the six million Jews killed in concentration camps and others subjected to forced labor. Germany also repaid $1.1 billion to the United States for $1.3 billion of Marshall Plan aid and donated $75 million to Harvard University to start the German Marshall Fund of the United States, a foundation promoting better understanding between Europe and the U.S.[2]

The unrivaled population giant of Western Europe, especially since 1990's surprise reunification of her East and West, Deutschland is the financial locomotive of the European Union—she shovels in more dues than anyone else and helps keep Europe chugging along. There's a reason why modern Germany found herself in the Ms. Moneybags role, besides the fact that she has a bigger economy than any other EU player—$2.7 trillion at the 2005 official exchange rate—making Germany's the third largest economy in the world after the U.S. and Japan. The underlying dynamic shaping German-European relations since the war is the unspoken rule that if Germany wants an active role on the Continent, she has to pay up, shut up, and play by the rules, which are dictated mostly by the U.S. and France.

GERMANY AND THE INFLUENCE OF THE U.S. AND FRANCE

The United States was the dominant force in the rebuilding of West Germany. For decades after the war, hundreds of thousands of Americans, mostly military personnel, lived in West Germany, overseeing the birth of the new nation. U.S. funding helped reconstruct it, and the U.S. guided the hands writing the new constitution. Americans influenced decisions from industry to energy and stamped American values onto the German republic, which the U.S. controversially brought into NATO. But the country that guided Germany back into Europe was France. French leaders approached Germans in 1950 with a plan to pool coal and steel resources. As with the U.S. their plan to bring Germany back into the loop wasn't entirely altruistic. The motives were threefold. First, if France and Germany shared the resources needed for war, they would be less likely to go to war again. Second, France realized that with Germany on her team she would have more power in international dealings. And third, France was about to go bankrupt from payments to farmers; German funds could be used to bail out French agriculture.[3]

Guilt-ridden by the events of the Second World War and shocked by the loss of East Germany to the Soviet bloc in 1945, West Germans became workaholics, plunging into their jobs with zeal, turning the country into a workhorse, and transforming the economy into Europe's most productive. The German Economic Miracle made their country one of the world's wealthiest, but the economy began sputtering in the 1990s. The reason: the sudden reunification with East Germany made Germany's population shoot up by 16 million overnight. By 2003, over $770 billion had been sunk into gluing the two halves together—and East Germany is still lagging behind.

West German states toss about $70 billion to Eastern states every year—a bone of contention for West Germans.[4]

SO HAPPY TOGETHER?

Fifteen years have passed since the fall of the Berlin Wall, but East and West still don't fully function as one, and resentment hangs in the air. Wessies (as West Germans are nicknamed in Germany) are still paid about 25 percent more than Ossies (East Germans), and Ossies have a much higher unemployment rate (around 18 percent). Living is cheaper in the East, but many young

Ossies head west. The government moved the capital east from Bonn to its previous home in Berlin, but that was mostly symbolic. Ossies say that since reunification their culture has been swallowed up by the West's. Their dreams about the happiness of reunification have rather faded as eastern cities become dilapidated and factories close up. Wessies are annoyed by how the reunification drains the economy, which was charging full steam ahead until the East and West got back together.

The economy, which Germans talk about obsessively, appeared to be leading Germans into yet another of their collective funks, when two things considerably brightened the scene: First, Germany landed the 2006 World Cup soccer tournament—and the country went goofy "footballing" the place up, including installing soccer balls atop buildings and billboards; the world's biggest soccer ball exhibit traveled around the country. Second, after an embarrassingly long tussle, Christian Democrat Angela Merkel finally got Gerhard Schröder to leave the chancellor's seat and offer it to her. Thus far, much to everyone's amazement, Chancellor Merkel is proving to be not only Germany's most popular leader in ages, but a dynamic force on the world scene.

ANGELA MERKEL: LETTING THE CLOUDS DISAPPEAR

A physicist by training and chemist by profession, Angela Merkel leapt into politics in 1989, shortly before the wall came crashing down. Her success is remarkable: after first landing a job as a government spokeswoman in the newly democratic East Germany, when Germany reunified, she was quickly plucked to be part of Chancellor Kohl's cabinet, as minister of women and youth. When the Christian Democrats took a nosedive in 1998, after a major scandal (see "Helmut Kohl," page 56), she tidied up the mess as head of the party. In her first stab at running for the chancellorship, she gained the chair—a historic moment marking the first time a woman and an East German took the top leadership role. Once rather dowdy, she got a makeover and promptly captivated leaders worldwide. She bluntly told President Bush that Guantánamo was an outrage (though she did support the Iraq invasion), and she demanded that Condoleezza Rice take action on CIA "special renditions"—or kidnapping terror suspects. She's calmed ruffled feathers at the EU, hammering together a budget, and has helped unite her country in spirit; after her first hundred days, she had the highest approval rating of any chancellor since 1949.

Nobody is missing Chancellor Schröder, who promised to cut taxes but instead raised them, and who just could not fit the key in the economic ignition. Most Germans supported his opposition to the war in Iraq; what's bringing them down is that Schröder was apparently two-faced about that as well. The media reports that Germany was helping the U.S. in Iraq, with agents providing information about targets. The chilly gusts once blowing in from Washington have definitely warmed, the economy is slowly picking up, and unemployment is slowly going down. Germans, for the moment, appear to be nearly in a good mood.

COMRADE CHIC

Once shoved under the rug, East German culture is now in vogue. There's a veritable "Ostalgie" trend in Germany—a nostalgia for the East reflected in everything from propagandistic art and posters to Communist-era music and sweets. At Ostalgie clubs, partygoers sport "People's Army" jackets, Soviet badges, and Young Communist uniforms. *Goodbye Lenin!*, a 2003 film by Wolfgang Becker, also spurred the nostalgia movement. The plot: an elderly East German woman falls into a coma in the late 1980s; when she recovers, Germany has been reunified, but her son, shielding her from shock, re-creates life as it was before his mother (and East Germany) fell.

For all the optimism of the moment, Germany has yet to confront her own frail self-esteem—a tightly wound, sensitive issue. Decades of war guilt have created a society that feels uneasy, even in the best of times. Any expression of satisfaction (outside of sports) sets off alarm bells and fears of rekindled nationalistic pride. When former president Johannes Rau recently chided Germans, saying they should not be proud to be German, it sounded far too harsh; when leaders opine that today's Germans shouldn't feel guilty, their comments seem insensitive to all the suffering that German military exploits caused. Germany has apologized, Germany has paid—but everyone knows that the death, destruction, and pain can never be erased with money or words. Then again, nearly sixty years after Hitler's death, maybe it's time for the world to forgive Germany, starting with Germany forgiving herself—while knowing full well that nobody will ever forget.

History Review

For most of history, Germany wasn't Germany; she was hundreds of fiefdoms, kingdoms, and principalities headed by German-speaking nobles, kings and knights, all under the umbrella of the Holy Roman Empire. Supposed to heed the authority of the emperor, many gave little more than a tip of the hat, and the territories had their own laws and levied their own taxes, making travel across them a deeply confusing affair. Just as puzzling were the boundaries, which were always snaking in new directions as knights won new towns; at times German fiefdoms extended east into today's Baltic States and Poland, north into today's Denmark, south into today's Switzerland, and west into today's France.

Despite the geographical mayhem, German principalities garnered a reputation for several things. German speakers became famous as traders, forming the powerful Hanseatic League—a medieval maritime trading group of outposts and ships that shuttled goods across northern Europe from today's Poland to Sweden, Germany, and Russia, expanding the network into the sixteenth century. Moreover, from the fifteenth century on, the German heartland emerged as the publishing hotbed of Europe, with Frankfurt its epicenter, pulling in thousands with her twice-yearly book fairs.

German territories were also the first planting grounds for religious war. The criticisms lodged against the Catholic Church by Martin Luther in 1517 stirred up such a reaction that new "Protestant" followers and devout Catholics waged vicious battles over Luther's "heretical" ideas. Pope Leo X condemned Luther in a papal bull (an edict), and Luther responded by burning it. Soon the Lutheran religion (and other Protestant variants) flourished in northern German states, while southern German states remained Catholic. Religious conflict spread like a raging venereal disease and was just as deadly. In the name of God—or rather the name of how God should be worshipped—most of Western Europe was sucked into the Thirty Years War, which sent millions to the Great Beyond.

A third of German-speaking people lay dead by the time the Thirty Years War fizzled out in 1648.

JOHANN WOLFGANG VON GOETHE (1749–1832)

In 1774, Goethe—perhaps Germany's most beloved writer and a hugely influential eighteenth-century voice—published his novel *The Sorrows of Young Werther*. The tale of unrequited love was so heart-wrenching that young men across Europe were swept away in melancholy and killed themselves. Goethe also wrote lyrical poetry (sometimes set to music)—the dramatic epic *Faust* being such a famous example that the word "Faustian" came into common usage as shorthand for not looking at future consequences. A scientist intrigued with metals, optics, and the study of animals; a philosopher fascinated by the possibility of evolution; a conductor, a lawyer, and a professor, well-rounded Goethe eventually moved into the ducal castle at Saxe-Weimar, where he became the duke's top political adviser and theater director.

German speakers kept trading, expanding territories, and fighting over religion, and boundaries kept moving across the entire Holy Roman Empire. By the time Napoleon arrived on the scene and dismantled the HRE, over 300 German kingdoms, principalities, and states spread out across Europe. The 1815 Congress of Vienna, which rearranged the lands held by the defeated Napoleon, recombined territories, whittling the number of states down to thirty and placing all of them under the umbrella of a new entity: the German Confederation.

GRIMM TALES: JACOB AND WILHELM GRIMM (1785–1863, 1786–1859)

Wilhelm and Jacob Grimm were newly unemployed professors, fired from their jobs after opposing right-stripping moves of the King in Hanover. Their growling stomachs drove them to devise a new moneymaking plan. They interviewed some three dozen locals, soliciting local folktales, which they began publishing in 1812. Originally not bedtime stories, the racy tales were modified and cleaned up by the Grimms, who ultimately implanted images of Cinderella, Snow White, Sleeping Beauty, Rapunzel, and hundreds of others in the minds of babes. Some call their tales Freudian myths; we shan't go into our theories on the meaning of the frog that, when kissed, turns into a handsome prince.

The ink hadn't dried on the Confederation's map when a power struggle emerged. The top dog and biggest German "state" by far was the Austrian Empire, which included today's Hungary and Czech Republic and beyond. Number two in both size and population was much smaller Prussia, a northeastern state that held today's Berlin and part of Poland. Run by the Hohenzollern dynasty, militaristic Prussia had no intention of being overshadowed by the Austrian Empire, which by then was militarily flabby and politically weak. Or rather, Otto von Bismarck—who became Prussian chancellor in 1871—had no intention of riding in the passenger seat.

"Laws are like sausages. It's better not to see them being made."
—Otto von Bismarck

Statesman and strategist Bismarck was a master manipulator, playing psychological chess while other European leaders were shooting marbles. His first priority: booting Austria from the German Confederation. Tricking the Austrians into fighting a quick war alongside Prussia for northern Danish duchies, Bismarck found a technicality in the victory to declare war on Austria. Prussia quickly won, and Bismarck's condition for peace was simple:

Austria had to leave the Confederation. Then Bismarck's eyes turned to France, which held the coal-rich Elsass-Lothringen region (aka Alsace-Lorraine). For this, he tricked Napoleon III into starting a war. Prussia quickly won, and France handed over the region. Bismarck then proceeded to part three of his plan: in 1871, he announced the unification of Germany as the German Empire, with Prussian king Wilhelm I as her royal head and Bismarck as political leader. From then on, Bismarck contented himself with statesmanship and alliances, fine wines, and cigars, and Western Europe found herself in deep peace until 1914.

In the late nineteenth century, Germany was roaring along—and advancing so rapidly she was scaring the neighbors. The German industrial machine was churning, and the standard of living soared as farmers moved to the cities, which were orderly and even boasted modern plumbing. The muses were alive: Hermann Hesse published his first works; Nietzsche became the controversial philosopher of the hour; and the operas of Richard Wagner blew the world away, underscoring the genius of German classical composers going back to Beethoven, Schubert, Handel, and Bach. Karl Benz unveiled his new machine in 1885—an automobile powered by an internal combustion engine—and Gottlieb Daimler invented the gas-powered motorcycle that same year; luckily, chemist Heinrich Hertz invented aspirin and helped alleviate the headaches from the new urban racket. Contact lenses, X-rays, and Zeppelins were but a few more German creations of the era.

> Headstrong Kaiser Wilhelm II took the German imperial crown in 1888. Threatened by Bismarck, he forced him to resign, the first of the Kaiser's many mistakes.

Few doubted the brilliance of the German mind, but not all trusted it. Many warily eyed Germany's growing military might. In 1906, the anxious British unleashed their new weapon: HMS *Dreadnought*, a huge, fast, and terrifying warship that had the potential to blow everybody else's navies out of the water. The great arms race was under way.

Peace was shattering: the volatile Balkans erupted in several wars over nationalism and territorial squabbling, and conflicts brewed up in African colonies. Armies were building up, revving their motors. And cocksure Kaiser Wilhelm II kept shooting off his mouth, further destabilizing an already twitchy Europe.

* * *

The Kaiser was hunting in Norway in 1914, when he heard the news: a Serb had killed Austrian archduke Franz Ferdinand. His advice to Austrian emperor Franz Joseph, the archduke's uncle: put the Serbs in their place. The Kaiser, after all, was itching to take his new weapons for a spin. On July 18, 1914, Germany and Austria invaded Serbia—an act that would kick off a chain of events from which Germany still hasn't fully recovered. The First World War had begun.

The "Summer War" dragged on for four dismal years, causing the worst physical destruction, loss of life, and financial drain that Europe had seen. The stagnant, trench-heavy war finally heaved its last gasp in 1918. Seen as the instigator of the most brutal military showdown then known to man, Germany was the target of postwar wrath. At the Treaty of Versailles in 1919, the victors— Britain, Russia, France, and the U.S.—went overboard: they ensured not only that Germany paid, but that she was utterly devastated.

> *"They [will] be shunned and avoided like lepers for generations to come."*
> *—Woodrow Wilson in 1919, on the future of the German people after World War I*[5]

In 1919, the new Germany was unveiled as the Weimar Republic. The weak government, with a $33 billion war reparation bill hanging around her neck, was destined to fail; she started unsteadily and soon slipped into chaos, with uprisings, strikes, assassinations, and chronic shortages of food and fuel. The currency became worthless as a result of hyperinflation; lifetime savings vanished as the value of the mark dropped from a prewar exchange rate of 4.2 marks per dollar to about 4.2 trillion marks to the dollar.[6] Germans pushed wheelbarrows of cash to the shop to buy bread. Some found a better use for the marks: burning them for oven fuel.

> *Bertolt Brecht's* Threepenny Opera *(1928)—a cabaret-style satire—jabbed the corrupt Weimar Republic and swept Berlin as the most popular play of the 1920s (the opening song later became Louis Armstrong's "Mack the Knife").*

In 1923, a short, bitter Austrian who headed a new political party plotted to toss the regional Bavarian government. Brandishing guns, he and dozens of colleagues broke into a beer hall where the Bavarian prime minister was holding a meeting. "Silence!" he yelled, shooting his gun into the air. "The revolution has begun!" Police put down the attempted coup, and Adolf Hitler—mastermind of the failed beer-hall putsch—spent the next year in prison, dictating his memoirs to cellmate Rudolf Hess. Published in 1925 under the name *Mein Kampf* (My Struggle), his book didn't sell diddly then, but would later become a school textbook and a bestseller—though it's said few people ever got through it. Future book sales made Hitler a millionaire.

> *Originally, Hitler's manuscript had the pithy title of* Four and a Half Years of Struggle Against Lies, Stupidity, and Cowardice. *In the Netherlands and Czech Republic it's illegal to own a copy of Hitler's autobiography, whatever it's called.*[7]

The Depression of 1929 only worsened conditions in the Weimar Republic. Amid the gloom, however, one ray of hope beamed through. A rousing orator coaxed Germans out of their collective depression, vowing that Germany would be great again. Little by little Germans started listening.

ADOLF HITLER (1889–1945)

Born in Braunau, Austria, the offspring of a government employee and his niece, Adolf Hitler—whose father changed his last name from Schicklgruber—was beaten by his father, but coddled by his mother, who led him to believe he was brilliant. Orphaned at eighteen, Hitler moved to Vienna, where he fancied his calling was to be an artist—but the Art Academy didn't agree, rejecting his application several times. Moving to Munich, he fought in WWI and was temporarily blinded by British mustard gas. He heard of Germany's defeat while in a hospital bed, blaming Jews for his blindness and for the war that Germany had just lost. Believing Jews to be the root of all evil, Hitler vowed to deport them from Germany. After the war, he was transferred to German military intelligence. His assignment: spread anti-Semitic feelings and infiltrate the nationalist German Workers Party.[8] In 1920, he took over the party and added "National Socialist" to the name; three years later, he led the failed putsch in Munich that landed him in jail. Released in 1924, Hitler found the party had crumbled in his absence, but he rebuilt it—complete with a propaganda machine. He didn't appeal to intellectuals or the wealthy—and was generally loathed in Berlin—but the budding politician changed tactics. The masses didn't respond well to a simple attack on Jewry, but they swallowed his anti-Semitic propaganda when he slammed the ailing Weimar Republic as well. In the 1930 elections, Nazis took 18 percent of the vote, becoming Germany's second most popular party. In January 1933, Hitler was appointed to sit in the chancellor's (prime minister's) seat. Dozens of Hitler's political enemies died within two days, killed by henchman Heinrich Himmler. Several weeks later, the president passed away as well. Hitler absorbed that role into his new one—Führer. Within weeks, all other political parties were banned, thousands were arrested, and tens of thousands of books blazed in squares. The Führer called for a boycott of all "non-Aryan" goods and posted storm troopers outside Jewish stores under signs demanding "Germans defend yourselves! Buy only at Aryan stores!"[9] Half the German Jewish population soon fled, their properties seized by the government. Meanwhile, most of the world looked at the strange little man as a passing fad, a nonthreat, a joke.

KRISTALLNACHT

By 1938, Hitler had stripped away Jews' citizenship and rights, and had begun deporting some out of the country, though not yet to death camps. His program intensified that November. When Herschel Grynszpan—a German Jew living in Paris whose family had been deported to Poland—shot embassy secretary Ernst von Rath, Hitler used the murder as an excuse to step up his anti-Semitic program. That bullet shot in Paris echoed across Germany in the shattering of windows. During the "Night of Broken Glass" (*Kristallnacht* in German), Hitler launched his first full-scale pogrom. Over two days of rioting, amid the crashing of windows of Jewish businesses, homes, and synagogues, Nazi forces rounded up 30,000 Jews, bludgeoned some to death, and sent the rest to concentration camps. The Holocaust had begun.

Hitler quickly demonstrated his intentions to make the 1919 Treaty of Versailles null and void: he rearmed the military with Panzer tanks; he built a new navy; and he tested new fighter planes and fire bombs in practice runs in Sweden and real battles in Spain—all with nary a peep from the international community. (See "Spain," page 147.) He annexed Austria—expressly forbidden by the 1919 treaty; the lone protest came from Mexico. He demanded Sudetenland, in northwestern Czechoslovakia; the leaders of Britain and France handed it to him. Eyebrows indeed rose when Hitler took all of Czechoslovakia in March 1939. But it wasn't until Nazis marched on Poland on September 1, 1939, that the world sat up and took notice. Two days later, Britain, France, and Australia declared war.

From there it was dominoes falling. In April 1940, Nazis invaded Denmark and Norway; in May, they stormed Belgium, the Netherlands, Luxembourg, and France. In September, the blitz on England began. And soon millions of Jews and war prisoners were hauled to concentration camps. By 1942, some camps had chambers where most new arrivals were gassed, in other camps they were worked to death.

> *Eleven million died in concentration camps, including 6 million Jews. Hitler is held responsible for the deaths of between 45 million and 60 million people who perished during World War II.[10]*

Too many soldiers, too many arms, too many sophisticated weapons, and too many people willing to try them out: all were factors in the war that kept going for six years. Thankfully, petroleum supplies began to dry up, slowing down the pace of the fighting. Horrifying new weapons—among them atomic bombs—dramatically pounded in the last nails. The nadir of human existence finally ended.

> *Hitler is believed to have committed suicide on April 30, 1945, in a bunker not far from Berlin's Brandenburg Gate. Details of the death are sketchy— including whether it was by cyanide or by a shot from a pistol—since Soviets were the first on the scene. They claimed to have cremated the corpse.*

In February 1945, Allied leaders met at Yalta to figure out how to crawl out of the black hole of war and revive Europe. Churchill and Roosevelt erred grievously by allowing Stalin to be involved in the reconstruction plan.

> *From 1945 to 1949, West Germany put many remaining Nazis on the stand in the highly publicized Nuremberg Trials, finding most of them guilty.*

THE BERLIN AIRLIFT

It's hard to say exactly when the Cold War began, but many point to Berlin in 1948, when all of Germany was divvied up and occupied by the Four (Allied) Powers—the United States, Britain, France, and the Soviet Union. Located in Soviet-controlled East Germany, the capital Berlin was divided into four occupied sections as well, with the Soviets occupying East Berlin. The troubles began when West Germany introduced a new currency, the deutschmark, to stabilize the economy. Stalin responded by closing all East German roads that led to West Berlin, strangling the other quadrants by cutting off all food and fuel. Stalin figured that the Americans, British, and French would simply give up their quadrants. Instead they dropped the needed goods into West Berlin by plane. The Soviets looked on open-mouthed as food drop missions continued for the next 462 days. Expensive, inefficient, and dangerous, the airlift was the only way to keep West Berlin (surrounded as it was by Soviet-occupied territory) from becoming engulfed by Communism; West Berlin was so potent a symbol that it was deemed worth the effort.

Berlin was split between the Communist East and Democratic/capitalist West for the next forty-two years, which mirrored the situation in all of Germany. Communist East Germany officially became known as the German Democratic Republic; West Germany was called the Federal Republic of Germany—the name used for the whole country today.

The United States took an active role in designing West Germany's future, and the Soviet Union shaped East Germany, establishing multifamily households and monthly work plans, and requiring that East Germany join up in the armed alliance of Communist countries—the Warsaw Pact, which was the Communist answer to NATO. East Germans weren't pleased. During the first twelve years, 2.5 million East Germans snuck over the border. In 1961, without warning, the East German government hastily erected a thick, fortress-like forty-three-kilometer long wall topped with barbed wire, lit by floodlights, and patrolled by guards and dogs. This literal manifestation of the "Iron Curtain" prevented further defection.

1968

It began as just another Vietnam protest, but West Germany's 1968 demonstrations marked the start of a new era. Millions of young Germans took to the streets, rebelling against the establishment ("the swine system") for linking arms with the U.S. and NATO and condemning the older generation for following Hitler's mad dream. Seen as a social revolution by many, the often violent 1968 protests resulted in more educational freedom, more honesty, and a desire to improve Germany's world image; even women's liberation came out of that era. Some of the most vehement '68ers became politicians, Chancellor Gerhard Schröder and Foreign Minister Joschka Fischer among them; others became radicals, who terrorized Germany for the next twenty years.

For decades, the two halves of Germany ignored each other. West German chancellor Willy Brandt, however, thawed the ice in 1969, and continued warming up the East through the next decade. "Ostpolik," as the diplomacy was called, and the roaring economy were the only happy things of the 1970s, as terrorism raged across Germany.

> *Palestinians killed eleven Israelis at the 1972 Munich Olympics, and hijacked a plane. The urban guerrilla group Baader-Meinhof and the Red Army Faction (RAF) kidnapped businessmen; assassinated politicians, lawyers, and industrialists; robbed banks; and attacked U.S. Air Force bases, killing at least fifty.*

RED ARMY FACTION (RAF)

Among the protesters marching in 1968 were wealthy Andreas Baader and intellectual Ulrike Meinhof. Their rage was extreme and contagious, and by 1972, they'd assembled several dozen fanatical followers. Frantic that Germany was becoming part of the U.S.-guided military industrial machine, Red Army Faction (RAF), as Baader-Meinhof was later called, took aim at German and American military and industrial targets. Their most impressive year was 1977, when, in six months, RAF assassinated a German federal prosecutor and two colleagues; offed a bank president; killed four high-placed business consultants; kidnapped and murdered an industrialist; and hired Arab guerrillas to hijack a Lufthansa plane, killing the pilot and holding passengers for days. By 1988, the group was mostly dead, imprisoned, or missing in action. East Germany's secret police may have armed and trained the group.

With rebellions and protests throughout Communist countries, pressure was building to open the East. In 1989, Soviet satellite Hungary allowed holidaying East Germans (and others) to flee from Hungary into Austria. In East Germany, Honecker gave a little and allowed East Germans to travel to West Berlin, but his gesture of November 9, 1989, was misconstrued; border guards thought the countries were no longer divided. Both sides were equally surprised when the wall tumbled down, and the sudden event led to what had long been regarded as a dream: the unification of Germany. On October 3, 1990, East and West Germany, separated for fifty-one years, came together as one.

Hot Spots

BERLIN: THE EYE OF THE KALEIDOSCOPE

Nobody can accuse Germany of being in a rut. Over the past century, the country—like a hot-to-trot clotheshorse heading out to a singles' bar—has tried on more looks, personalities, and agendas than any other country in the world. No place better epitomizes the kaleidoscope of Germany's identities than Berlin. The center of opulence in the early twentieth century transformed into a city of poverty after World War I—a raucous era when husky-voiced women and transvestites sang in smoky cabarets, and edgy artists unleashed experimental creations. Berlin soon emerged as headquarters of the Nazi war machine, and what had been Berlin lay in rubble after the firebombs of World War II. Occupied and divided, Berlin was schizophrenic in the postwar era, and the West German government moved the capital to Bonn. Starting in 1999, with German reunification, Berlin again bloomed as Germany's capital. Now it's a city of renovation, creation, and cranes. Cheap rent and a slew of cool bars draw arty types from designers to DJs, novelists to playwrights—and the city explodes with culture. Over 150 museums and galleries, three opera houses, dozens of theaters, a pulsing nightlife, chic restaurants, an underground arts scene, secondhand clothing stores (and those with original fashions that look secondhand) are just a few reasons alternative types looking for the un-mined creative hot spot of Europe are donning thick coats and setting up here.

> More Turks (2.5 million) live in Berlin than in any other city except Turkey's largest, Istanbul. Many were invited in a few decades ago as guest workers.

The Holocaust memorial: Finally opened, the $30 million Monument for the Murdered Jews of Europe in central Berlin consists of 2,700 columns of varying heights that have been treated with graffiti-resistant coating. That coating was yet another delay in the construction of the monument that had been in the works since 1988. The problem: the manufacturer had also manufactured the gas that killed millions of Jews in concentration camps.

Hamburg: Elegant, filled with parks, and boasting a wild bar scene, the city has plenty of touristic charm, but that wasn't the lure for 9/11 ringleader Mohammed Atta, who studied engineering here and worked for the city planning office. Employers say he was kind, hard-working and devout; he had a prayer rug at his desk, and never failed to give thanks to Allah five times a day.

Prussia: The kingdom that stitched Germany together was dissolved as a geographical entity in 1934.

Bavaria: Best known for Oktoberfest, when her beer halls are even more festive than usual, and for rigid Edmund Stoiber (whom you won't see at the beer halls), heavily Catholic Bavaria is the overachiever of Germany, with the lowest unemployment rate and the scariest ideas; the Bavarian government recently proposed "tagging" Roma for easy identification.

The Rhine: Europe's busiest waterway, and, until recently, the biggest sewer in Europe, the Rhine provides both drinking water and an industrial dumping ground. It's being cleaned up; aquatic life is returning, as are the fishermen. Eel anyone?

> *Green-friendly: Germany is one of the world's environmental heroes, and her popular Green Party keeps an eye on sustainable development. Recycling is second nature, the public transport is excellent, and all of Germany's nuclear plants are to be phased out by 2020. And, by and large, Germans simply don't litter.*

Dresden: This beautiful city in eastern Germany seems jinxed: it was firebombed by the U.S. and Britain at the end of WWII, with 35,000 civilians incinerated in the resulting, citywide inferno. Rebuilt to her original plan and unveiled in stately splendor in 2001, Dresden was ravaged by floods the next year, but the old gal has been shined up yet again.

Frankfurt: Rising along the River Main, the financial heart of Germany has a stunning skyline that resembles New York City's, hence her nickname "Mainhattan." Every October, she hosts the world's largest and most important book fair.

The ground: Weighing in at 500 pounds or more, Allied bombs are still embedded in German soil. Almost 2,000 have been unearthed in Berlin alone since 1945, and there are still 15,000 more to find in that city—and some are live. Now over 2,500 people are searching them out across Germany, digging up about 20,000 tons of the tickers every year.[11]

Desks: Chunks of the Berlin Wall serve as paperweights all over the world. If you don't already own one, don't bother now: so many fakes have been peddled that it's said the wall has been sold three times.

DREAMS COME TRUE

Mad King Ludwig (1845–1886) of Bavaria had the grandiose dream of building enchanting mountaintop castles that would capture music in architectural form. Built as tributes to his favorite composer, Richard Wagner, Ludwig's castles are splashed with scenes from Wagner's operas; even caves are built into the spindly towered fantasies. Security-wise, they were worthless, and in fact may have cost Ludwig his life. He was found mysteriously drowned in Starnberger Lake. His family, livid about his extravagant follies that were eating up all their money, was suspected of plotting his death. Ludwig's castles, particularly ornate Neuschwanstein, turned out to be a brilliant long-term investment: today they are Germany's biggest tourist draws.

Garching reactor: Germany plans to phase out all nuclear reactors for electricity, but has no current plans to shut down this twenty-megawatt nuclear research reactor, fueled with enriched uranium, at the Munich Technical University. This sort of reactor flies in the face of nonproliferation agreements; some worry that it could be used to build nuclear bombs.[12]

Nuremberg: The city where Hitler pushed through legislation to strip Jews of their legal rights was also where Nazi war criminals were tried.

Autobahn: Twelve thousand miles of mostly speed-limitless highway, the Autobahn—the world's first interstate—was commissioned by Hitler in the 1930s to give jobs to the Depression-era unemployed. Polish Jews and POWs completed it in 1941, but the armed forces didn't use it for the original plan: the asphalt couldn't support their tanks.

Hotshots

Angela Merkel: Chancellor, 2005–present. See box on page 42.

Horst Köhler: President, 2004–present. Christian Democrat Köhler should be able to help the economy; he was former head of the IMF.

Gerhard Schröder: The former chancellor is now heading a pipeline project to bring natural gas from Russia to Germany.

Joschka Fischer: A former taxi driver, and formerly Germany's most popular postwar politician, Fischer headed the Green Party and served as foreign minister under Schröder. Left both posts in 2005. No word if he returned to his cab.

Edmund Stoiber: Minister-President of

© Klaus Franke/dpa/Corbis

The lady chancellor is cheering up Germans.

Bavaria, 1993–present. White-haired and super-tan, conservative Stoiber lives up to the image of the Super-German Type A, working eighteen hours a day. It's paid off: the popular Christian Democrat from Bavaria has helped make his state Germany's wealthiest.

Neo-Nazis: The recent appearance of neo-Nazis, said to number around 30,000—mainly in the East—presents a tough problem. The government deprogramming school hasn't attracted many, and courts have ruled that it is unconstitutional to ban the neo-Nazi parties. In 2000, young neo-Nazis were behind the murder of an African man and a bomb explosion in Düsseldorf; many believe they are heading to Sweden and France.

Helmut Kohl: Chancellor, 1982–1998. Portly four-term chancellor, power-monger Kohl was a heavyweight in almost every way. He approved deployment of NATO nuclear missiles at German army bases, headed the republic when the Berlin Wall fell, and oversaw the reunification between the two halves of Germany. He lost to Schröder in 1998, and fell hard. He was implicated in a campaign finance scandal the next year, which had some calling for him to take a vacation in prison. The scandal shook his Christian Democrat Party; the power party of postwar German politics, their popularity plummeted until Angela Merkel was called in to clean up the mess.

Scientologists: Were they trying to infiltrate the top of Germany's power pyramid, or just trying to get leaders to take free personality tests? Who knows if the German press was on to something or exaggerating the numbers, but recently there was such a scare about scientologists trying to influence German politics that it turned into an international brouhaha.[13]

News you can understand: *Deutsche Welt*, one of several interesting papers that publish in English: (www.dw-world.de).

3. UNITED KINGDOM
(Britain)
Playing Both Sides

FAST FACTS

Country: United Kingdom of Great Britain and Northern Ireland
Capital: London
Government: Constitutional monarchy
Independence: Unified in tenth century (established as UK in 1927)
Population: 60,610,000 (2006 estimate)

Head of State:	Queen Elizabeth II
Head of Government:	Prime Minister Tony Blair (1997); may be shoved out soon
Elections:	Monarchy is hereditary; prime minister is head of majority party or coalition in House of Commons
Name of Parliament:	Parliament (House of Commons and House of Lords)
Ethnicity:	92% White (84% English, 9% Scottish, 3% Northern Irish, 5% Welsh); 2% Black; 2% Indian; 1% Pakistani; 1% mixed; 2% other (2001 census)
Religion:	72% Christian (Anglican, Roman Catholic, Presbyterian, Methodist); 23% unspecified; 3% Muslim; also Sikh, Hindu, Jewish
Language:	English (the Queen's, and heavily accented variations)
Literacy:	99% (claimed); functional illiteracy 22% (says UN)
Famous Exports:	Jerry Springer, Ozzy Osbourne, Charlie Chaplin
Economic Big Boy:	BP (oil and gas); 2004 total sales: $285.06 billion[1]
Per Capita GDP:	$30,900 (2005 estimate)
Unemployment:	5% (November 2005 Eurostat figure)
Percentage in Poverty:	17% (2002 estimate)
EU Status:	EEC member state since 1973
Currency:	British pound (sterling)

Quick Tour

So much of Britain is charming, if hard on the wallet and often plagued by gray skies and rain. Yet how lovely is the land when you can see beyond the cleared splash from the windshield wiper. Country villages ringed by pastures and dotted with lakes, Scotland's blindingly green hills punctuated by cemeteries and golf courses, Northern Ireland's crackling-fire inns downwind from whiskey distilleries, and Wales's battered coasts are but a few things that lured tourists long before the Harry Potter craze.

> Kids tracing Harry's steps as he learns to fly in magic school helped the UK soar to the sixth most visited country in the world, with 24 million visitors in 2004.[2]

London's regal Tower Bridge

Photo by John Humphries

GEOGRAPHICAL CONFUSION: UNITED KINGDOM VS. GREAT BRITAIN VS. IRELAND

Popularly called Britain, the country officially known as the United Kingdom is made up of four parts: England, Scotland, and Wales (all sharing the same island, and collectively known as Great Britain), plus Northern Ireland, the six British-run counties on the island of Ireland. All of Ireland was once part of Great Britain, but the bulk of that island became a separate, independent republic in 1921. The people who live in Britain are known as Britons or Brits, unless one particular group is specified—e.g., the English, the Scots, or the Welsh. In this book, Britain and the UK are used interchangeably.

With her swanky hotels (popular hangouts for well-heeled Londoners), nostalgia clubs (where partiers don smoking jackets and false eyelashes and dance to old jazz), and chic bars (that can now stay open past 11 PM), history-steeped London is the tourist magnet, with millions stopping by to gaze at Big Ben. Recently, more has changed than the guards. The city that landed the 2012 Olympics is now Europe's cultural epicenter, where flashy designs command eyes to London's catwalks, witty writers launch new genres, theater thrives in the West End, and edgy artists try to "out-edge" each other in a battle to break taboos. No other European country culturally influences the world more than Britain, which now holds up Coldplay, Beckham, and Potter as her symbols.

BRIT POP

London runways yank the heads of fashionistas worldwide with creations of Alexander McQueen, Shelley Fox, Phoebe Philo, and Boudicca, while British books shoot to the top of world bestseller lists, be they magic-infused fiction or cheeky "chick-lit" tales of urban singlettes fleeing from credit card bills and defying societal expectations, such as Helen Fielding's diary of Bridget Jones. Theater lovers may choose experimental works meant for heady contemplation, but the biggest hits are raucous musicals: *Jerry Springer—The Opera* (highlights included singing and dancing Ku Klux Klan members) packed houses for several seasons, even at the previously stuffy National Theatre, and Monty Python is stealing the West End with its musical *Spamalot*, featuring kicklines of knights. While contemporary British culture may be madcap, the visual arts—helped along by advertising magnate Charles Saatchi, patron to daring "Young British Artists"—most often cause eyebrows to raise and mouths to drop, or at least try to. Damien Hirst, whose work includes oversized, overflowing ashtrays and chunks of dead fish, was outdone by the Chapman Brothers, Jake and Dinos, who buy up rare works, such as Goyas, only to deface them with drawings of clowns, and who affix plastic penises to dolls' heads. They've been left in the dust by the latest in expletive artists, whose deep statements seem increasingly on par with those of teenagers who write graffiti on bathroom walls. But they are popular. The national art museum Tate Modern displays many of the subversive works, and the East End's Hoxton district is in the arts spotlight, made trendier by gallery White Cube.

With the European Union's third largest population, Britain commands respect as a cultural center and finance headquarters—the London Stock Exchange is Europe's biggest—but her weight in the world arena has changed. Britain is no longer the hungry imperial whale prowling the seven seas and swallowing more land than any other colonial power; nor is she now the manufacturing heart of Europe. The land whose thinkers unveiled the basic workings of the planet (gravitational forces, for one) and whose creators introduced many of the world's most important devices isn't Invention Central any longer. But the island kingdom still stands tall on the global power team. Granted, these days clout comes less from how Britain acts than how she reacts, and less from what Britain is than who she knows and can influence (or vice versa).

HELPFUL BRITISH INVENTORS

James Watt:	Revolutionized steam engines
Thomas Crapper:	Invented the modern toilet
Richard Trevithick:	Invented the steam locomotive

Sir Alexander Fleming:	Discovered penicillin, ending syphilis plague
Alexander Watson-Watt:	Invented radar
Tim Berners-Lee:	Invented the World Wide Web

Geographically and ideologically, the UK bridges the gap between the European continent and the United States, Britain's good mate and fighting partner. The Anglo-American relationship rattles Europe's elite—some hiss that Britain is "Atlanticist" (too close to the *other* side of the ocean)—but it aptly reflects British ambivalence about being part of Europe and the EU.

BRITS AND YANKS

Never mind that little eighteenth-century tiff when American colonists flipped off the king, resulting in the War of Independence (1775–1783). Now Britain is America's best friend. Clasping hands in wars and in pursuit of global corporate democracy, the two powerbrokers are united in love of oil, arms sales, and doing whatever they deem proper, especially if there's a buck or two to be made. Yanks fought alongside Brits in both world wars; had they not been so chummy, Americans may never have entered the European arena, where the arms she shipped and the troops she sent were crucial in evening the score. America and Britain forged powerful alliances such as NATO, standing out as the most vocal "white hats" in the Cold War, and encouraging those under Communist regimes to rise up and rebel (though rarely helping those who did). Recent Anglo-American activities have been most questionable—whether you're looking at costs, ethics, or motives. Brits fought alongside Americans in 1991's Persian Gulf War, which drove Iraq out of Kuwait, and the Anglo-American duo continued to fly fighter planes over Iraq for a decade, imposing no-fly zones in that country without international authority to do so. The U.S. and UK jointly launched the "War on Terror" with the 2001 bombing of Afghanistan that dismantled the Taliban (temporarily) and unleashed anarchy in its wake. But their most controversial move ever was the 2003 invasion of Iraq. Framed as part of the "War on Terror" and sold with dire warnings from both President George W. Bush and Prime Minister Tony Blair that Iraq possessed weapons of mass destruction (WMD) that it could—and probably would—unleash on their countries, that war, launched despite international protests and millions marching in the streets, made both countries look like warmongering fools when no WMD were found and Iraq erupted in chaos. The leaders' claims were bogus, and so was the packaging: Bush and Blair had been planning a regime change in Iraq at least eight months before the 9/11 attacks occurred or the "War on Terror" was unveiled. A divisive issue in Britain, where the citizenry split was 50-50 on going to war, the Iraq war triggered serious debate over the benefits derived from loyally and habitually backing us Yanks.

> *Bush and Blair, both deeply religious, have said that God told them to at-*
> *tack Iraq, leading one to wonder whether they're both delusional or*
> *whether God is not a skilled military strategist with an exit plan.*

The UK looks puny now, as compared to the behemoth it was during the nineteenth century, when nearly 40 percent of the planet's land was stitched into the British Empire's tapestry. But in many ways, this is Britain's golden hour—well, at least until you peek under the rug. Forget the 1970s and 1980s, when the British economy was so shaky that the government pathetically cut the free milk program in schools, unemployment hovered around 14 percent[3], and the major trade unions crippled the country with continual strikes.

> *That depressing period triggered more than the birth of angry punk music,*
> *as epitomized by the Sex Pistols. Two of the country's lingering problems*
> *emerged then as well: soccer hooligans—who take the game so seriously*
> *that they attack people and rip up property after a match—and the increas-*
> *ingly popular anti-immigrant British National Party (linked to neo-Nazis)—an*
> *instigator of ethnic violence.*

The British pound is one of the world's strongest currencies, and the British economy is vibrant. Previously aging, stodgy, and dour, leaders are now young, modern, and slick. The media, with its wide-ranging focus, is the most insightful on the planet. Power-wise, Britain hasn't flexed more muscle since the end of World War II. And, most amazingly, Brits have learned to cook, with celebrity chefs Jamie Oliver, Nigella Lawson, and Gordon Ramsay leading the charge. While many extol the culinary leap that proves that British haute cuisine extends beyond shepherd's pie, celebrity cooking shows have had an unexpected effect. Many Britons—perfectly capable of overboiling peas back in the days when that *was* the cuisine—now suffer performance anxiety; over two-thirds have stopped throwing dinner parties due to high expectations.[4]

Of course there's a flip side. The strong pound buys luxury on holiday, but life at home is staggeringly expensive. The snazzy bars and designer hotels that helped make Britannia so cool charge $20 for a martini and $500 for a night's stay. London is creatively rich, but creative types need to be rich to live there. Housing prices are so steep that only writers who've nailed Nobels can afford to buy property. A taxi to Heathrow from downtown rings in at $100, a low-key night on the town costs double, at least. And, lately, there's a national erosion of trust. Tony Blair is now seen as a man who has lost touch, is spouting fountains of misinformation, and won't relinquish his chair—even to Gordon Brown, the man he's been promising it to for years (see "Hotshots," page 81). And Tony's constant cootchie-cooing with George W. Bush is a serious liability. Thanks, at least in part, to Britain's always-at-DC's-side stance, radical Islamists are striking out in the UK—as evidenced by the attacks on July 7, 2005.

7/7

The fear of suitcase bombs left at bus stops, common in the 1980s, had subsided with the mellowing of the IRA, and it was just another commute to London that Wednesday, July 7, 2005, the opening day of the G-8 summit in London. At 8:50 AM, three bombs exploded, ripping open several subway cars on the underground; moments later, another bomb blew up on a bus, propelling it into the air. Thousands were trapped in the subway for hours, as emergency workers pulled out hundreds of injured and fifty-six dead. Although al-Qaeda claimed responsibility, the government initially denied that the work of the four foreign-born suicide bombers—three of Pakistini descent, and one a Jamaican—was at all connected to bin Laden's group or offshoots. The official report, released the following May, also skimmed over intelligence fumbling—the terrorist threat level had been lowered a few weeks before the July 7 attacks, and even though two of the men had previously blipped on intel radar, they weren't monitored. Under immediate heat from the public and media, which dismissed the reports as a whitewash, Downing Street soon announced that indeed there did appear to be al-Qaeda links, making this the first admitted al-Qaeda attack on British soil. The media and public are still pressuring the government to admit that the attack was related to British foreign policy, particularly the war in Iraq.[5]

The UK is home to some 2 million multiethnic Muslims; about 10 percent are considered radical. Until recently, Britain had extremely liberal asylum laws and welcomed those facing death sentences in other countries.

Although Brits displayed their famous stiff upper lip, and most went back to work the next day—Mayor Ken Livingstone made a point of taking the subway—Britain, where London is a melting pot and the city's 40 percent ethnic minorities are part of the city's cultural tapestry, was stunned. Radical Islam had been a growing concern—particularly Abu Hamza al-Masri, the fiery Egyptian imam at London's Finsbury Park Mosque, who instructed followers to attack and kill politicians, bankers, video shop owners, alcohol vendors, and non-Muslims.[6] Arrested in 2004, al-Masri is now serving seven years in prison for racial hatred and incitement to murder, but seeds he planted may still grow.

Predictably, the racist British National Party, which holds Islam to be a "wicked, vicious faith,"[7] had a field day. Buses soon carried their advertising banner—with the slogan "Maybe now it's time to start listening to BNP!"—and in the next general election, the party doubled its seats in local government.

BNP: NAZIS, RACISTS, AND CLOWNS?

The European Parliament described the hard-right, foreigner-loathing British National Party as "an openly Nazi party";[8] founder John Tyndall proudly referred to *Mein Kampf* as his "bible";[9] and anti-Fascist magazine *Searchlight* has been warning about the racist party's rise for fifteen years. Now headed by reputed neo-Nazi Nick Griffin (who denies that description), the party has widened its focus and is now targeting foreign-born immigrants and their descendents. BNP wants to padlock the doors and shove non-Europeans back to the countries of their "ethnic origins," with an envelope of money as incentive. A fundamentalist Christian party that only allows UK-born whites to join, the party stirs up emotions. In Oldham (in England's north), BNP lambasted Asian immigrants one night in May 2001; hours later, neo-Nazis, white hooligans, and other BNP supporters charged into Pakistani neighborhoods chanting, "If you hate Pakis, clap your hands," and throwing bricks through windows and into faces. Riots erupted, as whites and Asians hurled 700 petrol bombs at each other, looted stores, and torched over sixty cars—causing $14 million in damages in seven hours. By daybreak, hundreds had been arrested, dozens injured, and the streets—littered with scorched car shells and smashed windows—looked like a war zone. Two weeks later, the British National Party took 16 percent of the Oldham vote. While growing support of BNP alarms many, the good news is that once in office BNP politicians are often inept. As *Observer* columnist Nick Cohen observed: "One [BNP city council member] resigned after smashing a bottle into the face of another BNP member. A second left because he didn't have a clue about local government—'There's meetings that go right over my head and there's little point in me being there,' the poor dear complained. In Stoke-on-Trent, the city's first BNP [city council member] spoke only twice during two years in office (and one of his 'speeches' was an interruption to ask what 'abstain' meant)."[10]

Even Brits who aren't racist tend to harshly judge their own. What to Americans may seem an egalitarian society largely isn't, say Brits. The English, who for centuries ground down the Irish, the Scots, and the Welsh, do equal time in flicking off fellow Englishmen. One's accent—the vowels or consonants one swallows, even the way one refers to restrooms (the upper classes say "loo," those below them say "toilet")—conveys one's life story, including income, alma mater, the neighborhood one hails from, and the clubs one belongs to. The class system, ingrained in Victorian times, still plays out today—in opportunities available and in debates over schools and who is allowed entry to the most prestigious universities—making mobility in British society feel tightly restricted.

> *Brits, particularly the English, are painfully polite (as illustrated in the hilarious cultural critique* Watching the English *by Kate Fox), but there's also the problem of "yobs," who step beyond drunken buffoonery. According to the government, every year some 125,000 Brits have their faces slashed, their eyes blackened, or their noses and jaws bashed in bar brawls—including 5,000 or so "glassings," when bottles and champagne flutes turn into weapons.*[11]

Social problems don't stop there. Recent reports show that many Brits can't read—or at least not much beyond the *Sun*'s page 3, the best-read page in the UK, since each day it features a pinup of a topless gal. (Tellingly, Rupert Murdoch's paper claims the highest circulation in Britain—nearly 4 million.)

CN U RD THS?: LITERACY MATTERS

British politicians are persuasive debaters whose words and delivery are crafted by years of study and rhetoric at fine institutions. The British media is brilliant: sharp analysis, snappy style, and reporters in far-flung corners give the news here an edge unrivaled anywhere. The education system is often considered one of the world's best, with Oxford and Cambridge being the gems that add luster to the British claim of intellectual superiority. British writers are perhaps history's most gifted and revered; the elegant words of Shakespeare, Dickens, Austen, and the Brontës are still held dear centuries after the paper they scribbled on has crumbled to dust. So it's particularly disturbing that reports indicate that Britain has a very high "functional illiteracy" rate: 24 percent can't read this sentence, having trouble reading much more than "Stop," "Go," and "Vote here."[12]

> *Forty percent of Britons never read books, and 13 percent of Britons say they simply never read anything whatsoever.*[13]

Those who can read have certainly noticed that once-popular and hugely influential global player Tony Blair is sinking, and taking his New Labor Party with him. The prime minister's approval rating in May 2006 dropped below 30 percent, largely due to disgust with his wartime politics. The New Labor Party, for the first time in a decade, took second place in the country's local elections—being beaten out by the Conservatives, aka Tories. Blair reacted by rearranging his cabinet and tossing Foreign Minister Jack Straw. According to the *Washington Post*, insiders link the surprising dismissal of Straw (who'd just visited Iraq with Secretary of State Condi Rice) with the minister's comments about Iran. An attack on Iran was "inconceivable," said Straw, and the prospect of the U.S. launching a nuclear attack on that country, said Straw, is "completely nuts."[14]

History Review

Romans and Vikings, druids and dragons, knights and magicians, murderous queens, loony kings, and torturous deaths—British history has them all pressed into its pages, along with wars with the French, wars with the neighbors, and battles against poverty and disease, which, given the bone-dampening weather, always seemed to be more deadly here. But regardless of what the territorial holdings were that year—an island or an empire—the common thread of British history has been the continuing monarchy, a rule unbroken except for five years, when harsh Oliver Cromwell stepped in after the civil war to serve as lord protector (1653–1658) and act like the cruelest of kings. (See "Ireland," page 117.)

A FEW MEMORABLE MONARCHS

King Arthur: First mentioned in a Welsh poem from AD 596, Arthur and his Round Table may be merely a myth; most "history" about them was written seven centuries after the Round Table disbanded.

King John (b. 1167; King 1199–1216): In 1215, he was forced to sign the Magna Carta, the first document giving rights to the common man.

Henry VIII (b. 1491; King 1509–1547): Married six wives but had to start his own church to do it.

Mary, Queen of Scots (1542–1587): Never sat on the English throne, but Catholic Mary tried to snatch it from her cousin, Protestant Elizabeth I; when the plot was revealed, she was beheaded after paying the executioner to make it a clean chop. He didn't.

Elizabeth I (b. 1533; Queen 1558–1603): Who knows if she was really chaste (she so loved to flirt), but the Virgin Queen—as she was known, since she never married—pointed British navigators to far parts of the globe.

James I (b. 1566; ruled 1603–1625): The Scottish king first united Scotland and England when he inherited the English throne too. Demanded adherence to Anglican religion; dissenters fled first to Holland and then to North America, where they were best known as the Pilgrims.

Charles I (b. 1600; Ruled 1625–1649): Unpopular Charles so angered everybody that Britain fell into a forty-eight-year civil war, which led to Oliver Cromwell and cronies taking over.

King George III (b. 1738; King 1760–1820): Afflicted with insanity-causing porphyria, Crazy King George battled more than mental demons; he also fought in the French and Indian War, which zapped the treasury and caused him to raise taxes in American colonies, which led to the Revolutionary War, which led to more wars as other colonies tried to wrest free. During the last nine years of his rule, he was blind and so bonkers that he was imprisoned in his own castle.

Queen Victoria (b. 1819; Queen 1837–1901): Her offspring and descendants married or became crowned heads across Europe (even Queen Alexandra, of Czar Nicholas fame, was related) but the longest-reigning British monarch is best known for Britain's colonial acquisitions and technological advances.

Considering they're surrounded by water, Brits were sure slow in hopping onto their ships, entering the colonization race a century after Portugal and Spain. They set up colonies from snowy Canada to balmy Florida, then hit the Caribbean, snatching up small isles. When they reached South America, the Spanish and Portuguese had gobbled up almost everything; the British grabbed but one tiny tract (British Guiana), before planting the flag in Central America, including Belize, from which they depleted nearly all wood. By the mid-1700s, they were shoving the French, the Dutch, the Portuguese, and the Spanish out of the way and grabbing whatever they could in Asia. By the 1800s, the sun no longer set on the British Empire, which included land on every continent.

EXPLORERS: BRITS BEHAVING BADLY?

A few who took to the seas:[15]

Sir John Hawkins (1532–1595): Charming chap; introduced the slave trade in Britain and looted Spain's treasure-laden ships, bringing Spain and England to war.

Sir Francis Drake (1540–1596): Pirate and slave-trader Drake could do no wrong by Queen Elizabeth I, especially after he sank the Spanish Armada in 1588, when it sailed into the English Channel.

Sir Walter Raleigh (1554–1618): Poet Raleigh, legend has it, gained favor for tossing his cloak over a puddle that lay in the Virgin Queen's path. Looked everywhere for fabled El Dorado, where rivers flowed gold, from Spain to America's east coast starting the colony at Raleigh, North Carolina, along the way. Later a royal spy, he penned books about travels and world history.

Captain James Cook (1728–1779): Sailed to Tahiti to calculate size of the solar system, then mapped Antarctica and the northern Australian coast; died in Hawaii fighting with natives over a stolen canoe.

David Livingstone (1813–1873): Scottish missionary, physician, and early slavery abolitionist Livingstone explored nearly a third of Africa, then disappeared. The *New York Herald* sent explorer Henry Stanley to find him, which he did in 1872, after two years of searching, greeting him with the famous line "Dr. Livingstone, I presume?"

Richard Burton (1821–1890): Military man and spy, Burton sniffed out secrets in India's souks and explored Arabia and Egypt, writing breathtaking books about an exotic Muslim world unknown to the West.

The colonies spurred a revolution back home. North America and India were rich in white gold—cotton—and clever Brits devised new machines to more easily turn the fluff into cloth. Spinning jennies, steam engines, and water-powered machines sparked the Industrial Revolution that brought the masses from their cottages, where they had worked by the hearth, to cities where they sweated in factories as cogs in the machine.

Even though her textile business was booming, Britain's wars (mostly with France) were costly, and King George III's new sugar tax, then stamp tax, then tea tax, brewed up such anger in the colonies—culminating in the Boston Tea Party of 1773)—that Britain lost America. Fighting began in 1775, the Americans declared independence in 1776, and in 1783, the Brits recognized it and shoved off, relying even more on India to keep Britain in cotton.

THE DAYS OF BRITISH EXPANSION

By the end of the 1800s, the empire's holdings included:

Canada, Australia, New Zealand: Now independent, but Queen of England is still head of state
Hong Kong: Returned to China in 1997
Cyprus: Independent in 1960
Malta: Independent in 1964
Most of India: Independent in 1947

South Africa, Rhodesia, Kenya, Sierra Leone, Egypt, Sudan, British Soma-
liland: All of Britain's African colonies became independent in the 1960s and 1970s
The Falklands, Belize, Honduras, Bahamas, Gibraltar: The last remains of
the British Empire, they're still holding, but who knows for how long

---

The nineteenth-century British military forces were formidable: under
Wellington, they halted Napoleon's grand ambitions at Waterloo in 1815.

In 1837, eighteen-year-old Queen Victoria took the throne, where she would remain for sixty-four years, during which time over half of the country's residents moved to London or industrial cities Manchester and Birmingham. During the Victorian era of engineering marvels, Britain leapt into the future, pulling the rest of Europe along with her. The electric telegraph opened up new worlds as Brits strung cables under the Atlantic. Just as revolutionary was the steam locomotive, which crossed over massive iron bridges, shortening journeys that once required days to mere hours, delivering hordes of workers to cities, and replacing canal barges as haulers of coal to steel factories. Huge steamships plied oceans in two weeks, explorations into Africa and Asia brought more riches, and riveting adventure books were the rage. The world suddenly seemed so close at hand (and so intriguing) that fashionable Victorians decorated with wall-size ornamental screens displaying maps. And new ideas percolated everywhere.

CHARLES DARWIN (1809–1882)

Heir to the founder of Wedgwood pottery, Charles Darwin could have spent a leisurely life flitting about collecting butterflies and plucking pansies on the moors. Instead, he triggered the biggest leap in human self-understanding when he published *The Origin of Species by Means of Natural Selection* in 1859. Invited in 1831 to be the captain's companion on the HMS *Beagle*, which voyaged to South America, Darwin was sick for most the journey, but threw himself into nature exploration once the ship anchored and he stopped throwing up. Most interesting: the finches and tortoises on the Galápagos Islands off Ecuador, where locals knew which island a tortoise or bird was from by subtle differences in markings. Back in England, Darwin became intrigued with the idea that species adapted to their surroundings, and that those with the qualities most suited to their environment were most likely to survive. He threw himself into a frenzy of writing and research about natural selection, ultimately proposing that humans had evolved from primates. Realizing that his theories would deeply offend the Christian Church, he sat on his manuscript for twenty years. He might never have published it, had not a letter arrived in 1858, from a scientist in Asia, Alfred Russel Wallace, laying out almost exactly the same premise as Darwin had in his unpublished book. Honorably, Darwin sent Wallace's paper in for publication, but soon thereafter he finally lugged his own dusty manuscript to the printer. Predictably, the church condemned his ideas, but Darwin's book about our ancestors the apes wasn't as controversial as it might have been; he had friends in publishing circles and one, Thomas Henry Huxley, launched a lecture series about it, softening the blow.

Darwin's ideas opened the door to eugenics, selective breeding to emphasize positive characteristics, which intrigued the Nazis. The man who first peddled eugenics, Sir Francis Galton, was Darwin's cousin.[16]

Times were still hazardous, particularly for the urban poor; cholera raged, along with typhoid and deadly flus. Syphilis brought death and insanity to millions; workers lived in overcrowded, rat-ridden dwellings; and Jack the Ripper made the night seem much darker, even after the streets glowed with gaslights.

No writer better summed up the horrors and inequality of that era than Charles Dickens, who personalized the issues of class stratification, poverty, ghetto housing, and urban grime in his novels, including Oliver Twist *and* Nicholas Nickleby. *Dickens was well versed in societal ills, and not just because of his experience as a reporter—his father's debt had landed the entire family in the debtors' prison. Dickens's fiction produced tangible effects: in 1862, American George Peabody, who was living in London, donated 500,000 pounds to renovate the real-life slum that was the setting for* Oliver Twist. *Peabody Building Housing Blocks, as the neighborhoods of workers' dwellings became known, later became favorite haunts of Jack the Ripper.*

Parts of London were a scourge, but Scotland (or Alba as she's known in Gaelic), was worse, especially after the English began fixing her up. Shortly after Scotland unified with England in 1707, the English banned northerners from wearing tartans or even playing the bagpipes, stripping the clansmen of their cultural past. Worse, the English embarked on so-called improvements. Justifying the moves as a means of modernizing the subsistence farming society, wealthy Englishmen, who had dreams of transforming Scotland into hunting estates and sheep farms, ran farmers off the land and into the cities. Their method was simple: torch the Scots' houses and farms, killing their cattle, ruining their crops, scorching the soil, and ensuring that there was no timber left for rebuild-ing, as the farmers fled, choking, into smoke that sometimes spread for hun-dreds of miles. The Clearances drove tens of thousands of Scots from their homeland between 1785 and 1854, killing many in forced evictions now re-garded as genocide.

The Irish, too, were being uprooted from their land, which had been officially stitched to England in 1801. During the Irish Potato Famine (1845–1847), a mil-lion Irish starved to death, while English landlords shoved the weakened peo-ple, who couldn't pay rent, off their farms. Another million Irish fled for North America. (See "Ireland," page 124.)

Even the Welsh, who'd been bonded with England since 1535, were having their worst run-ins with the English, who owned the coal mines in Wales that pow-ered the Industrial Revolution. Armed uprisings and rebellions over poor working conditions and highway taxes became common, particularly in the 1830s.

> *The queen ineffectively addressed the problems, although she personally donated substantial sums of money to help the starving in Ireland, a land she so adored that she'd wanted to set up residence there. Mostly a figure-head, her concerns had little effect.*

The most dramatic display of how life evolved in the Victorian era was the Great Exhibition of Works of Industry of All Nations in 1851—which showed glimpses into cultures as much as it showcased machines. Six million visitors roamed through the Crystal Palace—a bubble of glass and steel iron erected in Hyde Park—where 100,000 exhibits came from all corners, from China to Italy, Turkey to the United States. Looms and ornate tapestries, giant harvesters and hookah pipes, life-size dinosaurs and homes carved from coal, thrashers and envelope-making machines, newfangled kitchen appliances alongside those from ancient Egypt, intricate paper screens and the latest fashions in nightcaps, as well as operas, circuses, dog shows, cat shows, flower exhibitions, displays of rare gems, flush toilets, carriages pulled by giant paper kites, the world's biggest diamond, the world's biggest organ, the world's biggest fountain (with water shooting 250 feet high)—all could be seen here at the world's largest fair, which was thick with pickpockets and caused traffic jams across London for six months.[17]

The event was trumpeted as proof that Britain was the world's most ad-vanced society—and it was certainly the most powerful of the era, although Brits of that age could scarcely be called the most humane. And no one epito-mizes that period's avarice and cruelty more than diamond magnate Cecil Rhodes.

CECIL RHODES (1853–1902)

The sickly son of a village vicar, Cecil Rhodes sailed to the warm Dark Continent to recuperate at his brother's South African farm. Arriving during a diamond rush, the young lad bought a hefty portion of the Kimberley mines, which (it turned out) held most of the world's most adored sparklers. Wealth wasn't enough, although he had even more after buying up nearby gold mines; Rhodes wanted land, power, and British domination of the world. "I contend that we are the finest race in the world and that the more of the world we inhabit, the better it is for the human race,"[18] he wrote in *Confession of Faith*, a book he penned at the age of twenty-four. Though he never succeeded in bringing the whole world under British control, he brought part of Africa under it, being de facto founder of three colonies, Nyasaland (today's Malawi), as well as Northern and Southern Rhodesia (today's Zambia and Zimbabwe, respectively), which he named after himself. In roping the colonies together, his hired armies killed a thousand Africans, and Rhodes single-handedly triggered a three-year war with Dutch living in Africa—the nasty Boer War (1899–1902) that killed upward of 75,000—after a botched raid to seize Dutch-held lands. Just as loathsome: he turned the Africans who lived near his mines into imprisoned slaves. Workers were forced to live in his heavily policed mining compounds, which they weren't allowed to leave, even when deadly epidemics broke out. According to his live-in companion (Rhodes was rumored to be gay), Dr. Leander Starr Jameson, "Cecil's favorite Sunday pastime was to go into the De Beers' native compound, where he had built them a fine swimming bath, and throw in shillings for the natives to dive for."[19] Rhodes died of a heart attack in 1902, but left many legacies, among them the Rhodes Scholarships at Oxford, until recently exclusively for men, and the De Beers Diamond Company, which hoards most of the world's diamonds and has been charged with antitrust activities and artificially manipulating the market. The land grabs Rhodes initiated while he was prime minister have repercussions today. In 2002, Zimbabwe's president, Robert Mugabe, snatched those lands back, this time taking them from the whites and giving them to the blacks.[20] One more continuing Rhodes ripple: he's now an idol to neo-Nazis.

The nineteenth-century British were the most benevolent of colonizers, which, granted, is not saying much. They built roads, schools, and hospitals; introduced new agricultural crops; and planted the seeds of democracy and liberty. However, slavery was common, as were massacres; wars were purposely whipped up; diseases were (inadvertently) introduced; resources were entirely depleted; religion and culture changes were forced upon the locals; and most riches from the colonies went to the British Treasury. At their worst, the British imperialists were brutal. They burned textile plants in Madras, India, so that India couldn't compete with Manchester's factories; they introduced opium to the Chinese to even out the balance of trade; the (Dutch and German) Boers in South Africa were marched to the world's first concentration camps, where about 20,000 died during the Boer War, after the discovery of gold on Boer property. And even when they weren't colonizing, Brits had a knack for showing up in foreign lands—the Middle East, for instance—and rearranging the power politics and map lines, frequently making vows they didn't keep.

BRITS IN THE SANDS

No Europeans loved the Middle East more than the British, who began seriously mucking around there in the early 1900s, the first Westerners (since the tenth-century Vikings and, later, Marco Polo) to explore Mesopotamia, Persia, Syria, and Palestine. Of the three British explorer-spies most associated with the area, two were women. Gertrude Bell (1868–1926) and Freya Stark (1893–1993) spoke Arabic and Persian, and both worked with the Royal Geographical Society, which held the world's largest collection of maps, and worked closely with the military. Gertrude Bell was extremely powerful, holding many British government posts; she literally drew the doomed boundaries for Iraq, and in 1921, she convinced Churchill—then colonial secretary—to renege on Britain's promise to make Kurdistan (in northern Iraq) a separate country for Kurds. Freya Stark was a brilliant travel writer, although also a WWII spy. T. E. Lawrence, aka Lawrence of Arabia, gathered Arabs to fight with the British against the Ottoman Empire during World War I. He promised the Hashemite clan (today the rulers of Jordan) that they would rule the entire Middle East if they joined in battle. The British government, however, didn't follow through on his promise, which is unfortunate because Jordan, the only land the Hashemites held on to out of the deal, is the most peaceful and democratic country in the Middle East today.

Due to the secret Sykes-Picot Agreement struck during World War I, the British and French supervised Middle East territories after the Ottoman Empire fell in 1918. Both made a terrible mess of the area, drawing bogus borders, bringing questionable groups to power, and planting the seeds for unrest that still haunts the region. Brits pulled together warring factions when they drew the map for Iraq, which led to the problems today, but the classic example of bewildering British diplomacy was the Balfour Declaration of 1917. The British then controlled Palestine (the territory that holds today's Israel, Gaza, and West Bank) and Zionist Jews wanted part of it as a country for Jews. British foreign secretary Arthur Balfour responded on November 2, 1917, ambiguously writing, "His Majesty's Government view with favour the establishment in Palestine of a national home for the Jewish *people, and will use their best endeavours to facilitate the achievement of this object, it being clearly understood that nothing shall be done which may prejudice the civil and religious rights of existing non-Jewish communities in Palestine . . ." Jews interpreted the letter to mean that the British supported creation of their country; Palestinians took it to mean that they didn't. Scholars and politicians have been scratching their heads over the letter and its implications for ninety years.*

With diamonds and gold from South Africa, tea and spices from the East, and a nasty habit of "borrowing" treasures such as the Elgin Marbles (elaborate friezes taken from Greece; see "Greece," page 218), nineteenth-century Britain grew yet more powerful and moneyed, but the twentieth century steamrolled the kingdom's ego back to proper size—and her geographic size shrank too, as colonies and other holdings began snapping off like brittle leaves. One of the most troubling was Ireland, the predominantly Catholic island to the west, whose problems Britain had long ignored. After decades of rebellions, terrorist attacks, and fighting (on both sides), the British government gave up and accepted Irish home rule in 1921, but with one condition: the six counties in Northern Ireland, where Britain had sent Protestant settlers, would remain under British rule. That arrangement has been a point of bloody contention ever since. (See "Ireland," page 117.)

Scotland and Wales reluctantly remained part of Great Britain, however, in the 1990s, both regained more autonomy and their own parliaments.

BRITS IN INDIA

Nowhere are the effects of British colonization more keenly felt than in the South Asian subcontinent that, for centuries, made the British Empire even richer. During the British Raj (the period of British rule that unofficially started in the seventeenth century with the British East India Company), Brits turned India into their plantation, using Indians as poorly paid, heavily taxed laborers, and forcing them to turn over their farmlands to plant cotton and tea—moves that killed hundreds of millions from famine. Brits also transformed the social system. In 1858, Brits executed and exiled the Muslim mughals who had ruled the land for centuries and made Hindus the dominant force they remain today. By the twentieth century, high taxes, particularly on salt, prompted Mahatma Gandhi to lead mass protests, including one to the sea to make his own salt, and to launch the "Quit India" campaign against the British government. The British clamped down on the press and prohibited protests—and a British massacre of demonstrators only heated up calls for independence. Brits finally offered independence if Indians fought in the Second World War; millions of Indians volunteered. With independence drawing near, Muslim leader Muhammad Ali Jinnah won a last-minute legislative victory—a decree that the Indian territory would be split, with a new country for Muslims. Before granting independence in 1947, Brits divided the land into India and Pakistan. The work was done so sloppily that farmers were separated from their crops and houses were split from their villages, one reason that borders have been in dispute ever since.

The first half of the twentieth century rocked Britain, as it did most of Europe. British military prowess kept the country from capture during both world wars, although Brits fought in both with high losses. The Great War killed 750,000 Britons, and the Depression of 1929 hit Britain particularly hard, as the economy was already wobbling. And then, under Prime Minister Neville Chamberlain, Britain went weak.

Nobody wanted a return to war, and nobody could afford one. And the terms inflicted on Germans after World War I had been too tough, as most leaders agreed by the 1930s. The Weimar Republic had gone bankrupt paying war reparations; German cash was worthless. Many believed that Germany's territorial losses as outlined in the 1919 Treaty of Versailles had been too harsh as well. So when Hitler showed up in 1933, talking about taking back "lost" areas that held large German populations, he didn't sound all that unreasonable at first, except perhaps to those in the countries he wanted to take back. Austria happily joined up with Germany in 1938—and Brits said nothing even though that union had been forbidden by the Treaty of Versailles. But when Hitler fixed his gaze on the Sudetenland, the northwestern corner of Czechoslovakia, President Edvard Beneš wasn't keen to give it up. "Sorry mate," was the message from British prime minister Chamberlain, seconded by French president Édouard Daladier. As the countries that had helped create Czechoslovakia in the 1919 treaty, Britain and France had few qualms about taking her apart. In what now looks like quivering appeasement, Chamberlain and Daladier simply forked the Sudetenland over to the Führer, thinking it would placate the man whom they regarded as a harmless nut. It didn't. And Winston Churchill had been saying it wouldn't from the start.

The Second World War hammered Britain, bleeding it economically, killing 355,000 Britons, and subjecting Brits to the terror of being pummeled by thousands of Nazi bombs daily. During the Battle of Britain—the three months in 1940 when Nazis most viciously attacked the island—over 23,000 British civilians died.

> *"The Battle of Britain is about to begin. Upon this battle depends the survival of Christian civilization. Upon it depends our own British life, and the long continuity of our institutions and our empire. The whole fury and might of the enemy must very soon be turned on us. Hitler knows that he will have to break us in this island or lose the war. If we can stand up to him all Europe may be free . . . Let us, therefore, brace ourselves to our duty and so bear ourselves that if the British Empire and its commonwealth last for a thousand years, men will still say, 'This was their finest hour.'"* —Winston Churchill, speech in the House of Commons, June 18, 1940

Britain did not back down: the British Bulldog, as Prime Minister Winston Churchill was known, never seriously entertained the thought of surrender. With newly invented radar, valiant fighters, and Churchill's resonant voice calming the masses nightly from the radio, the Brits won the Battle of Britain, becoming the only European country to fight back a full-blown Nazi invasion—except, that is, for brave little Malta, the British colony that suffered bombing for five months straight and didn't give up. (See "Malta," page 392.)

WINSTON CHURCHILL (1874–1965)

Pasty-faced, homely, and prone to long bouts of sheer gloom, Winston Churchill so altered the fate of Britain—and Europe—that many historians regard him as the single most influential person of the past century. Jowly Churchill, who rarely strayed far from a fine cigar, was a correspondent for London's *Morning Post* in South Africa during the Boer War (1899–1902); when he was captured, his dramatic escape made for page-turning journalism and turned his byline into a household name. He used fame to springboard into politics, and during the First World War he became head of the navy, a position he was removed from after ordering the landings at Gallipoli (off Turkey), a mistake that cost 21,000 British lives. He slunk back into Parliament, and in 1925, was appointed Chancellor of the Exchequer (head of the treasury). Churchill brought back the gold standard—a huge error that had esteemed British economist John Maynard Keynes ridiculing Churchill and calling his policies "feather-brained." Churchill was right about one thing: the looming threat of Nazis. Through the 1930s, Churchill's frequent tirades about Hitler only bored his fellow parliamentarians, who thought Churchill obsessed. After Hitler took

Poland and Britain declared war on Germany in September 1939, Churchill's foresight was rewarded. Chamberlain's government crumbled, and the king asked Churchill to head a new one. Appointed prime minister on May 10, 1940, Churchill proved to be Hitler's strongest psychological enemy and the British symbol of strength. The prime minister's fire was in his words, particularly those broadcast in radio addresses often heard across the world. Against a backdrop of whining air-raid sirens and exploding bombs, Churchill's voice might as well have boomed from the heavens; so inspirational and calming were the speeches he wrote himself that he came to personify steely defiance against Nazis. While his oratory skills helped steady the Brits, his military alignments helped win the war. Hours after Pearl Harbor was bombed on December 7, 1941, Churchill sailed for America, speaking before Congress on Christmas Eve and pulling the United States into the war, where her forces helped to bring Hitler down.

Though the Allies won the war, Churchill lost his office in 1945. He nevertheless predicted what the Soviet Union was up to, coining the term "Iron Curtain" in a 1946 speech in Missouri. In 1951, he returned to Number 10 Downing Street, but this time he accomplished little, proving to be a greater leader in war than in calm. In 1953, he won a Nobel Prize, not for peace, but in literature for his nonfiction works including *A History of the English-Speaking Peoples*.

Britain built herself back up with Marshall Plan funding from the U.S., almost a quarter of which went to the UK. Having worked well together during the war, Brits and Americans continued gathering intelligence—this time under the guise of Echelon, an intelligence operation run jointly by the British GDHQ and the American NSA, the agency recently rapped for tapping Americans' telephone conversations.[21] The two countries are also the big boys of NATO, the formidable coalition of Western powers with a nuclear arsenal (hidden across Europe) that is credited with stopping further Soviet advances into Europe during the Cold War. Through pretty much every military venture the U.S. has stepped into for decades, Britain has been by her side. The relationship is well matched: Brits realized that if they wanted to stay on top of the power heap, they needed to stay partnered with Yanks, and Yanks understood that Brits helped legitimize their actions, making them bilateral at least.

The United States is the biggest arms dealer on the planet, but Britain is number two, selling about $9 billion a year. Along with France, Britain is one of the two EU countries with nuclear weapons.

THE SWINGING SIXTIES

Though Britain had firmly established herself as a literary and drama gold mine several centuries back, she lagged in the music department—unless you count whining bagpipes and somber church organs—until the 1960s. Who knows what triggered it—Bo Diddley and Elvis, or the underground culture of acid and pot—but never in twentieth-century music was there a more happening scene. The Beatles set poetic lyrics to loud guitar, but kept a popular touch. The Kinks added backstreet raspiness and raunch, and the Rolling Stones put it into an explicitly sexual style, complete with Mick Jagger humping the mic. Twiggy introduced minis, and Carnaby Street and Biba were the places to shop, whether for Yardley lip gloss or Mary Quant geometric-print clothes. The scene lasted into the 1970s, when drugs, religion, bad relationships, and burnout seemed to drag everyone down. But during that era Britain stole the show from Paris—and she still hasn't given it back.

Britain's Victorian-era status and strength, however, weren't regained until the 1990s. And the path to getting there included numerous right-wing Tory (Conservative Party) governments, including three terms of Margaret Thatcher, the Iron Lady who made weapons of her will and her handbag—which she was known to whack on the table during summits, to great effect.

MARGARET THATCHER
(PRIME MINISTER, 1979–1990)

The grocer's daughter made the leap to Iron Lady during one of the toughest patches of modern British history. The economy was a wreck, unions were striking, and Argentines were trying to snatch back the Falklands. She was tough on all counts, privatizing state-held companies, dispatching police to break up strikes, and sending British troops to regain the Falklands in 1982—sending them there, it was later revealed, with nuclear weapons ready to launch. Nobody ever called Britain's first female prime minister a weak, flaky dame, especially when she was wielding her purse. She was famously friendly with President Ronald Reagan and signed Britain up for President George H. W. Bush's Persian Gulf War in 1991. She also made Britain's biggest arms deal of all times, selling $50 billion worth to the Saudis. Fifteen years after she stepped down, Thatcher still divides Brits. Some say she was the best thing to happen to the UK; the rest say she was the worst.

Britain isn't a two-party system like the U.S., but the race tends to end with either the Conservatives (on par with U.S. Republicans) or Labor (on par with Democrats) taking the prime minister's seat. Tony Blair, leading a flashed-up New

Labor Party in 1997, beat out the Conservative Party that had ruled for most of the postwar era. In the same way that George W. Bush makes a mockery of traditional Republican values (against big government and nation building, for starters), Blair confuses the issues Labor used to stand for. The Labor leader is a hawk (traditionally a conservative stance) who wants more nuclear energy (ditto) and who pushed a privacy-stripping national ID card. Labor might point out that times have changed—and indeed they have. The Conservative Party is most vocal about the travesty of Iraq and the unprepared state of troops being sent there—and the Conservatives are emphasizing small-scale renewable resources, solar panels, and wind turbines on houses. You know the world has gone wacky when environmental group Greenpeace gives a green light to Conservatives, the party that beat out Labor in 2006 local elections. Look for the name David Cameron—the youthful head of the Conservative Party looks likely to next lead the Brits.

Hot Spots

London: The land of designer hotels, designer martinis, designer magazines, and designers is more multicultural and hopping than ever—especially now that the place isn't forced to shutter down before midnight.

Northern Ireland: In the six counties still bound to Britain, flare-ups continue despite the 1998 Good Friday Agreement, but tourists are tiptoeing back in again—with good reason. The place is gorgeous, with rugged coasts, castle ruins, and mansions turned into inns. Nevertheless, the extra costs for police and security to keep the peace make it a financial burden for Britain. Almost half the Brits want to cut Northern Ireland loose. (See "Ireland," page 117.)

SCOTCH WHISKY VS. IRISH WHISKEY

Connoisseurs and nationalists get very upset if you confuse the best-known drink of Scotland with that made in Ireland. The easiest way to distinguish them is by the spelling: if it's "whisky," it's from Scotland, if it's "whiskey," it's not. Scotsmen light up when they talk about their whisky, which draws its unique essence from the magic combo of burnt Scottish peat and pure Scottish water; you'd think it was an elixir, the way they gush. Whisky is typically made from barley (or rye) dried over a peat fire that imparts a smoky taste; it's often a single malt, meaning it comes from one distillery. Irish whiskey tends to be blended—a cocktail of whiskeys from different distilleries—peat fires aren't normally used, and it's usually sweeter. Some of the finest Scotch whiskies, say connoisseurs, are Oban, Talisker, and Lagavulin. One more mistake not to make: never call a Scotsman "Scotch."

Scotland: With heather-clad moors and abundant fauna, Scotland is the nature reserve to the north, a land where the posh smoking-jacket crowd heads for deer stalking, salmon fishing, and grouse shooting—and where ex-Beatles buy islands. The salt-sprayed land of kilts, bagpipes, and yummy haggis—a sheep's tummy stuffed with oatmeal and a medley of chopped guts—Scotland and her distinct culture survived centuries of English domination. Gaelic was lost as the dominant tongue, but the thick brogue and feisty spirit live on. Rich with legends and rituals, the country's most famous event is August's Edinburgh Festival, where streets and every available venue fills with music and theater. But nothing is more festive than the *ceilidh*—a social gathering where Scots swirl each other around roaring pinewood fires to traditional shoe-stamping music of fiddle and accordion, with skirts swinging high and whisky glasses clinking. Nationalists still talk of shaking free of England, using money from oil pumped off Scotland's coast, but calls for an independent Scotland have grown fainter since 1999, when she gained her own parliament and more autonomy.

Wales: Setting of Arthurian legend, Wales served as resource central with coal mines and steel mills—many now closed—and is the quietest and most isolated of the British bunch. But lately you can hear very loud mumbling in this land that has her own language (only 20 percent now speak it), her own church (Nonconformists who sent Anglicans packing), and her own history (they're still miffed that the English snagged the title "Prince of Wales" for the Crown Prince). Sick of urban crime and spiraling house prices, many Londoners are moving west. "They sell their houses in London for a million pounds," explains one Welshman, "then come and buy one of ours, making quite a little profit in the move. Then they throw a thousand-pound check ($1,900) to the church, and more to the civic boards, and then they're sitting on the school governing bodies and all the boards and running your town." His claim may be exaggerated, but that's why many Welsh see the movement of Londoners into their turf as another English invasion.

Sellafield: This sprawling nuclear recycling complex emits the most radioactivity in Europe (making even faraway Norwegian crabs radioactive), and the site is more contaminated with radioactive waste than the ground around Chernobyl.[22]

Loch Ness: You know *what* they are looking for: the dragon-serpent known as Nessie. The question is *why* so many people have become so obsessed with the creature that they've moved to the Scottish loch and devoted their lives to looking for her, when there are so many more worthwhile pursuits—such as trying to communicate with extraterrestrials. (See "Sweden," page 250.)

Hotshots

Tony Blair: Prime Minister, 1997–present. Heading the New Labor Party, slick Tony is an Oxford-trained barrister whose courtroom abilities translate well in Parliament, where he wows with his speeches. Self-assured and cocky, he ruled the roost during some of Britain's happiest hours—but he also made her an international terrorist target. He began to be known as "Tony Bliar" after he exaggerated Iraq's WMD capabilities in his famous "forty-five minutes" speech, and hid info about the 7/7 attack, and he continues sliding down popularity charts as death counts in Iraq soar. All sides are screaming for him to step down, including his colleague Gordon Brown, to whom he fibbed as well (see below). The Bible never strays far from his bed; he believes that all the world's questions are answered in its pages—though he apparently skips over the ones that say "the end."

> *Blair's apparent fondness for Bush resulted in his detractors branding him a poodle, and he was spoofed in a 2002 George Michael animated video, which showed Bush tossing a bored dog a bone, which Blair continually retrieved.*

Gordon Brown: Chancellor of the Exchequer (powerful finance minister), 1997–present. "Beep beep, Tony, outta my way!" he seems to be saying, sometimes subtly and sometimes not. A Scotsman who heads the country's treasury department and is quick to point out what a fine job he's done (and largely, he has), Brown has his eyes on Britain's highest power seat—and it's not the first time he's gazed at it. In 1994, Brown dropped plans to put his name in the hat for the Labor leadership, after Blair promised he would leave the prime minister's post on turning fifty.[23] Apparently Blair hasn't seen a calendar; his half-century birthday was in May 2003. With Labor's popularity plunging, by the time Blair steps down he may have ruined Brown's shot at the seat. Beep beep, Tony, beep beep.

LADY DIANA (1961–1997)

It was a little too chocolate-box to have been true, cynics said from the start. On July 29, 1981, Prince Charles, aged thirty-two, and Lady Di, a blushing twenty-year-old former kindergarten teacher and daughter of an earl, captured the collective heart of dreamy romantics everywhere with their fairy-tale wedding. Di looked smashing in ivory taffeta and antique lace, her twenty-five-foot train trailing down the aisle of St. Paul's; Charles looked regally somber, with his decorated chest dripping with shiny medals, while 3,500 invited guests and some 750 million viewers across the world toasted the royal matrimony that finally brought youth and modern style into the castle. The union quickly produced two handsome male heirs—William and Harry—and the occasional peep into a royal world that appeared less than idyllic. Charles was distant and boring, Di was bulimic and lonely, Queen Elizabeth was as cold as a medieval stone castle on a stormy December night. The divorce that gossips had long predicted became reality in 1996. Charles suffered a drop in popularity as a result; Di publicly embraced worthy causes, such as land mine removal, and privately embraced a few men who raised royal eyebrows. Her final beau, Dodi Fayed—son of Harrods owner Mohamed Fayed—died alongside her one night in late August 1997, when the Mercedes S280 they were in spun out of control in a Paris tunnel. The death was blamed on the intoxicated state of driver Henri Paul, who was fleeing paparazzi, but there have been plenty of rumors otherwise. Mohamed Fayed is but one who says the couple was murdered.

That's Sir to you: Every so often British monarchs look down and recognize the immense talent in the kingdom. A few who have knelt before Her Royal Highness to be knighted: Sir Roger Moore, Sir Elton John, Sir Paul McCartney, Sir Richard Branson, Sir Mick Jagger, and Dame Judi Dench. There have been a few questionable calls, among them Romania's late dictator (Sir) Nicolae Ceauşescu.

Queen Elizabeth II (b. 1926): Reigning monarch since 1952 and winner of the royal big hat award, she throws the occasional rocking jubilee, but keeps very mum about the assorted scandals that have hit since the marriage between Di and Charles went down the tube.

Prince Philip, Duke of Edinburgh: Formerly Prince of Greece and Denmark, Philip tossed away the titles, his Greek citizenship, and his Greek Orthodox religion to marry then-princess Elizabeth II. The flirtatious prince is known for his humor—some call it dry, others dreadful. He told deaf children standing near a drum set, "Deaf? No wonder you're deaf standing so close to that racket!" He asked a blind woman with a guide dog if she'd heard "Now they have eating dogs for the anorexic." And pity the poor boy who confessed his dream to be an astronaut. Scoffed the prince, "You're too fat!"

Prince Charles (b. 1948): Heir apparent, His Royal Highness Prince Charles Philip Arthur George, Prince of Wales and Earl of Chester, Duke of Cornwall, Duke of Rothesay, Earl of Carrick, Baron of Renfrew, Lord of the Isles, Great Steward of Scotland, and Knight of the Garter is beginning to look a bit tired; it must be exhausting just remembering his title, and perhaps his regalia just doesn't shine as brilliantly as it once did. But while patiently waiting for his chance on the throne, he busies himself writing articles and letters to Parliament with suggestions, and now he has a new hobby: organic food. Charles oversees the 1,100-acre organic farm at one of his estates and sells the chem-free greens under the label Duchy Originals, with tens of millions in profits going to nonprofit organizations.[24] No wonder they invite him to head so many—200 at the last count.

Camilla Parker Bowles, Duchess of Cornwall (b. 1947): The stars uncrossed in 2005, when Prince Charles wed long-time lover Camilla. The couple was forced to repent publicly for their previous adultery, and there was talk that the wedding might cost Charles the crown, but the prince never looked happier. The marriage was met with lukewarm response by the tight-lipped British public, mildly appeased that, should Charles ascend, Camilla won't be queen; she'll only be a princess consort.

Prince William (b. 1982): Handsome elder son of Charles and Di—his mother nicknamed him DDG for "drop dead gorgeous"—William likes to cook, but probably won't indulge in his father's habit of donning kilts for public affairs. "It's a bit draughty," he explained to *Vanity Fair*. One might not think he'd mind the breeze; he's been known to show the "full monty" at parties while strutting to the seventies hit "YMCA." Some object to the nudity, others to the song. He may someday steal the throne from his father—well, at least, if it is put to public vote.[25]

Prince Harry (b. 1984): The young 'un has a wild look in his eyes, is a demon on the polo field, and had a little "cannabis incident" when he was in boarding school. Caused a furor when he showed up at a 2005 costume bash in Nazi uniform. He soon apologized (via publicist); Charles demanded he take a tour of Auschwitz.

HONORING THE SCOTS

A few fine minds born in Scotland:

Adam Smith	**(1723–1790):** Supporter of free trade and capitalism, economist Smith essentially created modern economics with *An Inquiry into the Nature and Causes of the Wealth of Nations*.
Samuel Johnson	**(1709–1784):** Penned the first widely used dictionary, published in 1755 as two heaving volumes.
James Boswell	**(1740–1795):** Boozy travel writer and attentive biographer of Johnson.
Robert Louis Stevenson	**(1850–1894):** The sickly traveler best known for *Treasure Island* and *The Strange Case of Dr. Jekyll and Mr. Hyde*.

| Alexander Graham Bell | (1847–1894): He invented the telephone when in the U.S. but Scots claim the Edinburgh-born inventor as theirs. |
| Sir Arthur Conan Doyle | (1859–1930): Physician, war correspondent, historian, and spiritualist Doyle brought Sherlock Holmes and Watson to life in 1887. |

Besides writers Jan Morris, Dylan "Do not go gentle into that good night" Thomas (1914–1953) and Roald "Charlie and the Chocolate Factory" Dahl (1916–1990), the most famous Welsh are entertainers—actors Richard Burton (1925–1984), Anthony Hopkins (b. 1937), and Catherine Zeta-Jones (b. 1969), and singers Shirley Bassey (b. 1937) and Tom Jones (b. 1940) among them.

Posh and Becks: Reigning celebrity couple. Take a dashing, talented soccer player (David Beckham), hook him up with a luscious sexpot (Victoria Adams, aka Posh Spice) of pop-music fame, and what do you get? Too much ink wasted on trivial matters, such as what Posh packed on her trip to Madrid and with whom Becks slept last week.

The Tories: Losing ground and face for a decade, the Conservative Party, which dominated British postwar politics, is making a comeback. Sticking new heads on the leadership spears has helped: David Cameron (b. 1966) is making the party sexy, environmentally friendly and youthful, targeting the young voters. Even though he's get a rep for being slippery—Labor calls him "the Chameleon"—Cameron has all the right creds, and the ladies find him adorable: a *New Woman* poll voted him one of the world's sexiest men.

London mayor Ken Livingstone: Not a wallflower

© Rune Hellestad/Corbis

Animal Rights Activists: Hard-core activists are making death threats against heads of research centers that test on animals.

Ken Livingstone: Mayor of London, 2000–present. Love him or hate him, rebel mayor Ken Livingstone stands out. He landed the 2012 Olympics for London and responded to the July 7 attack by making sure the city immediately got back on its feet and the subways; he even launched a promulticultural campaign in the bombings' wake. His controversial 2003 "congestion charge" is now popular—it reduced traffic in the capital by 18 percent—he chastised the U.S. Embassy for refusing to pay it. Never called shy, this son of a sailor and a circus performer marched in protests against the Iraq war and called George W. Bush "the greatest threat to life on the planet"—hours before the president rolled into town. Named 2003 "Politician of the Year" by the Political Studies Association, he got in hot water in 2006 for likening a Jewish reporter to a "concentration camp guard" and for saying he "longed for the day when the Saudi royal family are swinging [i.e., hanging] from lampposts." A disciplinary board suspended him from office for a month for his comments to the reporter—but the media stood up for him, and his suspension may go the way of London's double-decker buses which now only run on historic routes.

ISAAC NEWTON (1642–1727)

Sir Isaac Newton, grandfather of the Enlightenment and the first of his family to read, set the world spinning in numerous new directions. The boy who had showed little academic promise—teachers said he was dull—was suddenly struck by a force of brilliance in his late teens. Some say his curiosity was aroused by strange symbols in an astrology book that kept him awake for days and made him a channel for revealing the hidden knowledge of the universe. In bouts of mania he invented the reflecting telescope, figured out the nature of color, devised calculus, and established laws of physical motion and gravity—most realizations coming to him in the three years leading up to his twenty-fifth birthday. He explained the orbits of comets and the pull of the moon on the oceans; he had ideas for improvements to everything from clocks to windmills; and in 1686, his most famous book *Mathematical Principles of Natural Philosophy* was published, inspired by the descent of an album.

Best known for his ideas on gravity, Isaac Newton received weighty approval from Brits in 2003: when the BBC conducted a vote on the World's Greatest Briton, Newton won it.

News you can understand: *The Guardian* (www.Guardian.co.uk), *Economist* (www.economist.com), BBC (www.news.bbc.co.uk)

4. ITALY
(Repubblica Italiana)
Fractured Beauty

FAST FACTS

Country:	Italian Republic; Repubblica Italiana
Capital:	Rome
Government:	Republic
Independence:	1871 (unification completed); 1946 (king abdicated, republic born)
Population:	58,134,000 (2006 estimate)
Head of State:	President Giorgio Napolitano (2006)
Head of Government:	Prime Minister Romano Prodi (2006)
Elections:	President elected by electoral college and assembly of delegates for seven-year term; prime minister appointed by president, confirmed by parliament
Name of Parliament:	Parlamento

Ethnicity:	Italian (and clusters of German, French, Slovene, Albanian, and Greek Italians)
Religion:	Predominantly Roman Catholic (also Protestant, Jewish, and Muslim)
Language:	Italian (official) and numerous dialects; German (Trentino-Alto Adige); French (Valle d'Aosta)
Literacy:	99% (highly questionable statistic)
Famous Exports:	Columbus, Lamborghini, molti scandali
Economic Big Boy:	ENI (oil and gas); total sales 2004: $79.31 billion[1]
Per Capita GDP:	$28,400 (2005 estimate)
Unemployment:	7.5% (December 2005 Eurostat); south has 20% or higher unemployment
EU Status:	Founding member
Currency:	Euro

Quick Tour

From the chiseled Alps in the north to stone farmhouses with woven grape pergolas, from gondolas that sail past sinking palaces to Rome's crumbling *Colosseo*, Italia is a feast for the eyes. It is also a daily extravaganza of food. While every culture values eating, here all existence can be summed up in two words—*Buon appetito*—uttered before every meal. As one Italian explains, "If you have food, and a good appetite, then your life must be all right."

MANGIA, MANGIA!

Forget money, palazzos, *amore*, fast cars. Whether fiery penne alla arrabiata, cheesy polenta, or prosciutto-wrapped melon, nothing is more important to Italians than food. This is the land where *si mangia bene* (one eats well) is the highest compliment and where proverbs exalt the dinner table as the only place where one doesn't age. Simple flavors—sweet tomato sauce or ricotta-stuffed ravioli drizzled with sage butter—reflect more than close ties to the earth: a whole system of laws, some written and some verbally imposed, guides food from garden to stomach. Heaven forbid that the beloved *mozzarella di bufala*—served at room temperature—comes cold or from a cow. A stale pastry at a café warrants a ticket from food police. So aphrodisiacal are white truffles shaved over pasta that law prohibits them from being carried on trains, and cappuccino is a breakfast drink only; don't even try ordering one after lunch. Sprinkling cheese on fish is taboo, and risotto is made only from Arborio rice, so adored that smuggling it out of the north was once punishable by death (Thomas Jefferson risked it nonetheless). Never mix basil and oregano; wine should be bottled and grape leaves trimmed only during a rising moon. Above all, dining must never be rushed. It's no surprise that Italy spawned the anti-microwave, antiprocessing, anti–fast food movement called Slow Food.

The court jester of Europe, Italy is just hard to take seriously. Known for switching sides midwar, Italia is a place where leaders rarely last a year, porn stars are thrust into the senate, and corruption courses through her veins like a vital nutrient. Custom-made for a holiday poster—Roman ruins, Tuscan villas, and fab food all rolled into one—the country isn't as lighthearted as it appears. Finally booted from office in April 2006, former prime minister Silvio Berlusconi, Italy's longest-running leader since WWII, was a dangerous clown; the country's approach to unwanted refugees is medieval; and the land that holds many of history's architectural treasures is the target of scary terrorist threats. And let us not forget the ever-present Mafia, whose activities have been even more frightening lately.

BUMBLING BERLUSCONI

A flamboyant billionaire who owns most of Italy's national TV stations, major magazines, and book-publishing houses, an advertising agency, a newspaper, and the AC Milan soccer team, ex-PM Silvio Berlusconi of the Forza Italia Party was conflict of interest personified. He sacked journalists who criticized his laughable political performance, while his TV stations distorted his impact, showing him addressing cheering crowds in packed auditoriums when in fact he was droning on in a half-empty room.[2] Formally accused of numerous corruption charges, including bribing judges, Berlusconi shoved through laws in his own self-interest, such as the one granting him legal immunity while in office (another legalized cooking books). His hatred of Italy's judiciary was illustrated when he tried to do away with bodyguards for judges—necessary in Italy's Mafia-ridden society—effectively signing their death warrants. Even though 70 percent of Italians opposed it, he signed Italy up in loud support of the 2003 invasion of Iraq and sent some 3,000 troops in for postwar cleanup. But Berlusconi, formerly a lounge singer on cruise ships, is best known as a leader whose foot was perma-lodged in his mouth. Always a joking fool, he likened himself to Jesus, announced that Chinese Communists boil their babies, appeared on camera flipping off Spain's foreign minister, offered a German parliamentarian a lead role in a movie about Nazis, suggested that Mussolini had only sent Jews on vacations, and made light of dead refugees floating in Italian waters—for starters. He turned the 2006 elections rancorous, and among other things, called supporters of opponent Romano Prodi *coglioni*—or "dicks." Demanding a recount after Prodi won the election, Berlusconi has threatened to lethally weaken the Prodi administration, and even though he finally lost his grip in 2006, one thing is for sure: Berlusconi will be back, alas.

In the five years of Berlusconi's reign, little was accomplished in Italy. The economy ground to a screeching halt, intelligence powers expanded—Italians are now believed the most "bugged" in Europe—and the number of terrorist threats from radical Muslims exploded, some of them pointing a finger at "the incompetent Berlusconi" as the reason they were considering an Italian attack.

Since 2001, Italian police and carabineers have cracked several militant cells, including one that planned to pump cyanide gas into the U.S. Embassy in Rome.

Meanwhile, Italy has serious problems. Among the most pressing are the boats of dead and dying refugees showing up on Italian shores. With 2,500 miles of coast, the country draws hundreds of thousands of Albanians and Africans, but allows few in legally; the 20,000 or more *clandestini* who slip in each year typically can't find work, and make do by prostituting themselves, pushing drugs, stealing, or selling toys in squares and fleeing at the sight of police. Given the thousands of ships and rafts of wannabe immigrants in Italian waters every year—one report estimates that 2 million would-be immigrants will soon be heading toward the peninsula—the problem is not going away. But Berlusconi's government didn't seriously address it, except by giving the Italian coast guard and navy the legal power to force vessels to turn back before they reach port. One member of Berlusconi's coalition, Umberto Bossi, suggested that Italy simply sink any immigrant-filled ships that come near.

When Berlusconi finally handed over the car key in spring 2006, low-key and brainy prime minister Romano Prodi, who'd held the premiership from 1996 to 1998, inherited a boatload of problems, including the fact that his coalition is destined to be weak and short-lived. The world's fifth largest industrial economy is merely limping along. The unemployment rate is near 8 percent (20 percent in the south), industry is not competitive, government and business alike are riddled with corruption, and the country's biggest corporation, the milk empire Parmalat, is mired in fraud charges. Crime is rising, the Mafia is wearing new hats, and the country is so divided in incomes and opinions that some have suggested politically sawing it apart.

THE MOB'S NEW TRICK

Known for running heroin, trafficking sex slaves, siphoning off government-funded projects, and demanding "protection" payments, the Mafia has learned new tricks. Long involved in trash collection, they are now toxic-waste disposal professionals. Beginning in the 1980s, recycling laws required industries to safely dispose of lead, arsenic, carcinogenic chemicals, and radioactive materials. Costs for disposing of the materials were high—until mobsters showed up with proper permits (provided by corrupt officials), offering services for a tenth of the price. Winning contracts from paper mills, tanneries, and chemical companies, the Mafia load trucks with carcinogenic cargo. Sometimes they offload the poisons in municipal landfill sites not meant to hold hazardous waste, but the thugs don't care—they own the sites. Sometimes the waste is dumped into the ocean or thrown into deep holes that leech into water supplies. Recently, the Mafia sank to a new low: they mixed the deadly sludge with fertilizer and, posing as salesmen, gave it to farmers to try free of charge. Thousands of acres of prime farmland were contaminated, cows and buffalo in some towns produced toxin-laced milk, and the cleanup cost billions. Cancer rates also soared—in some areas around Naples, they quadrupled within a few years.[3]

In April 2006, police finally nabbed Italy's most wanted: Bernardo "The Tractor" Provenzano, kingpin of Sicily's Mafia and on the run for forty years.

The land that led the Renaissance now funnels creativity mostly into design, writing, and slick cars, but her creative ability to solve problems is sorely lacking. *Bella Italia* is nevertheless beloved: for her food, her culture, her enduring Roman architecture, and her Renaissance art—not to mention her flirtatious men, who are frequently mistaken for angels by those who don't speak Italian and don't know what the li'l angels are saying.

VOCABULARY BUILDER

Three of the most popular phrases in melodic Italian start with *va* which means "it goes":

Va bene:	All goes well!
Vá via:	Go away!
Vá fa 'n culo:	Up yours!

History Review

Ancient Greeks were among the first to settle what is today Italy, but the group that most put its stamp on the land was the toga-wearing, wine-swilling Romans. It wasn't just their poets and historians or their architectural skills that made them hugely important. Nor was it their fighting ability and expansionist nature per se. The most enduring legacy that Romans left to not only Italy but all of Europe was their stone roads, which, for the first time, connected much of the Continent as one. That all roads lead to Rome underscored the cohesion of their society, as did the fact that they created the first enduring transit ways. Countries left out of the Romans' developmental loop—Ireland, for example— were left out of progress for centuries.

> *At her height, the Roman Empire stretched from England to North Africa, Portugal to Yemen.*

Some historians sniff that the Romans weren't as great as the Greeks, merely being history's thieves—conquering ancient Greek colonies, kidnapping the culture, giving it a few twists (such as new names to Greek gods), and calling it their own. While they did indeed carry on with many Greek ideas, designs, and political practices, the Romans went further, both in the practices they introduced—building with arches and cement, for example—and in the territories they conquered. Greeks were shoreline developers who relied on their ships; Romans marched their armies inland.[4]

Romans established Latin as a unifying language; introduced engineering marvels, including central heating and water-distributing aqueducts; and entrenched social practices from public baths to drunken orgies and tossing enemies to the lions. They advanced military organization, legal systems, urban planning, and government administration. Although early Romans were polytheists—worshipping Venus, Jupiter, Bacchus, and Mars—the late empire under Constantine I turned Christian, leading to another of Rome's legacies: a Europe connected through Christianity. And the Romans brought real-life drama to a new height; it's amazing they could get anything done with the soap operas they were living.

JULIUS AND OTHER CAESARS

Julius Caesar: **(ca. 100–44 BC):** The dictator launched the takeover of the Greek Empire, had a mad fling with Cleopatra, and was killed in Senate by his former pal Brutus.

Augustus: **(63 BC–AD 14):** Named heir by Julius, Augustus permanently transformed the republic into a monarchy. A reformer who presided over a relatively peaceful era, he turned cranky in his final years—kicking out poet Ovid, for one.

Tiberius: **(42 BC–AD 37):** Paranoid Tiberius had the powerful men around him knocked off, leaving only nephew Caligula as heir. Bad call: Caligula probably killed him.

Caligula: **(AD 12–41):** Nuttier than the rest, torture and incest fan Caligula once sent his military to attack England, then changed his mind and sent them to pluck seashells on the French seashore instead.[5] Loved his horsey so much he appointed him senator and legal adviser.

Claudius: **(10 BC–AD 54):** Regarded as daft, the lame stutterer made it to emperor only because he was viewed as nonthreatening. Blew through wives, having his third killed after she had an affair. Promptly married his niece, who poisoned him.

Nero: **(AD 37–68):** Mother-killer Nero was despised by his people, and his era was plagued with problems; Rome burned down under his rule—he was probably the arsonist.

Hadrian: **(AD 76–138):** Expanded the empire to her farthest reaches.

The Roman Empire split into western and eastern parts after Constantine I (AD 272–337) founded an eastern capital in today's Istanbul in the year 295. He called it New Rome, but it was dubbed Constantinople and became the great center of the Byzantine Empire. Rome continued as a western power seat, and Constantine greatly affected that city too. After a vision of a cross in the sky with the words "in this sign you will conquer"—a sight that turned him into a Christian—he donated a palace to the bishop of Rome, who became increasingly powerful as the Catholic leader, better known today as the pope.

The empire officially limped on until 476, but the fire was pretty much out by the third century when Vandals, Visigoths, and other ruffians began swooping in. For the next 1,400 years, the Italian peninsula was a geographical free-for-all. Sicily and Naples (together confusingly known as the Kingdom of the Two

Sicilies) were run first by Arabs, then by Spaniards; Rome and nearby lands were Papal States; the north was a medley of Austrian and German territories; even the French staked out land in Italy's checkered history.

The most powerful city-states were in the north, the mightiest and most advanced being Venice, land of courtesans, scholars, explorers, and scribes. Lying between West and East, the city of canals was a major trading center where Arabs sold spices hauled from the East; the architecture was a blend of Arabic and Roman; the aristocratic society was enlightened; and artisans excelled at lace-making and glass-blowing. Ruled by doges (dukes), Venice had remarkable naval prowess, and eventually controlled Crete and coastal territories along the Adriatic (including today's Croatia, Slovenia, and Dalmatian Islands). The wealthiest Italian city-state and one of the most splendid European kingdoms, it was a hotbed for publishing, as well as for music.

MARCO POLO (1254–1324)

Venetian Marco Polo, son of an affluent merchant who traveled the Silk Road to the Far East, imprinted images of Asia on the medieval masses. After one journey, Marco's father and uncle returned bearing a letter from Mongolian leader Kublai Khan, asking the pope to send 100 Christian educators to teach about Western life. Unable to fulfill that request, the Polos returned several years later hauling extravagant gifts and a letter from the pope, and escorting young Marco Polo. Trekking across today's Persia, Afghanistan, Himalayas, and China, young Polo jotted notes about stones that burst into flames, pavilions that streamed with honey and wine, processions of hundreds of elephants, feasts for six thousand, money made of paper, and a sophisticated postal system. Seventeen years later, the Polos returned to Venice with their tales, which put them on the local lecture circuit. While fighting for Venice in a battle against Genoa, Marco was imprisoned for several months in 1298, during which he dictated his stories to his cellmate. Published as *The Travels of Marco Polo*, the book instantly elicited awe and disbelief. Skepticism about magic carpets and elephants being transported in the talons of giant birds ran so rampant that even his children thought he was joking. Called to his death bed in 1324, they begged him to admit his tales were all lies. His final words: "I have only told half of what I saw." Modern historians greet his stories with suspicion, pointing out that despite his supposed travels to China, Marco forgot to mention tea, chopsticks, bound feet, or the Great Wall.

By the fourteenth century, Florence rose to international stature, grew rich from the mercantile trade, and became a banking center, trading in the internationally accepted florin. A design competition held in 1402 for the bronze doors of the Florence Baptistry is viewed as the starting point of the Renaissance. For the next two centuries, the creative spark blazed across the peninsula (and Europe), although the flame burned nowhere brighter than in Firenze. Sinewy marble sculptures by Michelangelo, subtly powerful paintings by Leonardo da Vinci, the pointed writing of Dante, and the domed architecture of Brunelleschi were but a few remarkable achievements of the cultural movement that drew from classical Rome and Greece. Funded partly by the Church, the art of this golden era was also helped along by the Medicis, a family of bankers and de facto rulers of Florence. The Medicis ruled the Tuscan city into the eighteenth century and produced two popes (Leo X and Clement VII) and two queens of France (Catherine and Maria). The family that fed, financed, educated, and housed Michelangelo, Leonardo, Botticelli, and Donatello also enriched the city with churches, monasteries, libraries, and academies—all helping to make Florence the show stealer of the day.

HISTORICAL THINKERS AND CREATORS

Galileo (1564–1642): Dropped balls off leaning tower of Pisa to test theories of gravity; forced to recant his theory about heliocentricity.

Brunelleschi (1377–1446): Capped Florence's Duomo, taking inspiration from an egg that he smashed on the table to demonstrate how the dome would be done.

Dante (1265–1321): Inspired by neighbors, friends, and popes, he caught the worst qualities of humanity and displayed them in descending levels in his *Inferno*.

Michelangelo Buonarroti (1475–1564): *David*, the Pietà, and the Sistine Chapel, with its famous finger-touching "Creation of Adam," keep his name from fading; restorers do the same for his paints.

Leonardo da Vinci (1452–1519): Leonardo had creative attention deficit disorder, jumping from designing war machines (tanks, helicopters, submarines) to anatomical studies, from engineering and architecture to splendid paintings. Best known for *The Last Supper* and Mona Lisa's coy smile, he tried out new pigments—that's why few of his works live on.

Botticelli (1445–1510): *Birth of Venus* made fat beautiful; obese women have been describing themselves as Botticellian beauties ever since.

Machiavelli (1469–1527): The Florentine diplomat dealt with some of the most conniving people of the day, including the murderous Borgias, and advised rulers about the subtleties of statecraft in *The Prince*. Fell victim to a power play: he was imprisoned, tortured, and exiled after being fingered as anti-Medici, which he probably wasn't.

Florence: Where the Renaissance lives on

The Medicis' power in the gossipy city, known for competing families and guilds, was not universally respected. In 1478, another powerful family—the Pazzi—with help from an archbishop and a nod from the pope, attacked the Medicis while they were in church, killing Giuliano, the clan's coruler. Surviving the ordeal, Lorenzo the Magnificent (1449–1492) became known as the Savior of Florence. The corpses of the Pazzis and the archbishop were soon dangling from Palazzo Vecchio, as was the fashion of the day.

Generous Lorenzo should never have opened his purse for radical priest Savonarola, who ran the Medicis out of town in 1494. The righteous holy man took over as the dictator of Florence, closing down wine taverns, dress shops, gambling houses, and bookstores. In 1497, he ordered all Florentine riches destroyed. Paintings of nudes, nonreligious books, splendid hats, ornate dresses, lusty poems, mirrors, and makeup were torched in the main square, vanishing in the Bonfire of the Vanities. Florentines quickly regretted that move and rose up against the zealous reformer. In 1497, Savonarola was excommunicated, and he was hanged the next year, his corpse burned in the same square where the city's treasures had gone up in smoke.

BIG MOUTH PATRIOT FILIPPO MAZZEI (1730–1816)

Surgeon, diplomat, essayist, and winemaker Filippo Mazzei from Tuscany, upon invitation from the likes of Benjamin Franklin, arrived in Virginia (with tailor, cook, servants, farmworkers, and cuttings of vines) in 1773 to start the colonies' first official vineyard. Thomas Jefferson urged Mazzei to take the plot alongside Monticello. Mazzei planted grapes and became a passionate pamphleteer and orator for the revolutionary cause, loaning sacks of money to Jefferson to aid the colonists; two centuries later, Mazzei (who also wrote a book in France about the American Revolution) was commemorated with a U.S. postal stamp. At the time, he caused numerous headaches. After a botched diplomatic venture in Paris (Ben Franklin was finally sent to seal the famous money-borrowing deal) and a stint as a thinker for the Polish king, Mazzei holed up in Tuscany (some say he was secretly shipping arms back to Virginia), plotting a return to his American vineyard. Receiving a feisty letter from Jefferson (in which the vice president lambasted George Washington and President John Adams), Mazzei trotted his translation to the newspaper in Florence. The letter was picked up by the Parisian press, and then London's, the insult-peppered letter becoming spicier with each translation. The next year, 1797, when the "Mazzei Letter" was printed in the New York *Minerva*, it triggered an uproar—particularly as the newly passed Alien and Sedition Act outlawed criticism of government, and the vice president had heaped it on thick. Humiliated, Jefferson rented out Mazzei's vineyard to Germans whose horses trampled the grapes, stamping out the wine-making experiment and Mazzei's reason for returning. As for Mazzei's loan to the cause, among Jefferson's last words was a plea to repay the family Mazzei, finally accomplished quite a few decades later.[6]

The crazy-quilt peninsula continued unraveling for centuries. With rulers from all across Europe, city-states were further divided by Guelph and Ghibelline factions; the former swore loyalty to the pope, the latter to the Holy Roman Emperor. Napoleon stitched the many pieces together in 1804, but that union was fleeting. However, peninsular unification appealed to some. Count Camillo Cavour, prime minister of Piedmont, hooked up with guerrilla fighter Giuseppe Garibaldi to kick out foreign leaders and rope together the assorted states as one country. Kicked off in 1859, the consolidation, (helped along by Garibaldi and his "Red Shirts"), was completed in 1871. Victor Emmanuel II, former king of Piedmont, became monarch of the new country—Italia—where only 3 percent spoke a common tongue.

The Vatican was furious about losing its Papal States to the incoming monarchy and issued a bull (edict) demanding that Catholics not recognize the new government. Popes were so mortified about what might happen if they left the Vatican that not one ventured out for six decades, until Mussolini granted the Vatican independence in 1929, making it the world's smallest independent state.[7]

IL DUCE: BENITO MUSSOLINI (1883–1945)

History portrays Mussolini as a fool, but the Nietzsche fan fancied himself an intellectual. As with Hitler, a frustrated painter, Mussolini was a creator—Il Duce was a novelist—and one can't help wondering whether the world might be a less pained place if they'd both received (or deserved) a little more artistic respect. Mussolini's novel *The Cardinal's Mistress* was published in 1908, but was a bit thin on plot (a cardinal falls in love and wants out of the church, but the pope won't let him go) and rather purple in style: "Like a boy he knelt at Claudia's feet . . . 'You will be the Madonna of the temple within me. I will be your slave. Strike me, despise me, beat me, open my veins with a subtle dagger, but grant me the revelation of yourself . . .'"[8] Dismayed by dismal sales, the Socialist jumped into politics, but broke with that party and started up a Fascist newspaper in 1914. Three years later he was drafted into WWI. At first aligned with Austria and Germany, Italy in typical style switched sides and went in with Britain and France. Mussolini didn't see battle. Wounded in a drill, he returned home to perfect his writing and right-wing platform. Italy too was wounded. Financially handicapped from the beginning, Italy plowed into debt buying weapons for the Great War, and by 1918 owed about $4 billion. What's more, the country didn't get lands she'd been promised if she fought with the Allies.[9] In 1921, Mussolini won a parliament seat during the anxious time when the country's weak capitalist system looked likely to collapse. Mussolini stirred nationalist sentiment and boosted the sagging Italian ego. Not as captivating as Hitler, he was nevertheless rousing in his speeches and presented an alternative to the Communism that many feared. In 1922, he marched on Rome with his Fascist "blackshirts." After he was made prime minister by weak-kneed King Victor Emmanuel III, he climbed up as leader of Italia, killing opponents, shutting out other parties, censoring the press, and creating the myth of Il Duce, a relentless workaholic with the ability to work magic for Italy on the international stage.

So much for Mussolini's magic; the dictator made trains run on time, but he made Italy's name mud. Italy succeeded with her 1935 invasion of Abyssinia (Ethiopia) after Mussolini ordered the army to use nerve gas on locals who were mostly fighting with spears, bringing the scorn of Europe upon Italia; he soon introduced work camps, torture, and death by impalement. Mussolini stripped Jews of civil rights and their jobs in 1938—before Hitler—and annexed Albania the next year. He signed up with Hitler in WWII, but Italian forces were so hideously disorganized that Nazis frequently had to bail them out.

King Victor Emmanuel III (upon whom Mussolini had bestowed the titles of Emperor of Ethiopia and King of Albania) passively aided Mussolini during the first eleven years of his "reign." But in July 1943, after the Allies took Sicily, Il Duce's Fascist colleagues (including his foreign minister/son-in-law) worked with the timid king to eject Mussolini from office and into prison. Italy soon switched teams, signing an armistice and theoretically batting for the Allies. Hitler was livid, and the king and acting leader General Pietro Badoglio ran out, leaving the baffled military headless. Nazis stormed in, turning wine villas into fortresses as they battled incoming Allies; they lined roads with land mines and blew up bridges upon retreat. Although Mussolini didn't stay behind bars for long—Nazi paratroopers launched a dramatic escape—he'd lost his popular appeal. Setting up in the north, Mussolini behaved as if he were still in power, but Hitler was calling the shots, including organizing deportations of Jews. While trying to sneak off to Switzerland in April 1945, Mussolini and his mistress were shot and killed by partisans near Lake Como. For days, Il Duce's rotting corpse hung upside down in Milan, where the public defiled it, until American forces finally cut down the dead leader and buried him.

> *Art lover Hitler spared Florence massive destruction, wanting to preserve her Renaissance glory. Nevertheless, he ordered bombing of all bridges spanning the Arno River, except for the Ponte Vecchio—the old covered bridge, which he demanded be saved, not suspecting that the communication wires for Florence's resistance twisted underneath. After the war, bridges were rebuilt as they had been, using many of the same rocks, pulled out of the river.*

After twenty-four years of Fascism, Italy crawled into the postwar era as one of Europe's most impoverished countries. In 1946, Italians voted to boot the king and become a republic. The new republic revived in the late 1950s and 1960s. Marshall Plan funds ignited an industrial boom in the north, where car manufacturers Fiat and Alfa Romeo revved up the economy; most funding for the south was sucked off by the Mafia, leaving the Mezzagiorno behind in the race. All across Italy, family-owned businesses emerged in the neighborhood borgos, and still today Italians are more likely to be self-employed or to work for a small company making clothes, leather goods, or furniture than to work for a large corporation or factory.

> *Tuscan wine estates ran on a quasi-feudal system started in Renaissance times. Called* mezzadria, *literally "halfers," it relied on tenant workers whose wages were half of the wine, olive oil, and produce from the estate, where they had houses and small plots. Mezzadria was outlawed in the 1960s, and peasants moved to cities. Unable to afford laborers for their vineyards—and believing forecasts that predicted the Italian wine market was doomed—many nobles sold off their estates; many northern industrialists bought them up for a song and entered the wine game. Though outlawed,* mezzadria *is now making a comeback.*

In the violent 1970s, Italy was rocked by Gli Anni di Piombo, or "Years of Lead." Mafia kidnappers and radicals from right and left (including the Marxist Red Brigades) assassinated politicians and bombed museums and trains. The Red Brigades alone are accused of killing 350 people, including Prime Minister Aldo Moro.

> *Although officially denied, there is a persistent belief that NATO and the CIA were at least peripherally involved in assorted bombings and attacks of the period. A NATO program called Gladio, its existence confirmed by former prime minister Giulio Andreotti, was devised to keep power out of the hands of Italian Communists (and to a lesser extent Socialists), whom it was feared would open Italy to the Soviet Union. By blaming high-profile attacks on left-wing guerrillas, it was believed, Gladio could knock out support for the Italian Communist Party.*

Somehow, despite *i molti problemi*—the stinky politics, the nonstop scandals, the Mob, the disorganization that just seems to be the Italian way, and the illegal immigration that adds another dysfunctional thread to the social fabric—Italy just keeps chugging away, finding the meaning of life in a plate of good food and amazing the 30 million tourists who visit each year, and who can't fathom the chaos hidden behind all the beauty.

Hot Spots

Mama's House: Everyone within driving distance returns to Mama's for Sunday dinner. The distance is getting shorter. Given the state of the economy and house prices, few Italians are moving out in their twenties; some never do.

> *Italy has the highest "stay at home" rate in Europe: 95 percent of adults under thirty still live at home.[10] The average age for an Italian to fly the coop: thirty-four years.[11]*

Roma: It's said here in the city of seven hills that when Rome's Colosseum falls, civilization goes with it. In the meantime, the capital awash with leftovers from Imperial Rome is still one of Italy's liveliest. Visitors shuttle from the Pantheon and the Vatican's Sistine Chapel to the Trevi Fountain, where they pitch coins to ensure return.

Milano: The fashion and finance center was heavily bombed during the war, but has a few remaining bits of architectural heritage.

Tuscany: With the red-capped Duomo, sculpture-filled squares, and the Uffizi—which celebrates the Renaissance both inside (with its museum) and out (with its long-columned loggias)—Florence grabs the spotlight in this gorgeous region, but the vineyard-covered countryside, where one awakes to crowing roosters and mist hanging over valleys, is one of the most serene places on earth. Golden-hued Siena holds the Palio, a much-hyped competition between neighborhoods, when horses race in the square as they have since da Vinci's day. Florence and Siena have been feuding since then too; during one territorial standoff, a race between two roosters redrew the map.

Mezzogiorno: The troubled, poorer southern half of Italy is known for half-built structures where people live; building owners don't pay taxes until building is finished, so they delay completion permanently. It has higher unemployment rates, bigger families, and tends to be more religious than other regions. Among the charms: the Amalfi coast, with its hairpin roads, is dazzling; island Ischia draws jet-setters; and chaotic, crime-ridden Naples has a frenzied allure.

Drivers in Naples often race through red lights. The reason, explains one Napolitano, is that traffic lights are usually broken and permanently red, so there's no point in stopping to see if one actually works.

Sicilia: Birthplace of the Mafia, Sicily bears the brunt of Italians' prejudice, even though its cuisine—astoundingly fresh fish, handmade pasta, and flowery white wines—may be the country's finest. Phoenician ruins stand among Arabesque palaces, palm trees line imperial squares, and, off the main drags, poverty runs rampant.

Albania: When the Communist dictatorship fell in the country across the Adriatic, 24,000 Albanians appeared on Italy's doorstep—in three days. The Italian government welcomed them, issuing work visas, and the president urged Italians to take them in as guests. Six months later, another 15,000 showed up. This time Italy sent out riot squads and the Albanians were herded into a stadium, where food was air-dropped to them. Five days later, they were airlifted back to Albania. During the previous six months, said Italians, crime had skyrocketed; the government issued a statement that Italy was not a land of immigration. However, some Italians and Albanians do get along. Albanian-organized crime and the Mafia in Puglia work together to smuggle cigarettes and Eastern European sex slaves.

Puglia: The heel of "the boot" boasts some of Italy's tastiest cooking (skip the horsemeat), but scummy port city Bari is smuggling central.

Aviano air force base: This northern base, a center for NATO operations during the 1990 operations in Yugoslavia, is often in headlines. In 1998, a U.S.

fighter plane sliced the wires of a cable car at a nearby ski slope; twenty died when it crashed. The base was previously embroiled in scandal when it leaked that the U.S. was transporting nuclear arms via Aviano, violating Italy's law banning nuclear weapons on her land.

The Vatican: Sure, you can visit the world's smallest sovereign state that is home to 932 residents and has her own post office, police force, newspaper, TV and radio stations, and which generates, mostly through international Catholic donations, some $250 million a year. Millions of visitors each year take in the splendor of the dome at St. Peter's Basilica; the column-lined St. Peter's Square (watched over by Swiss guards in colorful Renaissance garb); and the beauty of Michelangelo's ceiling in the Sistine Chapel. But what really happens behind the wall of this 108-acre state remains as much of a mystery as ever. Some are still trying to uncover the Holy See's role in World War II. Some assert that the Vatican helped hide thousands of Jews; others believe the Vatican ran "ratlines," sneaking Nazi war criminals out to Australia and the Americas. Other mysteries include the Vatican's role in laundering money through its bank, and the sudden death of Pope John Paul I, who lasted only a month—some say he planned to tidy up the scandal-ridden financial institution.

The dinner table: Mind the rules here. Nearly as important as food is the order of dishes, always beginning with antipasti and ending with the salad, an eating peculiarity that—along with the *passeggiata*, that after-meal stroll—may explain why Italians are so rarely fat.

The Autostrada: Marriages suffer under Italy's latest attempt to enforce speed limits. Using license-plate numbers, snap-the-speeder technology sends a photo of the offending vehicle straight to the offender's house. The fines aren't the problem; it's who's in the passenger seat. Wives aren't happy to see it's not them.

ITALIAN FILM

Federico Fellini, Vittorio de Sica, and Roberto Rossellini unleashed a new genre of dramatic postwar cinema with *La Dolce Vita*, *The Bicycle Thief*, and *Rome, Open City*. More recently, Roberto Benigni cowrote, directed, and starred in *Life Is Beautiful*. The film, about a father who tries to spare his son the horrors of the Second World War, swept the Cannes Film Festival and won Benigni an Oscar for Best Actor. Another heart-stirrer is *Cinema Paradiso* by Giuseppe Tornatore, which, like *Mediterraneo*, also won an Oscar.

Runways: Gucci, Pucci, Prada, Ferragamo, Armani, Valentino, and Dolce & Gabbana help make Milan's catwalks more daring than the runways of Paris.

The Garden: The Italian obsession with food may be rooted in the country's peasant past, but even wealthy Italians pride themselves on their green thumbs. Give a man a foot of land, and he'll put in a small garden and vineyard, grind pesto from smashed basil, pine nuts, and parmesan, and concoct honeyed drinks from white grapes he's dried. A good Italian, even if living in the heart of the city, has found somewhere—balcony, rooftop, or windowsill—to grow tomatoes (one kind for salads, another for sauce) and to pluck fresh herbs. Genetically modified varieties have no place here, where antique seeds are saved and no gift is finer than olive oil straight from the cold press.

VINITALY

It sounds like a big Bacchanalian bash, but it's serious biz when 2,000 wine producers uncork their stuff, some 30,000 buyers swarm around for a taste, and potential billions of dollars are up for grabs. That's what happens every spring in Verona, where the concrete convention center is tarted up with plastic vines and wooden tables for VinItaly, the biggest wine sale of the year in the world. With the possibility for vintners to sell out that year's entire stock in 120 hours, the five-day event of swirling, sniffing, and spitting is surprisingly sobering. Few Italians can be found flirting (not even with the lovely wine pourers hired for the event), interupting their *coitus attemptus continuus* inclinations for the business at hand—that's how important it is.

Hotshots

Romano Prodi: Prime Minister, 1996–1998, 2006–present. Former professor Prodi is Berlusconi's opposite: intellectual, left-leaning, calm, and somewhat dull. He probably can't last long with Berlusconi barking from the sidelines and trying to pull the rug out before Prodi even steps in, but this former president of the European Commission will likely nudge Italy closer to the rest of Europe and distance her from George W. Bush.

Giancarlo Fini: Head of the National Alliance, former journalist Fini is softening the image of the neo-Fascist movement moving closer to the center, and condemning Il Duce's Fascism as "absolute evil." Apparently it's working; he's one of Italy's most popular politicians.

WRITERLY SORTS

Nobel Prize–winning storyteller Umberto Eco will never be accused of being a minimalist, given works such as the 800-page *The Name of the Rose*. Left-wing satirical playwright Dario Fo, part of Italy's "laughter culture," cracks his whip at corrupt society, and daring Oriana Fallaci was once was the world's most unflinching journalist—she posed many a difficult question to world leaders, and occasionally had a romantic fling postinterview. Former leftie Fallaci has done an about-face; now she harpoons Europe for becoming Arabized—"Eurarabia," she calls it. In her recent book *The Strength of Reason* and her post–September 11 diatribe *The Rage and the Pride*, racist statements, including a claim that Muslims "multiply like rats," offset her insights about radical Islam's growing hatred of the West. Her books sell wildly in Italy.

Alessandra Mussolini: Italian parliamentarian in European Parliament, 2004–present. Doe-eyed, pouty-lipped, and hot-tempered Mussolini, granddaughter of Il Duce and niece of Sophia Loren, is a walking contradiction. A Fascist who protects women's rights, Mussolini posed nude for *Playboy*'s centerfold in 1983. The former actress with a degree in medicine now heads her own party, having broken with the National Alliance when its leader apologized for her grandpap's activities during WWII.

> *Ms. Mussolini called for sex offenders to be chemically castrated, pushed for Italian mothers to give their last names to their children, and loudly protested a rape ruling in Italy. The judge said it was impossible to rape a woman wearing jeans. Mussolini strode into Italian parliament with other female parliamentarians, wearing jeans and waving a banner that read "Jeans: an alibi for rape."*

Licio Gelli: A former Blackshirt in Mussolini's Fascist volunteer army who helped support Franco during the civil war in Spain, Gelli apparently worked with the SS, but his recent activities are more shadowy. He's believed to have been part of NATO's Gladio operations to block Communist support in Italy by agitating unrest, and was also linked to the CIA, perhaps as part of his illegal Masonic lodge Propaganda Due, whose members numbered among Italy's most powerful and wealthy. Convicted in 1982 of fraud in the Banco Ambrosiano, he escaped to France before completing his sentence. After being rounded up, he was hauled before the courts for the murder of the head of the Vatican bank, and his name comes up in nearly every

Alessandra Mussolini,
a feminist Fascist

Courtesy of European Parliament, Photo Department

Italian scandal over the past thirty years. Among those he's rumored to have worked with in the U.S.: General Alexander Haig and leading neocon Michael Ledeen.

Pope Benedict XVI: On April 19, 2005, white smoke puffed from the chimney of the Sistine Chapel, announcing the appointment of the 265th pope—one whom many had hoped would modernize the Church. Instead, Cardinal Joseph Ratzinger, aged seventy-eight, a hardliner from Germany, appeared at the Vatican balcony—and he may prove even more traditional than his conservative predecessor, John Paul II. The new pope opposes the ordination of women, stem-cell research, and gay marriage, and considers religions other than Roman Catholicism to be "deficient." Some have raised questions about his past. As was common during the Nazi era, he was a member of the Hitler youth group. Some speculate that his ultraconservatism will polarize opinion within the Church. Many, however, supported his move to quickly canonize his predecessor.

While Italians generally highly respect their pope, few adhere to the Church's edicts on contraception and abortion. In Italy, abortion during the first trimester is provided free; a recent proposal that women pay after more than one termination triggered outrage.

DRINKING MATTERS

Briskly herbal Campari or bubbly Prosecco, start the meal; anise, astringent Cynar (made from artichokes) or citrusy limoncello often end it. Made from dried grapes, the adored honey-like Vin Santo from Avignonesi, released from nine years in oak during the waning moon, hails back to the Renaissance; the "mother yeast" has been "living" for 600 years. Seeking romance? Try clove-scented but puckerish Strega—aka "witch." The yellow color comes from saffron, the recipe from covens' love potions.

News you can understand: *Colors* is the best magazine coming out of Italy—and surprise, it's not owned by Berlusconi. Published by Benetton, the bilingual magazine innovatively covers the most basic of topics—food, water, shelter, drugs—and plugs readers into the distant corners of the world. Eye-opening, award-winning, and right-on: www.colorsmagazine.com

5. BELGIUM

(België, Belgique)

Falling Apart

FAST FACTS

Country:	Kingdom of Belgium; Koninkrijk België, Royaume de Belgique
Capital:	Brussels
Government:	Parliamentary democracy under a constitutional monarch
Independence:	October 4, 1830 (from Netherlands); monarchy since 1831
Population:	10,379,000 (2006 estimate)
Head of State:	King Albert II (1993)
Head of Government:	Prime Minister Guy Verhofstadt (1999)
Elections:	Monarchy is hereditary; prime minister, leader of majority party in legislative elections, appointed by monarch, approved by parliament
Name of Parliament:	Parlement
Ethnicity:	58% Flemish; 31% Walloon; 11% other

Religion:	75% Roman Catholic; 25% Protestant/other
Language:	60% Flemish (Dutch derivative); 40% French; 1% German
Literacy:	99%
Famous Exports:	The Smurfs, Tintin, ecstasy
Economic Big Boy:	Delhaize Group (supermarket); 2004 total sales: $23.67 billion[1]
Per Capita GDP:	$31,900 (2005 estimate)
Unemployment:	8.5% (December 2005 Eurostat figure)
EU Status:	Founding member (member of EEC since 1957)
Currency:	Euro

Quick Tour

With her charming medieval villages, thick forests, and swan-filled canals, België, at first glance, appears to be wholesome to the point of eliciting snores. Known for divine chocolate, sparkly diamonds, and comic books, Belgique—where the Smurfs were invented—is also headquarters for the European Union and NATO, which makes her sound snoozier.

FUN IN BELGIUM

The best things to do in Belgium are drink, eat, and sleep, and Belgians provide compelling reasons to indulge in all three. The country serves up 400 beers—brewed by Trappist monks, spiked with sour cherries, white, gold, red, or syrupy black, and all of them best drunk in the country's many cozy pubs. Fabulous eateries abound, from sleek oyster bars with waterfalls caught behind glass to homey inns with buckets of mussels served in creamy beer sauce; weight gain is inevitable in Belgium, particularly if one partakes in a multicourse, multihour Burgundian lunch—a blur of courses including white asparagus, lobster tarts in buttery sauce, partridge with port, and endless bottles of wine. Hotels may be marble-wrapped suites, fetching converted railway stations set deep in woods, or castles where peacocks wander the grounds. The combination of beer, feast, and deep snooze is more beneficial than it sounds: Belgians are considered the healthiest people on the planet. Well, they certainly aren't the skinniest.

Despite the initial goody-goody appearance, boring the country is not. Belgium is riddled with corruption, seediness, ethnic tensions, and hair-raising scandals, at least a few involving alleged pedophilia rings.[2] Carcinogenic dairy products, bribe-greased arms deals, and hissing secessionists are just a few reasons why this odd little country appears to falling apart.

BRUSSELS VS. WALLONIA VS. FLANDERS VS. WALLOONS VS. FLEMISH

Brussels is Belgium's capital and is bilingual: French and (Dutch-derived) Flemish are both official languages. The rest of the country is divided into two distinct regions. In Wallonia, the industrial south that boasts the wooded Ardennes, they speak French. In Flanders, the northern half that holds diamond center Antwerp and former mercantile capitals Bruges and Ghent, they speak Flemish. Differences between the Walloons and the Flemish, who are forever bickering, don't stop there—which is one reason the country is served by seven different legislatures, some Flemish, some Walloon, some combined. The right-leaning Flemish are akin to the Dutch, while the left-leaning Walloons are more like French. Wallonia used to be rich, but the coal is gone, steel mills are closed, and unemployment is around 18 percent; now the wealthy Flemish complain about subsidizing unemployed Walloons. Language differences fuel their mutual dislike. Flanders won't pay for libraries with many French books or let school buses with names written in French into their districts. Walloons construct pricey bridges to connect French-speaking neighborhoods, and French speakers in Flanders boycott local taxes because they're written in Flemish. The only groups winning in the constant battles are the separatist groups, who churn issues up even more.

> *Eight people died in a 2001 train crash simply because the signalmen—one Walloon, one Flemish—couldn't communicate.*

With a tiny population of 10 million—about that of Paris—there are a surprisingly high number of scandals and unsolved mysteries in Belgium, home of Agatha Christie's detective Hercule Poirot, a character the country desperately needs in real life. Bizarre crimes pop up with alarming regularity—whether you're talking about the Protestant minister who, along with his daughter, chopped up their family[3]; the father who pimped out his twelve-year-old to the local mechanic, lumberjack, antiques dealer, and family doctor; or the unsolved murder in Brussels of astrophysicist Gerald Bull, who was building a supergun for Iraq. Not long ago, the government ordered dairy products laced with dioxin to be stocked on store shelves, even after the EU had ordered them off; the foreign minister was accused of selling passports to known East European mobsters; a half dozen ministers—including a former head of NATO—were convicted in an international stinker involving bribery and arms that some believe may be linked to the never-solved 1991 murder of politician Andre Cools, who was reportedly about to name names. A high-ranking Belgian official stepped down after attending a reunion of the Nazi SS, and far-right anti-immigration group Vlaams Blok (Flemish Block) became Northern Belgium's most popular party, peddling a list of "Seventy Points" that smacked of racial cleansing. The revelation that many Belgian soccer games in the 2006 season were rigged—a Chinese mobster "bought" agents, coaches, and players—was simply par for the course.

The scandal that most disgusted and disturbed Belgians, and still makes them shudder today, is the multilayered crime of Marc Dutroux—a crime that most believe still hasn't fully been solved and that some, including Dutroux and accomplices, say leads right to the top.

BELGIAN DARKNESS

A father of three, electrician Marc Dutroux was reportedly a teenage prostitute who supplied cocaine at sex parties, dealt in stolen cars, and may have trafficked sex slaves from Eastern Europe. That's the nicer part of the résumé of this predator, first tried for rape in 1983. He ditched that charge, but in 1989 was found guilty of kidnapping and raping five young girls. Slapped with a thirteen-year sentence, he was out after three years. Dutroux constructed a dungeon of tunnels, cages, and cells in the basement of his house, where six young girls, all of whom he tortured and raped, were held for months during 1995 and 1996. Four of the six died. He killed two, but another two died, probably in early 1996, while Dutroux was in prison for several months for car theft. Those girls, both eight years old, starved to death in the well-hidden dungeon; even though police had searched the house twice, looking for clues of the missing children, they hadn't found the girls hidden under the floors where they walked. (Dutroux later killed the friend whom he'd asked to watch over the prisoners.) After eluding police for months—and briefly escaping from prison—he was finally tried, nearly eight years after his arrest, and found guilty, in June 2004, of child rape and murder. Dutroux now faces life imprisonment, but he maintains that he was abducting the children for a pedophilia ring. In 1999, a series of witnesses gave statements about being procured for such a ring—saying that torture, murder, and snuff movies were part of the package.[4] Some even stated it was part of a satanic cult. Whatever was happening, Dutroux and a codefendant, businessman Jean-Michel Nihoul, maintain that the ring involved the highest levels of Belgian society.

Little België (or Belgique, as the Walloons call it) has more problems than sickening crime. Racism and separatism are also simmering behind-the-scenes issues—and they sometimes boil up in port city Antwerp, Belgium's second largest metropolis, the world's biggest diamonds trade center, and a major distribution center for rave-drug ecstasy. About 20,000 Jews, many Hassidic and working with diamonds, make Antwerp their home, and the majority live in the old Jewish quarter. Right next door is the Arab quarter, home to many of the city's 30,000 Moroccans and Turks—a location that makes for ongoing tension. A wave of anti-Semitic acts hit Antwerp recently, but Arabs say they are victimized too, sometimes at the hands of right-wing nationalists.

Arabs in Flanders have a high unemployment rate—20 percent overall, more than 30 percent among the young. The issue fires up anti-immigration groups, but Arabs say the problem is that the Flemish won't give them jobs.

They point to November 2002, when a Moroccan schoolteacher was killed by a Flemish dockworker. Furious Arabs rioted in the streets, knocking out store windows and overturning cars—and more violence ensued as police battled rioters. Saying that police targeted Arabs, a newly formed group called the Arab European League organized teams with video cameras to patrol the streets and videotape any perceived aggression. The patrol teams themselves were considered aggressive, and the government shut them down. Nevertheless, the incident gave more attention to the head of the Arab European League, Dyab Abou Jahjah, who is quickly

Coutesy of Arab European league

Dyab Abou Jahjah, noisily demanding Arab rights

becoming a spokesman for disaffected Arabs living in Europe—and speaking out about their rights to preserve their culture in Europe, from dress to sharia law. The Belgian prime minister views Jahjah and his Arab European League as "a threat to society,"[5] and Jahjah's group was recently slapped with charges of running a private militia.

THE MALCOLM X OF BELGIUM?

Whatever you think about Lebanese-born Dyab Abou Jahjah—a former Hezbollah member who the Belgian government would like to send packing—you have to admit that the handsome, well-spoken activist raises interesting questions. Among them: Should immigrants be forced to adopt the culture of the countries they move to? And, more pointedly, where does freedom of speech cross the line and become unacceptably offensive? Jahjah points out that European society "is fundamentally monocultural," and says that if Arabs don't forgo their culture they are "economically and politically excluded" from European life. He's working to change that—demanding that Arab-Muslim cultures be given their own schools and be allowed to wear headscarves (banned in French schools) and practice their laws (which may include killing homosexuals and adulterers and chopping off the hands of thieves). Those ideas aren't well received here, but the Arab European League's reaction to Danish cartoons mocking Allah was even more extreme. Spearing the rhetoric about freedom of expression, the AEL posted a number of outrageous cartoons on its site—including one of Hitler in bed with Anne Frank, and another of Jews fudging numbers in the Holocaust count. The point of the cartoons, Jahjah later stated, was to sarcastically "confront Europe with its own hypocrisy." The cartoons look like they will result in yet another lawsuit for the AEL—this one in the Netherlands, where the AEL has set up a branch.

Volatile Antwerp is also the epicenter for radical separatists who want to nab Brussels and secede from Belgium. Spearheading that movement is popular anti-immigrant party Vlaams Blok (Flemish Block), which has links to the Nazi party and views Belgium as an "artificial" country. Party spokespeople have questioned the Holocaust (and even the authenticity of Anne Frank's diary), and the party's program calls for blocking future mosques, forcibly repatriating immigrants, and booting the king—for starters. The most popular party in Flanders in 2004, it overtook Antwerp's city council but was isolated in Flemish parliament when all other parties shunned it and wouldn't form a coalition. Then, in November 2004, high courts ruled that it was racist, effectively shutting it down. Not to worry; the group simply formed under a new name—Vlaams Belang (Flemish Interest).

Antwerp is but one city that illustrates the behind-the-scenes strife shaking up the whole country. Belgium is a chocolate-coated jalepeño: pretty on the outside, exploding from within. Walloons and Flemish are at each other's throats, Arabs and Jews don't get along, Vlaams Blok wants to secede—and kick out the Arabs—and the government is trying to block Vlaams Blok's attempts to tap separatist rage.

Yet with her prominent role as backdrop for the European Union and NATO, Belgium is an undeniable international power. She is forming a separate military alliance with Germany, France, and Luxembourg, and occasionally rivals the Netherlands as a rising voice in international justice, both moves that the Bush administration has tried to shut down.

WAR CRIMES LAW

When Belgium resident Martine Beckers answered the phone in 1993, her sister—living in Rwanda—told her that she was about to be killed by a gang of machete-wielding Hutu. Unsure what to do, Beckers called the Belgian police, thus planting the seed for what would become Belgium's most infamous law: the 1993 Belgian War Crimes Law, which directed Belgian courts to try cases of international genocide and attacks on civilians. Neither the police nor the law could prevent the death of Beckers's sister, but the law opened the door for trials of Rwandans, including two nuns who were tried in Belgium in 2001, and found guilty of inciting murder. Cases snowballed and the scope widened. Suits were filed against Israel's prime minister Ariel Sharon, Iraq's Saddam Hussein, and Cuba's Fidel Castro. In 2002, a suit was filed against former president George H. W. Bush, Colin Powell, Norman Schwarzkopf, and Dick Cheney for their roles in the deaths of civilians during the 1991 Gulf War. Then, in 2003, a new case was filed against President George W. Bush, Secretary of State Colin Powell, Secretary of Defense Donald Rumsfeld, General Tommy Franks, and British prime minister Tony Blair for their involvement in Iraq. In June 2003, Rumsfeld threatened to move NATO out of Belgium if the law wasn't amended; in July, he froze the U.S. financial contribution to building a new NATO headquarters in Brussels that carries a $350 million price tag.[6] The law was hastily amended, and now it can be used only if a Belgian citizen is a victim or suspect of a war crime. Charges were also dropped against the U.S., UK, and Israeli officials.[7]

History Review

Nudged up against France, Germany, and the Netherlands, today's Belgium has tolerated all the neighbors barging in to run the place or their warriors traipsing across it like it was the back door to France. Made wealthy in the Middle Ages by textiles—woolen fabrics, delicate lace, and fine tapestries put Brussels, Ghent, and Antwerp on the trade map—the area was ruled by the French House of Burgundy in the fourteenth century. The region became an opulent arts center, and the countryside was dotted with castles, where people partook in the enduring feast known as the Burgundian lunch. The Austrian Empire pulled the area into her geographic weave in the 1400s, which led to it being later yanked into the Spanish Netherlands—a move that came complete with the Spanish Inquisition; thousands were killed for perceived heresy. (See "The Netherlands," page 178.)

Pieter Brueghel the Elder (1525–1569): Perhaps the first European to paint landscapes that weren't merely biblical backdrops, Brueghel—the star of sixteenth-century Flemish art—turned his paintbrush to vibrant village life, capturing it in bawdy detail that was nearly scandalous (see *The Peasant Dance*), especially considering that the Spanish Inquisition was hanging around. Whatever corner of his paintings a viewer takes in, another vignette unfolds, telling us more of life in that day than whole history books.

The Spaniards reintroduced Catholicism, and the Church assumed great importance. Napoleon invaded in 1792, and sold off church property—about half of the land—and just outside Brussels he met his demise in 1815 at the Battle of Waterloo. The European leaders who redrew the Napoleonic Empire at the 1815 Congress of Vienna hoped to prevent future invasions. For security, they lumped the Catholic region of contemporary Belgium and Luxembourg together with the Protestant Netherlands. Nobody much liked the arrangement, particularly the French-speaking Catholics in the south, who were given a backseat to the Protestant Dutch speakers in the north.

In the late 1700s and early 1800s, a revolution was stirring in textiles. Long a cottage industry, new machinery triggered a costly change; factories could now make fabrics much more cheaply. The British, supplied with cheap resources from the colonies, made the bottom line drop even further. Peasants lost much of their textile income, and bad weather hurt their crops. Their unhappiness was a factor in the region's independence movement.

Calls to shake loose from the Netherlands hit a high note one night in 1830. After taking in the opera *La Muette de Portici*, about a revolt in Naples, the audience was stirred to action. The uprising that began at the opera spilled onto the streets, where the hungry and unemployed were incited to loot the houses of noblemen, symbols of the Dutch king's hold on the south. The new country of Belgium officially broke ties with the Netherlands a few weeks later and borrowed a German prince, Leopold of Saxe-Coberg-Gotha, to head the new state under the name King Leopold I. His son, King Leopold II, who became monarch in 1865, made Belgium wealthy when he opened up the Congo and led the late nineteenth-century "Scramble for Africa," when European countries divvied up the Dark Continent for themselves.

KING LEOPOLD II (1835-1909)
AND THE BELGIAN CONGO

Long of face and even longer of snowy white beard, Leopold was a dreamer even before he climbed upon the throne at age twenty-nine, taking over a thirty-five-year-old country that was already fraying.[8] Walloons and Flemish were quarrelling even back then, and secular liberals and Catholics were sniping. To escape from the problems at hand, Leopold invented health ailments as reason to travel to exotic locales from Egypt to China. Independently wealthy, especially after investing in the Suez Canal, he wanted to expand Belgium's boundaries. Advisers cautioned against such silly notions, but Leopold had his own money to find a colony where Belgium could plant her flag. Alas, all the ones he wanted to buy—the Philippines, Angola, New Zealand—weren't for sale. Hearing stories about the Dark Continent's Congo River, he decided to develop it. In 1876, he sent a mission there, claiming the Belgians would save the Africans from slavery. The masses loved the idea, but Leopold did just the opposite. His men ravaged the land and turned the locals into the most cruelly treated of slaves. Leveling their villages for rubber plantations, the Belgians demanded that the Congo people harvest the plants. Those who resisted were killed; those who didn't keep up with the workload had their hands chopped off. Millions of Congolese people died before English maritime journalist Edmund Dene Morel unraveled what was going on in 1900. He discovered that the ships returning from the Congo were loaded with far more riches than claimed—and those that went out carried weaponry. This wasn't free trade, as the king claimed, this was slavery, and Morel went on to make a huge stink about it. The British government finally sent its consul to report on the situation, but by then—almost three decades after the Belgians first set foot in the Congo—most of the original population had been wiped out. The Belgians finally looked into it. The government's report, published in 1905, was so damning that Leopold donated much of his land to the state in exchange for the government keeping the report under wraps. The matter was hushed up until the 1980s, when a Belgian ambassador discovered the report and the ugly truth finally slithered out, shocking the Belgian people as much as anyone else.[9]

The Belgian king had a royal fit in 2003, when the BBC wanted to air the documentary White King, Red Rubber, Black Death about the genocide in the Congo. The program was indeed broadcast—but was heavily edited.

During the First World War, Belgium declared neutrality, but the Germans ignored that as they marched into France. Belgium became a permanent front,
where troops dug into trenches for four years. During World War II, Germans
again invaded Belgium to enter France. Again, Belgium played a crucial role geographically. She was the setting for the horrific Battle of the Bulge, Germany's last
major move to reclaim lost territory in December 1944. Aiming to take Antwerp,
Germans surrounded the thinly protected line of Allies in the snow-thick forests of
Belgium and Luxembourg. Some of WWII's most desperate fighting ensued—
and at times it looked like the Allies couldn't hold out. Ultimately, the Allies held
their ground, but the battle marked the most brutal for American troops, who suffered about 75,000 casualties. (See "Luxembourg," page 273.)

> Nazi-occupied from 1940, Belgium had her fair share of collaborators,
> many executed after the war.

During the war, the king refused to cooperate with Nazis and was deported
to a German prison. But his quick surrender to the Germans brought charges of
treason from some Belgians—a charge that was officially found unwarranted.
Nevertheless, he was exiled in Switzerland, and a vote on the future of the
country showed that few wanted him to return. He passed the monarchy on to
his son, but the role was no longer terribly powerful. In 1950, the people voted
for a constitutional monarchy, which made the king even more of a figurehead.
During the 1960s, the strategically located country finally became a beneficiary
of her geography instead of a victim of it. NATO and the European Economic
Community (now known as the European Union) both set up headquarters in
Brussels, making the city a prosperous seat of power.[10]

Hot Spots

Antwerp: The world's fourth-biggest port and a center for fashion design.
Also a major transshipment point for drugs, arms, and stolen goods of all
sorts.

Brussels: Now called the Capital of Europe, since the EU took up residence here, she's home to wonderful restaurants and one of Europe's prettiest
squares—flashy La Grand-Place. Noted for art nouveau design, antiques markets, and a few stunning neighborhoods (some dotted with lakes), Brussels
lost many historical buildings in the 1990s, when developers erected modern
structures for the EU. Over 12 percent of offices in Brussels are devoted to EU
institutions.[11]

La Grand-Place was destroyed in 1695, when French armies tried to knock down City Hall. That edifice remained, but neighboring buildings crumbled. They were rebuilt as headquarters for mercantile guilds, all trying to outdo each other in gold-heavy baroque style. In the 1800s, Karl Marx lived here, penning his Communist Manifesto while staying in a room above what is now the Swan Restaurant, a bourgeoisie favorite.

Bruges: Once a wealthy textile town, this canal-happy city crams in more tourists per square inch than Paris.

Ghent: This lost-in-time town with rich medieval architecture, including a majestic castle, graceful church spires, and authentic store fronts, takes the noose as its symbol. Holy Roman Emperor Charles V tried to humiliate rebellious fifteenth-century residents by marching them through the city wearing only nooses and shirts; now they reenact the scene annually.

Hotshots:

Guy Verhofstadt: Prime Minister, 1999–present. Right-leaning in theory, his administration legalized euthanasia and gay marriage, and closed down Belgium's seven nuclear plants. Keeps tossing more autonomy to Belgium's disparate regions.

Photo by Star

La Grand-Place: Great for mussels in Brussels

King Albert II: Reigning monarch, 1993–present. This monarch has had a tough life: his mother, Princess Astrid of Sweden, died in a car crash when he was one—his father was driving—and six years later, the royal family was locked up in Germany while Nazis occupied Belgium. He's a tad wild: loves motorcycles and riding them fast; married Italian noblewoman Paola Ruffo di Calabria in 1959, but admits to having a daughter by a Belgian baroness.

Georges Simenon (1903–1989): Celebrated pen behind the fictional detective Inspector Maigret, Simenon cranked out more than 500 books (plus innumerable short stories) by the time he died at eighty-six. He claimed to have sex at least three times a day, perhaps not always with his wife: he was known as "the man of 10,000 women."[12]

Tintin (1929–1983): In 1929, Georges Remi (aka Hergé) gave birth to the modern comic book when he inked boy reporter Tintin, fluffy canine Snowy (aka Milou), and scotch-swilling sailor Captain Haddock, who in their first adventure battled Communists in the Soviet Union. Over the course of twenty-two volumes, the trio (along with the Thompson Twins and Professor Calculus) uncovered treasures and took on evil forces everywhere from Peru to the moon. The crew died when Hergé did, in 1983 at age seventy-five.

René Magritte (1898–1967): He brought the absurd to the everyday (and vice versa) in precise images that always contained a slip of logic and a joke. A man looks into a mirror and sees the back of his head, or perhaps the sky is raining blank-expressioned businessmen. The Belgian art world didn't get his reality-questioning works. In 1927, critics so slayed his first Belgian show of surrealistic paintings that he moved to France, where his works still weren't fully appreciated for another two decades. By the time he died in 1967, however, the innovator was acclaimed the foundation stone of pop art.

PETER PAUL RUBENS (1577–1640)

Born in Antwerp, Peter Paul Rubens, the seventeenth century's most famous artist, certainly got around—studying in Venice, Genoa, and Rome, then heading to Spain and London—and made a huge name for himself wherever he set up his easel. Best recalled for his 2,000 oil paintings—some of corpulent women, some with religious themes, and some now fetching upward of $60 million—the court painter was also a skilled diplomat: in 1630, he negotiated peace between England and Spain, who'd been going at it for five decades. After marrying a sixteen-year-old when he was fifty-three, Rubens created many of his finest works and sired five more children while living in luxury. His rich style of living came with a price—gout took him out.

6. IRELAND
(Éire)
Getting Her Due

FAST FACTS

Country:	Republic of Ireland; Éire
Capital:	Dublin
Government:	Parliamentary democracy
Independence:	1921 "Irish Free State," limited independence from United Kingdom; 1948 republic formed, called Éire
Population:	4,063,000 (2006 estimate)
Head of State:	President Mary McAleese (1997)
Head of Government:	Prime Minister Bertie Ahern (1997)
Elections:	President elected by popular vote, seven-year term; prime minister nominated by house of representatives, appointed by president
Name of Parliament:	Oireachtas
Ethnicity:	Celtic, English

Religion:	89% Roman Catholic; 3% Church of Ireland; 2% other Christian; 3% other; 3% none (2002)
Language:	English (official), Irish (Gaelic) (official)
Literacy:	99% (2003)
Famous Exports:	Ryanair, Guiness, the IRA
Economic Big Boy:	CRH (construction); 2004 total sales: $13.55 billion[1]
Per Capita GDP:	$34,100 (2005 estimate)
Unemployment:	4.3% (January 2006 Eurostat figure)
EU Status:	Entered EEC in 1973
Currency:	Euro

Quick Tour

Make way for the new Éire. After centuries of wallowing in depressing financial and historical muck, Ireland has picked herself up, shined herself off, and she is now displaying herself as the sparkling gem that she is. Ireland's economy is racing, her world status is rising, and for the first time in 170 years, more people are running to the island of soft folded hills than are running away.

> A previously unfathomable quarter of a million immigrants moved to Ireland between 1995 and 2000, many of them Irish who'd long before moved away. And the numbers keep rising.

Everything looks greener than ever in Éire: new businesses are shooting up, new housing is going in, and the country is overflowing with good spirit and a mood of prosperity. With their newfound wealth, the Irish are downright giddy. A chat in the pub will reveal that plenty of those not long out of college have bought their own car and house—in cash—and are now perhaps buying a new home for their parents. There are so many jobs to be had that, until recently, recruiters were signing up employees straight off the plane. And the GDP keeps booming: average income was $30,000 in 2003, and two years later it was $5,000 more. The Irish now make more money than anybody else in the EU except Luxembourgers, and Ireland has the lowest unemployment rate in all of Europe.

> The Irish are cutting impressive figures in the global arena. Former president Mary Robinson headed the UN Commission on Human Rights and is one of the world's most respected politicians. Long noted for amazing writers—

James Joyce, Oscar Wilde, Samuel Beckett, and Lady Gregory among them—Ireland is now reaching millions more with the music of U2, Sinéad O'Connor, the Cranberries, and Bob Geldof, who weave politics, folklore, society, and history into song.

The good news is that the "Emerald Tiger" has finally slipped out from Britain's long, oppressive shadow and is jigging with business partners all over the world. And the best news is that the heated situation in Northern Ireland has cooled off—well, sort of, pretty much, at least for the moment, maybe. And the latest news is that the *Economist* says that Ireland is the best place in the whole world to live (although the London-based magazine hasn't moved there yet).[2]

Never has Éire been trendier, as evidenced by earnings from tourism. In 2004, tourism kicked about $6 billion into the Irish coffers, making it one of the country's biggest moneymakers. In 1992, income from tourism amounted to about $2 billion. Now over 7 million visitors touch down on the Enchanted Isle every year.

Photo by Franz Bauer

Fetching Ireland: Beauty starts at the coast and rolls in

THE SURREAL DIMENSION

The wind howling through the glen sounds like muffled voices, mushrooms sprout from the rain-sodden ground almost magically, fog tangles eerily among gnarly witchy-fingered branches, and the quaint stone cottages puffing smoke during the day seem scarily isolated at night. There's something about Ireland that seems supernaturally charged. Whether it's the remnant of folktales implanted in young minds or a way of explaining the unknown, many Irish, particularly those in rural areas, believe in magic—leprechauns, wood sprites, and screaming banshees; across the countryside, lone undisturbed mounds rise up midfield and are thought to be fairy rings; salt is thrown into borrowed milk; dried herbs hang over doors to keep phantoms from entering. You don't have to go far to find seemingly rational people who swear they have encountered the wee folk. (See www.irelandseye.com/leprechaun for a webcam look at a fairy circle.)

Ireland is the EU's poster child for success. No other EU country has ever used funding from Brussels to stimulate her economy to greater effect. Wisely spent EU money, good marketing, and a surge of foreign investment—in the 1990s, IBM, Intel, and other computer firms suddenly wanted a piece of the Dublin action—helped the Irish economy explode. Financially, Ireland is considered the most global economy—she even weathered the 2001 "dot.com crash."

The bad news is that the EU funding that helped make Ireland sparkle is getting cut, but the good news is that it doesn't really matter. The other bad news is that it's hard to imagine that Ireland will ever be fully content until her North and South are again united as one. And that just may never happen, which may be good news or bad news, depending on which side you're on, and pretty much everybody takes a side around here. Or at least they used to. Lately the calls for a united Ireland—a cause that hundreds of thousands died for historically—are dying down. The Irish, now content with their country, are more likely to shrug off the North as a problem that, if absorbed, would cast a shadow on their very bright light. Even in Northern Ireland, Sinn Féin's Gerry Adams—once an ardent supporter of secession from the UK—is saying union with Ireland is no longer a pressing goal. And as for the Brits, over half of them are saying it's time to cut Northern Ireland free. Northern Ireland, once the object of desire of Brits and Irish, now appears to be the headache nobody wants.

IRELAND VS. REPUBLIC OF IRELAND VS. NORTHERN IRELAND

Ireland is a gorgeous chlorophyll-happy island lounging between the Atlantic Ocean and the Irish Sea. The island is divided into two countries: the bulk of it, twenty-six counties, is the Republic of Ireland (Éire), which became independent from Britain in 1921. Six counties to the northeast—Northern Ireland—belong to an entirely different country, namely the United Kingdom, aka Britain. Most residents of the Republic of Ireland are Catholic, but the dominant group in Northern Ireland for centuries was Protestant. Catholics live in Northern Ireland, as well; their call for equal rights in the 1960s led to civil unrest there, although relations have been testy for centuries. The problem wasn't as much religion as it was allegiance—Protestants usually wanted to keep ties with Britain, and Catholics usually wanted to politically bond with the Republic of Ireland. However, the Northern Ireland situation has improved since the 1998 Good Friday Agreement, which gives more power to Catholics and Protestants and more autonomy to Northern Ireland as a whole. Now Northern Ireland has the option to leave Britain and become part of Ireland—if the majority votes to do so.

Beyond economics, all of Irish society is transforming. The school system is now secular, being run since the 1970s by the government, not the Church; and the agriculture that once employed most Irish workers has been shoved aside by industry—Ireland is now the second largest producer of computer software, behind the United States. In the land where not long ago, you could not buy condoms—the train to Northern Ireland was nicknamed the "pill train" because you could get birth control there—contraception is now widely available, having been legalized in 1993.

> The issue of contraception was so touchy that when Mary Robinson, then in Irish parliament, first presented the idea in the 1970s, not one parliamentarian supported her move to legalize it.[3]

Divorce is now legal in some circumstances; women—who until two decades ago were forbidden to sit on juries—are now powerful forces in organized voting groups. The Catholic Church, while still respected, is now taking a backseat.

> *Sign of the times: The late-1990s Channel 4 Irish comedy* Father Ted, *about a household of inept priests who are always competing with other clergymen, was a social marker. It wasn't long ago that knocking the sacred cow of religion was unthinkable.*

Granted, there's a bit of a moral vacuum at the moment, with Ireland finding herself more moneyed and with few social constraints outside the new no-smoking laws. Binge drinking is up; so are heroin use and drug use in general. Marriage is postponed, the birth rate is dropping, and divorce is on the rise. Well, good-bye banshees and little people; Ireland has finally entered the modern world.

History Review

Ireland's history isn't so obvious these days. It's cloaked in the misty hills that fall to the coast like crumpled green velvet, hidden in the gray stone cottages and old country inns with creaking clocks and blazing fires, buried in the graveyards with looped Celtic crosses blackened by time, and it's hard to make out in the caves where walls are scrawled with mysterious ancient languages that nobody can read. Passing buildings splashed with bright murals that look cheery until you notice their angry slogans, you can still sense it—and if you're looking at the caged and barbed-wire reinforced police stations in Northern Ireland, built to withstand rocket-launched grenades, you feel it quite strongly. But wherever you are, the political-religious tension that has so long defined Ireland—never mind all the agreements and the cease-fires and even the healing effects of increased wealth—is still there staring at you, even in the quaintest of glowing gaslit pubs.

VOCABULARY BUILDER

Gaelic, the original Celtic tongue, is also the language of Irish nationalism, and its words and phrases still pepper Irish speech today. Suppressed by the English and a symbol of poverty and disobedience, Gaelic went hand-in-hand with louder calls for independence.

Éire:	Ireland
Taoiseach:	Prime Minister
Craic:	laughs with friends
Seanachai:	storyteller whose fireside tales brighten rainy nights
Giodam:	sprightly stroll
Mìshaolta:	otherworldly
Pòtaire:	drunkard

If only the Romans had showed up in Ireland, her entire history might have been different. The Roman conquerors made it to England, where they built walls and roads, and linked trade to the Continent; but the third-century adventurers never made it across the Irish Sea, leaving Ireland's environment wild, undeveloped, and unconnected. The Vikings tramped through, however, starting in the eighth century AD, being keen fans of Ireland's churches. They weren't fond of the Catholic religion, but Vikings loved the gold that dripped from church walls, which they looted along with other church treasures.

> The Vikings did, however, put Ireland on the commercial map. Dublin was originally a Viking trade post.

The English were also drawn to Ireland in part because of the Church. Protestant from the sixteenth century on, the English and Scots dismissed the Catholic Irish as superstitious savages, and apparently not having heard the commandment "Thou shall not steal—especially from a church," Henry VIII sent his men to plunder the holy houses as well. Henry's new Anglican religion eventually set up house on the western isle, where it was called the Church of Ireland—which became a huge issue, because the Irish were required to tithe to the Protestant Church even though they were Catholic.

> Book of Kells: Considering how many times the Catholic Church in Ireland was ravaged, it's almost a miracle that this ornate copy of the Gospels from the eighth century still exists. With shimmering gold woven into its pages, the flowery Latin script flows between fantastical images of serpents and beasts. The Book of Kells is housed in Dublin's Trinity College.

In the early seventeenth century, the English sent thousands of Protestants to colonize the northern part of the island—and their arrival and treatment of the Irish as wild cannibals didn't play well, leading to a fiery Irish uprising in 1641, which the English easily stamped out. When the English civil war kicked off at about the same time, the Catholic Irish, continuing on a losing streak, cast their lot for the king. The war's victor, parliamentarian Oliver Cromwell (who celebrated victory by executing the king), exacted cruel revenge on the undeveloped Catholic backwater which he loathed. To solve the "Irish Problem," Cromwell yanked away almost all Irish rights and passed laws stripping Ireland of her culture, from language and music to jigs and traditional clothes. Catholic Irish couldn't buy houses or land, attend schools, or enter professions such as law.

Britain's treatment of Ireland was lampooned in the eighteenth-century novel Gulliver's Travels *by Jonathan Swift, who satirically writes of two islands, one happy and perfect, and the second residing under the first and receiving all the upper one's slop. His best-known stab at the Englishman's skewed view of the Irish, however, was his essay "A Modest Proposal," in which he sarcastically suggests that the Irish eat their young, thereby staving off hunger and keeping the population under control.*

The Irish were banned from passing on Catholicism to their offspring, and their children were often plucked from their homes and shipped as slaves to sugar plantations in the West Indies. Cromwell's army crushed any dissent, offering forgiveness to those who surrendered but typically executed them nevertheless.

Secret words: Education for Irish Catholics was banned, but clandestine classes, called hedge schools, took place hidden away in the woods.

There was little the Irish could do. The Protestant North politically signed Ireland over to England in 1801, by which time the powerless Catholic Irish were mostly peasant farmers who rented from English landlords running agricultural estates from offices in London. The situation turned more drastic in 1845, when the potato blight struck the peasants' sole crop. The English didn't initially fathom the severity of the disease that turned potatoes to black mush overnight; they shrugged off the reports of mass starvation as just another exaggerated Irish fantasy. One lord suggested quite seriously that the starving should drink water flavored with curry powder as a substitute for real food. Many English who owned Irish estates evicted tenants who, given crop failure, couldn't pay. The blight ruined crops for several years, but 1845 is the year most painfully recalled, for the million Irish who starved to death and for the million who boarded leaky ships, or anything else that might float, and headed across the ocean to the United States, an exodus that led the way for millions more over the next century.

Much funding for the IRA came from the United States, home to many Irish whose families bolted during the Potato Famine.

The callous treatment by the British, who let the Irish Catholics starve (some call it genocide), was worsened by the fact that plenty of food was available in Ireland; Irish Catholics simply had no money to buy it. The British finally shipped in dried corn, but the Irish had no mills to grind it. The Protestants in the North not only survived, some thrived, planting even more bitterness in the hearts of Catholic Irish.

> *In the 1860s, emigration and death by starvation halved the Catholic Irish population.*

The Potato Famine was the turning point. Those who had survived the famine had little love left for the British, whose grasping hands now appeared as poisonous as the ruinous blight. The Irish language, which had been nearly eliminated, was shaken from slumber, and the Gaelic revival was coupled with a nationalist movement demanding independence, known as Home Rule. Starting in the late nineteenth century, the land known for her forty shades of green was often splattered in red from the bloody battles fought over it, and if the Irish had once been underdogs, their rebels were now often aggressors.

Secret societies pushed for Irish independence. Fenians (aka the Irish Republic Brotherhood) and the Invincibles were but two of the underground groups born in the mid-nineteenth century. Fenians kicked up revolts, attacked landlords, and planted the occasional bomb, and the Invincibles murdered British politician Lord Cavendish in 1882—all moves that stirred up anti-Irish sentiment among the English and antirebel sentiment in the Irish, many of whom found the rebels' actions extreme.

The biggest battles for freedom brewed up in Dublin. During the 1916 Easter Uprising, the Irish seized the Dublin Post Office and declared Ireland independent. After the British army arrived, there was a major showdown and 1,500 died. Initially most Dubliners, who loathed violent methods, shunned the rebels, booing and hissing when the British paraded them to prison. But their hushed execution without trial brought many Irish around to their cause, and the rebels were soon seen as heroes.

> *The Fenians, and members of other secret independence societies, pulled together as a military force: the Irish Republican Army (IRA), or Óglaigh na hÉireann, which would fight battles in the name of the Republic of Ireland from 1916 to 1921. Many of those fighters put down their weapons after a treaty with the British was signed, but the name IRA continued to be used by fighters who opposed the treaty. After 1969, "IRA" was used by the paramilitary group operating mostly out of Northern Ireland that aimed to free Northern Ireland of British rule.*

In 1918, all of Ireland's elected politicians were from Sinn Féin, the pro-independence political party founded in 1905. Sinn Féin's first act was to cut ties to the English parliament, set up a legislature in Dublin, give it a Gaelic name—Dáil Éireann—and proclaim Ireland independent. That wasn't well received in London, and a war ensued for the next three years.

AN EYE FOR AN EYE, A LIFE FOR A LIFE

The year 1920 was nastier than most. The British unleashed paramilitaries—called the Black and Tans—whose job was to make life in Ireland miserable. They succeeded in their goal. In the course of a few weeks:

- the IRA killed fourteen undercover detectives
- the Black and Tans opened fire at a soccer match, killing twelve
- Irish rebels killed eighteen Black and Tans
- Black and Tans torched downtown Cork

By 1921, England was ready to deal. The twenty-six counties in the south, about 85 percent of the island, were given Home Rule—essentially becoming a self-governing independent country, though still part of the British Empire. Six counties in Northern Ireland—where the Protestant majority lived—would remain part of Britain.

> *Poor Michael Collins: A hero of the Easter Uprising, but a young and inexperienced diplomat, he was sent to broker the 1921 deal with the British. He is said to have scratched his name on the Anglo-Irish Treaty with a sigh, saying, "I have signed my death warrant." He was right; within nine months, Collins was dead.*

Ireland was (sort of) free, but Ireland divided wasn't the answer desired by the Irish masses. Nevertheless, one faction—Fine Gael—accepted the 1921 treaty. Another faction—Fianna Fáil—didn't. Emotions ran so fierce that the treaty led to a brutal year-long civil war. The protreaty faction won, but the disappointment over a split Ireland never subsided. Meanwhile, a virulent anger was festering in Northern Ireland. Some Catholics moved south to independent Ireland, but those who remained in the north had few rights.

> *Even into the 1970s, good Protestants were taught that Catholics (who went to different schools, lived in other parts of town, and even had their own taxi services) were semicivilized beasts who didn't even know how to use knives and forks.*

More than 3,600 people died during the three decades euphemistically termed "The Troubles." The conflict started in Northern Ireland in 1969, when Catholics led a passive protest in Belfast demanding equal rights, and Ulster (Protestant) militiamen attacked them with wood beams, iron rods, bottles, and chains. The Troubles had begun—and they carried on for the next thirty years, centered mostly in Belfast and Derry (aka Londonderry).

> *Loyalists called the Northern city Londonderry, underscoring their link to Britain; Republicans called it Derry, emphasizing their disrespect for London.*

MEET THE FIGHTERS

Whether they want Ireland united or to keep the North linked to Britain, most Irish and Northern Irish don't condone violence on behalf of the cause. But chances are some of their ancestors died in the never-ending battle.

Nationalists, Republicans: Typically Catholic, want Ireland and the North politically united.

Loyalists, Unionists: Typically Protestant, want Northern Ireland to stay linked to London.

Irish Republican Army: Nationalist paramilitaries who sprung up in 1969, bombing cars and buildings and typically harming civilians, want to unite Northern Ireland with the Republic. Called a cease-fire and disarmed in 2005; good thing—everybody's sick of 'em.

Real IRA: A more-radical IRA cell that branched into its own group, keeps on bombing, as do other offshoots.

Sinn Féin: The political arm of the IRA, whose leader, Gerry Adams, says he has no control over the IRA, although few really believe him. He says the IRA is giving up the fight to unite Northern Ireland with the republic, and we really want to believe him. *Sinn féin* means "we ourselves" in Irish Gaelic.

Ulster Defense Association, Red Hand Commando, and others: Loyalist Northern Ireland paramilitaries, as violent as the IRA, who go through waves of calm and violence. Like to leave territorial markings in the form of the "Ulster flag"— a bloodred imprint.

Northern Irish Police: Catholics accused these Protestant police of discrimination. Police stations were the targets of intense IRA bombings and now look like fortresses.

Most of the deaths (many were civilians) were the responsibility of two parties: the Irish Republican Army and the equally violent protestant Ulster Defense Association and Ulster Volunteer Force.

A FEW TROUBLING MOMENTS

Bloody Sunday, 1972:	A symbolic anti-British protest in Derry (aka Londonderry) turned nasty; thirteen protesters killed, allegedly by British troops.
Bloody Friday, 1972:	IRA sets off car bombs all over Belfast; twenty-two bombs explode within seventy-five terrifying minutes.
Orange marches, annually:	Every spring, hundreds of older Protestants march to the beat of drums through Northern Ireland's Catholic neighborhoods in an aggressive display of sectarian hatred.
Ulster bombings, 1974:	Protestant Loyalists explode bombs in the Republic of Ireland; thirty-three die.
IRA killing, 1979:	IRA hits Lord Mountbatten, the queen's uncle.
Food strike, 1981:	Ten IRA prisoners starve themselves to death, including first Sinn Fein minister, Bobby Sands.
Brighton bombing, 1984:	IRA bomb blasts Brighton's Grand Hotel, where Margaret Thatcher is staying; four die, including political VIPs.
Downing Street mortar attack, 1991:	IRA launches mortars at 10 Downing Street, the residence of the PM.

By the 1990s, pretty much everybody was Troubled-out. There had been far too many funerals, and attacks on those attending the funerals; too many had suffered, and nothing had been accomplished. Sinn Féin leader Gerry Adams began talking with Irish nationalist John Hume, the IRA declared a cease-fire, the Ulster Boys followed, and the United States flew George Mitchell in for peace talks. Despite plenty of stumbling along the way, and plenty of stumbling since, the 1998 Good Friday Agreement was hammered out. Fliers were slipped under every door across the Irish isle, explaining the treaty and urging voters to turn out. They did so in huge numbers, and an overwhelming majority voted yes to the Good Friday Agreement. The era of bombs left in briefcases at bus stops (a signature of the IRA) and protesters beaten with iron rods (a signature of Ulster thugs) had theoretically ended. However, radicals from both sides keep the conflict alive, as does the good reverend Ian Paisley, whose motto, when it comes to negotiating with Catholics, is "No Surrender!"

> *The British government has been slowly giving Northern Ireland more inde-*
> *pendence, but many think the chains that bind Ulster to Britain will never be*
> *fully unlocked. One factor: Northern Ireland industries pay huge taxes that*
> *London would miss. On the other hand, the costs of maintaining police and*
> *military there continually drain the British coffers.*

Hot Spots

Dublin: A century ago, the Republic of Ireland's capital was a battlefield that many fled; now it's simply a blast, and exploding with immigrants. Computer geeks abound here, where the country's wealth is concentrated.

The countryside: Job possibilities and income levels still lag in rural areas, but gee they're pretty . . .

The Irish Sea: It's the world's most radioactive, thanks to Britain; nuclear compound Sellafield releases its waste into the waters between Britain and Ireland.

Northern Ireland (aka Ulster): Blustery coasts, crumbling castles, and enchanting inns are some of the reasons tourists have been taking a peek in these parts since the Good Friday Agreement was signed. They might not be seeing the high walls that still divide Protestant and Catholic neighborhoods.

Hotshots

Mary McAleese: President of Republic of Ireland, 1997–present. It's a veritable trend; twice in a row, women have sat in Ireland's presidential seat. Barrister McAleese, of Fianna Fáil, is sharp and looks good on TV. No wonder—she's a former broadcaster.

Mary Robinson: President of Republic of Ireland, 1990–1996. (See box on page 130.)

Courtesy of Realizing Rights/The Ethical Globalization Institute

Former president Mary
Robinson brought Ireland
into the present

HERE'S TO YOU, MRS. (MARY) ROBINSON

No one in modern Irish history did more to catapult Éire into the present than former president Mary Robinson. Holding law degrees from Trinity College Dublin and Harvard before she was twenty-five, she won a Labor seat in the Irish parliament the next year, where she stood out as a reformist. Winning the presidency in 1990, she pushed women's rights, legalized contraception and divorce, and was so effective in her seven-year term as president that she had the approval of 97 percent of the Irish. She hit all kinds of buttons, meeting first with Gerry Adams and then the British queen. While giving a firsthand report on Rwanda, the typically reserved lawyer broke into tears, moving audience members to the same. After the presidency, she headed the United Nations High Commission for Human Rights (1997–2002) but the Bush administration, furious about her criticisms of the Afghanistan war, ensured that her first term was her last. Now she's president of the Ethical Globalization Initiative, a humans rights organization that she founded.

The U.S. government may have saved Robinson's life by shoving her out of the High Commission for Human Rights. She was replaced by Brazilian Sergio Vieira de Mello, who was killed several months later when the UN headquarters in Iraq was bombed.

Bertie Ahern: Prime Minister of Republic of Ireland, 1997–present. "The Teflon Taoiseach" has reigned during Ireland's most glorious hour; he's the only prime minister in Irish history to be elected to two consecutive terms.

OSCAR FINGAL O'FLAHERTIE WILLS WILDE (1854–1900)

With drooping almond eyes and a long face under a flip of dark hair, Oscar Wilde looked melancholy even before 1895, when everything went to hell. Born in Dublin to a wealthy surgeon, Oscar stood out at Trinity College for his crackling wit, dandyish appearance, and fondness for decorating with peacock feathers—and, of course, for his gifts with the pen, which garnered him a slew of awards. Wilde married wealthy Constance Lloyd, sired two sons, and ventured into books: first poetry, then fairy tales, and finally the stinging high-society novels and plays that made him famous. *A Picture of Dorian Gray* came out in 1891, to popular acclaim, and in 1895, *The Importance of Being Earnest* was performed to rave reviews in London, but Wilde's high lifestyle soon spiraled downward. Manuscripts he was working on were stolen and, worse, his double life emerged. (Apparently, he wasn't joking when he wrote in *Dorian Gray* that "the one charm of marriage is that it makes a life of deception necessary for both parties.") When the Marquis of Queensberry—father of Wilde's young lover, Lord Alfred "Bosie" Douglas—publicly accused Wilde of homosexuality, the playwright sued for libel and lost. After Wilde lied in court about his dealings with Bosie, the tables turned and he became the target of London prosecutors. Found guilty of "gross indecency," he was sentenced to two years hard labor in Reading Prison. Upon release, Wilde slithered off nearly penniless to live in Paris as Sebastian Melmoth. Shortly after writing *The Ballad of Reading Gaol*, he died of cerebral meningitis—but thanks to a wealthy fan, he ultimately ended up with a fancy tomb in Père Lachaise.

Bono: Born in 1960 in Dublin as Paul Hewson, U2's humanitarian lead singer brings politics to music and makes huge donations to fight HIV and poverty; he also brought U.S. Secretary of Defense Paul O'Neill on a tour of Africa as part of his campaign to convince rich nations to drop outstanding Third World debt. Wanted to become president of World Bank, but Paul Wolfowitz beat him out.

Seamus Heaney: Winner of the 1995 Nobel Prize for Literature. Poet, essayist, and professor, Heaney captures the divide between agricultural and industrial Ireland, as well as that between the Six Counties and the Republic.

Maeve Binchy: Former London correspondent for the *Irish Times*, Binchy turned to fiction, writing over a dozen novels about everyday Irish life that far outsell fellow Irish bards Beckett, Joyce, Yeats, and Wilde.

James Joyce, aka Séamas Seoighe: Between his binge drinking, eye problems, financial woes, blowouts with publishers, familial fights, schizophrenic daughter, and parapatetic wanderings across Europe, it's a wonder the ex-pat from Dublin got anything done, but he did. Among his more easily digested works: *A Portrait of the Artist as a Young Man*, *Dubliners*, and (less so) *Finnegans Wake*. His magnum opus, however, was the groundbreaking novel *Ulysses*. The book that covers one day in eighteen chapters took seven years to write.

7. SPAIN

(España)

Living It Up

FAST FACTS

Country:	Kingdom of Spain; Reino de España
Capital:	Madrid
Government:	Parliamentary monarchy
Independence:	Unified 1492; Franco dictatorship ended 1975
Population:	40,398,000
Head of State:	King Juan Carlos I (1975)
Head of Government:	Prime Minister José Luis Rodríguez Zapatero (2004)
Elections:	Monarchy is hereditary; leader of majority party approved by monarch, elected by parliament
Name of Parliament:	Cortes
Ethnicity:	Historically Mediterranean, but millions of Latinos from the Americas, Moroccans, Algerians, Africans, Eastern Europeans, and retired Brits have recently immigrated, some legally

Religion:	94% Roman Catholic; 6% other
Language:	Almost all speak Castilian Spanish. Regional languages: 17% Catalan; 7% Galician; 2% Basque
Literacy:	98% (2003 estimate)
Famous Exports:	Opus Dei, singer Manu Chao, tapas
Economic Big Boy:	Repsol (gas and oil); 2004 total sales: $2.54 billion[1]
Per Capita GDP:	$25,200 (2005 estimate)
Unemployment:	8% (January 2006 Eurostat figure)
EU Status:	Founding member (EEC member since 1986)
Currency:	Euro

Quick Tour

For a place that took a siesta through most of the twentieth century, España—the European Union's second-largest country by area, and historically one of its poorest—is waking up in grand style. After the death of General Francisco Franco, who lorded over Spain from 1939 to 1975, the country swiftly transformed from a lumbering, backward dictatorship into a plugged-in liberal democracy. Now one of Europe's most dynamic countries and quickly rising in international stature, Spain is also incredibly popular, pushing past the United States to become the second-most-visited destination in the world.

> Tourism rakes in some $40 billion for the Spanish economy[2] and employs about 11 percent of the population.[3]

CONTEMPORARY BIG NAMES FROM SPAIN

Pedro Almodóvar:	Campy filmmaker Pedro Almodóvar brought Penélope Cruz and Antonio Banderas to fame and won two Oscars. In 2002, he walked off with Best Original Screenplay for *Talk to Her*; in 2000, he won Best Foreign Film for *All About My Mother*.
Joaquín Cortés:	Flamenco dancer Cortés stomps across the world's best-known stages in outfits designed by Armani and had a steamy love affair with Naomi Campbell.
Javier Solana:	Former secretary general of NATO; is arguably the European Union's most powerful man as de facto foreign minister of the EU.

Judge Baltasar Garzón:	He demanded the 1998 extradition of General Pinochet from Britain, and summons bigwigs from Kissinger to Berlusconi to his court. They rarely appear.
Ferran Adrià:	The chef at El Bulli (in Roses) is the toast of the world culinary scene for inventions such as the Rice Krispy paella.
Telefonica:	Waiting months to be hooked up, being forced to pay for pricey services you don't have, waking up to find that your telephone number has been inexplicably changed—such are the joys of inept telecom Telefonica (which netted over $1.4 billion in 2005). With 100 million customers worldwide, it's expanding into the U.S. Yikes!

Enchanting Ávila: Saint Teresa floated here

As the 50 million visitors who swoop in every year can testify, there's too much to love about Spain, Europe's most festive land. Modernist architecture that swirls in Barcelona, palm trees that sway in medieval squares, the classical guitar echoing through alleys, tiled tapas bars where hams hang overhead, fab wine that's affordable, sunny beaches, and fun-loving locals are but a few enticements. Spain's biggest draw is variety: from the foggy Ireland-green hills of Galicia (home to redheaded bagpipers) and the parched white villages tumbling down the Andalusian hills (dotted with palaces of Muslim Moors), to the rugged Mediterranean coast and folded valleys of dairy farms in the north, Spain is a patchwork of different histories, personalities, and terrains, and each corner possesses its own distinct style, spirit, and flavored spirits. That the different territories are now allowed to flaunt their distinctiveness and speak their own languages is one alluring feature of New Spain.

PARTY TIME!

Nearly stamped out by dictator Franco, who viewed regionalism as a threat, the festivals (fiestas) of Spain are now symbols of a cultural renaissance. Every region, town, and neighborhood (barrio) has its own, some immortalizing historic acts, others tributes to saints, harvest rituals, or simply reasons to eat chestnuts, paella, or grilled leeks dripping in spicy sauce. Geese, pigs, or bulls run through the towns; balls of fire roll down the hills; locals put on plays lampooning the town's least beloved. Men don branches on their heads and run into lakes, cobblestones are carpeted with bright flower petals and aromatic herbs, statues move, or a Madonna is "stolen." Some fiestas are mock battles, where goatskin bags transform into wine-shooting artillery or the air is filled with flying tomatoes. A young maiden might be kidnapped so the town can search her out, men might be ceremoniously caked in flour, women might dance around costumed as mules, boys might crawl around looking up dresses, or the streets might be turned over to the white-haired for the famed "Dance of the Chickens." But the most dramatic festival, and certainly the smokiest, is the annual spectacle in Valencia, Las Fallas, where hundreds of giant satirical sculptures of political figures (each costing tens of thousands of dollars and taking a year to create) are set ablaze in every barrio. The fires dance eerily through the night, and by morning the disliked figures, and the sentiments they represent, are reduced to ashes.

The crazy quilt of varying cultures is also Spain's greatest weakness. Some call España an artificial country of seventeen disparate regions, first stitched together by power-hungry and religion-driven monarchs Isabella and Fernando, and later pounded into one faux nation by Franco's strong arm. Madrid is headquarters of national government, but each of Spain's regions has its own parliament and a great deal of autonomy. Yet some regions—Catalonia (which holds Barcelona) and the Basque country among them—still want more independence, and sometimes threaten to secede.

> The biggest thorn in Spain's side for decades has been ETA—Euskadi Ta Askatasuna (Homeland and Freedom)—a separatist group that wants the Basque region in northern Spain to secede, bond with adjacent regions in France, and start its own country. Formed in 1959, the group has killed hundreds, but may be starting to mellow with age.

Ironically, what most pulled Spain together as a nation recently was tragedy—the bombings of March 11, 2004, which killed 191, injured over 1,400,

and caused a political upheaval in their wake. The government of the conservative Popular Party (Partido Popular), poised to win an upcoming parliamentary
election, instead went flying as the people showed they were fed up with then-
prime minister José María Aznar's dicey leadership abilities and his party's numerous manipulations and lies. The Aznar administration's deceitful behavior
leading up to the election wasn't new: it had also tried to cover up its bungled
handling of the 2002 *Prestige* oil spill.

*Over 90 percent of Spaniards opposed the 2003 war in Iraq—millions
marched in antiwar rallies that were among the world's biggest—and were
against sending Spanish troops there. Prime Minister Aznar ignored them
and shipped off the military for Iraq's postwar reconstruction. Aznar never
even broached the topic in the Spanish parliament before the deployment;
he finally mentioned it in the Cortes some eight months after troops had
flown out. When Spanish cameraman José Couso died in Baghdad, after a
U.S. tank he was filming fired on his hotel balcony, the Spanish media boycotted Aznar. At that day's press conference, they piled their cameras,
recorders, and notebooks in the middle of the room, crossed their arms,
and glared as the prime minister slinked in, the trademark cocky expression
noticeably missing from his face.*

POLITICAL BOMBS: MARCH 11, 2004

Terrorism isn't new to Spain—the bombs and bullets of Basque separatist
group ETA have killed over 800 (mostly police, government officials, and journalists) since 1961. However, the country had never before experienced anything like what happened that Thursday in March. During Madrid's morning
rush hour, ten bombs on three trains exploded simultaneously, ripping open
carriages like sardine cans and leaving the tracks strewn with dead bodies and
bloody limbs. Within hours, a group affiliated with al-Qaeda—Abu Hafs al-
Masri—claimed responsibility for the attack that killed hundreds. But even while
smoke still billowed out from the trains and emergency workers hauled off the
injured and covered the dead, the Aznar administration had already made up
its mind: it was the work of ETA. The sophisticated operation—bombs were det-
onated by calls to explosive-rigged cell phones—didn't fit the Basque group's
MO—and ETA, which admits to its misdeeds, loudly denied any involvement. Investigators quickly discovered evidence pointing to Islamic radicals—a duffel
bag with a live bomb, a detonator, and an Arabic-configured cell phone, and a
nearby van loaded with detonators, cell phones, and extremist Islamic tapes—
but Aznar's Popular Party government wouldn't acknowledge the discoveries.[4]

Foreign minister Ana Palacio instructed all Spanish embassies to maintain that ETA was behind it,[5] the Interior Minister announced it was "absolutely clear" that the attack was all ETA's doing,[6] and Prime Minister José María Aznar demanded that the UN Security Council immediately condemn ETA for the Madrid attack (which the UN body did that day). Aznar personally called the heads of international media to insist this was a barbarous act of the Basques; his administration tried to suppress information contradicting that view. The reason Aznar kept up the farce: the parliamentary election was in three days. Aznar's government had retained power largely because of its hard line stance against ETA, with whom it refused to negotiate. An ETA attack would ensure victory in the upcoming election. However, if it was an attack by Islamic radicals, perhaps in response to Aznar sending Spanish troops to Iraq, then it would be a glaring liability. Despite the government's nonstop chanting of "ETA, ETA, ETA," word slipped out that it probably was not ETA at all. For their deception, as much as for their unpopular decision to get Spain involved in Iraq, the Popular Party lost the 2004 parliamentary election. Three days after the attacks, a record 77 percent turned out to vote—the numbers boosted by young voters who rarely show up—with most casting their ballots for the only national PP alternative, the Socialists. Some international pundits condemned Spain, saying voters had caved in to terrorism. The truth was that many Spaniards were sick of PP's incessant misinformation, and its response to the March 11 attack was but one pathetic example.

José Luis Rodríguez Zapatero appeared as surprised as anyone else when the Socialists won the election in spring 2004, but his administration quickly made several moves that impressed the public. Prime Minister Zapatero appointed women to half the seats in his cabinet—that's a first—and he made good on promises to end Spain's involvement in Iraq, pulling troops out the next month.

When Defense Minister José Bono informed the U.S. that Spain was bringing her troops back from Iraq, there was some serious static over the wire. Donald Rumsfeld reportedly called the pullout "cowardly," which prompted Bono to yell back that Spain indeed had cojones.[7]

The new government inherited a few problems—namely, an unemployment rate of 11 percent, an ill-defined immigration policy, and the question of what to do about ETA. The young government has made quick progress: unemployment is now at about 8 percent, a new immigration law extended citizenship to millions who had been working there illegally, and, in March 2006, ETA announced, for the first time ever, a permanent cease-fire.

The issue of foreigners arriving from all corners is entirely new to Spain, which until the 1990s had few immigrants from anywhere, except for teachers coming in from the UK. Now the masses are arriving by car, train, and plane—and on flimsy rafts or floating tires from North Africa. Latin Americans claiming Spanish ancestry—particularly Argentinians, Ecuadorians, and Venezuelans—have arrived by the hundreds of thousands. Since 2000, over 3 million foreigners have flocked here—600,000 in 2003 alone.

While many Spaniards are pleased with the Socialist leadership, the religious and the conservatives aren't necessarily among them. The Popular Party's leader, Mariano Rajoy, is organizing anti-Zapatero protests, denouncing him for even speaking with ETA. The religious are upset because Spain became the third European country (after the Netherlands and Belgium) to legalize same-sex marriages. Another issue: powerful Catholic sect Opus Dei, founded in Spain, doesn't have an instant "in" with this government. During Aznar's administration, it influenced numerous issues, including bans on stem cell research, and attempted to mandate teaching religion in schools.

RELIGION IN THE SHADOWS

Started in 1928 by Spaniard Josemaria Escrivá de Balaguer, who encouraged self-flagellation, the right-wing Catholic organization that some call "a church within the church" sounds like the ultimate do-gooder organization. Operating charities and foundations, Opus Dei (Latin for "God's work") aims to better the world by "spreading throughout society a profound awareness of the universal call to holiness." Opus Dei does so by empowering the layperson. But Opus Dei has many unusual practices; some call it a cult. One cause for criticism is its recruitment methods: prospective members, often students, aren't fully informed about what they're getting into, are encouraged to cut ties with their families and friends, and are told that if they don't join (or if they try to leave) they will go to hell.

Although Opus Dei members may number only 85,000, they are the rich and the powerful, politicians, judges, heads of intelligence, and newspaper publishers among them. "Supernumeraries," as married members are called, are encouraged to confess only to Opus Dei priests, attend mass daily, and make very large donations to Opus Dei. A smaller, very devout group are called "numeraries": they live in Opus Dei centers (where doors don't have locks), turn their income over to Opus Dei, list Opus Dei as beneficiary of their wills, allow Opus Dei to monitor all their mail and communications, take vows of celibacy, attend daily mass, and sleep on boards. They also observe practices that some consider "kinky": they wear spiked chains (*cilices*) that cut into their thighs, and they whip their buttocks with knotted ropes thirty-three times a week—and they typically ask to flagellate themselves even more.

Pope John Paul II loved Opus Dei—his press secretary was a member—and in 1982, he made Opus Dei the most powerful Catholic group by raising it to the status of prelate, which means it answers to nobody but the pope. Some say the elevation has to do with Opus Dei's donation of $1 billion to the Vatican Bank the same year, but that rumor, like much about Opus Dei, is hard to prove (or disprove). The pope was questioned about his move to make Opus Dei founder, Escrivá, a saint in record time—Escrivá died in 1975 and was canonized in 2002—but that's just one controversial move that has many non–Opus Dei Catholics wondering what is up with this shadowy group.

A final issue is Spain's involvement in the European Union, which she joined in 1986. The EU funneled billions upon billions of dollars into Spain, much of it going to infrastructure, and all of it helping to give Spain a vibrant economy that for much of the past decade grew at some 5 percent a year. With funding now being siphoned off by new EU members in Eastern Europe, it remains to be seen how well Spain will hold her own. Oh well, *que será, será*—they can deal with that *mañana*.

> Long dominated by France, Germany, and, to a lesser extent, Britain—the so-called Big Three—the European Union is now admitting that with their large landmasses and populations, Spain and Poland are also major EU players.

History Review

Settled by Romans, Celts, and Visigoths, the peninsula of Iberia was a disorganized mass of scattered kingdoms when eighth-century Muslim Moors invaded, conquering most of the land in seven years and creating a settlement that became one of the world's most sophisticated. Setting up headquarters in the parched terrain of the south, they made Córdoba the capital of the kingdom they called al-Andalus, which today is called Andalusia. Working alongside the locals, the Moors established a settlement that rivaled Alexandria and Baghdad in their heydays, lasted seven centuries, and far outshined any other society in Europe.

AL-ANDALUS (711–1492)

Scientific and philosophical scholars flocked first to Córdoba and then to Seville and Granada, as did linguists, architects, artisans, and scribes who translated the works of ancient Greeks and Romans, launching a renaissance comparable to the one born in Florence some six centuries later. Marble palaces and elaborate mosques with horseshoe arches appeared across the land; water from mountain snow and rivers was brought to homes via pipes. Irrigation and advanced agricultural practices coaxed forth new crops from the seeds Moors had brought; soon, the perfume of orange blossoms breezed through courtyards, and outlying hills burst with trees of almonds, dates, lemons, and limes alongside fields of sugarcane and rice. While the rest of Europe was technologically in the dark, the paved streets of Córboda were lined with lights; markets boasted silks, tapestries, swords, porcelain, and spices. The most popular shops were booksellers, whose trade was made possible by the eighth-century introduction of papermaking techniques and by the skill of copyists, who produced some 50,000 books every year. Ideas and research flourished, as thinkers scratched pens across paper in flowery scrawls of crescents and dots; by the tenth century, libraries abounded, some containing over 200,000 handwritten tomes, and the Koran, Bible, and Torah stood alongside books by Ptolemy, ancient histories, scientific treatises, and volumes of poetry. Hospitals performed operations for cataracts; schools taught algebra and spherical trigonometry; students learned Latin, physics, botany, and medicine, and studied maps of the seas and the stars. Observatories tracked celestial bodies and astrolabes guided ships on trade routes to the Far East. Just as impressive was the level of civility that typified much of the Moorish occupation. Women in al-Andalus were doctors, lawyers, librarians, and esteemed copyists of books; Christians, Jews, and Muslims lived side by side in relative peace, each pursuing their religion in their own places of worship. Non-Muslims enjoyed nearly all rights afforded to Muslims, even working in government and schools; they could also drink alcohol, eat pork, and ignore Islamic dictates. However, nonbelievers paid a high tax and males could be drafted unless they converted.

Catholics (including famous Spanish hero El Cid) gradually pushed the Muslims out and the occupiers' territory shrank. Retreating from such academic centers as Toledo, the Moors lost Valencia, then Córdoba, then Seville, the favored city of musicians, until finally all that remained by the 1300s was the southern region of Granada. The long-awaited final moment of the Catholic "reconquest" occurred in 1492, when the armies of King Fernando and Queen Isabella forced out the last Moorish ruler from the spectacular hillside palace of Alhambra; it's said that the sultan, Boabdil, took one final look at the lacy latticework and fine gardens of his home, let out a deep sigh, and departed in tears.[8]

> *Although the armies of Isabella and Fernando ran the last Moors out in 1492, legend has it that some Moors were soon invited back. The Spaniards couldn't figure out how to run their elaborate irrigation systems.*

Having united all of Spain under the strict veil of Catholicism—Muslims and Jews were booted unless they converted—Isabella and Fernando delved into the enterprises that made them best known: conquering the New World and introducing the Spanish Inquisition, both activities that further spread the Catholic faith and filled the treasury.

> *Launched at Isabella's behest in 1478, the brutal Spanish Inquisition lasted until 1808. At the onset, 200,000 Jews fled Spain, but some Catholics were accused of heresy as well. The accused, who had no idea who accused them, lost their property and riches upon being arrested. Subjected to grueling torture, they were burned if they still did not confess. At least 350,000 accused Spanish "heretics" died at the stake.*

EXPANDING THE EMPIRE VIA THE SEAS

Portugal said no, France said no, and so did England and Spain, but Christopher Columbus (aka Colón), an explorer from Genoa, would not drop his idea of a western route to the East Indies—nor would he stop pestering monarchs to fund his trip. Finally, after nearly a decade of his pleading, Isabella—feeling competitive with Portugal, whose sailors kept their sea route to the Indies a secret—gave Colón his three ships and his funding in 1492. Although Colón insisted, from his first voyage to his last, that he had found the East Indies, the discoveries and maps of Amerigo Vespucci in the early 1500s showed that Colón had discovered entirely new lands, starting with the Caribbean island of Hispaniola. Soon the race was on to ravage the unexplored world and steal her riches. Ponce de León claimed Puerto Rico for the crown; Velásquez took Cuba; and Balboa seized Panama. In 1519, Hernán Cortés struck the mother lode when he pushed into Mexico, killing Montezuma and claiming the gold of the Aztec kingdom of Tenochtitlan for Spain; four years later, Pizarro conquered the silver-rich Inca civilization of Peru. The most dramatic (and traumatic) voyage was that of Portuguese explorer Magellan, who sailed under the Spanish flag with five ships in a 1519 voyage that sought to find the Spice Islands by heading west. Rounding the southern tip of Chile, his ships sailed across the Pacific for three months without spotting land, and the sailors ate rodents to stay alive. After finally reaching today's Guam, he continued on to the Philippines, where his pride got the better of him. After converting a local sultan to Christianity, he offered to show the ruler how to fight his enemies the modern, European way. He launched a battle against nearby islanders, but Magellan's men were quickly beaten back and Magellan took a fatal poisonous arrow in the heart. The few remaining sailors pushed on, dropping anchor in Seville in 1522, with only eighteen of the original 240 crew members remaining to tell the tale of the world's first circumnavigation.

The brutal acts against Native Americans, who died from disease, torture, and the slave labor trade, did not go unnoticed. Spanish priest Bartolomé de las Casas made the indigenous peoples' plight widely known in his 1552 book A Short Account of the Destruction of the West Indies. *Still, the brutality continued until many of the original peoples were wiped out; Europeans shipped in African slaves to fill in the worker shortage.*

Spanish ships, heavy with riches, were continually raided by pirates off Africa's northern coast and by other Europeans, particularly the British; hundreds of others sank in storms at sea. Enough of the silver and gold nevertheless made it into Spain's treasury to make Spanish rulers the world's richest for a time. Under King Philip II, Spain kissed off her dominance of the sea, particularly as she kept losing ships in wars with the English and French—and in 1587, Sir Francis Drake sneaked into Cádiz and sank all the vessels in port. The most crushing blow: the loss of her formidable fleet the following year, when Spain's attack on England backfired, and her mighty armada, thanks to Drake's fighters and a nasty storm, was reduced to splinters on the rocks. New ships were built and new lands—including Naples, Sicily, and Portugal—were added to the empire's roster, but the problems of corruption and weak leadership continued.

THE NOVEL IDEA OF MIGUEL DE CERVANTES SAAVEDRA (1547–1616)

For a man who was the world's first bestselling novelist, Miguel Cervantes spent a lot of time in prison. In 1575, he was captured in Algeria, where he spent five years behind bars until ransom was delivered; other times he was rounded up for his dodgy practices as a tax collector. But prison served him well. Some say he wrote *Don Quixote* behind bars, while others say he merely conceived of the idea of a parody of a chivalrous knight there—but most agree that the book he produced was Europe's first novel when it appeared in 1605.

Readers so adored his book that part II soon followed, selling equally well, but that only infuriated Cervantes. The "sequel" was a fake, written by an unknown using both his characters and established plot. The author quickly followed up with his own part II in 1615.

Devastating wars, rebellions in the colonies, and (literally) imbecilic leadership continued to hack away at Spain's power—and by 1648, when the Thirty Years War drew to an end, France had shoved Spain aside to become the dominant European country. Spain simultaneously lost her holdings in the Netherlands. (See "The Netherlands: History Review," page 178.) Another blow: in 1704, Britain captured the Rock of Gibraltar, which lies off the south of Spain, a loss that infuriates Spain to this day. But what really did Spain in as a global power: Napoleon, whose army invaded in 1808. The Spanish military was called back from the New World to fight the French, and the South American colonies saw a chance to escape.

THE SPANISH WAR OF INDEPENDENCE (1808–1813)

Few Spaniards liked King Carlos IV (b. 1748, reigned 1788–1808), including his son. And while Prince Fernando VII (b. 1784, reigned 1813–1833) was unsubtly trying to grab the crown off padre's head—his father had had him arrested in 1807 for attempted murder—Napoleon saw his chance. In 1808, the French emperor kicked the royal family out, ordered his armies in, and placed brother Joseph Bonaparte on the Spanish throne.

That was the easy part. The rest was hell—so hellish that the Bonapartes were shocked, as no other country had reacted the same way. Before Joseph was fully seated on the throne, the people—from the peasants to the upper classes—rebelled, launching what the Spanish call the War of Independence, what the British (who dropped in to help) call the Peninsular War, and what the Bonapartes called an *absurdité*.

Spaniards loathed the wine-swilling Frenchman, whom they called Pepe Botellas—Joe Bottles—and who really annoyed most of them when he diminished the power of the church. Besides, they *did* like Prince Fernando VII—who for about one minute in the confusion had been king—and they wanted Fernando back, but he was imprisoned in France.

Fighting for his return, the feisty people formed their own government—from the local level to the national—and refused to listen to anything Joe Bottles said. It was the biggest popular struggle of the day, finally unifying the assorted Spanish peoples who fought in Fernando's name. Their new government, while fighting off the French, even wrote a liberal constitution that was widely embraced by the Spanish people—or at least by those who could read.

When the French finally departed in 1813, Spain was economically wiped out but poised to be a truly united country for the first time, with all anticipating the return of their beloved new king Fernando. Alas, Fernando came back and ruined the fantasy.

In 1808, Joseph Bonaparte abolished the Spanish Inquisition, which had been going on for 330 torturous years.

New King Fernando was in a foul mood. He'd been humiliated by Napoleon, who'd invited him to France and then tossed him in jail for five years. When Fernando returned to Spain in 1813, he flicked off the adoration of his people who'd fought off the French for him. He appreciated the little constitution they'd prepared even less: he ripped it to shreds. That didn't endear him to the masses, nor were they thrilled about what was happening overseas. One by one, Spain's New World holdings dropped off: Chile declared independence in 1810, followed by Argentina, Venezuela, Colombia, and Uruguay. Spain waged wars to keep the territories roped in, but fifteen years later only Cuba and Puerto Rico remained of Spain's empire in the Americas. Already going downhill, Spain plummeted to new depths over the next century and a half, as regionalism, value differences, and depression ripped the country apart.

For all the wealth it brought the Spanish Empire, colonization and the country's extreme religiousness actually set Spain back. Devout Spaniards ignored the scientific revolution, and Spain was not a land that produced many inventors. Like a child raised in wealth who doesn't learn job skills, Spain did not evolve with the rest of Europe, shrugging off the Industrial Revolution and the changing textile market. By doing so, Spain set herself back centuries.

Spain's national identity was further deflated in 1898, the year of *el desastre*—the disaster. The United States had long been eyeing the Spanish colony of Cuba—and since the days of Thomas Jefferson had made numerous offers to buy it. After a mysterious explosion on the USS *Maine* was dubiously blamed on the Spanish, the U.S. declared war. The modern American navy easily blew the Spanish rust buckets out of the water. Spain was devastated, economically and spiritually, after losing Cuba and Puerto Rico, her last colonies in the New World, as well as the Philippines. The national mood was downbeat, but at least one person benefited from the Spanish-American War of 1898:

Catalan architect Antoni Gaudí. After their foreign investments dried up, Barcelona's elite decided they had best throw their money into the architectural riches of their own city.

ANTONI GAUDÍ (1852–1926)

Barcelona was always an iconoclastic city that thumbed her nose at Madrid, including with unconventional architecture that competed with Madrid's neo-classical splendor. So it was fitting that an eccentric architect imprinted a style that would make Barcelona, a city where anarchists designed utopian neighborhoods and eighteenth-century inventors sank fortunes into constructing submarines, stand out all the more. Spiritual Antoni Gaudí drew his inspiration from nature, eschewing right angles and straight lines. His daring creations of swirls and meandering squiggles look like shells or storm-tossed sands, skulls or slayed dragons, candied ice-cream cones or icing-heavy cakes topped with strange details—such as dizzying ghostlike figures twirling up from terraces. Industrialist Eusebi Güell and the Catholic Church were his two most important employers. Güell kept the architect busy for thirty-five years with projects including Güell Park, a tile-happy, color-jumbled park complex of gingerbread-house buildings topped with domes, originally planned as a living community for Güell's workers. Another huge project came from the church: the Sagrada Família. During his final twelve years, Gaudí worked on nothing but the Swiss-cheese-textured temple of slender domes, becoming obsessive and going broke in the process. His habit of teaching trolley cars to stop for pedestrians did him in one morning in June 1926, when one ran him down. So ragged-looking was the then-impoverished architect that the hospital refused to take him in, mistaking him for a bum, but when he died three days later, most of the city turned out to mourn his loss. Now the biggest draw to the Mediterranean city, Gaudí's Sagrada Família still isn't done—completion is scheduled for 2023—but 2 million visitors in 2002 came to see the work in progress. A man who failed in love and threw himself passionately into architecture and religion, Gaudí is now in line to be Spain's next saint.

By the twentieth century, Spanish intellectuals were calling their country "irrelevant," and politics were a mess. Regionalism and religion split Spain, as did growing divides between wealthy and working class. Liberals were sick of having a monarch. After workers' strikes and armed uprisings, the beleaguered king consented to a democratic vote in 1931 and the left won; a rash of anarchists, Communists, and Socialists overtook Las Cortes. Parliament soon declared that Spain was a republic, and the king fled. The left released all political prisoners, taxed the landed rich, and outlawed the Fascist Party (the Falangists) of a rising military star, General Franco. Before long, the country blew up in a heinous civil war.

SPANISH CIVIL WAR (1936–1939)

Even those involved in this military debacle weren't entirely sure what it was about. Some say the Spanish Civil War was a class war; others claimed it was the result of the country's identity crisis when Spain's historical greatness was erased after losing her colonial holdings. Still others claim it was a violent illustration of the old issue of Spanish regionalism. What led up to it, at least, is clear: after the leftist National Parliament pushed out the king in 1931, a powerful faction of the country was furious, all the more so with reports of clergy being attacked by the left. The assassination of a right-wing politician by leftist police gave the right-leaning army cause to revolt. General Franco led a 1936 army uprising in Morocco that spread and brewed into war. The monarchists, Fascists, clergy, aristocrats, and army rebels fought as nationalists battling Republicans, a coalition of Socialists, Communists, anarchists, antimonarchists, anticlerics, and assorted liberals. Factions of the Republicans—for whom George Orwell and Ernest Hemingway fought— sometimes battled each other as well. Fighters were poorly armed—crooked forty-year-old rifles and rusty bullets were the norm—and military strategy was pathetic, but there was horrific brutality. Republicans lined up priests against church walls and shot them, and nuns were gang-raped. Nationalists attacked villages by night and left them filled with corpses by morning; they blocked food to Republican-held areas, starving residents to death. Both sides sought outside help: the Republicans sneaked the treasury's reserves of gold—about $600 million worth—off to the Soviet Union for safekeeping and as a credit against arms,[9] although the Soviets took all the money and supplied them with overpriced second-rate weapons left over from WWI. Franco invited Hitler's Nazis and Mussolini's Fascists to try out their new weaponry, most famously in the Basque country, where in 1937, they dropped dozens of incendiary bombs on the sacred town of Guernica, wiping out almost all 7,000 residents in waves of fire and smoke. Nazis and Fascists—Italian fighters alone numbered 60,000—and their modern armies tipped the balance, as they bombed cities from Seville to Madrid. By the time the foreign forces split for WWII, Spain had pretty much knocked herself out.

The war that more "happened" than it "began" and which "stopped" more than it was "won," effectively wiped out Spain within three years, and by the time Franco and his nationalists took power in 1939, millions across the country were starving, war widows walked the streets as prostitutes, and villagers set up slums of lean-tos outside major cities. At least 500,000 died during the war, although some say it was closer to a million, and the killing didn't stop when the war was over. Franco bore a grudge against those who had fought against him, and went on to kill at least 100,000 more Republicans, mostly in the Basque country and in Catalonia. Thousands were deported, thousands were turned into prisoner-of-war laborers, and thousands are still turning up in mass graves.

> *Nazis for hire: Picasso's disturbing painting* Guernica *is his tribute to the Basque town firebombed by the Nazis' Condor Unit in April 1937. The attack that killed most of the inhabitants in a city-wide blaze is a continuing symbol to the Basque separatist movement of their treatment at the hands of the central government in Madrid. Picasso refused to allow the wall-size painting to hang in Spain until Franco was dead. In 1981, it finally arrived in Spain, where it is mounted at the Centro de Arte Reina Sofia in Madrid. A tapestry of it hangs outside the meeting room of the UN Security Council.*

Spain's pitiful state spared her from being brought into the Second World War, when as in WWI, Spain remained neutral. Hitler didn't even bother to annex her. Although Franco sometimes infuriated the Führer by making him wait an hour while the Spaniard took a siesta, Franco is believed to have given safe haven to Nazis. So cozy was Franco's relationship with Hitler, at least from the Allied perspective, that Spain was slapped with economic sanctions after the war ended. Thus Spain was not eligible for U.S.-offered Marshall Plan funding. As a result, Spain fell under an economic shadow that lingered into the 1960s. One of the few things that kept the country going: loans from Argentina's President Juan Perón.

> *Perhaps Franco and Hitler were not as chummy as Allies believed. Franco did not enact anti-Semitic laws, and according to some reports he offered Spain as a sanctuary to at least 60,000 Jews.*[10]

Franco had a vision: one Spain, with one national identity and one political party—his. Other parties were banned, regional languages and celebrations were prohibited, the media was censored, and dissidents and those who had fought on the "wrong" side were eliminated. After the first few years of Franco's thirty-six-year reign, the country simply crawled off from the rest of the world.

> *Franco so feared rebellion that groups of three or more were not allowed to congregate in public spaces—he made sure there were few public spaces, as well—and the Spanish were literally kept under lock and key. Apartment buildings were maintained by doormen who kept the keys to all apartments and reported to the government on the comings and goings of the residents.*

By the 1960s, both economic and political changes were slowly under way. Franco's government, still mostly run by Fascist Falangists (some were Opus Dei members), was opening up to foreign investment and tinkering with economic reform and rapid industrialization. Before long, Spain was one of the top ten industrialized nations in the world, and her economy was galloping ahead, expanding by 6 percent a year.[11] Meanwhile, repressed regions started to fight back. Frequent strikes broke out in Barcelona. ETA emerged in 1959 and defied Franco's censure of all that was Basque, going on to kill the man named as Franco's successor.

> Until 1975, a Spanish wife was not allowed to work, own property, or travel without a note from her husband.

Waiting on the sidelines sat Prince Juan Carlos, grandson of King Alfonso XIII, who'd left Spain in 1931. Beckoned by Franco, who'd promised to reinstall the monarchy, the prince arrived in Spain in 1948, at age ten, without his parents. Franco supervised his education, and life, in Spain—but never did put him on the throne. The Bourbon had to wait twenty-seven years, but when Franco finally died in 1975—and the streets erupted in joy—Juan Carlos I was handed the baton. Some dubbed him "Juan Carlos the Brief," but the new king called for a nationwide referendum, asking the people what sort of government they wanted. The answer: a parliamentary monarchy with the king as head of state and a prime minister as leading politico.

> Spain's seventeen provinces have their own parliaments and numerous parties, but on the national level elections are essentially a vote between two parties: the right-leaning Partido Popular and the leftist Socialists.

In 1981, fanatical Spanish soldiers overtook the parliament and held its occupants captive for twenty-four hours, threatening to shoot them if the king didn't step down. Juan Carlos refused to abdicate or to leave the palace; instead, he phoned all his generals and convinced them not to support the power play. He succeeded. His smooth moves that day made his reputation soar. He and wife, Queen Sofia, remain popular and in power to this day.

Hot Spots

Madrid: Chosen as capital by King Philip II simply because it marks the exact center of Spain, hopping Madrid is home to splendid architecture, vast parks, and high culture, including the Golden Triangle of museums—the Prado, the Reina Sofia (home of *Guernica*), and the Thyssen-Bornemisza Museum. Beautiful Atocha station—part of which is a misty botanical garden—was the site of the March 11 attack that would have been worse if the trains had been running on time: the plan was for trains to be side by side when the bombs exploded.

Barcelona: The pretty Catalan city on the Mediterranean snatched international attention when she snagged the Olympics in 1992, an event that caused the city to finally develop her coastline. Courtyards are filled with orange trees, and romantic alleys wind past the medieval cathedral in the Gothic Quarter. Urban planners rave about the abundant squares that serve as living rooms in the densely packed city, but travelers to Barcelona must beware: purse snatchers, mostly Moroccans, run rampant.

Catalonia: The hilly northeastern corner that unfurls toward France is the wealthiest region in Spain, thanks to its industry and tourism. Catalans speak their own language; it's taught in schools, used on subways, and spoken on local TV. Catalonia's independent streak, and the substantial contribution the area makes to the country's coffers in Madrid, has given the region political chips: she's Spain's most autonomous.

Valencia: The air grows thick with smoke during the annual burning of effigies in Las Fallas, and at any time of year in the paella capital, her tapas bars provide hours of fun—particularly after a day spent delving into her flashy culture; the new art museum is built in the shape of an eye.

Basque country: Glittering beach town of San Sebastián and the Guggenheim Museum in Bilbao are two pulls to this northern region that runs between the jagged Pyrenees and the yacht-dotted Bay of Biscay that hugs France. Dubbed the culinary capital of Spain, the Basque country boasts hundreds of prestigious cooking clubs—and perhaps only a few dozen radical separatists.

Galicia: This misty northwest corner of Spain that hangs over Portugal is perhaps the least connected to the rest of the country. Ancient Celt settlers left a legacy of red hair, bagpipes, and, some say, magic. Known for fish and beautiful beaches, Galicia became world famous for the 2002 *Prestige* oil spill. The cathedral in regional capital Santiago de Compostela marks the destination of a popular pilgrimage across the Pyrenees.

Rock of Gibraltar: Despite the occasional nearly comical "invasion" by Spanish troops, who are quickly forced to turn back, this "rock" that's about fifteen miles from Africa has been legally British territory since 1713. Punctuated by military structures and caves, Gibraltar is home mostly to British residents who furiously wave the Union Jack; votes consistently show that locals want to stay part of the UK. Spaniards are furious that Brits won't get off the rock.

OTHER IMPORTANT ROCKS

Parsley Island (Isla Perejil): When six Moroccan military men "seized" it in 2002, Spanish warships went in to reclaim this smaller-than-a-city-block rock that's a few hundred yards off Morocco and home to a few flocks of goats; probable reason: fishing—there's a gold mine of silvery fish in these waters.

Ibiza: Two million partyers descend upon it en masse three months of the year. The third biggest of the Balearic Islands had its own chill-out and rave musical styles, and the Ibiza DJ collections—such as those from Café del Mar and Pacha—defined a recent era.

Valle de los Caídos (Valley of the Fallen): Rising up in Castilla y León, the haunting 492-foot-tall cross atop Valle de los Caídos was an excruciating labor of Republican POWs from the Civil War. Some talked of knocking the towering cross down when Franco died, but it still looms; Franco lies underneath it.

Maternity wards: With one of the world's lowest birth rates—less than 2 percent—there are now incentives to breed. In Valencia, parents of a second child are handed a check for about $3,500; in towns such as Calzadilla, they might be presented with a pig.[12]

ALHAMBRA

Peering down from atop Granada, the Alhambra is the final reminder of the era (711–1492) when Muslim Moors ruled much of Spain—a time not favorably recalled by Spaniards. Begun in the twelfth century, the sultans' compound of seven palaces is a labyrinth of scalloped arches, honeycombed domes, and glazed tile mosaics surrounded by glassy pools and lush gardens. Each palace had grand baths, heated floors, and piped water (a choice of hot, cold, and perfumed); private chambers even had flush toilets. Later battered by Napoleon's soldiers, the architectural jewel was crumbling when nineteenth-century American writer Washington Irving became entranced by the stories held within its walls and moved in to write about the place. The resulting book, *Tales of the Alhambra*, so popularized the compound that it was saved from the wrecking ball and refurbished to much of its former grandeur. Now it's an immensely popular tourist site.

Seville: Thick with the scent of orange trees, filled with tiny tapas bars, and surrounded by mountaintop Moorish forts, Seville is so enticing it's hard to pull away. She's still renowned for her cigars, her bullfights, and her legendary barber.

Hotshots

José Luis Rodríguez Zapatero: Prime Minister, 2004–present. He can't seem to get that "I can't believe I was elected" grin off his face, but the young Socialist in Madrid is making plenty of Spaniards happy—and may bring the country closer together than it's been in years. A lawyer and former member of parliament—in 1986, he was its youngest member, voted in at age twenty-six—Zapatero made a U-turn from many of Aznar's controversial policies, and pulled troops back from Iraq.

PM Zapatero changed Spain's pro-Bush direction

King Juan Carlos I: Ruling monarch, 1975–present. Born in Italy in 1938, Juan Carlos was raised in Switzerland, while his father, Don Juan, waited to be called back to Spain since Franco had promised to restore the king—though he never got around to it. In 1948, Juan Carlos was more or less handed over to Franco, but he had to wait until 1975 to wear the crown. Despite his playboy reputation, he's respected, as is classy Queen Sofia, a Greek princess whom he brought to Spain as his wife with the promise that someday he really would rule it.[13]

Crown Prince Felipe (b. 1968): The man *HELLO!* magazine calls a "royal heartthrob" is better known for whom he's gone out with (a Norwegian model, a German royal, a Greek aristocrat) than anything he's ever done (received a master's degree in law and international relations, trained in the Spanish army, navy, and air force). Predictably, he attracted the most ink of his life when he married lovely Letizia Ortiz, a divorcée and a commoner. Surprisingly, given the prince's previous harsh feelings toward the media—which he blamed for ruining a previous love affair—Ortiz had been one of Spain's most popular newscasters. The real irony is that the couple managed to keep their relationship a secret from the press until plans for the May 2004 wedding were officially announced.

José María Aznar: Prime Minister, 1996–2004. Exuding all the charm of a taxman (which he used to be), former Franco supporter Aznar led Spain during an era when unemployment was the EU's worst—often over 15 percent; Spain's coffers increased, due to billions of dollars of EU funding and privatization of state utilities. After mishandling the *Prestige* oil spill (which he claimed was small and contained), sneaky Aznar and cronies allegedly went on to wipe government

Courtesy of Secretaría de Estado de Communicación of Spain

computers clean of all information they had about the March 2004 attacks. Now a "Distinguished Scholar" at Georgetown University, he conducts political seminars—one prays not about emergency management.

PABLO PICASSO (1881–1973)

Pablo Picasso painted in numerous styles—from neoclassical to modern to the cubism he invented—and few painters have more influenced popular culture than the Spaniard who studied in Barcelona and headed to France in 1900. In Paris, where his friends were anarchists, artists, and poets, Picasso was under watch by police, who described him as "a so-called modern artist" who was "arrogant and stuffy,"[14] but his bold works soon attracted the likes of Gertrude Stein, who, with her brother Leo, became his first patrons. In his later years, his autograph on a cocktail napkin sufficed to pay tabs when he went out. Picasso's marriage to Russian ballerina Olga Koklova was only one of a series of bad, maddening relationships, but whenever he chucked one mistress, the short and squat but charismatic creator—"a raging bull with an insatiable sexual appetite"[15]—soon had another willing victim at his side. His coterie, painting style, and even his dog, it's said, changed with every new female acquaintance, but it was a male friend, the poet Casagemas, who inspired his Blue Period. The poet, shortly after lamenting his love life, pulled out a gun in a café and shot himself in the head. That was also the suicide method chosen by Picasso's second wife, Jacqueline; his lover Marie-Thérèse hanged herself, and his grandson Pablito killed himself by swallowing peroxide. Picasso produced 22,000 works before he died of a heart attack in 1973 in France; Picasso had vowed never to return to Spain while Franco was alive, and the dictator outlived the painter by two years.

General Francisco Franco Bahamonde (aka El Caudillo): Dictator, 1939–1975. Born in Galicia, the general who pushed the dominoes that led to the devastating Spanish Civil War was brave—at thirty-three he was promoted to general—but most of all he was lucky: his two rivals died before the Civil War had ended, he held on to power for thirty-six years, and he won two football lotteries. He's best known for kicking his country into the dark ages, but some rich conservatives recall him fondly.

ALIEN ARTIST: SALVADOR DALÍ (1904–1989)

It's hard to overstate the influence of his Costa Brava summer home in Cadaqués on the work of Dalí. There, where the winds whip through olive groves so fiercely that they twist boulders, and the clouds, thick with African dust, literally rain red, nature herself takes on a surreal form that Dalí captured on canvas. In the tiny fishing village where stone alleys lace up past tiny white houses stacked upon a hill, time has a way of slipping away, as illustrated in the painter's melting watches. The man known for his peculiar mustache—he saved his clippings from the barbershop and elaborately waxed the upturned tips—also brought oddities he'd found on his annual trips to Paris and Manhattan back to the village; long after his death, you can still find his remaining coterie of twins and hermaphrodites there. The painter married his muse, Gala, after she left her poet husband, Paul Éluard, and he paid plenty for that. Gala kept her boyfriends in fine style, buying a castle and yacht for her fave paramour Jeff Fenholt, star of *Jesus Christ Superstar*, but Dalí didn't much care. Those close to him say he never consummated the marriage. The surrealist, who amused himself in odd ways—he hired models to serve as his doting fans for Parisian events and to prance around like fairies in his hotel room—went down in history not just for his strange art but for being a sell-out. The Catalan lent his name to jewelry, perfume, sheets, and ties—and signed blank sheets of paper before they went to the printers. One suspects that the weirdo would get a big kick out of knowing how many of his works are now considered fakes.

Saint Teresa of Ávila (1515–1582): Reformer of Carmelite nuns and patron saint of spectacularly walled Ávila—perched on a hill not far from Madrid—Teresa, who was once paralyzed for three years, is said to have been able to levitate, and if you feel the energy in the room where she slept you might believe the claim. Franco apparently did, believing that she was responsible for his good fortune; he'd come upon a lucky charm of hers—her severed centuries-old hand during one of the Civil War battles. Franco was so superstitious and so attached to the limb that he refused all requests from the nuns of Ávila to get it back. Not until he died was her lucky hand pried out of his, and buried with the rest of her corpse.

DRINKING MATTERS

In the land of drinking festivity, "cidra" is stylishly poured from bottle high over glass, bubbling Catalan cava may cascade over stacked champagne flutes, and Costa Brava's old salts still drink wine the old way, streaming from forehead down nose. Spice-rich and vanilla-ish Quarenta y Tres—from forty-three ingredients—is the national drink, but all regions boast their own specialties, taken as an after-meal shot or "chupito." Smooth Pacharan is made from sloe berries, Izarra is herb-infused Armagnac, the Canaries' banana-derived Licor de Platano elicits loud coos, and Mallorca's spicy "ron" (rum) is so special they don't let it off the island.

News you can understand: *El País*, Spain's finest newspaper, is published in Spanish—but eight pages are available in English through the *International Herald Tribune*: www.iht.com/pdfs/elpais/ep1.pdf

8. PORTUGAL
(República Portuguesa)
Still Sleeping

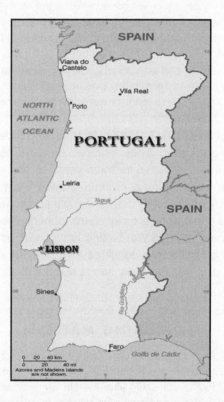

FAST FACTS

Country:	Portuguese Republic; República Portuguesa
Capital:	Lisbon
Government:	Parliamentary democracy
Independence:	1143, established; 1910, republic; 1974, overthrew tossed king, became dictatorship

Population:	10,606,000 (2006 estimate)
Head of State:	President Anibal Cavaco Silva (2006)
Head of Government:	Prime Minister José Sócrates Carvalho Pinto de Sousa (2005)
Elections:	President elected by popular vote, five-year term; prime minister (usually leader of majority party or coalition) appointed by president
Name of Parliament:	Assembly of the Republic; Assembleia da República
Ethnicity:	Portuguese-Mediterranean; African (less than 100,000); Eastern European
Religion:	94% Roman Catholic; Protestant, other
Language:	Portuguese
Literacy:	93% (male 95%, female 91%); some figures show 85% literacy or less
Famous Exports:	Magellan, lobotomies, vinho verde, the pitiful wailing of *fado*
Economic Big Boy:	EDP (electrical utility): 2004 total sales: $8.78 billion[1]
Per Capita GDP:	$18,600 (2006)
Unemployment:	7.7% (January 2006 Eurostat estimate)
EU Status:	EEC member since 1986
Currency:	Euro

Quick Tour

Edged by 500 miles of dramatic coastline, laced by rivers, and divided by mountains rising through her interior, La República Portuguesa is strewn with foggy fishing villages of twisting streets, tiny whitewashed towns tumbling down hills, and hamlets hidden in cork forests. The land of port, vinho verde, and two hundred dishes made with cod, Portugal is an eye-pleaser, from her train stations wrapped in painted tiles to her hidden bars, where one sits around wood barrels while her old-timers belt out sad ballads into the night. Stunning capital Lisbon weaves up and down hills, but most Portuguese live in small towns, where herds of belled goats jingle down dirt roads.

> *Agriculture, mostly in the form of small farms, still employs one-fifth of workers.*

Continental Europe's westernmost land shares the Iberian peninsula with Spain, the geographical sibling under whose shadow Portugal has atrophied for about five centuries; the country's weightiness was seen in James Michener's book, *Iberia*, which forgets to mention Portugal at all. Both countries entered the EU in 1986, but there are lots of differences—the most obvious being that Atlantic-hugging Portugal has a quarter of Spain's population, is less than a fifth of Spain's geographical size, and in Portugal they speak Portuguese. And unlike Spain, now a dynamo in Europe, Portugal has not yet gotten her act together—despite the billions of euros the EU has handed the country over the past fifteen years.

> Between 2000 and 2006, Portugal was allotted about $28 billion in EU funds to build infrastructure.[2]

Loud, happy Spain is paella and bullfights; gentle, reserved Portugal is the mournful wailing of *fado* and legendary sightings of the Virgin Mary. Spaniards are fiercely proud of their national identity—and particularly of their regions, which they extol as having the best food, architecture, and football team; the slumped Portuguese will tell you that their country is the graveyard of ambition, a kingdom of mediocrity where the national hobby is complaining, and the ambitious leave.[3]

Spain, under dictator Franco, was missing in action during much of the twentieth century; Portugal, under the forty-year dictatorship of António de Oliveira Salazar, simply disappeared—and in some ways she still hasn't come back: almost half of the Portuguese people reside outside the country.

TWIN BROTHERS OF DIFFERENT MOTHERS?

While Portugal was deep in her Salazar haze (1928–1968)—her press censored, her political system shut down, secret police roaming the streets, and thousands of dissenters thrown in jail—neighbor Spain was in her Franco daze (1939–1975) under similar repression. Both dictators isolated their countries and transformed their people into impoverished, malnourished masses, although in both countries a privileged elite made out (and still makes out) rather well. The two Iberian leaders weren't chummy, but each respected the other's territory and both dictators-for-decades flickered out in the 1970s.

Kidnapped and driven off into darkness after Salazar grabbed power in 1928, Portugal was absent from the Second World War and slept through most of the last century politically smothered. It wasn't until a military coup in 1974 pulled back the shroud that Portugal emerged, blinking, as the poorest and least-educated country in Europe. Despite some leaps, thirty years after democracy was restored, Portugal still isn't fully up to speed: some 13 percent of women still can't read,[4] less than half the children make it to high school,[5] and Portugal remains the low earner of Western Europe; even some Eastern European countries show a higher per capita income. That the country has come as far as she has—back in the Salazar days, about half of the population couldn't read, and almost all lived in dire poverty—is partly a result of over $25 billion doled out for educational funds by the European Union since 1989.[6]

Critics say much EU funding to Portugal was squandered, creating, for example, 60,000 government jobs that only further bureaucratize the place. Previous administrations were big spenders, investing in huge public works projects, such as the $1.7 billion Alqueva hydroelectric dam, which doesn't put much of a dent in the country's energy needs, while basic infrastructure is falling apart, as evidenced by the bridge that collapsed in Porto in 2001, killing seventy.

Most of Portugal's leaders since the 1974 revolution have appeared inept, but the hands-down most imbecilic was Pedro Santana Lopes, former mayor of Lisbon, who was hastily appointed to fill the prime minister's seat in 2004 after José Manuel Durão Barroso was tapped to head the European Commission in Brussels. Resembling Barney of Mayberry, Santana Lopes acted even dopier. Arriving an hour late for his inauguration, he bumbled through his speech and seemed to be drawing names for cabinet appointments out of a hat. The woman whom the government had boasted only hours earlier would be the first high-ranking female involved in military matters was instead appointed Minister of Arts and Entertainment. Defense Minister Paulo Portas received a second portfolio, being named Secretary of Maritime Issues, an announcement that, to judge by his televised response, was as surprising to him as anyone else.[7] So dismal were prospects for the new government that Lisbon magazine *Visão* noted that "expectations are so low that a few intelligent measures . . . can make it look good."[8] Alas, Santana Lopes didn't make any mildly smart moves—he was booted out of the seat within months.

> Santana Lopes is known for his bloopers, among them writing a fan letter to poet Machado de Assis, who passed away in 1908, and extolling the violin concertos of Chopin, who never wrote any concertos for violin.[9]

Thankfully, a new government is finally steering Portugal onto a steadier course. Prime Minister José Sócrates has tightened the economic belt, and has also made Portugal stand out for something besides soccer and buffoonery: under Socrates, the country is becoming a world model in renewable energy—building the world's largest solar station, erecting more giant windmills, and using lumber waste and other biomass to generate electricity.

Palácio da Pena in Sintra: Portugal's Sleeping Beauty

We don't expect Portugal to transform into an economic Germany overnight; besides, a certain backwardness is part of her charm. Some liken the country's rustic villages to Spain of a few decades ago, and many who set eyes upon her fall in love with the fair land that still feels like the final edge of the world. Portugal could use a bit more self-confidence and a lot more marketing. Spain is the second-most visited destination in the world, but gorgeous Portugal doesn't even place in the top twenty-five.

For centuries now, the underlying issue in Portugal has been her depressive passivity and dreaminess. The Portuguese tendency to lose herself in wistful thinking is so well known that there's a name for it: *Sebastianismo*, after sixteenth-century King Sebastião, who disappeared—and whose reappearance the people have been awaiting ever since.

DOM SEBASTIÃO (1554–1578)

He was sickly, barely educated, and mentally disturbed—never three winning qualities in a ruler—and then twenty-four-year-old King Sebastião became obsessed with Muslims. Previous rulers had already chased the Moors out of Portugal, but he still wanted to fight them, and headed across the Mediterranean to today's Morocco. Setting off for North Africa in 1578 with 24,000 soldiers—whom he didn't bother to train or equip terribly well—the king unleashed his pathetic army and was promptly defeated in the most devastating military disaster in Portugal's history; one-third of his troops were slaughtered.[10] The Muslims took hundreds of nobles as prisoners, demanding huge ransoms that drained the treasury. As for Sebastião, he probably perished in battle, but the news the Portuguese people received held a grain of hope: they were told he had merely vanished. The throne was empty and Sebastião had not left an heir. Spanish king Philip II annexed the country, and the Spanish rulers who followed stripped away Portugal's autonomy, raised taxes, and made the Portuguese miserable. Resistance groups formed holding out hope out that the missing king would reappear and restore Portugal to her previous status as Europe's richest land. Over the years, hapless Sebastião became a messianic figure; three centuries later, the faithful awaited his reappearance just as seriously, thinking only he could make Portugal great again, although he messed it up back when he had a real chance.

Portugal is called "the country of the Three Fs"—football, Fátima, and fado. *Football (soccer) is often the only way Portugal keeps her name in the news, with star players and events such as Euro 2004. Fátima is a pilgrimage site that lures millions, vividly illustrating Portugal's continuing bonds with Catholicism. Sad* fado—*originally wailed by widows whose husbands were lost at sea—may best portray the passive Portuguese spirit that mixes deep yearning with a feeling of betrayal by forces beyond their control.*

History Review

Some people get fine china when they trot down the aisle, but Teresa of León, the adored daughter of the king of Spain's León region, did much better in 1096. When she wed Henry of Burgundy, a daring knight in the service of her father, the newlyweds received a future country as their wedding gift. The present was a mixed blessing. The territory in the Iberian northwest was a battle zone between Muslims, who'd been running the area since the eighth century, and Christians, who were driving them off in the reconquest. Dutiful son-in-law Henry kept the territory secure and loyal to León, but not so his son. Afonso Henriques expanded his parents' patch of land to Portugal's current boundaries, and in 1143 declared Portugal an independent and sovereign country.

The Arab Muslims who landed on Iberia in the eighth century didn't much care for the wetter, cooler climate of northern Portugal, and settled into the south around the Algarve. Chased out entirely by the thirteenth century, the Moors had nevertheless helped local agriculture by introducing citrus crops and had shown the Portuguese how to make azulejos, *the painted tiles for which the country is now famous.*

UNKIND KIN

Poor Teresa. When hubby Henry died in 1112, she was given control of their land, but then the boys of her clan barged in. Teresa's nephew, the new king in the Spanish territory of León, wanted the land back and sent his army to reclaim it in 1127. Teresa clung tight to her wedding present—but then her son, Afonso Henriques, put together an army, and he too battled her beleaguered forces. Damned by the men in her family, Teresa finally relinquished control in 1128 and shuffled off to the fishing villages of the northwest.[11]

As a runaway Spanish territory, Portugal was always looking over her shoulder at the kingdoms of León and Castile, which eventually came together to dominate Spain. The Portuguese monarchy was so wary of the easterly neighbors that as early as the fourteenth century, Portugal forged a military alliance with England. That bond paid off. In 1385, England helped the Portuguese shove back the kingdom of Castile, thanks to skilled English archers. The Portuguese were so gushingly grateful that they signed the 1386 Treaty of Windsor, which solidified "an inviolable, eternal, solid, perpetual, and true league of friendship."[12] The treaty soon led, as so many do, to daughter-swapping. The Duke of Lancaster, who had negotiated the treaty, married off his Philippa to Portuguese King João I. But an even more lavish affair—one that further cemented the Portuguese-Anglo bond—was the 1662 wedding of King João IV's daughter Catherine of Braganza to King Charles II of England. The Portuguese princess came with an impressive dowry, the contents of which could not fit in one hope chest: papa shipped her off with $600,000 worth of gold, the Indian city of Bombay, the North African city of Tangier, and a lifetime supply of tea. Nevertheless, Charles quickly tired of her and was always trotting off having affairs.

Portuguese princess Catherine is credited with starting the English tea craze and introducing that breakfast essential, orange marmalade.

Fear of Spain did more than drive Portugal into England's arms. Claustrophobically wedged between her Iberian rival and the ends of the earth—waters off Portugal were believed to mark the edge of the world—the Portuguese went on a potential suicide mission and headed to sea. The motivation wasn't only lack of love for the Spanish, who blocked them from grabbing any additional land in Iberia. Conflicts between Christians and Muslims, including the Crusades, jammed up the overland spice trade across Asia. Parts of the Silk Road were blocked, attackers ran rampant, and some Muslims traders shunned business with Christians—all problems requiring finding new routes. A further factor: spreading Christianity. The Portuguese loathed Muslims, who had long ruled their land, and also wanted to butter up the Catholic Church, with which Spain was always currying favor.

The Portuguese Age of Discovery officially began when the Portuguese conquered Ceuta, a North African town popular with Arab traders. Along with English bowmen, the Portuguese attacked the settlement in 1415; few Portuguese died in the battle that left most of Ceuta's population dead in the streets. Beyond the corpses, however, they found hoards of spices, tapestries, gold, china, and silk, since traders used Ceuta as a storehouse between travels. The town never again filled up with such wealth. Once word of the Portuguese conquest got out, traders stopped coming.

Hoping to uncover other treasure troves, Prince Henry—told by an astrologer that he would lead men to discoveries—set up the world's finest maritime school in 1418, bringing together geographers, cartographers, astronomers, Genoese, Venetians, and Jews to study the mechanics of the discovery business. They pored over all the world's maps, plotting out known physical geography drawn from Marco Polo, Ptolemy, and seafarers' legends. They fashioned new instruments to measure geographical locations and consulted mapmakers about methods to best record what was seen. Henry's navigation school even invented a more maneuverable vessel, the caravel, better suited for exploration. Then, brimming with new knowledge, the explorers shoved off into the unknown, marking Porto Santo and Madeira in 1420 and the Azores in 1427 as their first claims.

> In Madeira, while clearing the brush, the Portuguese inadvertently started a fire that raged for seven years.[13] The result, once the blaze smoldered out, was potash-rich soil well-suited for growing grapes—launching the Madeira wine business—and was later used for gunpowder.

The voyagers possessed the era's most sophisticated technology and the most well-rounded knowledge of the physical world, but superstition still reigned; even the compass was suspected by many to be a likely toy of Satan. The most persistent folkloric beliefs concerned North Africa's Cape Bojador, a promontory to the south of Morocco that was feared to be the absolute end of the earth and proved to be a profound psychological barrier. Henry sent out over a dozen ships with the sole goal of passing it, but crews mutinied and captains buckled under the fear. Even respected navigator Gil Eanes reported upon return that the cape was impassable—but Henry sent him straight back out. Facing what he believed was certain death, Eanes pushed on, only to discover that the ship didn't plunge off the earth. The door to the rest of the world thus opened, and the rape of West Africa began.

> The brave Portuguese were shamelessly brutal as they uncovered what they called the Gold Coast, Ivory Coast, and Grain Coast for the treasures taken from those spots, slaughtering villagers who responded to their arrows with sticks and stones. The expanding Portuguese Empire grew wealthy from more than just metals, jewels, and tusks; the Portuguese also initiated the intercontinental African slave trade, later hauling their victims to Brazil, which they discovered in 1500.

Soon the Cape of Good Hope, Africa's southernmost point (and another psychological block), was rounded by Bartolomeu Dias—accidentally. In 1467, a violent storm blew his ship around the cape; even though the leap had been made, his frightened crew refused to push on. But the loudest "ka-ching" of all came from the 1497 voyage made by Vasco da Gama. Setting out with three ships and three years' worth of food, he too rounded the cape, then stopped at today's Mozambique and Kenya, searching for a pilot to lead him to India. He went through quite a few, but finally a Muslim guide sailed with him to Goa, in the south of the Indian subcontinent. And from the moment that da Gama dropped anchor, the fate of that part of the world changed forever.

> Despite his reputation as a sage "problem solver," da Gama was short on diplomatic skills, often leaving a river of blood wherever he stepped ashore. In 1502, passing a boat of Muslim pilgrims returning from Mecca, he first robbed them, then locked them in their hold before setting fire to the ship of 380 men, women, and children.[14] His actions at Calicut, India, were just as despicable. Upon arrival in 1502, he demanded that the leader hand over the sultanate. The leader instead sent out envoys to negotiate peace. Da Gama killed them and chopped them into pieces. Their boat, heaped with body parts, was sent back with a message that here were the ingredients for the Calicut leader's next curry.[15]

The Portuguese lassoed Malacca, the Spice Islands, Timor, and Macau. When Columbus discovered what he called the East Indies (and what we know today as the Caribbean islands), King João II demanded the lands be ceded to Portugal, since they weren't far from the Portuguese Azores. The Spanish, under whose flag Columbus had sailed, begged to differ, and the pope was called in to decide. In 1493, Pope Alexander VI drew a line in the Atlantic to demarcate how to divvy up new holdings. His decision: everything east of the line went to Portugal; lands to the west were Spain's. The next year, he redrew the line 1,000 miles farther east. Under this second Treaty of Tordesillas, Portugal bagged Brazil. Perhaps the change was due to divine vision, but it's more likely that the Portuguese had already stumbled upon Brazil, and gave the holy man a handsome financial incentive to pick up his pen again.

After breaking the Arab and Chinese hold on eastern markets, in 1505 Portugal declared a spice trade monopoly and tightly guarded the secret maps that showed the exact locations of the lands of nutmeg, pepper, and cloves. Every ship carried a map specialist who recorded new observations and kept maps heavily locked. One map keeper was a Dutchman, who bit by bit cribbed the maps; in 1596, he published the coveted Portuguese secrets, launching a nonstop spice war among Europeans.

PORT OF CALL

Port wine—fortified with brandy or other high-octane alcohol—made its official debut in the 1670s, after the British blockaded the French, foolishly cutting off their own access to wine. The Brits turned to Portugal, but found the wines to be swill, and jumped into producing wine themselves. To stabilize *vinho* for voyages, Brits added brandy—thus creating a libation called port, adored by connoisseurs. The British may have the reputation of being the world's biggest fans of port, savored as an aperitif or dessert wine with Stilton and fruit, but the French actually sip more rubies, tawnies, and vintage ports than anyone else.[16] Many ports are at their peak after aging over a century; some of the most valuable have been collecting dust since Napoleon's time.[17]

The sixteenth-century golden age, when Lisbon rose as Europe's major trade center for goods from the Far East, was punctuated by dark moments, including a 1531 earthquake that killed thousands. Still, despite battles on the high seas, the country flourished all the more after the discovery of gold in Brazil, until foolish King Sebastião's 1578 crusade sucked the treasury dry and left Portugal without a leader. Spaniards soon swept in. King Philip II ruled Spain and Portugal as one during the sixty-year period that Portuguese refer to as "the Spanish captivity." Spain gobbled up Portugal's remaining riches and dragged her into endless wars, including one against the English, long Portuguese allies. The Spaniards prevented Portugal from tending to her overseas lands, and the Dutch snatched up Portuguese territories in the East Indies and Brazil. In 1640, while Spaniards were distracted by internal uprisings, the Portuguese finally slipped off, grabbed a new monarch, and declared themselves independent; Spanish forces were spread too thin to grab the runaway back. Portugal remained free, but never regained her previous prominence or wealth, even with additional income from Brazil. In fact, Brazil, where Portugal set up cotton and sugar plantations, was in some ways a drain. So many Portuguese preferred living there that Portugal's population diminished drastically into the eighteenth century, when King João V formally banned further emigration.[18]

A subtle fear persists that Spain will reach out and grab Portugal again. In the early 1900s, Spanish king Alfonso XIII seriously considered forcibly annexing Portugal. Today the neighbor is conquering Portugal economically. Spain, Portugal's biggest foreign investor, has 3,000 Spanish firms operating there, and Spanish companies run about 15 percent of Portugal's banks.[19]

COLONIAL CONSIDERATIONS

At her height, the Portuguese Empire encompassed lands in Africa, Asia, and the Americas, but Brazil was her baby; the South American land where Portuguese royalty often took residence and where rubber barons grew so rich they built opera houses in the jungle became independent in 1822. Any holdings that remained into the mid-twentieth century were economic and military liabilities, but Portugal continued to cling, ignoring a 1960 UN mandate for European countries to give up their colonies. By the 1970s, military missions abroad were eating up almost half of Portugal's budget, and territories kept drifting away nonetheless. India grabbed Goa in 1961, and after Portugal's 1974 Revolution of the Carnations, she finally granted independence to Cape Verde, Mozambique, Angola, São Tomé e Príncipe, and Portuguese Guinea. East Timor proclaimed independence in 1975, and Portugal handed Macau to China in 1999. Only Madeira and the Azores, her first conquests, now remain of the once-vast Portuguese Empire.

Between 1755 and 1822, Portugal received three major blows from which she's never fully recovered: one was geological, one was military, and one was a political move with deep economic effects. During the eighteenth-century's downward slide, Portugal was knocked around in numerous shake-ups and anticlerical movements, and rattled in every possible way, including by a devastating earthquake—one of the world's worst.

LISBON'S DISASTER: NOVEMBER 1, 1755

On the evening of October 31, 1755, the sky over Lisbon took on a yellow tinge, a strange smoke rose from the ground, and as sunrise approached the following day, dogs began howling, cattle appeared nervous, birds stopped singing, and a sulphurous scent hung in the air. The day nevertheless appeared serene as the Portuguese headed out to celebrate All Saints Day in their churches, illuminated with candles and gas lamps. At 9:30 AM, the ground began shaking, rocking, and convulsing so violently that entire buildings collapsed, palaces fell, and churches crumbled down on the devout. Six minutes later, most of Lisbon lay in ruin, her streets littered with stones, wood, and corpses, and ripped open with cracks twenty feet wide. Her people's prayers were transformed into hysterical cries as thousands ran from the collapsed buildings that caught fire from the candles tossed about. Many fled toward the water to escape from smoke and falling debris. Thirty minutes later, the ocean pulled back—exposing the seabed littered with lost boats, skeletons, and treasures—then slammed the coast with a fifty-foot-high wall of water that battered all in its path. The tsunami pulled back, sucking thousands into a sickening whirlpool of broken bodies, trees, horses, shop signs, historical documents, explorers' maps, and smashed architectural treasures, and then disappeared in an eerie silence, only to hammer the coast twice more. The fires spread, starting an inferno that raged for seven days. In all, some 90,000 people (a third of Lisbon's population) were killed, 85 percent of the city was destroyed, and the faith of the fervently Catholic country was shaken—one factor in rising anticlerical movements.

Had there then been a Richter scale, the Lisbon earthquake would have registered almost 9—making the 1755 quake nearly 100 times more powerful than the 7.2 quake that shook Kobe, Japan, in 1995. Portugal actually laid the foundation for seismology. The prime minister sent out interviewers to ask about observations prior to the temblor, gathering detailed information about the behavior of animals and the physical changes that foreshadowed the quake.

The royal family survived—they'd left Lisbon that morning on a holy outing—and so did the prime minister, Sebastião José de Carvalho e Melo, later known as the Marquês de Pombal. The king became phobic about enclosed quarters, henceforth often insisting that the royal family sleep in tents, but the prime minister proved to be a coolheaded disaster management man. The Marquês de Pombal calmed survivors, preventing riots and looting, and dispatched rescue teams to "bury the dead, [and] feed the living." Within a year, Lisbon was rising again, the Marquês de Pombal supervising the redesign of the city into more orderly quarters and squares. His modernizing ideas entailed more than physical redesign: an anti-Catholic, he cut Portugal's ties to the Vatican, ground the Inquisition to a halt, banished Jesuits, and made education a secular affair—controversial moves that earned him enemies. An attempt on the king's life became an excuse for the Marquês to kill over 1,000 detractors, and he tossed thousands more behind bars. The Marquês de Pombal also ended slavery, shaped up Porto's wine business, and reinvigorated Portugal's economy. When devout Queen Maria (1734–1816) came to power in 1777, she reversed all of his reforms, released the political prisoners he'd locked up, and banished the Marquês to his villa in Pombal.

In the early nineteenth century, Napoleon fixed his gaze on the western strip of Iberia. Having already nabbed Spain, Napoleon's brother Joseph struck a deal with a Spanish general for the Portuguese conquest: one-third would go to France, one-third to Spain, and one-third to the general himself. Napoleon's forces entered the country in 1807, and Portugal's royal family fled to Brazil; the French lasted only four years and never fully settled in, thanks to the British who helped give the heave-ho. But Napoleon was yet another factor in Portugal's diminishing stature. Fighting the occupiers drained Portugal further, and the royals so adored Brazil that Prince João became emperor and nobody wanted to come back; the empire became the Kingdom of Portugal, Brazil, and the Algarves, and a wobbly regent babysat Portugal. João finally returned to Lisbon in 1821 to calm down a revolution, leaving his son Pedro as Brazilian emperor. Two years later, Pedro (facing a revolution himself) made Brazil independent, a crushing loss to Portugal, both economically and psychologically.

At the turn of the twentieth century, Portugal, now broke, was restless: revolts and riots often broke out, and church and monarchy served as scapegoats for the national decline. Intellectuals blamed the passive, nonentrepreneurial "Sebastianismo" spirit of the Portuguese people on brainwashing by king and clerics, and in 1911 legislators slashed the power of both. Parliament wrote a new constitution abolishing the monarchy, calling for separation of church and state, banning religious instruction in schools, and even forbidding soldiers from attending church. The government seized land held by the king and the Church, distributing it to peasants. Catholicism lost its hold—but only briefly.

FÁTIMA

Catholicism was nearly driven underground, and the time was certainly ripe for a miracle. On May 13, 1917, in the village of Fátima, three shepherd children claimed to have had a vision as controversial as it was extraordinary. The trio said they saw the Virgin Mary, although only two heard her speak. Over six months, according to the later written accounts of one of the children, Lucia dos Santos (1907–2005), Mary revealed herself six times, disclosing three secrets: in the first, she showed them hell, telling them that lost souls suffered in the flames because the living didn't sacrifice enough. The second concerned Russia, and how her rise would cause the death of millions and lead to a great war. The third—which some believe to be a ruse, with the "real" third secret still hidden—was not made public until 2000. The Church said that in the final secret, revealed to the children as a vision, a bishop in white is shot and falls, apparently dead. Pope John Paul II, who was shot in 1981, believed that he was the man in the vision. The current Pope Benedict, however, contradicted that version of the third secret in 1984, when the then-cardinal said the third vision concerned the last days of earth.

Lucia dos Santos became a Carmelite nun who was so respected that Pope John Paul II popped in for visits; like the pope, she died in 2005. Her cousins, Francisco and Jacinta Marto, died within three years of Mary's visits. Francisco, who Mary said would die soon and was not guaranteed entry to heaven, became severely depressed and stopped studying, doing little but praying; at eleven, he succumbed to the 1918 Spanish flu. Little Jacinta, only seven during the visions, was most profoundly affected by them— particularly the vision of souls suffering in hell. She took to making numerous sacrifices—among them, wearing knotted rope that abraded her skin and giving up water—and within three years, she too had died from the flu. Like Francisco, Jacinta was beatified by Pope John Paul II.[20]

The Catholic Church didn't officially endorse the Fátima visions for another thirteen years, but they quickly became a mainstay in the Portuguese belief system and culture; few dare question their legitimacy even now. At the time of the visions, 1917, Portugal certainly needed something to believe in; the new republic was self-destructing and anarchy prevailed. Secret societies of Catholics and monarchists in the north tried to reinstate the king, which led to a brief civil war. The economy and the political system collapsed. Even the military was a mess—it kept failing in attempts to overthrow the government. If there was ever an hour for Dom Sebastião to return, this was it. But instead António de Oliveira Salazar took center stage.

In 1926, the military finally succeeded in overtaking the government, but that immediately led to infighting. Eighteen months of flying generals later, a cabinet was finally appointed. And that's how an economics professor from the University of Coimbra entered the government: António de Oliveira Salazar was appointed finance minister in 1928. Within two years, he had reformed the Portuguese economy and was the hero of the merchant and working class. As his power soared, Salazar outlined his plan for continued success. He endorsed a new authoritarian government that would emphasize Catholic morality, hard work, and patriotic duty. Few opposed him; he was the only leader to have a vision at all. In 1932, he stepped in as prime minister, a role he held for the next thirty-six years. Salazar kicked off public works projects, including paved roads, but before long he gagged the press, banned other parties, and settled in as a self-serving autocrat, relying on secret police to battle opposition. Favoring the rich, he let the poor starve and hindered industrialization. The education system atrophied with millions never learning to read, and millions fled the country as she grew backward during his dictatorship.

> Salazar's only notable accomplishments were keeping Portugal out of World War II and signing her up for NATO. The coalition didn't care that he was a dictator: it wanted to build bases on Madeira and the Azores, seen as crucial to guarding the Mediterranean.

Salazar fell out of the power seat in 1968—literally—sustaining head injuries when he slipped out of his chair; he died two years later. Marcelo Caetano stepped in and continued the Salazar regime until 1974, when the military, sick of fighting losing battles in Africa, finally rose up and brought democracy to a people who were the most backward in Europe.

> In the 1960s, 8 percent of the Portuguese population moved to France, where many still live. Some 5 million Portuguese live abroad most of the year.[21]

REVOLUTION

On April 25, 1974, when "Grândola Vila Morena" played over Lisbon radio, few thought it was anything but a pleasant tune. But for a group of young Portuguese officers—the Armed Forces Movement—it was a coded call to overthrow the government, an act accomplished in mere hours and without bloodshed. The Portuguese greeted the revolutionaries with carnations, and thousands accompanied them into the villages to inform the peasants that they were free. The weeks of jubilant celebration that followed—and the common sight of officers walking around with flowers sticking out of their guns—gave the overthrow its common name: the Revolution of the Carnations. Under General António de Spínola, the military government disbanded the secret police, restored civilian freedoms, ungagged the press, allowed the return of political parties, and, within a year, set almost all of Portugal's remaining colonies free.

The military ran a liberal transitional government for two years, until a new constitution was hammered out in 1976 and presidential elections took place for the first time in fifty years. Among the additions in the 1976 constitution: women were given the right to vote.

> According to European Database, less than 11 percent of Portuguese women graduate from high school.[22]

Hot Spots

Lisbon: The hilly, Atlantic-hugging capital is Europe's most western and one of the prettiest, with a hopping nightlife and street celebrations that impart an ever-present sense of fun. Just watch out for them cabbies.

Porto: Portugal's second-biggest city straddles the Douro River, and is a lively transport hub in part due to its famous export, port. Restaurants, bars, and narrow paths are carved into the stone hills at the river's edge, making it all the more fetching.

Fátima: Millions descend on the site, many requesting miracles. "If you're sick or your football team isn't winning or you can't make a baby, you go to Fátima," explains one Portuguese.

Alentejo: Cork forests and cork factories are what the southern area is best known for; now it is also the home of burnt stumps and ashes after fires ravaged an area the size of Luxembourg during the summer of 2005. Also one of the country's poorest and most illiterate regions.

> Cork kicks in almost $1 billion of Portugal's GDP, and some 16,000 Portuguese work with the spongy substance made popular by blind monk Dom Pérignon, who first stuffed a plug of the peeled bark into a champagne bottle in 1650. Now Portugal produces over half of the world's cork.

Algarve: Book now to reserve your space on the crowded beaches in Portugal's south next summer.

The Azores: Flung 900 miles to the west of Portugal are the nine Azores, the volcanic islands that Portugal still won't cut loose. Now populated mostly by sheep and punctuated by the occasional military base, the islands still reflect their glory days as pit stops between Europe and the New World; navigators landed here with ships brimming with gold, silver, and other stolen treasures. The island of Angra was the biggest beneficiary of the wealth that came through: she still sparkles with stunning palaces, churches, and forts that are now on UNESCO's World Heritage list.

Hotshots

José Sócrates Carvalho Pinto de Sousa: Prime Minister, 2005–present. Without a head of government for months in 2004, the Portuguese voted in Socialist Sócrates, who pulled troops out of Iraq and daringly says he will float a new referendum on the country's antiabortion laws. The former parliamentarian who previously worked on environment issues and prison reform is more on the ball than any Portuguese leader has been in ages.

José Manuel Durão Barroso: President, EU European Commission, 2004–present; Portuguese Prime Minister, 2002–2004. The former Maoist, who recently made a leap to the hard right when he signed on with Social Democrats, has serious luck. It was a fluke when he became prime minister after 2002's surprise election. It was just as improbable that he would be selected as head of the European Commission, the EU's mighty policy-making arm.

Egas Moniz: Just call him "Dr. Lobotomy": in 1935, the Portuguese physician invented the practice of cutting out parts of the brain to "cure" schizophrenia and other behavioral problems.

Barroso, now president of
the weighty European
Commission

Fernando Pessoa (1888–1935): Portugal's most beloved poet suffered multiple personality disorder; he wrote poetry under different names and using different styles, and his assorted personalities also wrote scathing critiques of the poems written by the others. Almost all of the personalities were indeed talented.

José Saramago: Born in 1922, he is considered among the world's most gifted writers; a playwright, travel writer, novelist, and journalist, he won the 1998 Nobel Prize for Literature. Tellingly, he lives in Spain.

News you can understand: *Portugal News:* www.the-news.net

9. THE NETHERLANDS
(Holland; Nederland)
The Thinker

FAST FACTS

Country:	Kingdom of the Netherlands; Koninkrijk der Nederlanden
Capital:	Amsterdam; government seat: The Hague
Government:	Constitutional monarchy
Independence:	1579 (from Spain)
Population:	16,492,000 (2005 estimate)
Head of State:	Queen Beatrix (1980)
Head of Government:	Prime Minister Jan Peter Balkenende (2002)
Elections:	Monarchy is hereditary; prime minister appointed by monarch
Name of Parliament:	States General; Staaten Generaal
Ethnicity:	83% Dutch; 9% Moroccan, Turk, Antillean, Surinamese, Indonesian; 8% other (1999 estimate)

Religion:	41% none; 31% Roman Catholic; 13% Dutch Reformed; 7% Calvinist; 5.5% Muslim; 2.5% other (2002 estimate)
Language:	Dutch; Frisian
Literacy:	99% (2003 estimate)
Famous Exports:	Heineken, Philips Electronics, Unilever (Birds Eye, Slim-Fast, Wishbone)
Economic Big Boy:	Royal Dutch Shell (oil and gas); 2004 total sales: $265.19 billion[1]
Per Capita GDP:	$30,600 (2005 estimate)
Unemployment:	4.6% (January 2006 Eurostat figure)
EU Status:	Founding member (entered EEC 1957)
Currency:	Euro

Quick Tour

Don't be fooled by the flower markets awash with color and the skinny pictur-esque buildings scrunched along canals. Nederland is more than lovely: she's smart, rich, and is a showcase of sensible planning, a place where every square inch is accounted for and put to good use. For decades it appeared the efficient Dutch had figured out how to run a country that hummed along on her own. Affluent and tolerant, they had seemingly solved social woes with open minds—euthanasia and gay marriage are legal, prostitution and hash houses are licensed and taxed—and, having wrapped up domestic issues, they had plenty of time to ponder their role on the planet. Cerebral sorts, fond of debate, the Dutch love chatting through the night in candlelit restaurants, solving all the world's problems—even if nobody's listening.

> *Licensed cannabis cafés first appeared in the 1970s. The idea was to sepa-rate soft drugs from hard ones. Better to buy small amounts of hash from tax-paying café owners, the Dutch reasoned, than from street criminals who also peddle heroin and cocaine. The Dutch say the tolerant approach works. Relatively few of their youth smoke the herbaceous substances, and the proportion of those using hard drugs is negligible. Rates for all drug use are lower than in the United States. A 1997 study from the University of Amsterdam found that only 16 percent of the Dutch had ever tried cannabis, despite its wide availability, while 33 percent of Americans had; 4.5 percent of Dutch used marijuana at least once a month, compared to 9 percent of Americans. Later studies showed the same: Dutch cannabis use was about half of that in countries where it's illegal—perhaps information for American "war on drug" bureaucrats to put in their pipes and smoke.*

GLOBAL WEIGHT

Once a fearsome colonizer and maritime power, the Netherlands isn't the global power monger she used to be. With 16 million residents and a landmass that fits into France fifteen times, the country no longer has a booming voice in Europe or on the world stage. But the country has found weightiness in her new role as global justice center. The Netherlands is home to the UN International Court of Justice (the UN's judicial organ), the UN-sponsored International Criminal Court (an independent war crimes court), and international criminal tribunals, including the one that tried Yugoslavia's Slobodan Milosevic. She also flexes serious financial muscle with the banks Fortis, ABN-AMRO, and ING—and Royal Dutch/Shell is the world's second largest petroleum company. Philips Electronic and Unilever also add billions to the GDP.

The Netherlands, home to many philanthropists, is one of the world's highest per capita foreign-aid donors.

Much of the Netherlands is an anachronism: residents bike down cobbled streets or skate across icy canals to their jobs in the winter. Cities are architecturally old world, but have modern public transport; towns are pedestrian zones where shops sell warm-from-the-roaster coffee and jam bubbling away in copper pots—and shop owners still live upstairs. Wherever you are, you can count on one thing: the Dutch put their trash out in an orderly fashion—in the correct bags, on the right days. That's just how things work around here.

GEOGRAPHICAL CONFUSION: THE NETHERLANDS VS. HOLLAND VS. THE LOW COUNTRIES

Officially called the Netherlands, the country is also (erroneously) known as Holland. In fact, there are two Hollands: North Holland holds Amsterdam and, South Holland contains political headquarters the Hague (Den Haag)—but they are only two of the Netherlands' twelve provinces. Back when the catchy name was the United Provinces of the Protestant Netherlands, mapmakers may have found that it was easier to fit "Holland" on the map. The area was also called the Low Countries, since much sits below sea level; until 1830, Belgium and Luxembourg were bundled in the "Low Countries" package.

The popular image of an evolved society with all wheels smoothly turning recently had a wrench thrown into it. Suddenly, issues from immigration to renegade royals and—what?!—high-profile murders are rattling what long has appeared to be one of Europe's mellowest lands. With mosques and churches burning, the typically sedate Dutch found themselves with plenty of new debating to do, namely how to defuse a situation that, in late 2004, suddenly seemed to hold the makings of Europe's first religious war in four centuries. What struck the match was a most unlikely phenomenon in this permissive country: being killed for self-expression.

THEO VAN GOGH AND THE TEN MINUTES THAT ROCKED THE COUNTRY

Nobody can say that barrel-chested filmmaker Theo van Gogh—great-grandson of Vincent's brother—wasn't pushing it. Known for being blunt, the director was also racist. The group he most disliked were Muslims; he'd speared them in his newspaper columns and mocked them in his book, *Allah Knows Best*. But Van Gogh's most infamous work, a forceful ten-minute film called *Submission*, brought a backlash never before seen. The film, written by Dutch parliamentarian Ayaan Hirsi Ali—who, being of Somali descent, was born Muslim—told of routine abuses to Muslim women, the ritual of clitoral removal being one. Van Gogh didn't just make his point—he made it in a manner pointedly offensive to Muslims. In the most controversial scene, a Muslim wife describes abuse by her husband and his family (her brother-in-law raped her) while the screen shows a woman, shrouded in transparent veil; under it, viewers see her naked body covered in writing, detailing the Koran's many punishments for females. After *Submission* was broadcast on Dutch state TV in August 2004, both Van Gogh and Hirsi Ali were bombarded with death threats. Hirsi Ali hired armed security. Van Gogh didn't. On November 2, 2004, a man bicycled up to the filmmaker on an Amsterdam street, shot him half a dozen times, slit his throat, stabbed him, and, with the bloody knife, slammed a note into his chest that warned that the United States, Europe, the Netherlands, and Hirsi Ali would all "go down."

Van Gogh's slaying prompted the coolheaded Dutch to blow up. They hit the streets, banging pots and pans, yelling for vindication, and mourning the death of an era when they could safely speak their minds. Flames darted through mosques and a bomb exploded in a Muslim school. Radical Muslims retaliated, torching Christian churches and targeting Dutch schools. Violence continued for weeks as an issue came to full boil, namely, the problem of immigrants who don't want to assimilate, who drain the system, and who resort to crime—and who are increasingly putting the Dutch system under siege. And that's where politician Pim Fortuyn, a friend of Van Gogh's, enters the story. He was the one, say the Dutch, who first put his finger on the place that hurt.

As in Germany and Scandinavia, many immigrants from Turkey and Morocco were initially invited to the Netherlands as "guest workers" to perform menial labor during the economic boom of the 1960s and 1970s.

Given the Netherlands' previous sensitivity to ethnic and religious issues—prohibition of discrimination is the first item in the Dutch constitution—the world was agog when a bald, openly gay dandy pushed into the Dutch political scene and unleashed a slew of attention-grabbing sound bites and radical ideas. The Netherlands was "all full up"—"16 million is enough!" announced Pim Fortuyn, a former sociology professor turned political candidate and columnist from Rotterdam, the city that houses most of the foreign-born population. The country needed to bolt the door to immigrants, who were fueling a crime wave, opined Fortuyn; Muslims were disruptive, he said, calling Islam "a backward culture," unkind to women,

Pim Fortuyn shook up the PC

intolerant of gays. So outrageous were his pronouncements that the "Livable Netherlands" Party (which Fortuyn headed) quickly kicked him out. No problem: Fortuyn started his own party, Lijst Fortuyn, with a platform that was progay, prodrugs, proeuthanasia, anticrime, and against allowing 30,000 asylum seekers into the country each year.

PIM FORTUYN: STIRRING IT UP

The Dutch government is known for three things: compromise, compromise, and compromise. None of the country's half-dozen major political parties typically wins a majority, so odd coalitions form that compromise themselves right out. So plodding is the political scene that jaws dropped open in 2001, when mouthy Pim Fortuyn muscled his way in front of the cameras, wearing slick Italian suits, puffing cigars, and raising an issue that nobody else dared mention. The typically PC Dutch squirmed uncomfortably when the candidate put the spotlight on immigrants, saying many were welfare leeches, criminals, and illiterate in the Dutch language—ideas too sensitive to discuss before, even if government reports bore out some of his claims.[2] Fortuyn didn't endorse sending immigrants back, but he didn't want many more—and he wanted Dutch life preserved, as made plain in his book, *Against the Islamization of Our Culture*. "I am also in favor of a cold war with Islam," he said.[3] Even stranger than the emergence of this un-PC candidate was the fact that the Dutch were attentively listening. For months leading up to the April 2002 elections, few talked of anything but Pim, the country's most colorful candidate ever, who baited Muslim imams into insulting him and flounced out of TV interviews. Just before the election, the man who so riled up the country was shot down in broad daylight as he left a radio station. The Dutch were shocked to the bone—not only by the assassination, something that hadn't happened to a politician in the Netherlands since the seventeenth century, but by the assassin. The killer was not a Turk or Moroccan, but a young, soft-spoken vegetarian named Volkert van der Graaf—a homegrown white Dutch man. And Van der Graaf wasn't even religiously motivated. Fortuyn had promised a seat in his party to a prominent mink farmer, whom the gunman believed mistreated animals. He may have killed the politician, but he didn't shut him up. Fortuyn talks even from the grave, perhaps even more effectively than when he was alive. In the past century, only Hitler has affected the country more.

Fortuyn's death didn't hurt his showing. That April, his party took 17 percent of the vote, forming a coalition with the parliamentary winners, the conservative Christian Democrats. That government crumbled within 100 days—the belligerent Lijst Fortuyn members blocked progress—and in the 2003 election they lost two-thirds of their parliamentary seats. Nevertheless, the issues Fortuyn lit up are now burning: under Prime Minister Balkenende, the government slammed the brakes on immigration; failed asylum seekers are being deported, and Rotterdam is banning poor immigrants from moving in. "Multiculturalism" is a dirty word—more so after the death of Van Gogh, who, ironically, had just finished a film about Pim Fortuyn. Van Gogh did more than memorialize the murdered politician; in his death, Van Gogh became a martyr to Fortuyn's cause. And, as if fulfilling Pim's prophecies, radical Muslims are more aggressive than ever. Journalists, politicians, and professors are now under armed guard, after being issued death threats by Islamists. The threats appear to come from a group of some three dozen Muslim radicals known as the Hofstad Group, who are mostly under thirty—some are teenagers. They're not trained terrorists, but nobody doubts their potential danger. They've reportedly planned strikes on nuclear plants, and Van Gogh's killer was one of the gang.

ROTTERDAM: CITY OF THE FUTURE?

Flattened by Nazis during WWII, Rotterdam doesn't fit the quaint image of a Dutch town. In Europe's first city built for cars, the skyline is a glassy assemblage of angles, including architectural oddities such as geometric "cube houses"—diamond-shaped apartments perched on stilts. It also was a magnet for immigrants, partly due to a plethora of government-subsidized housing; over 30 percent of the city's population is now foreign-born. Gangs of immigrant thugs were a big factor in Fortuyn's stance and popularity. And when a government study was released in 2004, saying that if current trends continued, Rotterdam's population would be over 60 percent immigrant, the city council responded with land laws. Those moving to Rotterdam must now have residency permits, which are only granted to Dutch speakers who earn over $11 an hour—a ceiling that many foreign-born workers can't reach. "We have more unemployed people and crime than anywhere else," said Rotterdam city council member Ronald Sorensen, who is Fortuyn's political heir. "If people want to come to Rotterdam they must have a job. If they don't have one, then we don't want them."[4]

Oh, the Netherlands has her problems: crime in cities is rising, Amsterdam is clogged with glassy-eyed tourists, the parliament keeps falling apart, and even when functioning can make an insomniac snore; the Yugoslav and Russian mobs are moving in with their sex slaves, and newcomers use the wrong bags for their rubbish, and put them out on the wrong night. Despite all of this, the Netherlands remains special. Except for the weather—which ranges from goosebump gray to bone-numbingly cold—and except for the expense (laying your head anywhere on this densely packed bit of land isn't cheap), and except for the annoying egalitarian habit of splitting every bill down to the last eurocent (alas, there really is such a thing as "going Dutch") and except for that ever-present Dutch attitude of "We're more evolved than you" (well, maybe they are), the Netherlands may be the best place on the planet— except, of course, that the country is so frighteningly flat. There's just no place else quite like the land of tall skinny buildings peering over canals, where windmills and pot shops exist side by side, and where prostitutes press against glass not far from museums where tourists press up close to take in paintings by the masters. The Netherlands is that rare country where the medieval and modern often coexist in harmony, and where liberal notions spring from pragmatic honesty and acknowledgment of the moneymaking potential of vice.

NEDERLANDS: THE LANGUAGE FACTOR

Gutturally combining about twenty-three letters per word, the Dutch language is neither easy nor romantic—but one won't get a job here without speaking "Nederlands." Some "guest workers" brought in during the 1960s are fluent, but their families often aren't. Since 1998, foreigners who marry Dutch citizens must take yearlong language classes.

> *Vocabulary Builder:* Gedogen, *translated as "closing one's eyes," is a*
> *prominent feature of Dutch tolerance. One example: buying small amounts*
> *of marijuana at pot cafés is condoned, but it's illegal for anyone to supply*
> *the smoke to the café. But nobody looks out for backdoor transactions.*

History Review

For a small, soggy triangle of land, the Netherlands has made a huge splash in the world—and much of her rise came from water. The Dutch set sail in superior ships to pluck the planet's riches; watermills fueled early Dutch industry, gas finds in the North Sea brought much of the country's current wealth. More important: the sea's role in creating a cohesive society. Scarcity of dry turf created a highly organized, efficient society where land is valuable, population is dense, everything is planned, and everyone has a part and a say.

> *"God created the world, and the Dutch created the Netherlands."*
> —Dutch saying

LAYING THE FOUNDATION

The Dutch worked up from lowly beginnings. Over a quarter of Dutch land lies below sea level; for most of history they've been obsessed with pushing back water and creating new land. Early settlers built homes on mounds, minimizing chances they would float away, but in the twelfth century the Dutch launched civil engineering projects that are impressive even today. With a shared enemy in the encroaching sea, villagers worked together to devise clever schemes to keep water out. They stuck logs into marshes and elevated towns; they constructed canals that siphoned high rivers; they designed dykes to keep water back and windmills to pump water into canals. Amazingly, these were simple medieval folk who weren't fulfilling the orders of kings but initiating these clever public works on their own. More astounding: the Dutch not only controlled the surrounding water, they conquered it. Using pumps to dry out bogs, they filled them in, reclaiming the lost territory for farmland, pastures, and housing. For over nine centuries, the Dutch have created new land with the fill-in-the-swamp process they call poldering, which is still responsible for the continuing physical growth of the country today.

Oddly, Iberia was nearly as important as water in shaping the Dutch psyche. In the sixteenth century, the Spanish, Portuguese, and Dutch were all part of the same kingdom, a historical oddity that shows how convoluted the Habsburg Empire had become. Spain and Portugal each presented the Netherlands with something that profoundly altered the Dutch future: one was a zealot, the other a map.

For centuries, the Netherlands was part of the Holy Roman Empire, a grab bag of land that extended from Vienna in all directions across Europe. It wasn't a unified affair. Imperial territories were scattered into principalities and duchies; different corners of the Netherlands were lorded over by mighty counts, dukes, and bishops who didn't heed the Holy Roman Emperor, who typically sat far off in Austria. That changed under Charles V. Born in today's Belgium, he took a great interest in the Netherlands (which then included Belgium and Luxembourg). This was Europe's richest region, thanks to the extensive trade market the Dutch built up, transporting Eastern European grain and Portuguese wines. Because Charles was forever getting into wars, he slapped heavy taxes on the Dutch to fund military escapades.

In 1556, Charles divided his unwieldy empire, appointing his son Philip II as the King of Spain, Portugal, and the Netherlands—and the whole kit and caboodle got a new name: the Spanish Netherlands. Philip moved south to orchestrate from Spain—but tried to replant the Catholic Church in the Protestant Netherlands, then under the sway of Martin Luther and John Calvin. Rejecting Catholicism as too iconic, Dutch Protestants looted Catholic churches in 1566, toppling statues of saints and destroying holy treasures. Philip dispatched fervent Spanish Duke of Alva to take the Spanish Inquisition north. Over seven years, Alva killed tens of thousands of Dutch, nailing them to crosses, burning them at stakes, and cutting off food supplies until there was nothing left to eat but weeds. Alva imposed harsh taxes on everything: property, land transfers, and all sales. This caused the northern provinces of the Netherlands—under the leadership of William the Silent, Prince of Orange—to announce in 1568 that they were leaving the kingdom, and that triggered a war with the Spanish that dragged on for eighty years. Ultimately, the Netherlands won freedom; officially declared in 1581, independence was finally recognized by Spain in 1648.

Through Alva's sadistic attacks, Spain provided the impetus for the Netherlands to become independent, but Portugal provided something that led to spectacular wealth and ruthless domination of the seas. The Portuguese provided the Dutch with directions to the Spice Islands—accidentally.

OPENING UP THE SPICE CABINET

For over a century, the spice trade was dominated by the Portuguese, for a simple reason: only they knew the location of the Spice Islands (in today's

Indonesia) and other Asian trade centers for aromatics, and the Portuguese had no intention of parting with that valuable information. Enter Dutchman Jan Huygen van Linschoten, who wormed his way into employment on Portuguese trading ships, where he snooped through the secret archives, copying the treasured Portuguese information. In 1596, a Dutch publisher brought out *Itinerario*, van Linschoten's map-filled treasure book, which included detailed navigational charts. He might as well have published a map to El Dorado and Shangri-la. *Itinerario* launched a trade revolution: every Dutchman and his brother headed for the East Indies, and so did nearly everybody else, once the book was translated into their languages.

Dutch cities hired crews that raced towards the East Indies, but nutmeg and pepper soon flooded the market, deflating profits. Again the Dutch spirit of cooperation prevailed: the separate cities bonded together to form the East Indies Trading Company (VOC) in 1602. With power to acquire land, form colonies, negotiate treaties, and run its own army, the VOC was a state within a state. It was such a vicious operation that it's surprising the Dutch can talk about that era without wincing. It's not surprising, however, that in 2002, when the Dutch held a celebration of the four-hundredth anniversary of the VOC, the Indonesian ambassador refused to attend, saying the VOC days marked Indonesia's nadir.

WHAT PRICE SPICE?

Forget romantic notions of tropical islands with breezes perfumed by cinnamon and cloves. In the seventeenth century, when the Dutch launched their mad quest for the flavors that added zest to desserts and masked rotten meat, they opened up one of the most brutal chapters in history. The cruelty began on Dutch ships heading east. Allotted a chunk of bread, a round of cheese, and a bottle of water for the entire three-month voyage, many sailors died en route. Heaven forbid any rowdiness broke out: whoever instigated a brawl had his hand nailed to the mast or was pulled under the ship until his neck snapped.[5] The Dutch were even crueler to the Asians who grew the spices they coveted. Welcoming parties that canoed out to greet them with gifts were blasted to smithereens; inhabitants who didn't want to play the Dutch way—to accept low pay and trade only with the Dutch—were slaughtered. Never mind the teachings of Calvin or of humanist philosopher Erasmus, forget the idea of the evolved Dutch, once they left home turf: the 15,000 inhabitants of the nutmeg-rich Banda Islands were wiped out when they wouldn't guarantee a monopoly; 10,000 Chinese were eliminated when they threatened a rebellion on Java; some 30,000 were killed on Sulawesi, and another 100,000 were massacred on Sumatra.[6] They didn't have to touch the inhabitants of Bali: most killed themselves when the Dutch first set foot on their island. The Dutch also ran out the Portuguese and the British, burning and boiling them to ensure the Dutch retained a monopoly on spice.

The VOC went belly-up in 1798, but the Dutch folded most of what is today's Indonesia—and which was called then the Dutch East Indies—into their empire, which expanded further into Asia and into the Americas and Africa.

Back in the Netherlands, few had a clue what the VOC was up to abroad; all they saw were the treasures and the skyrocketing riches. A wealthy merchant class blossomed in the seventeenth century, and the country's religious freedom attracted everyone from French Huguenots to Portuguese Jews. The Netherlands was the only place in Europe where your station in life wasn't defined by birth: more important was your financial worth. The booming overseas trade and rise of the bourgeoisie triggered a golden age. Dutch women strolled the streets wearing Indian textiles, chintz, and Chinese silk. Ships hauled back stunning Oriental screens, tea sets of bone china, delicate Japanese flowers, and elaborate sculptures of teak. The fragrant spices—Javanese pepper, Ceylonese cinnamon, sassafras, ginger, and nutmeg—were only some of the faraway foods that made the Netherlands the best place to feast. In the land known for chewy breads, creamy cheese, butter, and every sort of fruit, vegetable, and meat, the Dutch could also polish off French wines, German beers, Caribbean coffee, Indian teas sweetened with sugar from Brazil, as well as Polish grain, and olives, dates, and figs from the Mediterranean.[7]

NIEUW NETHERLAND

The Dutch settled key areas of New York after hiring English navigator Henry Hudson, the first European to stumble upon the river he named after himself. Claiming the land in 1609, they liked the location—and liked the beavers even more; the rodents were then the rage for coats. Fort Orange is today's Albany; Wiltwyck is Kingston; and today's Manhattan, purchased from local Indians for sixty guilder, was New Amsterdam to the Dutch, who developed Broadway, ahem, as "Gentlemen's Street." The English snatched New Netherland in 1630, at the end of yet another Anglo-Dutch War, changing the name to New York; the Dutch got South American territory Suriname out of the deal. Long gone are most of the stunning wood houses the Dutch erected during their seventeenth-century stay, but a few names remain: among them, Haarlem and Staaten Island, the land named for Dutch Parliament, the Staaten Generaal.

The era was ripe for inventions and discoveries in unknown realms. Astronomer Christian Huygens invented the pendulum clock and identified Saturn's rings; Anton van Leeuwenhoek delved into cellular biology, after first inventing the microscope; Dutch scientist Cornelius Drebbel whipped up a perpetual-motion machine and the world's first submarine.[8] And sixteenth-century Dutch society went nutty for cut flowers, previously cultivated only for medicinal purposes.

ANOTHER STOLEN BEGINNING

Far more than simply a flower to the pragmatic Dutch, the tulip is a bulb. Sure, the countryside of mustard yellows and inky purples plays sweetly to the eyes, as do the markets where the brilliantly striped and subtly mottled blooms go for a pittance. But real money comes from the paper-wrapped progenitor, the onion-like bulb, sales of which bring in $700 million a year. The flower that's now a Dutch symbol didn't originate here; the tulip first poked up in Turkey. It ended up in Holland after the Ottoman Empire gave a gift to an Austrian ambassador, who took the beauties to Vienna's Imperial Garden. Botanist Carolus Clusius, who ran Vienna's garden, took a job at the prestigious University of Leiden in 1593, and planted a plot of them. His horticultural research soon became talk of the town. The wealthy started adorning their tables with cut blossoms, but Clusius refused to part with his precious blooms, no matter the price. Unable to bribe him, schemers simply dug up his bulbs from the beds, launching the tulip industry with their late-night theft. Because there were so few, the Dutch grew obsessed in their desire to possess them, and the value of the tulip bulb shot up, at one point reaching about $2,000 each. Speculators jumped in, and entire fortunes were made and lost during a few frenzied years in the 1630s now called Tulipmania—an era when the tulip was known as "the flower that drove men mad." Their insanity cost them: when the bottom dropped out, it had nearly the effect of the 1929 stock market crash.

The Dutch now cultivate some 3,500 tulip varieties, selling bulbs at much more reasonable prices.

The trademark of the Dutch golden age is the elegantly realistic style of painting that appeared in lobbies and drawing rooms. Wall-size portraits of militias and literary clubs replaced paintings of bleeding Christ and haloed saints as the merchant class replaced the Church as the main commissioners of art. Landscapes, cozy domestic interiors, and portraits hung from walls, even in middle-class dwellings; "Everyman" could buy art directly from the artist's studio or purchase affordable prints in markets—the first time that high-quality art trickled down to the masses.

* * *

Of all the Dutch masters—a group that includes Flemish artists Rubens, Van Dyck, and Pieter Brueghel (see "Belgium," page 105)—the most sought after of that era are Rembrandt and Vermeer, though in lifestyle the two couldn't have been less alike. Rembrandt (1606–1669) was flamboyant, well-regarded, and wealthy (albeit fleetingly) in his day, painting militias, as in *The Nightwatch* (1642), or portraits of Amsterdam's elite. Rembrandt was so in demand that he opened studios and instructed dozens of apprentices to imitate his style. Lesser-known, quiet Johannes Vermeer (1632–1675), now famous for his *Girl with the Pearl Earring*, lived in Delft, where his main client was but one wealthy merchant, and Vermeer's money was tight. Both artists turned their attention to daily life in the Dutch home, capturing spiritual beauty in the mundane, and both experimented with light and oil-rich paint that imparted a special sheen. Rembrandt, however, left us with some 600 paintings, 300 etchings, and thousands of drawings—although who knows how many are actually fakes. Vermeer worked more slowly, producing at most forty works, perhaps because he was often frolicking with his wife, who bore him fifteen offspring. And while Rembrandt painted over sixty self-portraits, no one is sure what Vermeer looked like. Both artists died in poverty and both would no doubt be astounded at the millions of dollars their paintings fetch today.

Civilized at home, the Dutch continued to be obnoxious at sea. By 1672, everybody was so sick of their high-handed acts that England, France, and German states attacked the Netherlands. Despite treaties, problems continued, especially with the British, who temporarily wrested away Dutch colonies in Asia. A bigger headache loomed on the horizon. Napoleon invaded in 1795, installing his brother Louis as ruler in 1806. That only lasted four years, but Louis made lasting changes, including founding the Rijksmuseum, where the works of the Dutch masters now hang.

When Napoleon fell, the Netherlands reassembled herself as a monarchy, but in 1830, Belgium and Luxembourg, which were mostly Catholic, pulled away taking a major chunk of land and much of the population. (See "Belgium," page 112.) Not to worry—besides holdings in the Americas, including Suriname and the Dutch Antilles, the Dutch clung to most of the East Indies (Indonesia), an area that increased their land holdings fifty-fold.

> *The northern part of the Netherlands is mostly Protestant; the southern part remains mostly Catholic and more demonstrative—for the Dutch.*

Successfully declaring neutrality in the First World War, the Dutch tried the same tactic again in WWII, but it didn't work. On May 10, 1940, Nazis attacked, soon occupying the country. The Dutch made efforts to hide Jews, but of the 140,000 Jews who lived there prewar, only 20,000 survived to its end, a source of lingering Dutch guilt. The Netherlands also lost the Dutch East Indies when the Japanese occupied the archipelago in 1941. The Dutch assumed that the islands would come back after the war, but the islanders had other ideas: a nationalist movement had taken root, and they proclaimed independence in 1945 as Indonesia. The frantic Dutch shipped out the military in the "Police Actions," during which they killed an estimated 100,000 Indonesians over four years.[9] The United States finally threatened to cut all Marshall Plan funding unless the Netherlands recognized Indonesian sovereignty, which they did in 1949. The events of those ruthless Police Actions are still coming out today.[10]

Typically coolheaded and rational, many Dutch are strangely emotional and irrational about Indonesia. To even talk about the Police Actions and the loss of the Dutch East Indies is to hit upon a national quirk. Another sore point: Srebrenica. When the details of the botched 1995 Bosnian peacekeeping effort emerged in 2002, the shocked Dutch parliament simply walked out.

SREBRENICA

In 1995, while serving as UN peacekeepers in the Bosnian town of Srebrenica, Dutch soldiers allowed Bosnian Serbs to take away Muslim men and boys, after being given assurances that the Muslims wouldn't be harmed. A slaughter ensued. In 2002, the Dutch government issued its report on the matter, stating that at least 7,000 Muslims were killed despite being under Dutch protection. The report faulted both the government, for sending in peacekeepers without adequate arms, and the Dutch military, which tried to hush up the affair.

Like Austria, Switzerland, and Scandinavia, the Netherlands accepted many Bosnians and other former Yugoslavian refugees during and after the war.

Hot Spots

Amsterdam: Ringed with canals that circle past some of the most eye-pleasing architecture on the planet, Amsterdam is also riddled with vice, much of it legal. Alas, Russian and Yugoslav mobs are moving in; some unconfirmed reports say over half of Amsterdam's bars and cafés are paying them for "protection."

Rembrandthuis: Now a museum, the five-story house on Amsterdam's Breestraat was Rembrandt's curse. A financial stretch, the home he'd bought with wife, Saskia, was where she died the next year giving birth to his son. House payments broke his piggy bank; this house was part of the reason that Rembrandt died a pauper.

Rotterdam: Site of the world's biggest port—80,000 seagoing ships and 110,000 barges call at the port of Rotterdam every year.[17] The Netherlands' second largest city is a major commercial hub. Whereas the most important cargoes were once Indonesian coffee and sweet-smelling spices, incoming ships today may carry drugs and slaves into this major smuggling point into Europe.

The Hague (Den Haag): Dutch special criminal tribunal prosecutor Carla del Ponte got off easy when Slobodan Milosevic died in his cell here—months before hearing his verdict on sixty-six counts of genocide, crimes against humanity, and war crimes involving the 1990s conflicts in the former Yugoslavia. Dutch (and UN) investigators say cause of death was a heart attack; Milosevic's family claims he was poisoned. Also controversial: the newly opened International Criminal Court, which the Bush administration refuses to endorse, since U.S. officials and military fear they might be tried as war criminals; U.S. aid to foreign countries now bears a clause that U.S.-related grievances won't end up here. Ironic, then, that President Bush's demands that Charles Taylor be tried in the Hague resulted in the Liberian being the ICC's first case.

Friesland: At this northernmost outpost, they speak a language unintelligible anywhere else, mustard-making is a local art, and the passion is to trek across the Wadden Sea that turns into sticky mudflats at low tide.

Maastricht: Limestone caves snaking underground are equipped as civil defense shelters, complete with ovens for baking bread and chapels for breaking it. Above ground, the town where European leaders decided to create the euro is brimming with fantastic medieval architecture and fancy castle restaurants. (See photo, page 186.)

Hotshots

Jan Peter Balkenende: With round glasses and a perpetual boyishness, the forty-seven-year-old prime minister/religious philosophy professor is often likened to Harry Potter, although he hasn't worked any magic on his government. During his cursed tenure, immigration woes blew sky high, the queen's husband, Claus, died, as did filmmaker Van Gogh, and the royals have been embroiled in scandals. The Christian Democrat opposes euthanasia, gay marriage, and hash houses, and has slowed flow of immigrants.

The United States insisted she didn't want any UN help on Iraq, but the Bush administration threw Balkenende into the UN ring in 2004 to announce that the U.S. had changed her mind. He sent over 1,200 Dutch troops to help reconstruct Iraq.

Queen Beatrix Wilhelmina Armgard (b. 1938): Monarch, 1980–present. Beloved and benign, Queen Beatrix of the House of Orange inherited the position passed down from William the Silent, who beat back the Spanish and unified the country five centuries ago. Reportedly the world's richest monarch—the family denies articles claiming she's worth about $3 billion[11]—she hasn't had to do much except fret about whom the kids plan to marry—and with all the fuss lately, you'd think she'd pay them to elope. Beatrix caused a scandal in her day by marrying Claus von Amsberg, a handsome German diplomat, in 1966, when the sting of World War II was still fresh. Despite being German by birth, Claus, who died in 2002, was also quite popular.

Prince Bernhard (1911–2004): Father of Queen Beatrix, German-born Bernhard was a major international player: he founded the secretive Bilderberg Group in 1954 and later founded the World Wildlife Fund. He was also involved in scandals, most notably in 1976 when he accepted some $1 million from U.S. aircraft manufacturer Lockheed to sway the Dutch government to order from them.

Johan Friso (b. 1968): Beatrix's middle son, Johan Friso, was long sus-

Courtesy of Netherlands Tourism Board, New York

Maastricht: Birthplace of the euro

pected of being homosexual, but proved otherwise when he began dating Mabel Wisse in 2003. No sooner had marriage plans been put on the table than the media dished out rumors that Mabel had dated the Netherlands' biggest drug baron. Worse, both Johan and Mabel lied about it to parliament. The prince gave up any shot at the crown when he wed his beloved Dutch jewel.

Crown Prince Willem-Alexander: Heir apparent. Likable Prince Willem-Alexander (b. 1967) was a bit of a playboy before he married Argentine beauty Máxima Zorreguieta in 2002. That marriage, too, caused a furor: Máxima's father was a minister in Argentina's 1970s military junta; Papa wasn't invited to the royal wedding.

VINCENT VAN GOGH (1853–1890)

Everybody knows he was a tortured creator who hacked off his ear, and that his love of absinthe may have been the reason his palette was so verdant and bright. But who knew that Dutchman Vincent van Gogh signed works with his first name, because so few could pronounce "Gogh" (rhymes with "lock")?[12] Or that he may have sired a child with a prostitute whom he wanted to marry?[13] The former preacher, whom the church asked to put down his Bible because he was thumping it too fervently, actually did have some friends—Toulouse-Lautrec among them—despite his incessant talking that drove many mad. Van Gogh had a dream: to start an artists' colony in Provence. That's how the Dutch painter ended up in the yellow house in Arles, where Gauguin came to stay for six weeks in 1888, during which time Van Gogh whipped up a whopping forty paintings while Gauguin churned out twenty. Cranky Van Gogh chased after Gauguin with a razor, but decided instead to slash off his own ear. He duly presented the bloody ear to his beloved at the nearby brothel—she fainted in response—and from that point on Vincent spent most of his time in a nearby asylum. "Vincent was hospitalized," wrote Gauguin. "He wants to sleep with the patients, chases the nurses, and washed himself in the coal-bucket."[14] His mental health deteriorating, Van Gogh shot himself in 1890; some say that his French physician, Dr. Gachet, was next to his bed, sketching Van Gogh when he passed away, and that Gachet sneaked out carrying several mysterious boxes, which some believe contained Van Gogh's notebooks.[15] Although the artist exhibited in only four shows while alive—selling only one painting—Van Gogh's posthumous success is the result of his sister-in-law Johanna, devoted wife of his brother, Theo. Johanna held on to Van Gogh's paintings, which, during his lifetime, were shrugged off as the works of a madman, which, admittedly, they were.

Curiosity: Most of the U.S. flight schools where the September 11 hijackers trained were owned by Dutchmen who don't know how to fly themselves.

Cees Nooteboom: Travel columnist, novelist, playwright, and poet known for such works as *The Roads to Santiago* and *All Souls' Day*, Nooteboom (b. 1933) is the best shot for a Nobel prize.

Paul Verhoeven: Director of twenty films, he bounces around in styles: *Soldier of Orange* was an acclaimed historical drama about the Dutch Resistance; *Basic Instinct* was a provocative psychological thriller; *Robocop* was schlock. Now he's delving into mysteries, specifically *One Step Behind* by Henning Mankell.

SHELL GAME

Royal Dutch/Shell—a Dutch-Anglo enterprise that made over $306 billion in 2005[16]—likes to advertise itself as the jolly green-friendly giant of oil, but that's whitewash. The company's most questionable dealings focus on Nigeria, where the petrol giant's heavily polluting operations leak almost 10,000 barrels of petroleum a year.[17] Royal Dutch/Shell has been accused of bribing officials,[18] supporting government attacks on whomever threatens the oil biz, and is allegedly implicated in the 1995 government-ordered hanging of eight Nigerian activists, including writer Ken Saro-Wiwa, who denounced the oil company's sloppy operations. In 2002, Nigerian operations were temporarily shut down by local women called the Mamas, who demanded the company give jobs to their husbands and sons, clean up the petrol-soaked ground, and extend electricity across the road to their villages. Shell called police and the showdown turned ugly: the women's group claims several female protesters disappeared and are believed to be dead. In January 2004, Royal Dutch/Shell admitted that, whoops, it had overstated oil reserves by 20 percent. Shareholders are furious about the 4.5 billion barrels of oil that apparently aren't really there.

Desiderius Erasmus: Scholar of the Dutch Renaissance, professor Erasmus (1466–1536) translated the New Testament, wrote assorted books and essays, and is described as a humanist. Hard to tell, given his scathing assessment of Dutchmen in his 1509 book *The Praise of Folly*: "[Dutch merchants] lie, perjure themselves, steal, cheat and mislead the public. Nevertheless . . . there is no lack of flattering friars to kowtow to them and call them Right Honorable in public. The motive of the friars is clear: they are after some of the loot . . . Perhaps it would be wise to pass over the theologians in silence. . . . They behave as if they are already in heaven; they look down pityingly on other men as so many worms."[19]

DRINKING MATTERS

The Dutch accidentally invented grape-based brandy: When a sixteenth-century shipper ordered that water be evaporated from Bordeaux to pack more onto ships, he created *brandewijn*—"burnt wine"—in the process. However, the sexiest Dutch contribution to the bar shelf is potent genever. The Dutch claim that it cures jet lag, knocks the nip out of winter, and is an alcoholic Viagra—and it's the libation poured out to celebrate weddings, holidays, and births. Similar to gin when young, genever doesn't stop there: special "genever bars" are brimming with neon-colored varieties flavored with coffee, cocoa, cinnamon, berries, and plums and decorated with rose petals or glittering flakes of real gold and silver. The dazzling colors and high-octane content (which gets you woozy fast) lend themselves to festivity, as does the centuries-old ritual for drinking genever: you must take the first sip from the glass—without hands—while bending over the bar.

News you can understand: Radio Netherlands runs a site that keeps one abreast of current events—and history—in English: www.radionetherlands.nl

10. AUSTRIA
(Österreich)
Dancing at the Edge

FAST FACTS

Country:	Republic of Austria; Republik Österreich
Capital:	Vienna (Wien)
Government:	Federal republic
Independence:	1156 Duchy of Austria founded; 1866 pushed out of German Federation; 1918 Republic proclaimed; 1955 independent of post-WWII Allied occupation
Population:	8,193,000 (2006 estimate)
Head of State:	President Heinz Fischer (2004)
Head of Government:	Chancellor Wolfgang Schüssel (2000)
Elections:	President elected by direct popular vote, six-year term; chancellor appointed from majority party by president
Name of Parliament:	Federal Assembly; Bundesversammlung
Ethnicity:	91% Austrian; 4% former Yugoslavs (Croat, Slovene, Serbs, Bosniaks); 2% Turk; 2% other; 1% German

Religion:	74% Roman Catholic; 12% none; 5% Protestant; 5% Muslim; 4% other
Language:	German
Literacy:	98%
Famous Exports:	Croissant, waltzing, Hitler
Economic Big Boy:	OMV (gas and oil); 2004 total sales: $9.62 billion[1]
Per Capita GDP:	$32,900 (2005 estimate)
Unemployment:	5.2% (January 2006 Eurostat figure)
Percentage in Poverty:	6% (2004 estimate)
EU Status:	Member since 1995; politically sanctioned for seven months in 2000
Currency:	Euro

Quick Tour

From Vienna's gleaming baroque palaces, topped with golden-winged sculptures, to the snowy hills of the Tirol, where skiers bundle into farmhouses for hot schnapps, from the medieval Christmas markets in Ganz to Carinthia's crystalline lakes and valleys filled with church steeples stretching towards God, Österreich is the old world personified. The land the Habsburgs built up as imperial headquarters is considered more German than Germany—even Austria's language is closer to true Germanic roots—and Austria is locked in her past.

THE COFFEEHOUSE

Whether you're sitting in a velvet chair in an austere, dark-paneled café, or at a sweet shop brimming with shiny chocolates, raisin-stuffed pastries, and candied violets in old fashioned tins, a coffee in Vienna is always a production. As though destined for royalty, it's served in fine china and delivered on a silver tray alongside a sweet, miniature pitcher of thick cream, small glass of water, and bowl of decorative sugar lumps—and whether you ordered a mélange, a cappucino, or a brauner, it usually comes slathered with a mountain of whipped cream. It might cost $4; it might cost $8. But that seems a trifle to soak in the artistry and high culture of this land, famous for Haydn's exacting symphonies, the lilting works of Mozart, Gustav Klimt's paintings of liquid gold, Sigmund Freud's heady analysis, and the waltzes of Johann Strauss. The European coffeehouse came to life here (after attacking Turks brought coffee beans), serving as center of literature and political discussion—and Vienna still emanates the brooding spirit of a self-absorbed artist: everywhere you look,

> moody pale-faced young people are carrying violins and cellos, most wearing the pained look of deep thinkers composing symphonies in their heads as they contemplate the coffee set before them.

Waiters still address customers as "sir" or "madam" in the chandeliered coffeehouses, where wall-sized portraits of royalty still hang—and where Austrians still while away hours reading newspapers of the world. At the annual Opera Ball, gentlemen in tailcoats still kiss the hands of ladies in puffy gowns before requesting a dance, and the countryside's wine gardens—*heurigen*—still serve the local plonk with sausage and cheese just as they have for a thousand years. Sunday is still the day when Austrians stroll in nature, as has been their habit for centuries; every day of the week, Mozart masterpieces still float through the alpine air in his hometown Salzburg (still as lovely as when he lived there), and every December 31, tens of thousands waltz to Strauss's *Blue Danube* in the squares.

ANTINUCLEAR AUSTRIA

Despite her reputation for being stuffy, bureaucratic, and entrenched in another era, Austria is progressive in many ways. In 1978, Austria outlawed nuclear power and is still vehemently antinuke: road signs indicate how many miles away one is from Chernobyl and from Czech nuclear plant, Temelin—a symbol of the Soviet legacy of shoddy plants. Austrians frequently demonstrate against the Czech plant, sometimes shutting down the border between the two countries in protest. Austria's righteousness is a bit hypocritical since Austria does receive electricity from nuclear power; energy from Hungary's nuclear plants is transmitted to Austria via electrical grids.

But for all the jewels of her history—the pageantry, enduring rituals, and architectural treasures—Austria is still remembered for her Nazi past—a shadow that lingers and a trapdoor that keeps opening no matter what Austria does to obscure it. Which is why what happened in 2000 caused a worldwide shock, the tremors of which are still felt.

READING BETWEEN THE LINES OF CENTRIFUGAL FORCES AND INEXORABLE PRESSURES

Austria's discomfort with her past is obvious in this strange summary of history from the Austrian Embassy site, which glosses over Austria's role in the two major wars that defined her:[2]

"In 1867 Emperor Franz Joseph acceded to demands for the creation of the Double Monarchy of Austria-Hungary. This conglomerate entity disintegrated at the end of the First World War, not least as a result of the centrifugal forces of nationalist self-assertion. Now the rump of what had once been an empire, Austria was proclaimed a Republic in 1918. But reduced to the dimension of a small state, it had difficulty finding its place in the new European order. In 1938 Austria succumbed to the inexorable pressures of Hitler's Germany and internal instability. With the help of the Allied Powers, Austria was revived as a Republic in 1945 but remained occupied by the armies of France, Britain, the Soviet Union and the United States until 1955 . . ."

As a result of World War I, which she initiated with Germany, the Austrian Empire lost her monarchy and 87 percent of her territory. As a result of World War II, during which Austria physically joined Nazi Germany and fought on the Nazi side, Austria was occupied by Allied forces for ten years and was forced to become officially neutral.

Since 1955, when Allied occupiers shoved off, Austria has in many ways been a model country. For instance, the government directly involves the people in decision making: *sozialpartnerschaft*, trade unions, corporate heads, farmers, economists, think tanks, and academics all work to shape national economic strategy. In the postwar era, Austria soared as one of Europe's most affluent countries, with nary a corruption scandal to show for it—and the European Union welcomed Austria as a member in 1995. Neutral Austria, edged by Communist countries, was the door to the free West—and welcomed many who escaped from Communism. Two hundred thousand Hungarians fled here after the Revolution of 1956; about 162,000 Czechs and Slovaks arrived after 1968's Prague Spring frosted over, 150,000 Poles showed up when Solidarity was banned in 1981; and a quarter of a million Russian Jews came through en route to Israel between 1973 and 1989. Fleeing civil war, 100,000 Bosniaks arrived in the 1990s, along with tens of thousands of other former Yugoslavians. Some moved on, but many stayed: 12 percent of Austrian citizens are foreign-born—one of the highest proportions in Europe—and over 700,000 temporary workers are from other countries.[3]

The Austrian government was the first to alert the world to the genocide in Bosnia during the 1990s.

But Austria usually doesn't make news for her generosity—her humanitarian "Neighbor in Need" funding during the Yugoslavian war, for example, or the Life Ball, Europe's biggest annual fundraiser for AIDS. The country remembered for starting World War I (with Germany) and then again embracing Germany as a World War II partner typically snags headlines only when she's done something else wrong. Most recently, that mistake came in the form of loudmouthed Jörg Haider. In 2000, the leader of the ultraconservative and nationalist Freedom Party—who had praised Nazis—leapt into national politics after garnering over a quarter of the Austrian vote. Austria soon found herself in the international dog house, collared with political sanctions and kicked around like a stray—and the experience still haunts Austria today.

HAIDER'S HOT AIR

Jörg Haider (pronounced HY-der) ain't shy.[4] The Porsche-driving, bungee-jumping, designer-clothes-wearing son of two Hitler enthusiasts first captured the attention of former Nazis as a teenager who gave rousing speeches lauding Austria's Nazi-supporting role in World War II. Many Austrians prefer to forget that era—or to portray Austria as a helpless victim—but for Haider, the alliance with Hitler's Germany was a source of pride. He joined the hard-right Freedom Party—an offshoot of a party begun by former Nazis—and was leading it by 1986. He began making news as governor of southern state Carinthia. Haider praised Hitler's labor policy, and called former members of the Nazi SS "dear friends" who were "decent people of good character" deserving Austria's "honor and respect." And all hell broke loose when he called concentration camps "punishment camps."[5] For his remarks, which he later retracted, he was ejected from the governor's seat in 1991, but eight years later he was voted back in. This time, he waved a new banner—Austria First—and launched antiforeigner tirades. With Austria's unemployment rate at 5 percent—the highest since the war—many were listening. The country should seal the borders, Haider opined, and send immigrants already there back home. France's Jean-Marie Le Pen had said the same, but Haider was the first elected official to push the idea so loudly while in office—and given his previous pro-Nazi statements, it rang an alarm bell across Europe. And that was before he'd even made a move toward the national arena.

Austrian politics usually work like a well-rehearsed waltz, with the same steps repeated every election. Left-leaning Social Democrats (drawing power from labor) usually win the majority of votes and take the more powerful chancellorship; the right-leaning People's Party (backed by big business and Catholics) usually takes the presidential seat, and the two usually dance together in a ruling coalition that never achieves much—except to keep out other parties. So much for snoozy predictability: in 1999, when Jörg Haider cut in with his radically racist Freedom Party, the music stopped. The world looked on in horror as he crashed Austria's exclusive power soirée. Nabbing a whopping 27 percent of the 1999 parliamentary vote, Haider's party kicked the People's Party to the number three spot. An unforeseen power shuffle ensued—some called it a coup—that tainted Austria's image around the world. That year, the Social Democrats and the People's Party didn't form their usual coalition. Instead, People's Party head Wolfgang Schüssel formed a coalition with Haider's Freedom Party; as a result, Schüssel nabbed the chancellorship, presiding over Austria's first conservative government in thirty years. The response: outrage, starting in Vienna, where thousands of demonstrators went berserk—an unusual event in a country where, until recently, protests rarely occurred.

Inaugurations are sedate affairs in Austria—usually. In February 2000, when Chancellor Schüssel stepped forward at the ceremony in Vienna with new coalition member Jörg Haider, thousands of Austrians blew up, pounding on drums, pushing past the top-hatted bouncers, marching into the ultra-refined Sachers Hotel, and bursting into the National Theatre to disrupt a performance. Protesters pelted police with eggs and attacked trams—and the politicians scurried away from the ceremony using Vienna's famous tunnels. Every Friday for the next year, thousands marched to show their disgust at Jörg Haider.

Austria was globally ostracized. Israel yanked bank her ambassador, as did the U.S. Austria was sneered at across Europe; ties with EU countries were cut and fierce words were exchanged. The European Union "will not behave with this government as if it were a normal government," declared French president Jacques Chirac.[6] "Europe can do without Austria," sniped Belgian foreign minister Louis Michel, declaring it "immoral" to go skiing there.[7] The heat was so intense that Haider quickly stepped down as party head and threw in another Freedom Party member in his place. That didn't appease the EU. Neither did the statement Haider and Schüssel signed denouncing the Nazis and declaring Austria's dedication to human rights. The diplomatic sanctions stayed in place, and Austria's only "sort-of friend," Germany, was not about to protest the matter.

Those working in Austrian tourism dubbed the international frostiness the "Haider Effect," as conventions and tour groups canceled long-held reservations. Tourism typically brings in over $15 billion annually to the country's coffers, representing nearly 7 percent of GDP.[8] That year it didn't.

With diplomatic relations on ice, Austria threatened to veto important EU legislation and withhold EU dues, but that just led to more barking from Brussels. In August 2000, however, the Austrian government announced that it would put some $80 million into a compensation fund for survivors of the Nazi concentration camps—later adding $360 million more for those whose lands had been seized. The EU agreed to lift sanctions. The experience, however, left Austria feeling utterly isolated. With Austria's political arena under international scrutiny, and a matter of lurid fascination to the world's press, Austria did what she'd done during the Kurt Waldheim affair in 1986. First she got angry, then she changed.

REEXAMINATION

Stately Kurt Waldheim, eloquent secretary-general of the United Nations from 1972 to 1981, was a source of pride to his compatriots, the first postwar Austrian to cut such a distinguished presence on the world stage. He returned to Austria to run for president in the mid-1980s, his victory assured on name recognition alone. But when he landed back on home turf, problems began. The press made accusations, never entirely proven, that Waldheim had been far more active with the Nazis than he had admitted. Austrians apparently didn't believe the rumors, or didn't care: in 1986, they voted Waldheim in with a landslide victory. The doors to the international community slammed shut the next day. Formerly one of the most powerful and respected men in the world, President Waldheim didn't dare set foot in the U.S. where he'd been barred entry and placed on the State Department's watch list; the only "country" that welcomed him was the Vatican. Austrians were outraged by the global chill—at first. But ire turned to introspection and soul-searching as Austrians explored what their country's role really had been during "Anschluss," as the 1938 annexation of Austria by Nazi Germany was called; it had been a taboo topic until then. The Waldheim incident triggered debate and belated acknowledgment of Austria's Nazi-supporting role. Schools, which had previously taught history only up until the First World War, encouraged a more open view; writers suggested a certain complicity; and intellectuals pointed out that many in Austria, suffering a national identity crisis after the empire was ripped apart, had wanted to bond with Germany. Austria's part in the Holocaust was acknowledged for the first time and she established her first programs to compensate concentration camp survivors and slave laborers.

Haider, it now seems, was just ahead of his time. His sudden popularity portended the rise of the radical right all over Europe. The man who personified the anti-immigrant right was soon joined by others across Europe: Vlaams Blok in Belgium, Pia Kjaersgaard in Denmark, Pim Fortuyn in the Netherlands, Carl Hagen in Norway, Umberto Bossi in Italy, and the British National Party's Nick Griffin—all heroes to neo-Nazis, who now add the anti-immigrant platform to their anti-Semitism. Public sentiment, however, turned against Haider. In the following election, the Freedom Party took only 10 percent of the vote. In the 2004 election for the European Parliament, it won a scanty 6 percent and lost four of five seats. Haider recently ditched the Freedom Party and started the Alliance for Austria's Future, under the antiglobalization banner. The new party is even less popular. Hard-right Haider, who so shook up Europe and Austria, now looks like a has-been. And that too may foreshadow trends across the Continent.

LOUDLY NOT NAZI

Between Haider and Waldheim and the high-intensity glare of the international spotlight, Austria has indeed changed. She finally came forth with funds for victims of Nazis and admitted to culpability in crimes against humanity that were previously shrugged off. Now Austria is making up for lost time: Austrian headlines all but shout about government acts officially honoring Nazi victims, from gays to women who perished under the regime, and the government is commemorating the late Nazi hunter Simon Wiesenthal, a Vienna resident, by naming a street after him. In fact, Austria is now making headlines for her vehement anti-Nazi stand. Austrian authorities arrested Holocaust denier and British author David Irving for speeches he'd made in which he questioned whether Nazi victims at camps had died in gas chambers. Irving, who'd been invited to Austria by a radical student group to speak in November 2005, is visiting much longer than anticipated. In 2006, he was sentenced to three years for two speeches he gave in 1998—in violation of Austria's 1992 law against "playing down" or "trying to excuse" Nazi crimes in broadcast or print. Even Irving is changing his tune, admitting he was wrong about denying that Auschwitz held gas chambers. But the "Nazi Issue" hasn't gone away. The new leader of the Freedom Party now begins speeches with "Heil."

The latest show stealer is journalist Hans-Peter Martin, a European parliamentarian who grassed on his colleagues in the notoriously wasteful European Parliament. Martin videotaped the reps signing in for Friday's work, then promptly leaving—but claiming that day's pay and the hefty $350 per diem. His colleagues were outraged—and Socialists were so red-faced that the party expelled him. Martin formed his own party, and in the 2004 parliamentary elections he was Austria's biggest winner, pulling in 14 percent of the vote. He may aim higher in Austria's next general election, once again shaking up the formerly staid world of Viennese politics.

History Review

Lounging against the snow-frosted Alps, Austria is now beloved as a stunning skiing getaway and haven for classical music. But most have forgotten that she was long the power seat of continental Europe. From the thirteenth century on, Vienna was headquarters of the Holy Roman Empire, the longest-lasting European empire in history—and at times the largest, stitching together lands from Spain to Yugoslavia, Poland to Sicily.

ROMAN EMPIRE VS. HOLY ROMAN EMPIRE VS. AUSTRIAN EMPIRE VS. AUSTRO-HUNGARIAN EMPIRE

The Roman Empire officially began in 27 BC; in AD 476 the last Roman emperor abdicated. The Holy Roman Empire, founded by Charlemagne in AD 800 with a push from the pope, eventually extended across most of Europe, and for six centuries was usually headed by the Austrian Habsburg clan. Napoleon ended the Holy Roman Empire in 1806; after 1815, the term "Austrian Empire" was popularly used to describe the Austrian Habsburgs' central and eastern European holdings. In 1867, the Austrian Empire was coruled by Hungarians, becoming the Austro-Hungarian Empire. In 1919, the whole kit and caboodle ceased to exist.

Headed by the Habsburg clan from the late 1200s onward, the Holy Roman Empire greatly enlarged—mostly through politically motivated marriages—and the riches of Vienna expanded with it. In 1529 and 1683, Turks besieged the opulent city, hoping to rope her into the Ottoman Empire. Twice beaten back from the walled kingdom, Turks nevertheless took most of the southeastern land, making Vienna the back door to Europe. Habsburg victories later pried Hungary and her environs from Ottoman rule, expanding the empire to the east, but Austria remains a symbolic bridge between East and West.

To celebrate one defeat of the Turks, Viennese bakers concocted the croissant, which Austrian Marie Antoinette brought to France when she married Louis XVI. Or so the story goes.

THE HABSBURG RULERS: A FEW STANDOUTS OF THE HOLY ROMAN EMPERORS

Rudolf I **(b. 1218) 1273–1291:** Started Habsburg rule, conquering Vienna by threatening to destroy vineyards and making the city the center of the Holy Roman Empire.

Rudolf II **(b. 1552) 1576–1612:** Bright but a tad mad and often depressed, Rudolf moved the imperial capital to Prague, where he invited scientists and magicians to explain the nature of the universe.

Charles V **(b. 1500) 1519–1558:** Ruling during the birth of Protestantism, Catholic Charles condemned Luther but let him live. Europe's richest man held so much land it was unworkable; his son Philip II got Portugal, Spain, and the Netherlands; brother Ferdinand got the eastern chunk. (See "The Netherlands," page 179.)

Maria Theresa **(b. 1717) 1740–1780:** Her hubby, Francis Stephen of Lorraine, became Holy Roman Emperor Francis I (1745–1765), but enlightened Archduchess Maria Theresa began reforms against serfdom, initiated public education, and abolished torture.

Joseph II **(b. 1741) 1780–1790:** Abolished serfdom and the death penalty, he allowed total freedom of religion.

Franz Joseph **(b. 1830) 1848–1916:** Senile by the end of his rule, Emperor Franz Joseph declared war on Serbia in 1914, igniting the First World War.

Karl I **(b. 1887) 1916–1918:** Poor man came to power during the First World War, and tried unsuccessfully to halt it and negotiate a separate peace with Allies. The last Austrian emperor, he was stripped of the title in 1918 and banished to Switzerland.

The lavish imperial capital, known for dancing Lippizzaner horses and devotion to high culture, hosted the nineteenth century's most important meeting of European heads: the 1815 Congress of Vienna, which redistributed the lands seized by Napoleon. The leaders remapped Europe, creating new kingdoms (among them the Netherlands, which combined Dutch lands with Belgium and Luxembourg) and tidying up amorphous fiefdoms. The most important creation was the German Confederation, which gave a solid outline to the jumble of German-speaking principalities, cutting it down to thirty-nine states: the Austrian Empire, which spilled into Eastern Europe, was but one state in this new confederation, but she dwarfed the others, and by size alone, she assumed the role of driving the car.

> *Austrian archduchess Marie Louise married Napoleon in 1810, giving birth to his heir Napoleon Francis Joseph Charles the next year. Napoleon II, more or less kept captive in his palace, died of tuberculosis in Austria at age twenty-one.*

The Congress of Vienna, however, did not address the main problem facing the Austrian Empire: her unruly mix of peoples. The Austrian Empire included today's Hungary, Czech Republic, Slovakia, Ukraine, Slovenia, parts of the Balkans, and several Italian states, as well as Austria—a dozen different ethnic groups, all forced to speak German and heed the archaic Austrian dynasty. Inspired by the French Revolution, the different ethnic regions began revolting and plotting how to take down the Austrian Empire. Throughout the 1800s, the Habsburgs battled to keep power, becoming increasingly weak. In 1866, the German state of Prussia invaded and won, booting the Austrian Empire from the German Confederation. Next, Hungarians demanded rule of the Eastern part of the empire; weary Austria added a hyphen, and the territory became the Austro-Hungarian Empire. (See "Hungary," page 307.)

During the late nineteenth century, so many tragedies befell the Habsburgs that you have to wonder if they were under a gypsy curse. The emperor's kind-hearted brother Maximilian ruled France's "new" colony, Mexico, briefly in 1863, but was assassinated by a firing squad; his poor wife, Charlotte, went bonkers. In 1889, unhappily married Crown Prince Rudolf killed himself and his eighteen-year-old lover at Mayerling, the royal hunting lodge. The emperor's other brother, Karl Ludwig, died from typhoid in 1896, after drinking from the Jordan River during a pilgrimage to the Holy Land. An anarchist fatally stabbed anorexic Empress Elisabeth in 1898, while she vacationed in Switzerland. The last heir, Archduke Franz Ferdinand, had tuberculosis and he too was doomed—but his 1914 assassination by a Serbian nationalist triggered more than national mourning. The bullet that pierced his jugular launched millions more as the Great War engulfed Europe.

> *Black Hand, a secret society of Serbian nationalists who wanted independence and to rule all Slavs, dispatched at least three would-be assassins from Serbia to Sarajevo to kill Archduke Franz Ferdinand, who was considering giving more representation to all Slavic peoples, not just Serbs, an idea Black Hand didn't like. All three potential killers, like the archduke, suffered from tuberculosis.*

ARCHDUKE FRANZ FERDINAND (1863-1914)

Had it not been for a series of untimely deaths, Archduke Franz Ferdinand, the heir apparent, would have been little more than a distant royal, a role that his uncle Emperor Franz Joseph would have preferred. The emperor didn't much care for his rebellious nephew, who refused to play by family rules, which included marrying only Habsburgs or other royals. Czech countess Sophie von Chotkovato was not deemed suitable, but the archduke insisted on marrying her in 1900 anyway. His future children lost all claims to the crown and Sophie wasn't even allowed to ride in the royal coach during state affairs. Franz didn't care; he was mad for his Soph—and it's a good thing he so enjoyed her company, since he was shunned by the class-conscious Austrian upper crust. Invited to observe military demonstrations in Sarajevo in 1914, the archduke might have said no, had not the invitation (for once) included Sophie. Although secessionist ideas were brewing up there, he accepted the offer. His murder was nearly thwarted thrice: the Serbian prime minister heard of the plot and ordered the arrest of the three men dispatched to Sarajevo, but his order was ignored. The assassins' first attempt—hurling a hand grenade into the ceremonial parade—missed the archduke, but injured those in the following car. The archduke insisted on being taken to the hospital to see the injured. The general in the car ordered an alternative route out of the city; when he realized the driver was going the wrong way, the general demanded that he turn the car around. During the slow reversing of the automobile, Serbian extremist Gavrilo Princip, who'd been sitting in a café, ran to the car and fired several bullets, fatally wounding the archduke and his beloved. "Sophie dear! Don't die! Stay alive for our children!" were the archduke's last words, but his wife of fourteen years was already dead. The date, June 28, 1914, was a fitting ending for the couple's story: it was a mere three days before their wedding anniversary.

Emperor Franz Joseph didn't attend the funeral. Neither did German Kaiser Wilhelm, who'd claimed to be a friend. Nevertheless, the assassination provided an excuse for the Austrian emperor to crush the call for Serbian independence. Everyone thought the military exercise would be over in a few months.

Nine million deaths and four years later, the "war to end all wars" had made a wasteland of Europe and resulted in yet another remapping of the Continent, this one more extreme. In 1919, the Austrian Empire was hacked apart, creating Czechoslovakia, a new Poland, a new Hungary, and the Kingdom of Serbs, Croats, and Slovenes (Yugoslavia). By the time the mapmakers at the Paris Peace Conference put down their pens, Austria had been whittled down to a sixth of her former size; her population shrank from 60 million to 7 million. Austria, once Europe's shining star, was flickering out.

The 1919 Treaty of St. Germain, signed by the Allied forces and the Austrian government, officially dissolved the Austro-Hungarian Empire and prohibited the new republic of Austria from politically or economically bonding with Germany again—a clause pretty much ignored when Germany annexed Austria in March 1939.

Gone were the king, most of the kingdom, and the former wealth. Austria, never self-sufficient, was cut off. Regions that previously supplied food, energy, and raw materials halted shipments; store shelves were soon bare, factories closed, furnaces grew icy from lack of fuel. Palaces were looted, trains stopped running, paramilitary groups roamed the streets, and it was cold everywhere. Unemployment skyrocketed, the government broke down, typhoid swept Vienna; the situation was so desperate that Allies eventually sent in food. Still, Austria was broke—so broke that she was unable to pay war reparations. The once-mighty empire hobbled into the 1920s, a shattered land marked by gloom.

SIGMUND FREUD (1856–1939)

When the father of psychotherapy stumbled into mental health in the late 1800s, treatment of the insane often involved removing sex organs; female hysteria was "cured" by slicing off the clitoris. Enter Dr. Freud, whose previous claim to fame had been finding the sex organs of eels.[10] Believing that behavior problems stemmed from childhood issues—including repressed desires to sleep with Mummy and kill Pops—that could be unleashed by unstifled chatter, Freud developed theories of the id (center of desires), the superego (the conscience), and the ego (the balancer of id and superego), as well as "penis envy," "castration anxiety," and the developmental stages oral, anal, and phallic. Psychoanalysis caught on in the early twentieth century, and was wildly popular through the 1950s. However, Freud-bashing is now the norm. His formulaic ideas and cold rapport with patients, who were prevented from making eye contact with the therapist, are denigrated as stiff. Some believe that Freud actually uncovered widespread child abuse,[11] saying that when he tried to report it, the response was so explosive that Freud repressed the information, and instead stated that patients were merely experiencing unconscious fantasies.[12]

Freud's daughter, Anna, pioneered the field of child psychology.

Slammed by the Great Depression, Austria was such a mess that Engelbert Dollfuss, of the Christian Socialist Party, easily stepped in as dictator. He shut down parliament, banned other parties, and doled out death sentences to political enemies. Tens of thousands fled and a brief civil war ensued, but Dollfuss remained in control. The chancellor had no desire to bond with Germany; he banned the Nazi Party. Nazis retaliated with terrorist bombings. In 1934, they took more drastic means. Nazis dressed as police entered the chancellery and fatally shot the chancellor, then seized Vienna's radio station and announced that he had resigned. Nazis were ousted after a few days, but some Austrians longed to join up with Germany. While Hitler was obviously anti-Semitic, so were some in Austria. Anti-Semitism was a platform of the Christian Socialist Party, and Vienna's mayor Karl Lüger had condemned Jews since entering office a decade before.

Hitler, shunned as a youth by Austria's art world, had long dreamed of annexing his homeland. Austria had gold, oil, minerals, and labor—and even though Anschluss was opposed by her leaders and by most intellectuals, Austrians didn't have much say in the matter. Chancellor Schuschnigg tried to avoid the annexation Hitler had in mind by scheduling a referendum for March 13, 1938. The choice before Austrians was whether or not Austria should remain an independent country. At the news, Hitler forced Schuschnigg to resign and sent Nazi troops into Austria the day before the vote. They were greeted by new Nazi chancellor Artur von Seyss-Inquart—put into office by Hitler—who invited Germany to annex Austria.

Some Austrians fled immediately and some killed themselves, but tens of thousands cheered Hitler as he entered Vienna and greeted his countrymen. He would later say that in Austria "there met me such a stream of love as I have never experienced."[13]

Austria had a new name—Ostmark—only one party (the Nazis), and a new leader in the wings. The Nazis held a vote on whether Austrians accepted Anschluss and Hitler, and thanks to vote-rigging and threats, 99.7 percent supposedly gave annexation a green light.

> The Habsburgs were among those who opposed Anschluss, but they had little say, having been stripped of their power in 1919. The UK, France, and the U.S. barely let out a peep. Only Mexico formally opposed the annexation, writing to the League of Nations in March 1938, warning that if the Great Powers didn't act to prevent Anschluss, "the world will regrettably sooner or later be engulfed by a catastrophe far greater."[14] Mexico was ignored.

Resistance movements sprang up immediately, and some 75,000 Austrian politicians and influential people were rounded up in the first few weeks. Among those sent to concentration camps: the chancellor, the mayor of Vienna, and assorted Habsburgs, including the two sons of Archduke Franz Ferdinand. But most severely targeted were Jews, who were soon stripped of almost everything, including the rights to hold property and work. Almost two-thirds of the 220,000 Jews in Austria quickly fled,[15] although they often had to pay fees upward of $100,000 to get out, and any property they sold went for a pittance.

MAUTHAUSEN

Hitler decided to renovate his hometown of Linz—and the granite quarry outside Mauthausen held the materials for his beautification plan. The Nazis bought the quarry weeks after moving in, and soon thereafter the first prisoners arrived from Dachau to build the mother camp of Austria. A grade three facility, it was where prisoners whose status was *Rückkehr unerwünscht*—return not desired—were sent for "extermination by work." Laborers were split into two groups: those who picked out granite with crude tools, and those who hauled the slabs up 189 precarious stairs, from which untold thousands fell. Mauthausen, like Auschwitz, became notorious: limb-eating Alsatian dogs were let loose on the quarry stairs; Dr. Krebsbach experimented with vaccines and lice; twisted SS guards dressed as damsels hacked up hundreds of workers with picks; weak prisoners were forced to run with enormous rocks tied to their backs until they collapsed from exhaustion and were shot for "attempting to escape." Over 100,000 died in Mauthausen.[16] When Americans neared the facility in May 1945, the Nazis gave orders to kill the remaining inmates in explosions of the quarries; however, 2,000 survived. Among them: Simon Wiesenthal, who would go on to be one of the great Nazi hunters.

"Austrians like to believe Beethoven was an Austrian and Hitler was a German." —German saying

How many Austrians willingly complied is up for debate, but there's little question that Austria was a vital cog in the Nazi machine; her factories, manned by slave laborers, churned out ball bearings and explosives, and her camps were some of the regime's most horrific. Allied bombing of Austria began in April 1945, and the Soviets marched into Vienna that month. After the war, the city was divided into quadrants Berlin-style, with the UK, France, the U.S., and USSR each taking a corner of the city and keeping them very much separate from one another. During that period, Viennese heard different versions of any event, and lacked even a shared newspaper. At least partly due to the Soviets' determination to drain Austria of her oil resources, Vienna remained occupied until 1955, when the State Treaty was signed, forbidding future unions with Germany, banning return of the Habsburg monarchy, and declaring that Austria would henceforth remain neutral. The Allies pulled out in November, an event celebrated by the reopening of Vienna's State Opera House, where Beethoven's *Fidelio* rang out for the opening night. Austrians, in culture shock, drifted into arias and concertos and denial about what had happened. Schoolbooks taught very limited history, and the country hid behind the slogan "Hitler's first victim." It was not a perfect fit.

> At least 80,000 Austrian Jews and others were shipped off to camps during the war. About 7,000 Jews returned, but most found that their homes were occupied, their businesses had been taken over, their savings were depleted, and their valuables were gone. Allies pressured the Austrian government into giving property back, but many Jews headed directly to Israel. Jews, such as the Rothschilds (who came to collect their stolen art) were coerced into making substantial "donations" to Austrian museums before exporting any of their treasures. In 1999, Austria announced she would begin returning the "donated" art.

RIPPING BACK THE VEIL

Austria had long shirked her part in World War II—and had largely escaped wide-scale restitution of war victims for one reason: back in 1943, the UK, United States, and Soviet Union reversed their former acceptance of the Anschluss, and dubbed Austria "the first victim of Hitlerite aggression." Never mind that it was largely realpolitik to undo repercussions of the Allies previous acceptance of Anschluss, and to help stir up anti-Hilter rebellions. After the war, Austria gratefully accepted this revision of history and long maintained that only a handful of Austrians collaborated with Nazis. One sign of change in views: in 1998, the government appointed a historical commission to investigate activities and paid compensations, which ultimately concluded that Austrians had been widely involved in the persecution of Jews. In 2001, under pressure from the U.S., the Austrian government issued a statement that "Austrians stand by the onerous heritage of their country" and announced that she would pay an additional $360 million to Austrians living in the U.S.

Austria remains a class-conscious society, one where double standards hold. While every Austrian is entitled to a roof over his head—provided free by the government if need be—that doesn't apply to immigrants. They don't qualify for low-income housing, are often overcharged for rent,[17] and one in three immigrants lives in substandard housing without running water, a situation found even in Vienna.[18]

Hot Spots

Vienna: The city split by the Danube still retains her regal air and the nobles rich enough to afford life here in the city, where the opera packs out every night. Headquarters for numerous international bodies including the International Atomic Energy Agency, OPEC, and the Organization for Security and Cooperation in Europe. Also home to escape tunnels, seen in *The Third Man.*

Salzburg: In the composer's birthplace, the hills are alive with the sound of Mozart. Most tourists, however, come to relive *The Sound of Music*, which was filmed here. Whatever draws them, almost everyone who sets foot here is charmed by the mountain-hugged town that first grew wealthy from salt mines.

Carinthia: Beautiful, pristine, and dotted with lakes, this southern alpine region holds many Slovenes, having formerly been part of Yugoslavia. It's now Haider territory, and as governor he keeps refusing to post dual-language signs in German and Slovenian, even though the national government demands it.

Innsbruck: The city's gorgeous, and researchers at the University of Innsbruck were pioneers in teleportation, beaming ions from one side of the Danube to the other in the closest thing yet to Star Trek's "beaming up."

Fucking: The tiny town in Upper Austria has had the name Fucking since the eleventh century, and they ain't changing it now despite the expense: the sign bearing the town's name is the most ripped-off sign in Austria.[19]

The liver: Who knows why, but Austria has the most deaths from chronic viral hepatitis.[20]

Courtesy of Innsbruck Tourismus Archiv

Alpine Jewel Innsbruck

Hotshots

Wolfgang Schüssel: Chancellor, 2000–present. Old Wolfie pulled a slick move to grab the power seat, and some still haven't forgiven him for it.

Heinz Fischer: President, 2004–present. Former leader of parliament, Fischer has a reputation for being diplomatic and moderate. He's also fluent in Esperanto, which must come in quite handy.

Hans-Peter Martin: Member of European Parliament, 1999–present. Widely published in *Der Spiegel*, former journalist Martin also wrote books about globalization (*The Global Trap*) and pharmaceutical giants (*Bitter Pills*) before taking on the corruption at the European Parliament.

Theodor (Binyamin Ze'ev) Herzl (1860–1904): Born in Budapest, the journalist, novelist, and playwright came to Vienna at age eighteen. Writing such plays as *The Ghetto*, about the difficulties Jews faced in European society, Herzl ultimately concluded that Jews are all one people who should have their own state. He proposed the idea to plenty of the day's powermongers—from Baron Rothschild to German Kaiser Wilhelm—but only the British government took him seriously, offering him an autonomous territory for Jews—in Uganda. That never went anywhere, but his idea for a Jewish state led to the creation of Israel forty-four years after his death.

Wolfgang Amadeus Mozart (1756–1791): The child prodigy who unchained classical music and gave it wings—best heard in his lively, fancy-fingered piano sonatas—causes inferiority complexes in even the most talented young 'uns and overachieving men. Composing at age four, Amadeus played minuets at five, had mastered violin and harpsichord the following year, and was writing symphonies and sonatas by nine. Dragged across Europe by Papa starting at age six, the tired lad who traversed the continent by stagecoach paid (and was paid) for his talents, performing upward of six hours a day for Europe's monarchs and high society; the whole family was often ill, and his mother died during a tour in Paris. His repertoire included three dozen symphonies, twenty-seven piano concertos, seventeen piano sonatas, and six operas (including *The Magic Flute* and *Don Giovanni*).[21] Europe's most famous child musician died, then slightly less famous, at age thirty-five.

*Whistle-blower
Hans-Peter Martin*

Courtesy of European Parliament, Photo Department

Gustav Klimt (1862–1918): Nobody made romance prettier than Austrian illustrator Klimt, who came to fame as a mural painter in Viennese theaters. His fluid, gold-infused style, best captured in *The Kiss*, was controversial at the time, and his art was endlessly criticized. Nazis made off with six of his best-known paintings, including *The Kiss*, now hanging in the Austrian National Art Gallery.

Johann Strauss II (1825–1899): His father was also a composer of waltzes, but nobody made them more famous than Junior, who became known as "The Waltz King" for his dozens of heart-stirring creations that brought waltzing to the ballrooms of Habsburg palaces. Now fiddles in perpetuity as a statue in Stadt-park. (Hear *The Blue Danube* at www.aboutvienna.org/composers/strauss jr.htm)

Russian Mafia: They love it here so much they've reportedly made it the place for annual meetings; Vienna is full of bought women they've hauled in from the East, whose plight pretty much goes unnoticed.

11. GREECE
(Ellas/Hellas)
Waking Up

FAST FACTS

Country:	Hellenic Republic; Ellinski Dhimokratia; Ellas/Hellas
Capital:	Athens
Government:	Parliamentary republic (monarchy last rejected 1974)
Independence:	1829 (from Ottoman Empire/Turkey)
Population:	10,688,000 (2006 estimate)
Head of State:	President Karolos Papoulias (2005)
Head of Government:	Prime Minister Konstandinos Karamanlis (2004)
Elections:	President elected by parliament, five-year term; prime minister appointed by president, to five-year term
Name of Parliament:	Parliament; Vouli ton Ellinon
Ethnicity:	98% Greek; 2% other (officially there is no ethnic breakdown)
Religion:	98% Greek Orthodox; 1.3% Muslim; 0.7% other (including Maronite)

Language:	Greek (official) 99%; also English, French
Literacy:	97%
Famous Exports:	Democracy, Zorba the Greek, the richest girl in the world, November 17 group
Economic Big Boy:	Hellenic Telecom; 2004 total sales: $6.18 billion[1]
Per Capita GDP:	$22,800 (2005 estimate)
Unemployment:	10.1% (Third Quarter 2005, Eurostat figure)
Percentage in Poverty:	21% (according to April 2003 Eurostat report)[2]
EU Status:	Member since 1981
Currency:	Euro

Quick Tour

You can see it in the mountain villages cascading white down to the sea and in the medieval monasteries wedged so high in the cliffs that basket and ropes are needed to pull visitors up. You can see it in hilltop ruins and fields of wild flowers thick with chipped statues. You can even taste it on the dinner plate, heaping with the traditional fare of stuffed grape leaves, feta cheese, and garlicky yogurt. You can hear it in the calls from the Greek Orthodox Church to steal back lands that once belong to ancient Greece, and it's obvious in the frequent run-ins with Turkey: Ellas is deeply lost in her history. The country that curls off the Balkans, breaking into thousands of islands, is obsessed with her spectacular past, and that's certainly understandable: ancient Greece was arguably the pinnacle of human evolution until (of course) our time. But Greek history is as much a crippling ball and chain as a sparkling crown jewel. The problem is not only that there's so much to live up to; the problem is there are too many reasons to bear a grudge—as evidenced by Greece's relationship with Turkey, a hate-a-thon that has gone on for centuries.

EPIC SNARLING

Greece and Turkey's problems go back to medieval times, but they've been really barking at each other since 1829, when Greeks—part of the Ottoman Empire from 1453—declared independence and launched a decade-long war that brought Western Europeans to fight for her freedom. Greece fought against Turkey four more times—once over regaining Crete—and wars have nearly started over oil exploration rights, airspace, Cyprus, escaped war criminals, and even uninhabited rocks in the Aegean. Every so often, however, the two foes show their kinder sides. On August 17, 1999, the ground under Izmit in northwestern Turkey collapsed in a 7.2-magnitude earthquake that killed 17,000 people. First to arrive: Greek doctors and emergency teams, bearing medicine, food, and blankets, and digging out the people who had been their enemies a few hours before. When Greece was shaken by a temblor several weeks later, Turkey returned the favor. Relations between the two countries, if not cuddly, have been warmer ever since—and they're even trading to the tune of $3 billion a year. Now, instead of trying to block Turkey's application to join the EU, the Greek government is (theoretically) supporting it, even though two-thirds of Greeks don't want Turkey in.

It's not that Greece is no longer great; she just isn't great like she used to be, exchanging great ideas for great fun somewhere along the way. The birthplace of democracy, individual rights, and freedom of speech is now best known for ouzo, bouzouki music, line dancing, and plate smashing—certainly festive pursuits, though not nearly as lofty. The sun-bleached villages and blissful islands thick with orchids, herbs, and olive trees are still as fetching as they were when robed thinkers, not camera-toting tourists, ambled over the hills—and the classical architecture, embodied in the Parthenon gazing down over the capital, still inspires awe even if today it is clouded by smog.

> With over 14 million visitors a year, tourism contributes over 10 percent to Greece's GDP.

GOOD PERSPECTIVE: THE ACROPOLIS

Peering over Athens from a rocky promontory stands the most potent symbol of the Greek golden age: the Acropolis (*akros* = highest, *polis* = city). Palace, fort, and temple for fifth-century BC Greeks, the site received its most memorable touches under Pericles, who gave it the Parthenon and the curving, columned façade, which looks perfectly straight when viewed from below and has inspired architects all over the world for 2,500 years. The Parthenon was turned into a mosque in the fifteenth century, and was damaged by Venetians in 1687; the only full-size replica stands in Nashville.

Despite clinging to historical relics, Greece fell far astray from the political path paved by her ancestors: for most of the twentieth century, Greek government appeared a mockery of the very ideas put forth by the Ancients. Riots, juntas, rigged voting, civil wars, loss of rights, and dictatorships defined Greece into the 1980s, making her appear more like a struggling South

American country during a bumpy patch than the land that was the birthplace
of Western civilization.

EUROPE'S LI'L HELLION

Until recently, Greece has been such a pain that the Hellenic Republic was
sometimes called the "spoiled child of Europe." She was the weak link in European security—making little effort to go after the assassination-prone November 17 group until 2002—and her airports were so lax that the U.S., for one,
issued travel warnings about going there. Greece got into a serious diplomatic
tiff with Macedonia over the use of the name, also the name of a region in
Greece. She kicked up problems in Cyprus, sending guerrillas there and supporting coups—and with a nod from the Greek Orthodox Church, Greek soldiers fought along with Milosevic's troops in Serbian slaughters of Muslims.
Greece was the site of a 1988 ferry attack (in which Palestinians killed nine
tourists), and at times her government seemed to love to goad the West by
chummying up with Soviets. And on numerous occasions, the international
community had to pull Greece and Turkey apart.

Greece appears to be mellowing and moving up in the world. Two things pulled
her out of the gutter. The first was joining the European Union in 1981, a move that
brought hundreds of billions in development funds and offered wider economic
markets. The second stimulus was an event that first started in Athens in 776 BC:
the Olympic Games. Preparations for the 2004 Olympics catapulted Greece into
the twenty-first century, bringing fancy new stadiums, an expanded subway, a new
airport, and tram lines. Kicking up a construction flurry, the event also gave Greeks
a new pride—and an international stature—that they haven't had since about the
time Constantinople fell. Some hailed the 2004 Olympics as the finest in recent
history; many were simply amazed that the construction for it finished on time.
Greece was so behind that the International Olympic Committee nearly yanked
the Games away at the last minute, and up until opening day, construction itself
was an Olympic event in the form of a round-the-clock work-a-thon.

> *Invented by ancient Greeks as an amusement for Zeus, the Olympics began
> in the eighth century BC, with chariot races, distance running, and discus-
> throwing—many events performed in the buff. The Games' flames were
> blown out in AD 393, when Romans took over Greece, but the jock-a-thon
> was revived in 1896—in Athens—by French baron Pierre de Coubertin,
> who required that athletes don clothes.*

Like the Olympics, which are integral to Greek identity, the Greek Orthodox
Church plays a profound role in defining Greece—and ensures that she clings to

memories of her past, including all misdeeds inflicted upon her. In May 2001, when Pope John Paul II visited Athens—the first pope to set foot in Greece in almost 1,200 years—his arrival was treated as a national tragedy. Orthodox clergy held an all-night pray-a-thon that he wouldn't make it, flags hung at half-mast, churches were wrapped in black, bishops led protest demonstrations of the faithful chanting, "down with the two-horned pope," and Orthodox archbishop Christodoulos loudly demanded that the pope repent for harming the Byzantine Empire in medieval times. The pope did indeed apologize for past acts, specifically the Crusader sacking of Constantinople in 1204, but even after the pope ate crow, Greek clerics snubbed the repenter; at least Christodoulos came forward to hug him. The rest of the room remained coldly silent, and the anger toward the Catholic Church burns on.

THE GREEK ORTHODOX CHURCH

The Orthodox Church is the official keeper of centuries of Greek history. The icon-heavy and ritual-rich branch of Christianity split with the Catholic Church almost 1,000 years ago and is more conservative than even the Catholic Church, and arguably more powerful—at least in Greece, where there is scarcely any separation of church and state, and religion is taught in schools. The Church is so important that clerics—routinely called in for government affairs and christening new buildings—are on the government payroll.[3]

The Church is now headed by Archbishop Christodoulos, who has a few secular issues on his mind—like yanking back all of the lands that were once ancient Greece, even if it takes a war to do it. He calls Turks "barbarians," wants to block Turkey's entry into the EU, and tried to prevent the first mosque from rising in Athens, which until recently was the only European capital where Muslims didn't have a house of worship. Lately, Christodoulos and the entire Church are in hot water. VIPs are accused of lurid crimes, from drug peddling, smuggling, and money-laundering to sexually abusing young boys, carousing with prostitutes, and bribing judges. It's serious, and bishops are flying. The archbishop presided over the March 2005 swearing-in of President Karolos Papoulis but, says the *Guardian*, Papoulis shunned kissing him. Not a good sign.

> The Greek Orthodox Church, whose wealth is estimated to be about $1 billion, owns vast amounts of Greek land; only the government owns more.[4]

Politically stable (for Greece), with popular conservative leadership, and still beaming over being the champions of the soccer tournament EURO 2004, Greece may be on a winning streak. Greece still has problems—a lagging educational system and high poverty rate are two—but at least now she has a reason to hope for the future and can stop dwelling solely on her glorious past.

History Review

From the scraps we have of antiquity, it's clear that ancient Greeks were latching on to ideas far ahead of their time—and which sometimes weren't proved true until thousands of years later.

> *The history of ancient Greece was lost for centuries. Islamic scholars living around the ninth century first translated the works of the wise; long ignored by Europe, the classical ideas and designs later inspired the Renaissance. America's founding fathers so adored ancient Greece that they toyed with the idea of making Greek the official language of the United States.*

DIFFERING PHILOSOPHIES

Still major names in philosophy, Socrates, Plato, and Aristotle took different approaches to explaining the world.

Socrates (470–399 BC): Believing "the life unexamined is not worth living," Socrates cross-examined everything and everyone so voraciously that there is a word—"aporia"—for the resulting bewilderment. A Delphic oracle declared him Athens' wisest, and he became arrogant in his "All I know is that I know nothing" conceit—and refused to write anything down. After two of his students overthrew Athens, he was found guilty of corrupting youth and forced to drink hemlock.

Plato (427–347 BC): Best known for his written discourses involving Socrates, Plato believed that our perceptions were foggy at best, like shadows flickering on cave walls. "Know thyself," he taught, believing true knowledge came from within; the senses merely led one astray.

Aristotle (384–322 BC): Plato's finest student, Aristotle, believed understanding came only from empirical observation, and laid the basis for the scientific method. Teacher to Alexander the Great, he left behind writing on topics from anatomy to astronomy, politics to poetry, and is the most widely respected of the three.

Prosperous city-states such as Athens and Sparta rose up around the sixth century BC across the Aegean, producing evolved societies whose citizens voted in leaders and thinkers postulated the existence of atoms, calculated earth's circumference, and correctly portrayed the galaxy as a collection of far-away stars. Greeks invented coins, pumps, sundials, and public works, leaving us the first written histories—as well as maps that were used into Renaissance times. Many of the most memorable achievements took place in Athens in the fifth century BC, during the Golden Era of Pericles.

> Greek city-states expanded territorially across the Mediterranean, creating a beachfront empire that included Sicily, south Italy, the southern Balkans, and North Africa.

GREEK GURUS

Homer: The blind poet is credited with transforming the Trojan War into the lyrical epics *The Iliad* and *The Odyssey*, but some historians doubt he existed.

Sappho: (c. 630 BC) From the island of Lesbos, she wrote love poems to women but threw herself from a cliff over a man.

Sophocles: (496–406 BC) Wrote 123 plays, only seven of which survive, including *Antigone*.

General Thucydides: (c. 455–395 BC) Preserved his battlefield memories in the multivolume *History of the Peloponnesian War*.

Hippocrates: (460–377 BC): Called the father of medicine, but some doubt he penned the Hippocratic Oath.

Pythagoras: (569–475 BC) Best recalled for his formula $a^2 + b^2 = c^2$ for triangles, he also experimented with musical tones (inventing the octave), exalted vegetarianism, and ran a philosophical society that reduced everything to numbers; initiates went for five years without talking.

Aeschylus: (525–456 BC): Famous for tragedies, he died comically when an eagle dropped a tortoise on his head.

Eratosthenes of Cyrene: (276–195 BC): Calculated Earth's circumference, off by only a few thousand miles.

Democritus: (460–370 BC): Theorized that atoms make up matter, stars are far-off planets, and the universe holds many worlds that might have life.[5]

Ptolemy: (c. AD 90–168): Astronomer and profoundly important cartographer, his maps were the best the world had until European discoverers revamped them.

Despite occasional claims of being descended from Zeus, early Greeks were mere mortals, and as such entered into occasional wars. Their first enemies were the Persians, who began conquering Greek lands in the sixth century BC. Closer to home, alpha dog Athens and militaristic Sparta were always going at it. Starting in 431 BC, the two knocked each other about for twenty-seven years in the Peloponnesian War; Sparta emerged victorious, but other city-states soon shoved her off the stage. Constant infighting made the city-states vulnerable, and in 346 BC, Thebes changed the dynamic when she hired an outside fighter to help her cause. Warrior Philip II of Macedon expanded Thebes' territorial holdings, and brought in his son Alexander, who forged even wider boundaries for all Greece.

> *Forgotten details: The Peloponnesian War ended in 404 BC. Peace, however, wasn't official for another 2,400 years. Mayors of former city-states Sparta and Athens, now stately cities, finally signed a formal treaty in March 1996.*

Greeks initially disliked the Macedonian, particularly when Philip took their cities and proclaimed himself leader, but he promised the return of Greek lands that were under Persian rule. Philip died shortly after starting that quest, but his son Alexander completed the mission in grand style. Twenty-year-old Alexander the Great (356–323 BC) won back Persian-held cities and conquered new lands from Egypt to Syria. By the time he died at thirty-three, Greek territories stretched all the way to India. The gem of the Greek acquisitions, however, was on the north coast of Africa: Alexandria.

ALEXANDRIA

In today's Egypt, Alexandria was a small village until 331 BC, when Alexander ordered that it be transformed into a metropolis. Palaces shot up alongside temples, theaters, markets, and mausoleums—and the lighthouse of Alexandria (one of the Seven Wonders of the Ancient World) was the world's first beacon for sailors and the tallest building of the day. The city, known for intellectuals, high culture, and kinky affairs, later boasted a well-endowed museum with on-site temples, gardens, a zoo, and the world's most extensive library, where scholars pored over 500,000 papyrus scrolls, maps, and documents from across Europe and Asia. The collected wisdom of the ancient world went up in flames, although exactly when it caught fire (probably in the first century BC or AD) and who to blame for the blaze that reduced knowledge to ashes is still a mystery (Julius Caesar is one contender).

> *The last of the pharaohs of Alexandria, Cleopatra (69–30 BC), had a zesty social life. Married to her brother (and rival), she disposed of him when Julius Caesar visited her city in 50 BC. Caesar was impressed with the hospitality: he received a present of a carpet with Cleopatra rolled inside. The two trav-*

eled the Nile for months, and soon the pharaoh was pregnant with the emperor's child. Cleopatra subsequently married her younger brother, continued sleeping with Caesar until he was murdered, then went for his successor Mark Antony, who handed her Crete, Cyprus, and Palestine as gifts. His foe Octavian declared war on Cleopatra, and, upon winning, threatened her with death. Rather than suffer whatever method he devised, Cleopatra came up with her own, killing herself with the poison of an asp, as befitted the seductress with a toxic effect on men.

Greek lands fell into Roman hands in the first century AD, although Greek remained the spoken language and Greek culture was mostly absorbed by the Romans; the same gods remained, but with new names. The polytheist religion was later swept aside by Christianity, the official religion of the Roman Empire, by the fourth century AD. In AD 330 the Roman Empire was split into two parts; the new eastern portion—the Byzantine Empire—boasted grand Constantinople, home to many ethnic Greeks, at her center.

CONSTANTINOPLE: THE LOST CITY

She was the Queen of Cities, the richest in Christendom, filled with palaces, markets, zoos, and the most beautiful churches—including the mosaic-thick, silver-rich Hagia Sofia, Church of Holy Wisdom. Founded by Constantine I in AD 330, Constantinople spread out along the azure Marmara Sea in today's Turkey. The capital of the eastern Roman Empire, Constantinople was a city where most, like Constantine himself, spoke Greek and where vestiges of Greek culture lived on, even after barbarian invasions brought the downfall of the Roman Empire and caused many to flee most Greek cities. In Constantinople, Christianity was embodied by the Eastern Orthodox Church, which split with the Catholic Church in 1054 over religious details, such as the question of whether laypeople could preach. Protected by two walls and a deep moat, the city was Europe's most formidable to enter. The walls were occasionally penetrated: in 1204, Crusaders sent by the Catholic pope sacked the city, looting churches, raping women, and establishing Constantinople as a new site of Catholicism for the next fifty-seven years—an event for which the Greek Orthodox Church would never forgive the pope. The Greek Orthodox Church won back control in 1261, but soon lost it again. In 1453, during one of the most horrifying battles of European history, Constantinople was besieged by Sultan Mehmed II's Islamic warriors for fifty-five days. Byzantines were greatly outnumbered—Mehmed had 200,000 fighters to their 20,000—but the city remained safe for weeks, thanks to her mighty walls. The Ottomans finally gained entry, not through fighting, but through a mistake: someone inside Constantinople hadn't locked a small gate in the thick wall,[6] and the Ottomans walked right in and claimed the crown city of the Byzantine Empire—and she remains part of Turkey today. Ottomans took Constantinople on a Tuesday, a day many Greeks still regard as jinxed.

Orthodox churches remained, and Greeks could freely practice their faith— as long as they paid hefty "non-Muslim" taxes. Ottomans so respected church leaders that they became paid employees of the Ottoman state. The church and the Greek language became symbols for Greeks of their lost culture—and of their dream that greatness would be regained.

Constantinople and most other Byzantine lands were pulled into the Islamic Ottoman Empire in 1453. For the next three and a half centuries, Greeks were obsessed with their past and with how to restore it. Although there were eras of relative peace, Ottoman rule was often a violent, unhappy affair for Greeks. In 1821, Greeks declared independence; European luminaries such as Victor Hugo and Lord Byron embraced the cause, and Britain, France, and Russia entered the battle, ultimately gaining freedom for Greeks in 1829.

Lord Byron (who died fighting) and other European romantics fighting in the Greek War of Independence weren't concerned with geopolitics or inhumane treatment; they came to the battlefield to preserve the ideals of Ancient Greece.

Leaving Constantinople and descending from mountain villages where families had hid for centuries, Greeks set about re-creating their country, starting with little more than the mainland. On reclaiming Athens, they discovered the once-great city was run down and deserted. Notably missing: the fabulous marble artwork that had wrapped the interior of the Parthenon. Greeks found out the Parthenon's interior was in London, thanks to a well-meaning earl.

LOSING THEIR MARBLES

The Elgin Marbles aren't small colorful orbs that tots shoot across the floor; they're intricate marble sculptures and friezes of war scenes and religious ceremonies, created in 440 BC, that were plucked from Athens in 1799. The Scottish Earl of Elgin, then British Ambassador to the Ottoman Empire, took the works for safekeeping, since Greece was then occupied by Ottoman Turks. He believed he was saving them, although omens revealed their removal was cursed. First, the earl had to pay exorbitant fees to get the friezes off the walls; then he had to buy a ship to send them. Alas, the vessel sank, and it took two years to salvage the pieces—the cost of which came out of the earl's pocket as well. Traveling back to Scotland by land, he and his new bride were captured by Napoleon's forces in France and thrown in prison. The Scotsman sent to negotiate their release was successful with the Mrs.; once he got her out of prison, the two had a spicy affair. When the Earl finally showed up with the marbles in London, the British Museum would only pay a pittance. The poor earl, by then divorced, died in poverty—but the marbles became the museum's most valued collection. Greece wants the babies back, but the museum won't part with them, despite pleas lodged by tearful Greek politicians (who begged to borrow them for the Olympics) and VIPs from Bill Clinton to Vanessa Redgrave. Pressure builds for Britain to shoot the marbles back to Greece; reports that the museum's caretakers have damaged the marbles aren't helping the Brits' cause.[7]

Athens' antiquities were further ravaged at the hands of the new Greek king, Otto Wittelsbach, who was foisted on them by Brits, French, and Russians. A Bavarian royal who cared little for Greek culture, he sent out construction to rip down most of the city's "barbarian" buildings. The Greeks' nineteenth-century return to their lost heritage was anticlimactic—and civil wars raged across the land. The romanticized past had disappeared, territory was scanty, many ethnic Greeks still lived under foreign rule, and the new Greece was divided, disorganized, and poor. Trying to unify Greeks, the first head of state John Capodistra proposed *Megali Idea*—a nationalistic plan for Greeks to reclaim their heritage by uniting ethnic Greeks everywhere and reassembling all the lands once included in ancient Greece—Crete, Cyprus, Constantinople, western Turkey, and chunks of the Balkans among them. The idea caught on, fueling assorted wars, and Greece gradually added parts of Bulgaria, Albania, and later Crete. Still missing were Constantinople and assorted islands, including Cyprus. When the First World War rolled around, Greeks—particularly Eleftherios Venizelos, Greek prime minister under King Constantine I—saw a chance to regain them. When Britain and France dangled the prospect of regaining Constantinople, Cyprus, and Thrace under his nose, Venizelos quickly signed Greece up to fight alongside the Triple Entente (Britain, France, and Russia). King Constantine I, however, wanted to stay neutral in the war his brother-in-law German Kaiser Wilhelm II had started. Venizelos was so determined to gamble for the lost lands that the king fired him. Britain and France intervened: they gave the king a choice—abdicate or watch Athens be turned into ruins—and occupied the capital to assure they meant business. The king gave the throne to his son Alexander, Venizelos was re-instated in Athens, and in 1917 Greece was dragged into the war.

At war's end, Venizelos discovered the promises made by the Brits and the French were mostly bogus. He could forget Constantinople, and the Brits fancied Cyprus, but the victors invited him to take the area to the west of Constantinople (Thrace) and several important cities on Turkey's coast—if he could. Greece continued to fight, this time in the nasty three-year Greco-Turkish War (1919–1922). One highlight: reclaiming Izmit in 1922, the Turkish army massacred the mostly Greek population, setting the city ablaze in an inferno that drove them into the sea. The war ended in a mass repatriation: 1.3 million Greeks living in Turkey fled to Greece and 800,000 Turks ran the other way, with thousands dying en route.

> Athens' population swelled by a million overnight, causing food and housing shortages, widescale unemployment, and unrest.

Bad news wouldn't let up: King Alexander died in 1920 from a monkey bite. His father Constantine I returned, only to be dethroned in 1922; he was succeeded by his son George II, who was deposed the following year. A military junta ran Greece until 1935, when George was restored to the throne by plebiscite. The Great Depression throttled Greece, dictator Metaxas took over in 1936, and then the Second World War rolled around. Exhausted, Greece did not want to fight: in 1940, when Mussolini asked to traverse the country on his way to battles, Greece replied *Oxi*—no way—and they still celebrate "Oxi Day" today. The refusal was costly: in 1941, Nazis, Italians, and Bulgarians marched into the land at their most brutal, ultimately leading to *katoxi*, the Nazi occupation lasting through World War II. Fierce resistance brewed up immediately, led by Greek Communists. Rightwingers and royalists later joined to push out the occupiers, and Greece was thrashed between the Nazis and the resistance fighters. In 1944, factions within the Resistance turned against each other, launching a brutal civil war that lasted for five years.

> During *katoxi, the Greek population shrunk by 8 percent: over a million died, many from starvation, which killed 100,000 during the first occupied winter.*

World War II was over, but as civil war raged on, British and Americans intervened in Greek politics. Fearing that the popular Greek Communists would lead Greece into the Soviet Union, both tried to quash Communism in Greece. Brits purged Communists from the Greek military; Americans doled out $400 million to fight Greek Communism. The two democracy-loving countries—believed to be running a shadow government within Greece—also suggested that the government fudge votes to ensure Communists would not win. The U.S. government, then under President Truman, also demanded that Greece issue "Certificates of Political Reliability" to Greeks who did not harbor left-wing sympathies. Without the certificates, required until 1962, Greeks could not vote or get a job.

Despite the maneuvering, the left remained popular: in 1964, Socialist George Papandreou was elected prime minister in what was Greece's first leftist victory. Immediately under attack by the powers that be, he was shoved out the next year. He looked likely to win the 1967 election, but surprise: two nights before the elections, three colonels staged a coup—and their junta took over Greece. The United States is widely believed to have ordered and backed the coup, and the U.S. quickly recognized the junta's legitimacy. Called "The Glorious Revolution"—by the junta, at least—the coup ushered in seven years of repressive, inhumane dictatorial rule during which foreign newspapers disappeared, Greece lived under curfew and martial law, and dissent wasn't tolerated: eight thousand Greeks died in the first "glorious" week.

On November 17, 1973, the army stormed a student protest—killing twenty youths by rolling over them with a tank. Worldwide wrath fell upon the already-loathed colonels. Desperate to keep control, the colonels embraced the cause of Cyprus, which Greece had been trying to annex for decades. The junta backed a coup on Cyprus, hoping to rope Cyprus to Greece. The coup failed and took the junta down with it.

> The 1973 tank-rolling incident bred militant discontent, namely the small but lethal November 17 group. Blaming the U.S. and Britain for the junta, the group targeted Western VIPs, killing at least two dozen, four American diplomats among them. Greece didn't crack down on the assassins until just before the 2004 Olympics, when most were rounded up, tried, and convicted.

Democracy returned in 1974, and Greek politics are now dominated mostly by two families: the Socialist Papandreou and the right-leaning Karamanlis, assorted members of each taking turns leading the country. (Greeks usually vote in line with their own families as well.) Socialist prime minister Andreas Papandreou most changed Greece when he led the country in the

1980s. He liberalized divorce, approved civil marriages, and abolished the dowry. Stridently anti-West, he loved to show up for photo ops with assorted aging Soviets, but he didn't pull Greece out of NATO or the European Economic Community; for all his words condemning America, he even approved a new U.S. naval base. That had everything to do with arming Greece: Papandreou insisted that the U.S. give Greece at least 70 percent of the billions in military aid she provided to Turkey—and the U.S. acquiesced.

> *Tensions between Greece and Turkey benefit American arms makers who've peddled everything from fighter planes to missiles to both since they joined NATO in 1952. Until recently, Turkey and Greece also received huge U.S. military grants. Now they're addicts; if Turkey buys tactical missiles with warheads that explode shrapnel, then you can bet Greece will too. Must be hard for Turkey to keep up lately: Greece signed up for a $17 billion arms variety pack of warships, fighter jets, subs, an AWACS plane, tanks, attack and transport helicopters, assorted missiles and antiaircraft devices—as security for the 2004 Olympics.*

Greeks have plenty of legitimate reasons for anger, but those feelings of historical injustice only hold their country back, just as inner turmoil has for a century. Greece now has cutting-edge infrastructure and weapons, but her society lags behind. Women got the vote in 1952, but Greece remains a patriarchal society where females may work but rarely attain leadership roles. Young Greeks often study abroad, since universities are filled to the brim, and 27 percent of Greeks under twenty-five don't have a job;[8] many shack up with their families until middle age. Poverty runs at around 21 percent, and while the official illiteracy rate is only 3 percent, some put the figure far higher—particularly in villages. Culturally, modern Greece has her own Madonna and Elvis equivalents—Anna Vissi (singer of "You Are") and Sakis Rouvis (a hip-shaking heartthrob)—but aside from the ancients, the most popular Greek writer is Nikos Kazantzakis, author of *Zorba the Greek*—who died in 1957. The most sought-after Greek creator these days is Nia *"My Big Fat Greek Wedding"* Vardalos—and she's a Greek-Canadian who grew up in less than Hellenic Winnipeg.

Hot Spots

Athens: Revered, polluted, overcrowded Athens—where the taxi you hailed continues to squeeze in more fares en route—is home to almost 4 million, almost a third of Greece's population, despite being designed for only 350,000. She's modernizing—and even has a female mayor, Dora Bakoyianni.

The Aegean: Greece is still fighting with Turks over uninhabited rocks here, and the fish for which Greece is renowned just aren't what they used to be: thanks to overfishing—and fishing with dynamite—stocks are depleted.

Islands: More than 1,400 trail off the mainland in almost every direction, but only 170 are inhabited, some by only a few dozen residents. Superstitions run strong, including the one that cawing crows foretell death. The mule trails that once led to the hills of irises are now covered by asphalt. Buses take tourists up and bring villagers down: they're moving to cities in hordes. Corfu, Mikonos, Santorini, and Crete are four islands where you're more likely to meet holidaying Brits and Germans than Greeks.

Athens: Birthplace of democracy, philosophy, plate-throwing

Crete: Not included in the package when Greece became independent in 1829, Crete triggered a Greek-Turkish war in 1897. Greece lost, but after yet more fighting, Greece won Crete back in 1913; it's now her biggest island and the site of a U.S. naval base.

Imia/Kardak: This pebble of a Greek island in the Aegean almost kicked off a war in 1996: a Turkish boat ran aground here, and when the Greek coast guard arrived, the boat owner refused help, saying Imia was a Turkish island. Turkish journalists inflamed the issue by sticking a Turkish flag on the rock. Both countries sent out warships, and the international community had to pry the two apart.

Mount Athos: No women are allowed on this northern Greek peninsula that is home to twenty monasteries and hundreds of monks; even female livestock are unwelcome.

Hotshots

Photo by Takis Diamantopoulos; courtesy of Greek Government Press Office

PM Karamanlis. In Greece, politics is all about family

Konstandinos "Costas" Karamanlis: Prime Minister, 2004–present. From the conservative New Democracy Party, this nephew of former prime minister Konstantin Karamanlis is the youngest Greek premier ever, and certainly the least experienced. Greeks give him a 47 percent approval rate, despite his stance supporting Turkey in coming into the EU.

George Papandreou Junior: Foreign Minister, 1999–2004. American-born Papandreou of the Socialist PASOK party is Greece's finest diplomat and one of Europe's leading men. Unlike his irascible father (former prime minister Andreas) or his grandfather (former prime minister George Senior), this Papandreou has tried to soothe relations in all of Greece's problem areas—Turkey, Cyprus, Macedonia, and Bulgaria—and made at least limited progress. Too bad his party PASOK was voted out in 2004, and his job went with it. No doubt planning a comeback.

Archbishop Christodoulos: Archbishop of Athens and all Greece, 1998–present. Born in 1939, the powerful and hotheaded head of the Greek Orthodox church is pushing the *Megali Idea* concept again, encouraging Greeks to reclaim land lost to Turks. "We are ready, if necessary, to shed blood," he says of reconquering ancient Greek territories. "We bless the sacred weapons when the moment demands it."[9]

Karolos Papoulis: President, 2005–present. White-haired Karolos Papoulis, seventy-five, has been active in Greek politics since he worked as part of the anti-Nazi resistance during the Second World War.

THE ONASSIS DYNASTY

No modern Greek family illustrates ancient Greek tragedy more vividly than the Onassis clan. Death, jealousy, the depths of loneliness and misery—all set against a backdrop of incredible wealth—are just a few highlights of the shipping family that is still being chronicled in *Vanity Fair*. Patriarch Aristotle Onassis was born poor, but jettisoned his family's tobacco business for an international shipping operation that raked in billions. His ability to attract the fair sex was even more remarkable: opera diva Maria Callas was but one who adored him— his first marriage broke up after his wife found him in the sack with the singer— and Callas vowed revenge when Ari dumped her for JFK's widow Jackie Kennedy. Maybe Callas got her wish. The 1968 Kennedy-Onassis marriage was soon on the rocks, Jackie's shopping extravagances but one problem in the marriage that cost Onassis over $20 million in its first year.[10] In 1973, when Onassis's only son Alexander died in a freak plane crash, Onassis again sought solace in Callas's loving arms, since his wife's arms were, as usual, an ocean away. When Onassis died after a gall bladder operation in 1975, Jackie was out of the will, though she reportedly shook loose some $25 million. About $500 million went to his sole heir, Christina—daughter of wife number one— whose jetsetter life was riddled with drugs and mean husbands. Even more alluring to high-society pirates, Christina, weighing in at around 250 pounds, didn't have glamorous looks and didn't fit with the in-crowd. In 1985, she gave birth to Athina, by Thierry Roussel, her fourth husband—another one fated to leave. Christina adored the child, dressing Athina up in Chanel and Christian Dior, adorning her dark curly locks with real diamonds, and holding up the baby as proof that life was worth living, at least for a while. In 1988, Christina died, alone, in Buenos Aires, apparently as a result of a heart attack and perhaps a drug overdose, although some suspect suicide or foul play. Athina, age three, stood in line as heiress to the modern world's biggest inheritance. In 2003, Athina came fully into her fortune, estimated to be around $2.7 billion. Far more grounded than her mother, Athina apparently prefers four-footed mammals over two-footed party animals. An avid equestrian, she fell in love with Brazilian horse trainer Alvaro Alfonso de Miranda and married him in 2005. Her father, with whom she battled for money, wasn't in attendance at the São Paolo wedding. Here's hoping that newlywed Athina doesn't forget her previous goal: to save the whales.[11] Lord knows, with her dough, maybe she can.

News you can understand: *Kathimerini.* Everything from politics to soccer: www.ekathimerini.com

12. SCANDINAVIA: DENMARK, SWEDEN, FINLAND, AND NORWAY
Quiet Leaders

Overview

Despite the biting weather and vicious Viking culture from which they sprang, Scandinavian countries are (usually) seriously civilized, amazingly evolved, and rather utopian—from their beautiful, squeaky-clean squares where candlelit booths flicker, to social welfare systems that keep residents cozy from cradle to grave. Wealthy and wise Scandinavia often plays global moderator, with Norway brokering deals between warring factions and handing out the Nobel Peace Prize, and all of them throwing out mountains of money and teams of advisers to assuage assorted world woes.

> Scandinavian countries, along with the Netherlands and Luxembourg, are the world's most generous per capita; they're the only countries to heed UN recommendations to donate 0.8 percent of GDP to humanitarian causes.

GEOGRAPHIC CONFUSION: SCANDINAVIA VS. NORDIC COUNTRIES

The term "Scandinavia" is confusing: geographically, it is Norway and Sweden; politically, it refers to Norway, Sweden, and Denmark; and in popular usage and lifestyle it often includes Finland and sometimes far-flung Iceland as well—all of which are called the Nordic countries. In this section, "Scandinavia" refers to Norway, Sweden, Denmark, and Finland—also called the Nordic countries here.

Nobel Prizes, annual awards that come with checks for 10 million Swedish kronor—that's over $1.3 million—are actually a shared two-country venture. Sweden funds the awards and hands out the Nobel Prizes in Literature and scientific areas. The Nobel Peace Prize is given out by Norway. When Alfred Nobel established his prize-awarding foundation, Sweden and Norway were one country.

Scandinavians are lucky: their sparsely populated corner of the world is resource-rich and stunning in its pristine beauty—filled with thousands of lakes, islands, cliffs, and fjords—and the residents are gorgeous, smart, and globally attuned. Their societies draw from Socialist models, with benefits such as free day care, numerous paid sick days, and subsidized health care, and Scandinavians are assured of having a job—the government will educate them, find them work, and even retrain them in new careers for free. There is a flipside: Scandinavians pay steep taxes—often upward of 50 percent—to ensure that welfare systems coddle one and all. Restaurant meals (perhaps fancy open-faced sandwiches or reindeer stew) sure are tasty, but they seriously hammer the wallet; prices for booze are frightening enough to make you run to AA, and expenses from cars to sweaters and from rent to heating bills make costs in the U.S. appear to be a bargain-basement deal. Besides, what good is living in such evolved societies, when you have to brave cruel, icy winds to get anywhere? (Those ubiquitous Volvos with heated seats help.) Nevertheless, Scandinavians are a contented lot, typically topping global "happiness surveys," and even though they're world travelers, few permanently stray from their gardens of Eden despite the teeth-chattering cold. In fact, the big Nordic problem is the opposite: immigration. The issue brings to light what may be the only serious flaw in these advanced countries: many Scandinavians don't want to share their snowy paradises, which have long been ethnically homogenous. And some politicians have become downright xenophobic and racist in their attempts to eject foreigners and prevent more from coming.

Until recently, Scandinavians rarely lived alongside people from other cultures, unless you count other Scandinavians—and it's very telling that Scandinavians do so: a Swede living in Denmark, for instance, is a foreigner. Africans, Middle Easterners, Asians, and even East Europeans were rarely found living in the Nordic countries until the 1970s; the numbers have escalated since. When the first mosque in Scandinavia appeared (in Sweden) in 1984, it was hugely controversial and spawned a number of anti-immigrant parties, some now wielding substantial clout.

THE VIKINGS

Never recalled for their delicate touch or flowery names (such as Gorm the Old and Harald Bluetooth), ninth- and tenth-century Vikings (Scandinavians pronounce it "Wikings") were remarkable in their ability to sail nearly anywhere, plunder without reservation, and establish popular trading posts. Swedish Vikings headed east along rivers, setting up Russia's Novgorod and Ukraine's Kiev, and marauded across Constantinople and Persia.[1] Danish Vikings headed west, sacking Ireland and roping England into the Danish Empire; they so frequently attacked France that the king finally handed them the French northwest coast, now called Normandy after the Norsemen. Vikings of Norwegian extraction colonized Iceland and Greenland and first touched down in Vinland—North America—six centuries before Columbus set sail. The Vikings were so brutal that they threatened to wipe out Western European civilization in the tenth century,[2] but their legacy lives on: trading posts they established are today bustling cities, and their divinatory rune stones are still being pulled out of cloth bags and deciphered. Even Viking god Odin is making a comeback in Nordic pagan circles.

The collective fretting about immigration isn't the only thing that binds them. Except for Finns (who have more in common with Estonians), Scandinavians are linked by similar languages, ethnic roots, and history. All (including Finland) are wealthy, nearly homogenous social welfare states, and are predominantly Protestant—although less than 5 percent typically attend church. All are heavily militarized, due in part to fears of Russia. They share the same cross design on their flags (but in different colors), and they madly celebrate the summer solstice in days-long midsummer festivals.

NORDIC PERKS

Living in the most northern region of the world does have its benefits— among them meteorological oddities. In the farthest regions of Norway, Sweden, and Finland, one can glimpse the world's most spectacular views of aurora borealis—waves of phosphorescent lights that streak across the skies. The northern extremes also have the most dramatic lighting. In winter the sun doesn't come up for weeks, and in summer it doesn't set for weeks in these "lands of the midnight sun." Being dominated by weather, Scandinavians emphasize the comfort of their homes—and holidays are times of days-long feasts. And once the sun makes its appearance, no group of people is happier as they set out on boats, set up in lakeside cottages, and transform small islands into concert sites and partygrounds. The highlight is June's summer solstice, when they dance around maypoles, pluck special flowers for love, eat barrels of fish, and drink copious amounts to celebrate the return of warmth.

Despite their commonalities—including the fact that their residents speak gorgeous English—don't mistake Scandinavians for one big happy family sitting around the fireplace knitting beautiful mittens. They battled each other fiercely for centuries—and rivalries still play out. The different countries all have distinct identities and plenty of differences, starting with Finland being a republic while the others are monarchies. Other contrasts:

- Denmark entered the European Union in 1973, Sweden and Finland waited for twenty-two years, and only Finland uses the euro; Norway refuses to join at all (and isn't covered in this book)
- Only Denmark and Norway are NATO members
- Sweden is now the most open to asylum seekers; Denmark is the most closed
- Formerly liberal Denmark is still the most easygoing about alcohol
- Finland used to be part of Russia
- Norway is the richest, thanks to her North Sea oil fields

CHANGING PARTNERS

The Nordic countries weren't always separate entities; for ages, they were part of Denmark or Sweden—Finland and Norway are very recent creations. In 1397, the areas that are today's Scandinavia united as the Kalmar Union, dominated by Denmark. That lasted until 1523, when Sweden broke away, taking today's Finland with her—and thereby launching a centuries-long war with the Danes; Denmark latched on to Norway for the next three centuries. Russia grabbed Finland from Sweden in 1809 (Finland shook loose in 1917); Sweden was so upset by the loss that she snatched Norway, which finally wriggled free in 1905. The Danish territory of Iceland, taken by Vikings in the tenth century, became entirely independent in 1944, and Greenland, self-governing since 1979, is still trying to give Denmark the full heave-ho.

Perhaps the best way to distinguish the different Scandinavian nationalities is to note where their citizens feel most at peace. Swedes find happiness in a sailing boat bobbing off the southern islands. Danes find it laughing in the pub (called *kro*) while drinking a bitter (beer) or Gammel Dansk (old Danish schnapps). Finns are happiest in their home saunas, from which they run naked into the snow.[3] Norwegians are most joyful atop a mountain, preferably alone.

13. DENMARK
(Danmark)
The Bridge

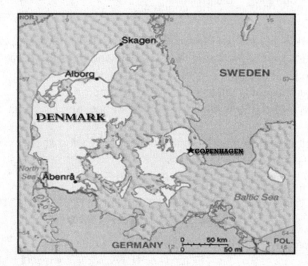

FAST FACTS

Country:	Kingdom of Denmark; Kongeriget Danmark
Capital:	Copenhagen (pronounced ko-pen-HAYG-en)
Government:	Constitutional monarchy
Independence:	Constitutional monarchy established 1849
Population:	5,451,000 (2006 estimate)
Head of State:	Queen Margrethe II (1972)
Head of Government:	Prime Minister Anders Fogh Rasmussen (2001)
Elections:	Monarchy is hereditary; prime minister appointed by monarch
Name of Parliament:	Folketing
Ethnicity:	Scandinavian, Inuit, Faeroese, German, Turk, Iranian, Somali
Religion:	95% Lutheran—less than 3% attend church; 3% Roman Catholic; 2% Muslim

Language:	Danish; English widely spoken; also Faeroese, Greenlandic, German
Literacy:	99% (2003 estimate)
Famous Exports:	Carlsberg beer, Lego, anti-Islamic comics
Economic Big Boy:	Moller-Maersk (freight company); 2004 total sales: $26.55 billion[1]
Per Capita GDP:	$33,400 (2005 estimate)
Unemployment:	4.4% (December 2005 Eurostat figure)
EU Status:	EEC member since 1973
Currency:	Danish krone

Quick Tour

She's delightfully nonjudgmental, she's pragmatically liberal, she's joyfully open—oh wait, that's *old* Denmark. Over the past five years, Danmark, the laid-back land where royals walked about town without guards and locals rarely locked their doors, has pulled a shocking about-face, swinging sharply to the closed-minded, finger-pointing, xenophobic right. Now the charming country that was long Scandinavia's most open-minded (she was the world's first to legalize gay marriage), is now the most uptight and downright racist of the region—so much so that the UN formally condemned her recent rabid political campaigns. Once known as the castled fairy-tale land of Hans Christian Andersen, Denmark is now best known for the nightmare she triggered when the most popular daily, *Jyllands-Postens*, printed cartoons denigrating Muslim prophet Muhammad. Muslims from Pakistan to Nigeria rioted in response, some attacking Danish embassies. And those comics were but one illustration of how sweet little Denmark has alarmingly changed.

> *The smallest of Scandinavian countries, Denmark likes to claim it is actually the European country with most land—and it is, if you add in Greenland, still a Danish territory.*

To understand what is so rotten about what's happened to Denmark lately, it's best to understand what the lovely country until recently was, and in some ways still is, which is to say a smattering of 400 whose island denizens appeared more like a homogenous family 5 million strong. Danes speak what they regard as a secret language, barely understood by other Scandinavians, and all it takes is a request from their beloved queen—for instance not to litter—for Danes to honor it. Whether in a fishing village of thatched cottages or in

Copenhagen: Flat but high-minded, previously

Copenhagen, the elegant capital of spires where the pavements nearly glisten, life is usually so carefree that Danes leave their swaddled infants unattended in baby carriages on the sidewalk when they dart into a shop.

Until recently, Danish life was so lacking in topics for outrage (besides the bingeing Swedes who come over and vomit in their streets) that Danes still brought up the 1963 scandal surrounding the visit of American actor Danny Kaye (star of the movie *Hans Christian Andersen*), who visited the Hans Christian Andersen Museum and caused a huge hullabaloo when he jumped into Hans's bed. "Yes, jumped right in his bed!" they'd repeat indignantly, likening it to the "horror" an American would feel if a Dane jumped into Lincoln's four-poster.

Danish life has long been (and continues to be) a festive affair. Christmas holidays kick off when Carlsberg makes rounds across the country, delivering kegs of free beer, Danes wander through candlelit squares or twinkling Tivoli Gardens sipping *gløg*—hot spiced wine with slivered almonds—before settling in for stellar Danish cuisine, perhaps duck cooked with cardamom, brandy, and prunes, and polishing off (or starting) their feasts with icy cold, caraway-spiked *akvavit*.

> *Nothing better captures the lavish art of Danish dining than director Gabriel Axel's masterpiece* Babette's Feast.

In the summer, Danes frolic along gleaming island waters while glowing bonfires dot the white-sand shores, and a thousand festivals are crammed into the few gloriously warm days. And any time of year, Danes pack into grand high-ceilinged cafés, chic clubs, and cozy pubs, tossing back schnapps with their beers and celebrating a worry-free lifestyle that allows them to take off several years—with pay—to launch new careers.

Typically the most daring of the Scandinavian bunch, Denmark was the first to leap into the European Union and NATO, and she was the first European country to wholeheartedly embrace green energy. Giant, high-tech windmills spin across the countryside, generating wind-powered electricity, and Danes built Europe's first large-scale solar energy plant; biomass is another power source, and steam from industrial plants is piped into villages to heat homes.

CHRISTIANIA

The best-known symbol of Danish tolerance is Christiania—an "alternative lifestyle experiment" on the outskirts of Copenhagen. In 1971, students, artists, and hippies moved into an abandoned army fort, transforming it into a self-sufficient eighty-four-acre village with houses, stores, gardens, and restaurants, complete with "Pusher Street," where residents openly sold hash. Initially determined to shut it down, the government instead decided the community was a "social experiment" and, in 1987, turned the land over to the "Christianites," requiring only that they pay taxes. The alternative community of 1,000 became a source of pride to many Danes as an illustration of their open-mindedness, and was a huge tourist draw. An icon of Danish liberalness, Christiania is now under attack. Shortly after the right-wing government marched into power in 2001, it banned hash sales and announced plans to renovate the lake-dotted hamlet and turn it into a condominium complex. Thousands of Danes marched across Copenhagen in protest, but the push is on to bring a screeching halt not only to Pusher Street but to the whole experiment.

The progressive country began shifting right in the 1990s, when thousands of Bosnians and Somalis flooded the country, seeking refuge from wartime strife—and bringing the number of Muslims to about 210,000, or 4 percent of the population. Now, about 8 percent of Danish residents are immigrants (although that figure includes other Scandinavians). In 1999, the government set up an integration and language teaching program; until then, most immigrants didn't learn Danish. Thus many—about 90 percent of Somalis, and half of other immigrants—had remained jobless. Immigrants drained welfare funds by some 40 to 50 percent, according to right-wing groups, who added that statistics showed that immigrants committed the most crime in Denmark. Impish social worker Pia Kjaersgaard began screaming about the refugees, but initially most Danes rolled their eyes at her anti-immigrant tirades; in 1996, however, the newly formed anti-immigrant Danish People's Party made her its head. Three years later, a fourteen-year-old Danish girl was locked in a shed and gang-raped by immigrant teenagers. Seven of the boys were found guilty in February 2000. But the group was sentenced to only nine months' imprisonment; since they'd already been imprisoned for that long, they walked free from court. Danes were outraged—and Kjaersgaard made it her cause célèbre. In following weeks, swarms of anti-immigration protesters took to the streets, their marches some- times turning violent—a most un-Danish phenomenon. The September 11 at- tacks gave the final push to full-strength xenophobia. Prime Minister Poul Nyrop Rasmussen called a snap election, believing the panicked country would stand behind him. He was dead wrong: opponent Anders "Fogh" Rasmussen (no rela- tion) correctly read the mood and campaigned with the slogan "Time for a Change" plastered across a photo of the convicted rapists walking out of court. Fogh Rasmussen took the election in a landslide. Another big winner: Pia Kjaersgaard, whose anti-immigration Danish People's Party suddenly made sense to 12 percent of the Danish population, making it the country's third most powerful party. In a flash, Danes were looking at the most conservative govern- ment in seventy-five years.

"When she retires, Muslims will be a majority in Denmark," reads the tagline under the photo of a wide-eyed blond child in a 2001 political poster for the Danish People's Party. Another poster showed a picture of Danish girls next to a gang of bloody Muslims. "Denmark now," ran the caption under the girls; "Denmark in ten years," ran the caption under the gang. The United Nations High Commission for Refugees was so horrified by the racist cam- paigns that it formally condemned them.

Doors are slamming shut to asylum seekers, undesirables are being de- ported, minority populations are targets of scorn, and a new law states that Danes can't marry foreigners unless they are at least twenty-five years old— and even then they have to plunk down $8,000 as a deposit against any future welfare payments. The country that was once synonymous with "evolved" and "egalitarian" is now best known for Pia Kjaersgaard's "shrill squawking" and comments such as "Muslims have a taste for committing mass rapes"—none of which helps to solve very real problems.

Fogh Rasmussen sent in troops for the American 2003 Iraq invasion and cleanup.

Denmark has been catching plenty of flak, not only for now having the world's most restrictive immigration policies, but for what smacks of inhumane treatment. In 2001, for example, the government temporarily boarded 300 refugees in container units—boxes used for shipping—providing only eleven bathrooms to share.[2] The United Nations High Commission for Refugees was only one agency that swiped at Denmark for that move. The Fogh Rasmussen government points out that Muslims are free to practice Islam, that Denmark has over 120 mosques and prayer rooms, and that the country has Muslim cemeteries and has passed antidiscrimination laws. But Denmark appears to be dividing—as evidenced in a new trend for white Danes to head to private schools. It remains to be seen where the dust from this major fallout settles.

History Review

One word aptly describes Danish history: "shrinkage." Denmark, now the tiniest of the Nordic countries, was once the largest. The alpha dog behind the fourteenth-century collective Scandinavian kingdom—the Kalmar Union—Denmark lost Sweden (and Finland) in the sixteenth century, lost Norway 200 years later, and lost Iceland sixty years ago. Just as painful: when German state Prussia snatched the duchy of Schleswig-Holstein in 1864, Denmark lost a third of her territory and almost half her people—most of them ethnic Germans. That geographical severing, however, resulted in a country that was ethnically homogeneous, a white-bread uniformity that continued for over a century.

> *A mighty naval power during the seventeenth century, Denmark has since had problems with her navy: she kept losing it. First the British ran off with it during the Napoleonic Wars in the 1800s. Then in 1940, when Nazis occupied Denmark, Britain snatched it again—making off with half the Danish merchant navy. In 1943, the remaining Danish fleet ended up underwater; rather than serve Nazis, the Danish navy scuttled its ships.*

DANISH STAR: TYCHO BRAHE (1546–1601)

Nobleman Tycho Brahe was a rash, passionate sort. In his youth, he dueled with a fellow student over a math formula, losing part of his nose in the fight. (Being wealthy, he bought a gold prosthesis, but it frequently fell off.) When he saw a supernova several years later, he became hooked on astronomy and talked King Frederik II into building him a deluxe hilltop observatory, Uraniborg, where he spent years tracking heavenly bodies and filling notebooks with Virgoan detail. The next king found his celestial studies boring, so Brahe huffed off to Prague to become Royal Mathematician for Holy Roman Emperor Rudolf II, and hired a German assistant named Johannes Kepler. The assistant stayed at home, poring over planetary studies, but Brahe was often dragged out to party with Rudolf; he died after one particularly rough night of drinking. For centuries, historians believed that the cause of Brahe's death was that his bladder had burst. Recent DNA tests show, however, that Brahe died by accidentally poisoning himself while treating a bladder malady: fittingly, the astronomer was killed by mercury.

Brahe died thinking that the universe was geocentric, but in his vastly complicated model, the planets revolved round the sun. Kepler used Brahe's notes to illuminate the motions of heavenly bodies, becoming far more famous, and accurate, than his boss.

Neutral during the First World War, Denmark stayed clear of the action, but neutrality didn't help in World War II. Hitler wanted Scandinavian iron ore and threatened to flatten Copenhagen; the monarchy allowed Nazis to come in without a fight, in exchange for remaining an independent, albeit occupied, country. Food and industrial goods were shipped off for the German war effort, but Nazis generally treated Danes well, as Hitler admired their Aryan good looks and planned to make Scandinavians part of the German gene pool. Jews were discriminated against, but were not forced to wear stars and were somewhat protected under the collaborating Danish government—at first. That soon changed. Resistance flared up in 1941, and by 1942, when Danish politician Christmas Møller escaped to England and broadcast calls to throw out Nazis, acts of sabotage and riots kicked up all over the place; Hitler was livid that the Danish government refused his calls to kill resisters. Fearing that Denmark was slipping away, Hitler blew his top when he was snubbed (he thought) by King Christian X. When the Führer sent the monarch a birthday greeting, the king telegrammed back three words—"my utmost thanks"—which struck Hitler as curt. Shortly after the so-called telegram crisis, Nazis booted the king and took over Denmark's government. Plans to round up Jews, however, were thwarted when Danish resistance spread the news in advance. Danes helped thousands of Jews flee the country and escape to neutral Sweden.

Touchy Areas: In the darkness of October 1, 1943, Danish fishermen ferried some 8,000 Jews to Sweden via a secret boat lift—that much is fact. The rest is hard to pin down. Some say Jews were forced to pay large sums and that some fishermen became quite wealthy from what was painted solely as a humanitarian effort. Another touchy bit of history: at war's end, the Allies were loathe to count Denmark as having been on their side, but Danish diplomats struck a deal. Denmark would be remembered as part of the Allied forces if the U.S. could set up more military bases on Greenland. Four U.S. military bases shot up on Greenland, and Denmark went down as an ally.

GREENLAND

Iceland is green, and Greenland is icy, as the saying goes—and Greenland (with a population of 50,000, mostly Inuit fishermen) lives up to the description. The ice-capped land holds 10 percent of the planet's water, tons of PCBs and radioactive waste—legacies of U.S. military bases there (Thule Air Force Base remains)—and an ongoing source of local anger at Denmark, which invited the United States to build the bases. That was a costly move—starting with the fact that the U.S. ignored Denmark's demands that nuclear bombs would not be transported over Greenland or stored there.

- **1953:** Inuit people were shoved out to make way for Thule U.S. Air Force Base, the most northerly U.S. military post—good for spying on Soviets; decades later, the Danish government forked over $70,000 in reparations for taking away Inuit villages and hunting grounds.
- **1968:** According to declassified U.S. government documents, a B-52 carrying four hydrogen bombs crashed near Thule, releasing at least one pound (and up to twenty-four pounds) of dead plutonium; one hydrogen bomb was never found.
- **1995:** The Thule cleanup crew for the nuclear accident, many sick with cancer, sued the Danish government, settling for over $15 million.
- **2006:** The U.S. awarded Raytheon a contract to set up advanced radar systems on Greenland as part of its national missile defense scheme, which makes locals shudder.

Denmark granted the island more autonomy in 1979, but many Greenlanders demand total independence, complete with mineral rights, since loads of oil may sit offshore. While looking for petroleum, perhaps they can find that stray H-bomb.

Hot Spots

Copenhagen: In the elegant waterfront capital that is home to harbor, canals, Tivoli Gardens, drug-free Christiania, and half a million Danes, property prices are rising as land grows scarce, and fear levels are up in the normally easygoing, pedestrian-oriented, and fashionable city. Still, Copenhageners know how to party, and new districts of cafés, clubs, and pubs are shooting up everywhere, including in the former red-light district Nørvebo. Word to the wise: it's easy to meet beautiful Danes while out on the town, but don't break into "Wonderful, Wonderful Copenhagen," or you'll hear about the Danny Kaye "scandal" for hours.

> *Rising above the sea in Helsingør, Kronborg Castle was Shakespeare's inspiration for Hamlet's Elsinore.*

Danish prisons: Is it that many guards are women, that inmates take anger management courses, or that the lodgings don't have bathrooms? Whatever the reasons, the few Danes who end up in prison tend to not stay long (most are in for less than a year), and relatively few come back (a 27 percent return rate).[3]

THE BRIDGE

Denmark is the physical, mental, and political bridge to the rest of Europe—more so since the 2000 opening of the Oresund Bridge that links Malmö, Sweden, to Copenhagen, Denmark—from which one can zip down to Germany. The $4 billion double-decker bridge, a joint venture of Danish and Swedish governments, carries a hefty toll of $35 per one-way crossing—convincing many commuters to stick with the ferry. Unexpected side effects have transpired, however; thousands of Danes are moving to Malmö, where housing is cheaper (by half) and Danes who want to marry foreigners can skip the immigration hoops.

Jutland: A peninsula surrounded by Denmark's 400 islands, Jutland protrudes from north Germany, and is known for white beaches, windsurfing, and music festivals. The biggest draw: Legoland, a fantasy theme park made entirely of Lego toys, including the train.

Faeroe Islands: The twenty-two islands lying between the Shetlands and Iceland were yanked into the family by Vikings, and they're still populated by sheepherders and fishermen, many of whom want independence, but that might be a dream; Denmark's subsidies are needed to keep the place running. On the other hand, oil may be gurgling offshore, so they might be able to make it handsomely on their own, should Denmark decide to let them go.

> *Who knew? The Faeroes are home to the world's longest continuously running parliament, which first started deliberation back in the tenth century.[4]*

Hotshots

The Danish royal family: Beloved head of state Queen Margrethe, famous for tossing back her head in a hearty laugh, is also a respected painter and illustrator of children's books. Like his mom, Crown Prince Frederik mingles with the masses. During his playboy years he was known as the "Turbo Prince," often spotted dancing in bars with a fetching model draped on his arm. In 2004, he married Mary Donaldson, a Tasmanian lawyer who isn't a model but who looks like one; no word on if they had to pay the new $8,000 marriage-to-a-foreigner fee. Prince Joachim married lovely Princess Alexandra, of Austrian-English-Polish-Chinese heritage—the first person of Asian extraction to marry a European royal—who learned the decidedly difficult Danish language in about six seconds, and soon produced two male heirs, although that took slightly longer. Alas, they recently divorced.

Anders "Fogh" Rasmussen: Prime minister, 2001–present. His sensationalist "Time for a Change" campaign hit the panic button, getting the conservative Venstre leader into office—and generating votes for the right-wing Danish People's Party too. His government curtailed immigration, passing laws that refugees will be deported if their home countries are deemed safe, limiting the immigration of clerics, and denying citizenship to foreign-born people over the age of sixty.

> *Rasmussen triggered an uproar in 2003, when he became Denmark's first prime minister to denounce the behavior of the Danish government during the Second World War.*

Housewife Pia Kjaersgaard is
tidying up Denmark

Courtesy of the Danish People's Party

Pia Kjaersgaard: Head of Danish People's Party, 1996–present. The social worker once delivered meals to the elderly and now dishes up steaming-hot ethnic hatred. Denmark's most frothing anti-immigrationist, Kjaersgaard wants Denmark to stop offering political asylum, shut down the Øresund Bridge, and kick up a "holy war against Islam"—for starters. The press appreciates her controversial statements, including her claim that Muslims are "bringing a medieval mentality to Denmark." Like she's not?

Even if the most famous Dane—Hamlet—was the fictional creation of a Brit, there are plenty of other famous Danes and famous Danish inventions, although the Danish pastry is not one of them; in Denmark they call it Vienna bread.

Hans Christian Andersen (1805–1875): Son of a shoemaker and washerwoman, Hans Christian Andersen had scant education, but at fourteen headed to Copenhagen, where he tried to make it as a singer-dancer-actor-artist-playwright and lived on the streets for years. He finally sold a musical play, which was performed by the Royal Theatre in 1829. Perpetually pooh-poohed by critics, and appreciated even less by women, Andersen found a fan in the king, who funded Andersen's travels across Europe. Returning from an inspiring journey to Italy, Germany, and France, Andersen began writing fairy tales. By the time he died, he'd completed over 150, including *The Ugly Duckling*, *The Emperor's New Clothes*, *Thumbelina*, and *The Princess and the Pea*; Andersen's works are said to be the world's most translated, after the Bible. He also applied fictional technique when writing his fantasy-filled autobiography *The Fairy Tale of My Life*.

Søren Kierkegaard (1813–1855): Wealthy, well-read, and a wicked wit at parties, philosopher Kierkegaard was prone to deep gloominess, which led to ideas about individuals living their own subjective truths—earning him the moniker of "Father of Existentialism." In the 1840s, he cranked out books that wove together philosophy, psychology, biblical analysis, and literary criticism, including *Fear and Trembling*, *Either/Or*, and *Concluding Unscientific Post-script*, all widely respected by philosophers today.

Isak Dinesen/Karen Blixen (1885–1962): Baroness Karen Blixen, who wrote as Isak Dinesen, hardly lived a life of noble boredom. After her father committed suicide, her life became a drama. A love affair with a Swedish cousin soured, so she married his twin and traded in her privileged lifestyle to buy a coffee farm in Kenya, the basis for *Out of Africa* (published in 1937). The marriage between the kissing cousins fell apart (the cad gave her syphilis), and then she lost the farm. Suffering from advanced syphilis, she returned to her family's estate in Denmark that symbolized all from which she'd wanted to escape. She was shocked, upon her return, to find herself a celebrity. Dinesen is pictured on the Danish fifty-kroner note and is the only non-royal to have rated a postage stamp. She is buried at her Danish estate, Rungstedlund, now a sanctuary for birds.[5]

CUT THE CRAP: DOGME FILMS

Sickened by Hollywood's formulaic scripts and technological slickness, Danish filmmakers in the Dogme 95 Collective wrote a list of ten commandments, demanding that only handheld cameras be used and pledging that their films would avoid special effects, artificial lighting, soundtracks, and faked actions such as murders; they even shunned makeup for actors. The best known of the three dozen Dogme films is *Festen* (*Celebration*) by Thomas Vinterberg, in which a family reunion transforms into a hilarious forum for airing the clan's filthy laundry. The popularity of Dogme's films made handheld shakiness fashionable and rather defeated their revolutionary aim, as mainstream filmmakers imitated the style; even John Travolta and Steven Spielberg are fans.

DRINKING MATTERS

It tastes like cough syrup mixed with motor oil, but many Danes won't travel without shot-size bottles of Underberg—the digestif so good for tums that the company guarantees its benefits. Divine: Xanté—like potable poached pears.

News you can understand: *Copenhagen Post*—"the Danish News in English": www.cphpost.dk

14. SWEDEN
(Sverige)
Suddenly Unsure

FAST FACTS

Country: Kingdom of Sweden; Konungariket Sverige
Capital: Stockholm
Government: Constitutional monarchy
Independence: June 6, 1523 (Gustav Vasa elected king)
Population: 9,017,000 (2006 estimate)

Head of State:	King Carl XVI Gustav (1973)
Head of Government:	Prime Minister Göran Persson (1996)
Elections:	Monarchy is hereditary; prime minister elected to four-year term by parliament
Name of Parliament:	Riksdag
Ethnicity:	Swedish; Finnish; Sami; other Scandinavian; Yugoslav; Greek; Turkish
Religion:	87% Lutheran; Roman Catholic; Orthodox; Baptist; Muslim; Jewish; Buddhist; others
Language:	Swedish; Sami; and Finnish
Literacy:	99% (2003 estimate)
Famous Exports:	Pippi Longstocking, ABBA, dynamite
Economic Big Boy:	Volvo (autos); 2004 total sales: $30.32 billion[1]
Per Capita GDP:	$29,800 (2005 estimate)
Unemployment:	6.2% (December 2005 Eurostat figure)
EU Status:	Member since 1995
Currency:	Swedish krona

Quick Tour

Land of snow-sprinkled spruce forests, shimmering mountains, and ice-glazed lakes, sparkling Sverige is a beauty, as are so many of her inhabitants, about half of whom live in tiny snowbound villages with populations of 1,000 or less. From the glaciers in river-threaded Sarek, Europe's largest wildlife park, to islands of quaint cottages, Sweden is a traveler's paradise. Draped over fourteen islands, grand dame Stockholm is artistically charged and technologically wired: the capital pulses with so many new designers, artistic sorts, boutique hotels, street markets, and information technology companies that *Newsweek* calls Stockholm the "new Seattle." To the west, fetching Göteborg, the country's major port, is home to dozens of festivals and to Volvo, the carmaker that eschewed assembly-line production, while Malmö to the southwest is the most racially diverse settlement in Scandinavia, with all the issues that come along with it.

THE MALMÖ EXPERIMENT

Malmö, a port city of 265,000 on the Oresund Sound and the shipbuilding center of Sweden, is Scandinavia's most dynamic urban area. One reason: the six-year-old bridge that stretches to Denmark, the first built between the countries. The Oresund Bridge triggered a flurry of change. Against a backdrop of red-brick buildings and medieval squares, universities sprang up alongside new businesses and high-rises, including Sweden's tallest, the new fifty-eight-floor Turning Torso—an architecturally twisting apartment tower that is now Malmö's trendiest address. But that isn't why Malmö sticks out. This is Sweden's biggest melting pot—a mix of Yugolavs, Iraqis, Poles, Pakistanis, Somalis, Turks, Bosnians, Iranians, Greeks, and more; in all, over 130 nationalities, speaking 100 languages, have settled here, most since 1980. Some are quickly employed; others await word on asylum applications, which can take a year. While some industrial areas are being revamped with chic cafés and filmmakers and artists are opening studios in Malmö, poor immigrants settle out in Rosengrad, where most are Arab, Muslim, and/or African, and unemployment can run at 95 percent.[2] With as few as 5 percent native Swedes in the classrooms of Malmö's state schools, this was multiculturalism put to the test. Many locals accepted and endorsed the changes—here you can find Swedes laughing it up with Iranians and Poles—but about 40,000 fled, although the population is now booming. Others joined anti-immigrant parties, which appeared in 1984, when Scandinavia's first mosque was erected in Malmö. Radical right-wingers don't fare well politically, but tension sometimes flares: the mosque was set on fire in 2003—but survived.

Sweden doesn't have a popular anti-immigrant party, and Denmark's self-appointed immigration expert, Danish Peoples' Party leader Pia Kjaersgaard, continually hisses criticisms at Sweden's doors-still-open refugee policy. She calls Swedish immigrant communities "Scandinavian Beiruts," filled with "gang rapes" and warns that Sweden is facing an "apocalypse." In response, Sweden's foreign minister called Kjaersgaard an "embarrassment" to Denmark.[3]

The largest Scandinavian country in area, population, and ego—and third largest area-wise in the EU—Sweden is one of the world's most generous countries, and not just for many millions of dollars in award money she's handed out with the Nobel Prize.

ALFRED NOBEL (1833–1896)

Alfred Nobel fancied writing poetry, so his alarmed parents sent him to Paris to work as a chemist. There he met the man who had invented nitroglycerin, an unstable, dangerous explosive. Nobel brought the chemical back to Stockholm, where his experiments often blew sky-high (his brother was killed during one explosion), until local authorities banned nitroglycerin within city limits. Nobel devised a way to stably contain it—in dynamite—an invention that made him wealthy, and his fortune soared after he invested in Azerbaijan's oil fields. He founded arms manufacturing companies worldwide—including Sweden's Bofors AB—but was also attuned to the push toward disarmament. When he died, Nobel requested that 94 percent of his estate be used to start a foundation that would award the world's highest achievers in physics, chemistry, medicine, literature, and world peace. His relatives hotly contested the will, as did Sophie Hess, his young lover, who threatened to publish spicy letters he'd penned. She was paid the equivalent of $120,000 to hush up[4,5]—and the first prizes were handed out in 1901.

Sweden also donates billions for victim relief in natural disasters and billions more to help out developing countries, including funds to upgrade water systems and promote sustainable agriculture development; the government even brings in workers and lawmakers from developing countries and trains them in areas from children's rights to energy management. Like Finland, a world leader in research and development, entrepreneurial Sweden innovates, most recently in alternative fuels. The world's biggest biogas plant is going up in Göteborg; using manure and wastewater, it will cut Sweden's carbon dioxin emissions by 15,000 tons annually. Drivers can pump ethanol at hundreds of gas stations, and Sweden is so aggressively developing renewable energy that it hopes to be petroleum-free by 2020.

> *Even the million bottles of booze confiscated annually by customs goes in the biofuel mix that now powers buses and taxes in Linköping.[6]*

Well, what else would you expect from a country long hailed as the world's model society? With low crime, high incomes, a soaring economy, and a government that pays for health care, day care, and education from the first cry of birth to the last gasp of death, Sweden was long the most vibrant example of the "welfare state" that blends the best of Socialism and capitalism.

> *Children are protected under Swedish law: in 1979, Sweden banned "smacking" children, becoming the first country to outlaw physical punishment of children, and the law was publicized on milk cartons; even advertising to children is banned. In 1999, Sweden introduced a law to limit prostitution. It didn't go after prostitutes; it hit johns with a maximum of six months in jail and a minimum fine of fifty days' wages. Swedish street prostitution dried up—although some say now there are more call girls.*

KILLING IKE'S SUICIDE CAMPAIGN

Contrary to popular belief, Swedes do not have a high suicide rate. According to the Swedish Institute, that legend started after U.S. president Dwight D. Eisenhower gave a blustery speech in 1960, striking out at Sweden for not fully committing to the Cold War—and for endorsing a system with Socialist elements that smacked too much of Communism for the black-and-white Cold War mentality. "Sin, nudity, drunkenness, and suicide," he asserted, were all results of Sweden's social welfare state.[7] Swedes don't deny the sin, nudity, and drunkenness parts (although nobody links them to the welfare state)—but they point out they don't score high on the suicide list. Perhaps Ike was a victim of geographical confusion; Finns and Danes are indeed prone to do themselves in, perhaps because it's so hard to keep up with the Swedes. It's even difficult to compete with them on happiness surveys: 96 percent of Swedes say they are happy.[8]

Designed with an egalitarian eye as a "home for the people," Sweden has high taxes—the wealthy may pay upward of 60 percent—but results are spectacular. Cities are well-kept, cultural programs and museums are well-funded, strikes are rare, roads are smooth, and everything from medieval squares to apartment laundry rooms are laid out in orderly fashion. With their country routinely topping quality of life charts—it's the best place to be a woman and a mother, says a recent "Save the Children" report—Swedes can't help but feel rather smug. For decades, theirs was the most successful socioeconomic experiment in the world, with Europe's lowest infant mortality rate, longest life expectancy (for males), and one of the planet's wealthiest societies.

Swedes can get government funding (and work space) for "study circles"— when five or more learn a new skill, be it mastering Mandarin, putting on a play, or learning how to crochet. Another "Swedish model" benefit: 480-day maternity or paternity leaves with full pay; each year, a parent can take off sixty paid sick days to tend to their kids.

DEVISING FRAMEWORKS AND INVENTING THINGAMAJIGS

Is it the cold, the vodka, or the long winter nights that keep one homebound and bound to create? Whatever the reason, Swedes are known as designers and inventors, particularly of systems and handy gadgets, from the cream separator to the adjustable wrench—and engineering accounts for about half of Swedish GDP and exports. A few of the big names historically:

- **Olof Rudbeck (the Elder) (1630–1702):** Identified workings of the lymphatic system.
- **Anders Celsius (1701–1744):** Invented the world's most-used temperature system.
- **Linnaeus (aka Carl von Linné) (1707–1778):** Developed classification systems for plants (and animals and minerals), launching botany and taxonomy and coining such terms as *Homo sapiens*. Also a stellar travel writer.
- **Fredrik Ljungström (1875–1964):** Invented steam turbine to produce electricity.
- **Sven Wingquist (1876–1953):** Invented ball bearings—crucial to Nazis in WWII.
- **Ruben Rausing (1895–1983):** Invented Tetra Pak drink carton.
- **Rune Elmquist (1906–1996):** Invented pacemaker.

Swedish grace: Swedes are also famous for their lean furniture design— and are credited with being the hands that married beauty and functionality in the twentieth-century home. Ingvar Kamprad took the idea of simple utility to new heights with his chain of u-assemble furniture—IKEA—becoming the fourth richest person in the world in the process.

The object of international media coos and the neighbors' envy, Sweden first tumbled off her pedestal around 1986, when an assassin shot down Prime Minister Olof Palme—an event that rattled Sweden to her core, especially since violent crime was little known in the land of 9 million. The Midas touch that Social Democrats, who had formulated the country's economic and social model, had exerted on the country vanished with him. Taxes kept increasing, industry stopped expanding, refugees from Yugoslavia, Iran, Iraq, and Somalia flooded in, and recession hit hard. By 1994, the "Swedish model" appeared to have fallen off the catwalk: the budget deficit was around $120 billion,[9] unemployment shot up from 2 percent to 14 percent,[10] industries packed up for Asia, and immigrants, homosexuals, and Jews came under attack.

NOT EXACTLY MODEL BEHAVIOR

When the Swedish economy nose-dived, racially motivated crimes blew sky high, as did crimes committed by immigrants. In 2000 alone, over 2,800 hate crimes were reported (many aren't), and the majority were Swedes attacking immigrants. A few incidents:

1991: Neo-Nazis kill Iranian immigrant.

1992: Housing for asylum seekers torched seventy-nine times.

1993: Neo-Nazis attack two Somalis and burn down a mosque. Neo-Nazi bands began gigging and selling white power recordings.

1997: University of Stockholm reports that one-third of young Swedes doubt the Holocaust occurred.

1998: Dance hall packed with young immigrants catches fire, sixty-three die, hundreds are injured; arson by neo-Nazis suspected.

1999: Car bomb injures journalist investigating neo-Nazi activity; neo-Nazis kill union leader; three neo-Nazis rob bank, killing two policemen.

2000: Neo-Nazis fatally stab nineteen-year-old Turk; seven "Middle Easterners" rape fourteen-year-old Swedish girl in parking garage; immigrants and Swedes kill seventeen-year-old Swedish neo-Nazi.

2002: Enraged Kurdish father shoots his daughter—execution-style, in front of the family—because she refuses to go through with arranged marriage.

2003: Mosque in Malmö set ablaze; several death threats to reporters investigating neo-Nazi activity; foreign minister fatally stabbed by Serbian immigrant.

Rape rates skyrocketed during the 1990s, with about 350 gang rapes out of approximately 2,000 cases reported each year. The government is considering teaching self-defense to schoolgirls.

Prime Minister Göran Persson's long-lasting Social Democrat administration, which began in 1996, helped put the economy back on track—as did soaring demand for Ericsson phones and Swedish Internet technologies. Slammed with numerous social problems, however, the Persson administration was slow to act. On the one hand, to counter doubt among one-third of young Swedes that the Holocaust had happened, the government launched an education campaign about World War II and the treatment of Jews, publishing a book, setting up an Internet site, and making Stockholm the venue of an international forum about genocide. But the government shut its eyes tightly to growing neo-Nazi activity. After a string of murders and bank robberies by neo-Nazis in 1999, the media were gravely concerned by government inaction. For the first time ever, editors of the country's four competing papers banded together to demand that the Persson administration wake up.[11] Their coverage included pleas that the public, afraid to testify in court cases, come forward with information about racists and Fascists. Under the headline "They Threaten Democracy," the papers listed the names and pictures of sixty-two "active Nazis." Many of the pictured were fired, and some left the movement.

WHITE POWER

Nobody knows exactly how many active neo-Nazis live in Sweden; estimates range from 1,000 to 3,000, which does not sound like many. But these young racists are armed, organized, and dangerous; they killed at least sixteen immigrants, homosexuals, and police in the 1990s alone, and send out nail bombs to politicians. A dozen neo-Nazi groups, most formed around 1994, are spread out across Sweden—from Karlskrona in the south to villages in the north—running Internet sites and publishing magazines that extol the Aryan race, explain weapons, and run photos of police and journalists. Neo-Nazis sometimes train with the Swedish military, and then make off with caches of arms. Neo-Nazis are musical too: the two biggest "white power" record labels—Ragnarock and 88 Musik/Nordland—are located here, and Interpol estimates they now make over $3 million a year; some believe most Aryan music comes out of Sweden[12] and that one in six young Swedes listens to "white power" rock. In 2003, rumors swirled that neo-Nazis are running training camps deep in the forests and are planning to launch a race war. On a brighter note, at least a few leaders have quit the movement, defecting to Sweden's very active antiracist groups—who are known to brawl with neo-Nazis in marches.

In 1997, Persson was hit by another unsettling revelation: Sweden had secretly conducted eugenics programs. Thankfully, at least one area was bright: the economy continued to grow and unemployment plummeted. But this administration has been continually troubled by acts that are atypical for Swedes—including 2001 protests in Göteborg against President George W. Bush, which threatened to turn into large-scale riots.

SECRET SWEDEN

In Sweden, you can read all the prime minister's mail and access anyone's tax returns. But the typically open Swedish government hid a few dark truths from the people. The government's previous Nazi-like eugenics policy was cloaked in total secrecy until 1997, when Polish immigrant and muckraking journalist Maciej Zaremba displayed the skeletons in the closet. Among the findings published in Sweden's largest newspaper *Dagens Nyheter*: at least 60,000 women (and men) were forcibly sterilized between 1935 and 1976, many for having gypsy-like features or being deemed of a mixed race by Sweden's state-financed Institute of Racial Biology.[13] The institute, initially set up to study hereditary diseases, began the clandestine eugenics program in 1935, and greatly expanded it in 1941, as part of a plan for the social engineering of an optimized society. Danes sterilized 11,000 as well.[14] Also an early proponent of eugenics: the United States, where sterilization programs were set up in such wholesome-seeming places as Vermont.

A Swedish government commission admitted that sterilizations occurred, but said only 15,000 of them were forced; it awarded about $ 20,000 to each surviving victim.

The fatal stabbing of foreign minister Anna Lindh in a department store in 2003 was just the latest appalling act in a land long believed to hold the secrets of societal success. Neo-Nazis were at first suspected, but her killer was a Serbian immigrant.

Lindh's assassin explained that Jesus had directed him to kill her; he's now residing in a psychiatric hospital.

Perhaps it's no surprise that Swedish cities are turning more violent, although the incidence of crime is still much lower here than in most of Europe. But bizarre acts are unfolding in Sweden's tiny villages as well—some making news for quirky charms, and some for dark acts.

SMALL TOWN LIVING

Tiny Uddebo in western Sweden is best known by the 400 residents for two things: the textile factory that makes plush bathrobes and the "chicken incident," when one of the locals went nutty and whacked grocery shoppers with a frozen fryer. Village meetings, well-attended since in Uddebo there's not much else to do, had grown boring, and residents wondered how to liven up the place and simultaneously put their small village on the tourist map. That's when they consulted Mats Theselius, one of Sweden's best-known designers, and that is also why extraterrestrials may someday be hovering in Swedish skies. His idea: an alien landing strip, circular of course, where extraterrestrials can easily touch down. Although Uddebo was never previously on record as a site of UFO sightings, many locals' memories have been jarred in the planning of the work, known officially as "the Uddebo Weave." Unclear is whether visiting ETs will be welcomed with one of Uddebo's thick bathrobes.

For all the knocks she's taken lately, Sweden is still racing ahead. Her growing economy is now hailed as Europe's second most competitive (just behind Denmark), her people are still happy whether on the slopes or throwing crayfish parties on the beach, and her immigrants—now known as New Swedes—are marketing their fresh perspective and putting out magazines such as *Gringo*. All supermodels must learn to mature; while Sweden took a few stumbles, she's once again showing her grace, improving not only herself, but relentlessly trying to lift up the world.

> *The Swedish government publishes numerous reports on how to tackle societal problems, the latest about how to end "honor killings" of women.*

History Review

Sweden, now a neutral country, sits on the outskirts of world rumblings today, but she used to be in the thick of it all. In the seventeenth century, the Kingdom of Sweden rose as one of Europe's great powers, running much of northern Europe's trade, holding territories that stretched into Russia and across the Baltic Sea, and forever getting in wars.

> *Swedish military might was helped out by rich iron-ore deposits and skill in producing formidable weapons. But the warrior was often benevolent; under Swedish rule, peasants in Eastern Europe were not serfs but free men, able to buy and sell land. Sweden introduced literacy to the masses in today's Estonia, Latvia, and Finland.*

By the nineteenth century, nonstop battling had bled the country of vitality; in 1809, Russia won the land that is today's Finland. That was a crushing blow—Finland comprised nearly half of Sweden's territory, and the two had been united for six centuries. Swedes hired one of Napoleon's generals, Jean-Baptiste Bernadotte, (who later become their King Charles XIV), hoping he could grab back the lost territory. In 1814, Bernadotte showed up with land, all right, but it wasn't Finland—he'd taken Norway, newly independent from Denmark. Norwegians, unhappy with the idea of Swedish rule, finally shook off in 1905, substantially trimming Sweden's size when they left.

> *Since 1814, when Sweden militarily locked Norway up in her kingdom, the country hasn't actively fought in a war.*

Surprisingly, given her previous clout, Sweden stumbled into the twentieth century an undeveloped and poor agricultural nation. But thanks to plentiful wood, iron, and water, she galloped through the century. Cheap hydropower fueled Sweden's steel mills, producing, among other things, ball bearings (a Swedish invention) and factories produced wooden safety matches (another Swedish invention). Another boon: Sweden wasn't devastated in either world war. Unlike Denmark and Norway, Sweden escaped Nazi occupation during WWII. Exactly how Sweden slipped out of the war pretty much unscathed is a matter for future historians to unravel—Swedes were aiding both sides—but it was more than just waving the neutrality flag. Germany needed Sweden's iron and ball bearings, which were instrumental in the construction of arms. Sweden had also allowed Nazis to practice military exercises and conduct weapons experiments there before the war,[15] actions that violated the Treaty of Versailles. Hitler adored Swedish good looks—tall, blond, and blue-eyed, Swedes were the epitome of the Aryan race—another factor that may have contributed to his decision to spare Sweden. Whatever other elements came into play—not the least of which was the desire to preserve the country in an era of gruesome insanity—Sweden remained officially neutral during the war, serving at times as a safe haven for Jews, as in 1943, when around 8,000 fled there from Denmark.

> *Heroes: Several Swedish diplomats, including Raoul Wallenberg and Per Anger, helped 100,000 Jews in Hungary escape. They opened "Swedish libraries" in Hungary that were actually safe houses, issued protective Swedish passports, and smuggled people out. The Swedish king also convinced Hungarian leader Admiral Horthy to stop the deportation of Jews.*

Postwar Swedish society was literally designed—most heavily by Social Democrats Gunnar and Alva Myrdal, who shaped "social engineering" policies around the world. Heavily taxing the rich, the Swedish government promoted a "middle way" between Communism and capitalism that emphasized equality between citizens and took care of them all from nursery to nursing home. And it seemed to work—so well, in fact, that other Scandinavian countries eagerly adopted the "Swedish Model" and many hired the Myrdals as consultants.

MEET THE MYRDALS: ALVA (1902–1986) AND GUNNAR (1898–1987)

She pushed disarmament, free day care, and education for the masses; he pointed out that racism in the U.S. held back blacks and that the key to Third World development was land reform. Together, social scientists, politicians, and diplomats Alva and Gunnar Myrdal (he was also an economist) were the power couple of social engineering, whose reports, books, and ideas had dramatic effects all over the globe. After publication of their 1934 book, *The Population Crisis*, both were instrumental in designing the Swedish welfare state and both won Nobel Prizes: he in 1974 for economics, she in 1982 for peace. Gunnar was profoundly important in race relations, particularly in the United States, where the Carnegie Foundation gave him $300,000 to investigate the social dynamics of American life. The resulting book, *An American Dilemma: The Negro Problem and Modern Democracy,* published in 1944, documented the shabby treatment of blacks in the mid-twentieth-century United States and greatly influenced the landmark court decision to integrate American schools.

Olof Palme made the Swedish model famous

Postwar Sweden zoomed to the top of the moneyed pack. Absolut Vodka, Saab, Volvo—and more recently furniture manufacturer IKEA and phone-maker Ericsson—are but a few of the names that made Sweden a global player. Pharmaceuticals are also big biz: Swedish drugmaker Astra hit the mother lode with Losec, an ulcer medication that is one of the most prescribed remedies on the planet.[16] Politically, Sweden stood out as well, particularly after Olof Palme stepped in as prime minister. He infuriated the United States (by opposing Vietnam) and Israel (by supporting the PLO) and the government in South Africa (by supporting Nelson Mandela and loudly opposing apartheid).

Courtesy of Image Bank Sweden

OLOF PALME (PRIME MINISTER, 1969–1986)

Handsome in a craggy-faced sort of way, Social Democrat Olof Palme put Sweden smack bang in the middle of the international power map. He promoted nuclear disarmament, was vehemently antiapartheid, and opined that Israel

was overstepping borders in the Middle East. When he likened the U.S. bombing of Hanoi to Hitler's persecution of the Jews, Nixon kicked the Swedish ambassador out of Washington. Although a pusher of peace, the Swedish prime
minister, who came to power in 1969, also pushed arms to plenty of questionable leaders, including the ayatollah in Iran, and he was chummy with Cuba's
Castro and the PLO's Arafat, to whom he gave financial aid. Friend of the poor
and the powerless, Palme welcomed refugees from Third World countries to
Sweden—and in 1985, he insisted that Sweden formally adopt the idea of "multiculturalism." Adored by some, loathed by others, he would never have been forgotten, but his assassination in February 1986 made him a martyr—and made
Swedish detectives look like fools. Nearly two decades and $50 million of inves-
tigations later—the manhunt was Sweden's most extensive ever—Palme's killer
is still at large, and even the weapon hasn't been recovered.

*Before Palme, a Swedish leader hadn't been assassinated since 1792,
when King Gustav III attended a masked ball where he was fatally shot.
However, UN Secretary-General Dag Hammarskjöld died in 1961, when his
plane mysteriously crashed over Northern Rhodesia, an event many believe
was no accident.*

After Palme died, Sweden never again found such a strong voice—unless
you count ABBA—although likable Anna Lindh showed potential, and it's said
Prime Minister Göran Persson was grooming her to take over his spot. That she
went down as Palme did—assassinated in public while without a bodyguard—
has underscored the fact that the country is changing in ways unforeseeable by
the original modelers of Sweden.

*Sweden doesn't belong to NATO, but she does have a well-trained military
and plenty of arms manufacturers, including Bofors and Saab Missiles. The
world's sixth largest arms industry (it sold about $700 million worth in 1999)
has sold killing machines everywhere from Singapore to Iran.*

Hot Spots

Stockholm: A tantalizing tangle of streets, stone stairs, ornate castles, and
floating hotels, Stockholm is the most cosmopolitan of Scandinavian capitals, a
magnet for architects and designers who rave about the international style and
French flair. Tourists and Swedes alike flock here during summer—for the Wa-

ter Festival of concerts and theater on the shores—and to catch rays on the outlying islands of white wooden houses.

Rinkeby: The Stockholm suburb of apartment towers houses "New Swedes"—Turks, Kurds, Iraqis, Iranians, Syrians, and Yugoslavs; the main square is now a colorful market selling exotic goods, and on Sundays it is encircled by Swedish evangelical types who sing Christian songs and implore the Muslims to see the light.[17]

Göteborg: The port city, Sweden's second largest, has it all: dramatic architecture, lakes, nature reserves, museums (World Culture to the Butterfly House), ferries to the nearby islands, and the country's biggest citywide party every August.

Stockholm: Site of summer fun

Photo by R. Ryan. Courtesy of Image Bank Sweden. Copyright Stockholm Visitors Board

Malmö: The edgiest urban center in Scandinavia—and arguably the most artistically charged. Also headquarters for the Skåne movement, which wants to reunite Malmö with her seventeenth-century owner, Denmark.

Göta Canal: Tourist ships cruise through the scenic countryside on this 120-mile canal, connecting the Baltic to the North Sea.

Internet Bay: Mobile phone technology was born at this IT center that nudges the Arctic Circle in Luleå; hundreds of new tech companies have launched here, hoping for a repeat.

The laundry room: No barging in with the laundry basket: one must sign up in advance for a two-hour spot, reserving it with your key, and do one's washing in private. The government provides laundry-instruction classes for foreign-born people and sometimes hires supervisors to ensure laundry rules are followed to the tee.[18]

Systembolaget: Buying booze is an ordeal. One enters a clinical state-run warehouse with short open hours, waits in line, fills out a form, and pays sky-high prices. The government says the hassle is an effective deterrent to alcoholism; Swedes are among Europe's lowest alcohol consumers—at least until they leave Sweden.[19]

Absolut Absurdity: Sweden is home to Absolut Vodka, but for decades it's been absolutely difficult to buy a bottle of the stuff. All liquor is incredibly pricey—averaging about $26 a bottle—and it's sold only through the state liquor outlet, closed on weekends. A beer in Sweden costs eight times more than in neighboring Denmark. (But in Norway the prices are even more sobering: a pint of ale goes for $10 and up.)

The Ice Hotel: Every winter in the Lapland district of Jükkasjärvi they chisel an elaborate hotel—with rooms, bars, chairs, tables, and beds—from ice. Don't wait too long to check in: by spring, it's a pool of melted memories.

Hotshots

The royal family of the House of Bernadotte: King Carl Gustav, cousin of Denmark's Queen Margrethe, is perennially Sweden's most popular man—impressive, since he's been ruling since 1973, stepping up at age twenty-seven. He holds no power, but is a perpetual do-gooder—he formerly headed the Boy Scouts—and looks dashing in full regalia when presenting the annual Nobel Prizes. Met his queen, a German commoner named Silvia Sommerlath, at the 1972 Munich Olympics, where she was a hostess. The royal offspring are jet-setters, but relatively scandal-free, except for the time Prince Carl Philip reportedly pranced around naked with his classmates at a religious retreat. The German celebrity press, however, was brimming with rumors of royal riffs, white-powdered noses, and illegitimate babies—so many untruths that the royal family finally demanded front-page apologies and admissions of fabrications. They got them.

Göran Persson: Prime Minister, 1996–present. The sole Social Democrat to keep strong hold on a Scandinavian government since the right-wing craze hit, he is Sweden's second-most popular man. Nobody is sure why: between neo-Nazis, immigration issues, and increasing violence, Sweden is getting slammed, and aside from the economy, Persson hasn't really tackled the demons. Pundits were open-mouthed when Swedes reelected him in 2001; hadn't they seen the popularity polls?

Anna Lindh: Foreign Minister, 1998–2003. Forthright, funny, and popular, the assassinated foreign minister had been chummy with Secretary of State Colin Powell, who claimed the three best things about Sweden were "ABBA, Volvos, and Anna Lindh." Lindh remarked, "Am I only third?"[20]

Henning Mankell: Adored crime-fiction writer Mankell explores how the Swedish Model has gone flabby in intricate mysteries about Midsummer's Eve murders, Latvian criminals, and ethnic clashes in Skåne, all solved by over-worked, dogged, and diabetic Inspector Kurt Wallender.

Ingvar Kamprad: *Forbes* says he started selling bulk matches as a kid and founded IKEA at seventeen. It paid off. He's now worth $28 billion.

August Strindberg (1849–1912): The man who was to Sweden what Ibsen was to Norway wanted to be an actor, but was so untalented on stage that he swallowed opium, hoping to end his life. Instead it launched a new career. During his opiate journey, he cranked out a play in four days. The playwright later convinced a pregnant baroness to dump her husband and marry him. Their stormy union inspired numerous works about twisted love, including *The Dance of Death* (1901) and *Miss Julie* (1888), in which the baroness starred. Strindberg despised Norwegian playwright Henrik Ibsen, who parodied him as a boozing poet in *Hedda Gabler*.

Greta Garbo (1905–1990): Husky-voiced and mysterious, Greta Garbo just vanted to be alone, and the star of *Anna Karenina*, *Grand Hotel*, and *Flesh and the Devil* rarely granted interviews to the press. At the height of her career in 1941, she called it a wrap and became a recluse in New York.

CELEBRITY CONFUSION:
INGMAR BERGMAN (B. 1918) VS.
INGRID BERGMAN (1916–1982)

Ingmar is the director (*The Seventh Seal*, *Wild Strawberries*, *Cries and Whispers*) who captures the torment in daily life and whose trademark is the dialogue-free half-hour scene of a wretched soul looking out a window. Ingrid was the movie star, cast opposite Bogart in *Casablanca*, who played a holy martyr in *Joan of Arc* and a prudish nun in *The Bells of St. Mary's*, but who was viewed as quite the opposite after she had an affair and a child with Italian director Roberto Rossellini, leaving her husband and child to marry him.

Astrid Lindgren (1907–2002): Housebound with a twisted ankle, Astrid Lindgren conjured up a rebellious adventurer named Pippi Longstocking, writing up the adventures as a birthday present for her daughter. Pippi had universal appeal. Lindgren wrote more than eighty books, selling over 130 million copies, and in 1999 was hailed "the most popular Swede of the century," even though she then lived in Norway.

Lars Norén: Formerly Sweden's most admired playwright, he befriended an imprisoned neo-Nazi, wrote a sympathetic play, and cast the neo-Nazi as a prison inmate in the National Theatre production. While out of prison, the actor robbed a bank and two policemen were killed. The play flopped too.

Lukas Moodysson: Films of Sweden's most celebrated director range from hilarious (*Together* parodied a 1970s Swedish commune) and moving (*Fucking Amal* concerned a teenage lesbian trapped in a small town) to tragic (tearjerker *Lilya 4-ever* focuses on a Russian prostitute bottoming out in Malmö). *Lilya* was so moving that it prompted new legislation about sex trafficking.

ABBA: Second only to the Beatles in record sales, ABBA got their big break from Eurovision, taking top prize in 1974 for "Waterloo"—a chart-topper followed by eight more. Their Stockholm studio was so flashy that Led Zeppelin rented it to record an album. ABBA broke up in 1982, but *Muriel's Wedding* reinvigorated CD sales, as did the hit musical *Mamma Mia*. In 2000, the band was offered $1 billion for a reunion gig, but turned it down.[21] Definitely not an influence for the "white power" movement.

Zvi Mazel: Israeli Ambassador to Sweden, 2002–2004. The career diplomat lambasted Swedish politicians and media as anti-Semites and "anti-Israelis," and went berserk in January 2004 at an art exhibition in Stockholm. When he saw the piece *Snow White and the Madness of Truth*—a controversial mixed-sculpture piece of a small boat, with a photo of a Palestinian suicide bomber, crossing a pool of red bloodlike liquid—Mazel threw a floodlight into it. Israeli prime minister Ariel Sharon applauded the move, and at least a few Swedes applauded when Mazel soon thereafter retired.

15. FINLAND
(Suomi)
The Attractive Outsider

FAST FACTS

Country: Republic of Finland; Suomen Tasavalta
Capital: Helsinki
Government: Republic
Independence: December 6, 1917 (from Russia)
Population: 5,232,000 (July 2004 estimate)

Head of State:	President Tarja Halonen (2000)
Head of Government:	Prime Minister Matti Vanhanen (2003)
Elections:	President elected by popular vote, six-year term; prime minister appointed by president
Name of Parliament:	Eduskunta
Ethnicity:	93% Finnish, 6% Swedish, Russian, Estonian, Sami, Roma
Religion:	84% Lutheran; 14% none; 1% Greek Orthodox; 1% other
Language:	92% Finnish, 6% Swedish (both official); Sami
Literacy:	100% (2003)
Famous Exports:	Lordi, Linux, Olympic gold medalist skier/singer/stripper Matti Nykänen
Economic Big Boy:	Nokia (mobile phones): 2004 total sales: $39.71 billion[1]
Per Capita GDP:	$30,600 (2005 estimate)
Unemployment:	8.2% (January 2006 Eurostat figure)
EU Status:	Member since 1995
Currency:	Euro

Quick Tour

Land of spooky black forests, the darkest winters, and 10,000 sparkling lakes, Suomi has always been the off-yonder Nordic country whose tight-lipped inhabitants rarely let out a peep.

> *The cliché: Two Finnish friends, who haven't seen each other in years, celebrate their reunion at a bar. The barman serves two shots. The first man says, "Cheers." The second man says nothing. The barman serves two more shots. The first man says, "Cheers." The second man says nothing. The barman serves two more shots. The first man says, "Cheers." The second man says nothing. After a long silence, the second man turns to the first. "Look, did you come here to drink or just to chitchat?"*

QUIRKY FINLAND

They're considered taciturn, but Finns—who hold an annual wife-carrying contest (the ladies are hauled upside down across their hubbies' backs) in Sonkajärvi—are secretly an oddly funny bunch, particularly after they toss back some vodka. Their hidden passions come out on the dance floor, which they rip up to the Finnish tango that blends waltz rhythms with lyrics about nature—it's so popular here that tango clubs open in early morning so night-shift workers can swing and swirl before heading home. Finnish male choir Mieskuoro Huutajat is all the rage, but they don't sing, they shout—sometimes from floating icebergs. One of their most popular numbers: the Finnish national anthem.[2] Another amusing thing about Finns: they adore Conan O'Brien, who flippantly campaigned for the (successful) reelection of President Tarja Halonen, because, he said, they look a lot alike. Constant jabs about Finland as part of *Late Night*'s "Conan hates my homeland" routine brought a flurry of mail from Finns, inviting him out. In February 2006, he flew to Helsinki to tape a show. The funniest thing: the *Late Night* show from Finland was hilarious.

> *Reindeer is a common Finnish dish served up sautéed, smoked and sliced, cubed in stew, or as a slab of reindeer steak. Hurry and get some while you can afford it: the price is skyrocketing.*

The most distant Nordic country in every sense of the word, Finland is the stunning surprise of Scandinavia. Never mind that she's still frequently forgotten on maps of Europe, that many assume her leading manufacturer—wireless telephone giant Nokia—is Japanese, or that many believe Finland was part of the Soviet Union (well, the Soviets sure yanked the chains). The former wallflower is the region's dynamic up-and-comer: technologically savvy Finns are the world's most plugged-in to the Internet[3] as well as the biggest users of mobile phones, not surprising, perhaps, since Nokia is the planet's largest mobile phone maker; the former toilet paper company now kicks in 4 percent of Finland's GDP and accounts for 25 percent of Finnish exports.[4] The least corrupt place in the world, Finland is one of the world's top three locations for doing business, says the Economist Intelligence Unit, and the World Economic Forum hails Finland's as the world's most competitive economy.

> *Ring tones—musical chiming for mobile phones—were born in Finland and quickly grew to be a multibillion-dollar business; according to the University of Oxford they generate 10 percent of revenues for the world's music industry.[5]*

The neighbors are openmouthed that the Finns are finally opening theirs—mobiles have made them far chattier—and are nonchalantly assuming a much more prominent position in the world. Finnish computer whiz Linus

Torvalds developed Linux—a revolutionary computer operating system that can be downloaded for free and threatens to replace Windows. Finland's razor-sharp minds are developing vaccines for AIDS, as well as alternative energies, and the country's educational system shines. Finnish students are Europe's brightest.[6]

WOMEN IN POLITICS

In 1906, Finland became the world's first country to give women the vote and the right to hold office—now, females hold over a third of Parliament's seats. It wasn't until 2000, however, that a woman—Tarja Halonen—stepped in as president. In 2003, Finland became the first European country to have women as both head of government and head of state. That arrangement fell apart before you could say "grrrl power." Prime Minister Anneli Jaatteenmaki resigned after being accused of blabbing state secrets about a hush-hush meeting between President Bush and the former PM who secretly supported the 2003 Iraq invasion, which, she said, compromised Finland's neutrality.

Courtesy of the Office of the President of the Republic of Finland

President Tarja Halonen: Conan's twin?

Finns have a rep for being coolheaded, but their favorite activity is to sit in a small wooden box that's hotter than hell. The Finns invented saunas and have been sweating in them for over 2,000 years; now there are over 1.6 million saunas across the land.[7] So adored is the ritual of over-heating in pungent rooms while beating themselves with birch sticks that apartment buildings often have a sauna on each floor; the wood-lined ovens are so frequently used that they caused an energy crisis in 2003. Finns love the startling cold, too—which is handy, since the temperature rarely exceeds 65°F even in summer and in winter can drop to 50° below—and Finns are prone to jump naked into frozen lakes straight from the sauna.

"*The mightiest enemy of the Finns is the gloom, the sadness, the bottomless apathy . . . The grip of depression is so firm that many Finns see death as their only salvation.*" —Writer Arto Paasilinna in his 1990 book, Collective Suicide.[8]

SERIOUS PROBLEMS

Life can get depressing around here, especially during winter's polar nights, and many of the country's residents suffer seasonal affective disorder (SAD). Much of the year is bitterly cold, and, in the north, opaquely black, and even if the snow-coated forests are spellbindingly beautiful (when you can see them), there's little to do except get divorced (Finland shares with Sweden Europe's highest divorce rate), take another sauna, talk on the mobile, or eat more herring (it's said Finns eat it in 105 ways). No surprise then that Finland had Europe's second-highest suicide rate (just behind Hungary), and that heroin use is on the rise.

Finland has been most defined by Sweden, which kept Finland as her eastern region for centuries, and by bossy Russia, which occupied her off and on since the era of czars. As a result of her two domineering neighbors, Finland hasn't even been a sovereign country for a century—declaring independence from Russia only in 1917. Swedes—or, rather, Finnish Swedes—still have a hand in the country. Though only 6 percent of the population, they tend to be government leaders and corporate heads—and since they speak Swedish (or, rather, the less melodic Finnish Swedish)—language issues sometimes split the country. A few decades ago, they split capital Helsinki—literally. Finnish speakers strolled on the south side of the main drag, while Swedish speakers ambled on the north.

Resentment toward Sweden lingers, but Russia was far worse. Russia kept the Finnish masses uneducated and "Russified" during the nineteenth century, and Soviets later kept a silent hold on Finland, preventing her from integrating with the West after World War II. (See "History Review," page 264.) Even now, Finland, which finally joined the European Union in 1995 (and is the only Nordic country to use the euro), is wary of joining NATO, partly out of fear of how Russia might react. Finland is so weary of being dependent on Russia for oil and gas that she recently commissioned another nuclear reactor—the first built in Europe since Chernobyl blew in 1986. Though some protested, even Green Party parliamentarians approved Finland's fifth nuclear plant—that's how much Moscow is distrusted around here.

Excessive logging and animal rights are hot issues in Finland. So is globalization: when World Bank president James Wolfersohn visited Helsinki in 2001, he was greeted with a cream pie in the face. The culprit, twenty-six-year-old Green Party leader, Markus Drake, defended his action as nonviolent protest. "I would not have thrown a hard pie," he told the local paper.

> *Apparently, others would. Police now sometimes don riot gear, and protesters sometimes show up sporting ice-hockey helmets.[9]*

Spectacular Finland is still the last frontier: only 2 percent of her population is foreign-born. In fact, with over a million Finns running out of the country during the twentieth century—many to Canada and Minnesota—net immigration only began in the past ten years. Many immigrants are returning Finns (others are coming in from Somalia and Iraq). Immigration problems aren't a major to-do in Finland yet, but the government recently converted a prison to a refugee detention center, perhaps expecting a future flood.

History Review

At the western edge of the landmass that contains Russia, and just across the Baltic from Sweden, Finland's location was long her curse. For the better part of six centuries, today's Finland was Sweden's eastern half; from 1809 to 1917 she was a Russian duchy, which further instilled a fatalistic outlook and a thirst for vodka.

> *"Closeness without conflict only exists in the cemetery." —Old Finnish saying*

Forced to fight numerous wars they never initiated, Finns developed a strong national identity in the 1800s, demanding that Finnish, not Russian, be their official language. In 1917, Finns snuck off during Russia's Bolshevik Revolution, founding Finland as an independent country. In what is still a national embarrassment, the fledgling republic immediately broke into civil war. Socialists were reds, the bourgeoisie were whites, and while the latter won, the former was the color of the land where bloody battles between 200,000 fellow Finns unfolded. At the end of 104 days, 40,000 Finns were frozen in snowdrifts and icy forests, dead from the cruel slap of winter and their countrymen's hands.

GREAT NAMES FOR BAD THINGS

Nobody beats Finns for devising original names for wars, and no wonder—they've been dragged into plenty of them, most against Mother Russia. During the Long Wrath (1570–1595), Sweden and Finns battled Russia; during the Great Wrath (1713–1721), Finns fought to break out of Russia's temporary hold; and during the Lesser Wrath (1741–1743), they rose up again against the

Russians occupying their turf. During the First Era of Oppression (1899–1905), Finns unsuccessfully tried to overthrow Russian rule, and during the Second Era of Oppression (1909–1917), they succeeded in escaping from the over-bearing Bear. Predictably, Russia came back: when World War II began, Soviets invaded, kicking off the Winter War (1939–1940), only to be shocked when the vastly outnumbered Finns—dressed in white and fighting on skis—shoved them back. To ensure the Russians stayed away, Finns handed 10 percent of the land and 20 percent of industry to Russia. That apparently wasn't enough. Russia returned in 1941, and since Russia was then playing on the Allied team, Finland reluctantly asked Nazis to help them fight in the War of Continuation (1941–1944). That war was aptly named. No sooner had the Finns and Nazis beat back the Russians than the Nazis turned on the Finns. The Finns showed their mettle and pushed out the Germans as well. But their brief partnership with Nazis cost them. Even though Finns were never aligned with the Nazi cause, and were battling solely for self-preservation, the Allies forced Finland to pay hefty war reparations and cede yet more land to Russia.

> *The crushing war debt forced mostly agrarian Finland to rapidly industrialize—and the country soon became one of the world's wealthiest.*

There isn't an official Third Era of Oppression, but there should be. From the end of the Second World War to the fall of the Soviet Union in 1991, Finland was still bullied by Russia. As a buffer between the West and the Soviet Union, Finland performed a delicate dance. The Soviet Union pushed Finland into signing a Treaty of Friendship, Cooperation, and Mutual Assistance, stating that if the enemy (NATO) invaded, Finland would fight with the Soviets. Even though Finland was theoretically free, she dared not get too involved with the West—and she became economically enmeshed with the Soviet Union. The Finnish government reportedly didn't make a move without first checking with Moscow, and the self-censored Finnish media rarely criticized Soviets. Even though Finland had been prospering, when the Soviet Union crumbled in 1991, she took Finland's economy down with her. Finland tumbled into a recession and unemployment shot up to 20 percent. The country, however, pulled herself back together quickly, and is now revved up and ready to go.

Hot Spots

Helsinki: The eye-pleasing city showcases architecture: from decorative art deco–like Jurgenstil to the sharp angles of Alvar Aalto, buildings are a mix of old and new, including the concert hall—a ruin topped with a glass roof. Traditions are woven into the urban tapestry: some women still head down to the piers to wash their rugs in the Baltic Sea.

Rovaniemi: Finns insist that this village on the Arctic Circle is the One True Home of Santa Claus. Of course, there's a post office near by—and a Santa Claus theme park.

Åland Islands: Summer finds these 6,000 islands off southwest Finland packed with bikers, golfers, and canoers paddling isle to isle. Ferries carry the less energetic, and the all-night party boards sell duty-free booze. Any time of year, the archipelago of Swedish-speaking residents is politicized; most locals want to return to original owner Sweden.

Photo by Paul Williams. Courtesy of Helsinki City Tourist and Conventions Bureau

Helsinki: Hotbed of saunas, tango, and wife-carrying contests

Estonia: Finns by the ferryload glide over here to stock up on cheap booze, and Finnish pensioners are moving to Estonia, where the climate must seem relatively balmy.

Hotshots

Tarja Halonen: President, 2000–present. Groundbreaking Social Democrat Halonen (who speaks six languages) has a string of firsts on her CV: first woman foreign minister, first woman president—and the first candidate to be presented with chocolates by American talk-show host Conan O'Brien. She thanked him for promoting Finland, saying, "I think that at least now many more

Americans know where Finland is." (We doubt it.) Local media harpoon her clothes—nobody calls her a fashionista—but she is a human-rights-affirming, land-mine-opposing, kindly nontraditionalist: she raised her children as a single mother, and didn't marry her live-in until after she stepped into office.

Matti Vanhanen: Prime Minister, August 2003–present. Former defense minister Vanhanen was suddenly yanked center stage when PM Jaatteenmaki stomped out of office. No word on whether he will seek an endorsement from Conan.

LINUS TORVALDS

The Finnish Swede who calls himself "Benevolent Dictator for Life," ranked on *Time*'s 2004 "Most Influential" list, and resembles the penguin that is his personal mascot, Linus Torvalds launched a revolution when he devised the kernel for a new computer operating system—as part of his master's thesis—and recruited input from computer nerds around the world. The resulting system, Linux, competes with Microsoft Windows—but unlike Windows, you can have it for free. Quite threatening to those money-grabbing capitalists in Seattle—all the more since Torvalds moved to Seattle's rival city Portland, Oregon.

Jean Sibelius (1865–1957): Finland's most-beloved composer, known for his original style and his symphonic poems, was also a wit. When a countess complained of the sinful behavior of youth, bragging, "I've been chaste for close to ninety years and who thanks me for it?" Sibelius replied, "Well I don't, that's for sure."[10]

Tove Jansson (1914–2001): Author of the famous *Moomin* books about big-snouted, heavily furred trolls, Jannson also illustrated some editions of *The Hobbit*.[11]

News you can understand: *Helsingin Sanomat.* The latest scandals in Helsinki, plus good coverage of Estonia and the occasional hilarious humor piece: http://helsinginsanomat.fi

16. LUXEMBOURG
Sleeping Beauty

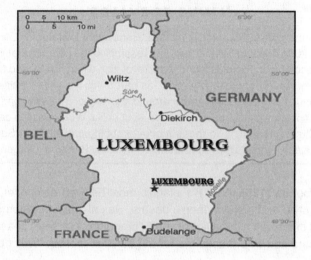

FAST FACTS

Country:	Grand Duchy of Luxembourg; Grand Duché de Luxembourg
Capital:	Luxembourg
Government:	Constitutional monarchy
Independence:	1839 (from the Netherlands); full independence 1867
Population:	475,000 (2006 estimate)
Head of State:	Grand Duke Henri (2000)
Head of Government:	Prime Minister Jean-Claude Juncker (1995)
Elections:	Monarchy is hereditary; prime minister appointed by monarch for five-year term
Name of Parliament:	Chamber of Deputies; Chambre des Députés
Ethnicity:	Celtic base; one-third of residents foreign-born, many from Portugal

Religion:	86% Roman Catholic; 13% Protestant; also Jewish and Muslim
Language:	Luxembourgish (national language); German and French
Literacy:	99% (2003 estimate)
Famous Exports:	BCCI scandal, idea for euro, Battle of the Bulge
Economic Big Boy:	Arcelor (materials); 2004 total sales: $40.98 billion
Per Capita GDP:	$55,600 (2005 estimate)
Unemployment:	5.5% (January 2006 Eurostat figure)
EU Status:	Founding member EEC
Currency:	Euro

Quick Tour

The belly button of Western Europe, landlocked Luxembourg is mountainous in her north, lushly forested to her west, and crossed by four rushing rivers. Skiing, hiking, and biking are big in the "green heart of Europe," and on weekends out-of-towners descend on the verdant land and clog up the most popular trails. Luxembourgers are quite religious, and they are among Europe's most knowledgeable on political issues—handy, since voting is compulsory here. They are also the Europeans who travel the most, and almost everyone is multilingual, speaking not only Luxembourgish but German, French, and often English as well.

> A third of the country's 400,000 residents are foreign-born and a third of Luxembourg's workforce commutes from Germany, Belgium, or France. Even more out-of-towners bank there: corporations are drawn by her buttoned-lip banking practices, but so too are the middle-class neighbors; Germans are particularly fond of Luxembourg's financial services.

Home to the European Court of Justice and a half dozen other EU institutions, Luxembourg is easily the most joked-about country in Western Europe: the grand duchy, thirty-two miles wide and fifty-one miles long, appears to be nothing but a big banking machine in a small boring land. But why should Luxembourgers care? They're the wealthiest people in the world, and Luxembourg, with her dense forests and castled hills, is one of the prettiest countries. So what if everybody mixes Luxembourg up with Liechtenstein or the same-named region in Belgium? So what if nobody outside their country speaks their

Courtesy of Luxembourg City Tourist Office

Luxembourg City: Home of the world's richest citizens

beloved Luxembourgish? So what if few realize how hard it was for the country, scarcely bigger than London, to maintain independence over the centuries? It just makes the place all the more special to the Luxembourgers, whose country is more like an exclusive—albeit friendly—club, where life is tranquil but sleepy. Nice restaurants abound in Luxembourg City, but the place shuts down too early, say those who like to stay up past ten. Maybe that's why Luxembourgers are Europe's biggest drinkers, knocking back nearly twelve liters of spirits per person every year.[2]

LUXEMBOURG VS. LUXEMBOURG VS. LUXEMBOURG CITY VS. LIECHTENSTEIN, ETC.

Luxembourg is a rich, independent country, and is one of the world's major financial centers; her capital is Luxembourg City. Belgium has a region called Luxembourg: this used to be part of Luxembourg the country, but was lost in 1839. An entirely different entity, Liechtenstein is the wealthy principality that lies between Austria and Germany, and is also tiny and rich. Rosa Luxemburg, the famous Socialist, wasn't from Luxembourg, Luxembourg, or Liechtenstein; she was born in Poland. As for the famous Luxembourg Garden, that's in Paris.

The land that fell out of a fairy tale isn't known for snow-white wholesomeness in the financial department. The world's seventh-biggest financial center, she's home to 200 foreign banking institutions. One of the most famous was "rogue bank" BCCI (a Pakistani-Arab Emirates institution closed in 1991 amid a huge flap about money laundering), but plenty of other iffy-sounding banks and businesses have their overseas headquarters here. High interest rates, low tax rates, and bank secrecy have made Luxembourg an attractive money launderette and tax-evasion center, although new laws have been enacted that are sure to prevent that—wink wink.

STICKY FINGERS, DIRTY MONEY, AND GENERAL GRIME

Who knows what is really going on in the back rooms of Luxembourg's banks, but a lot seems not to be aboveboard. Here are but a few clues that the business conducted out of the country isn't always squeaky clean:

1991: Important U.S. bank First American is found to be controlled by a money-laundering bank in Luxembourg; BCCI closed down after money-laundering scandal involving mujahideen financing and money laundering for Colombian drug cartel.

1994: Employees of KBLux bank steal equivalent of $9 million.

1999: Luxembourg's ex-prime minister Jacques Santer, the president of the European Commission, is forced to resign along with the whole European Commission on charges of corruption.

2000: Pressure from EU to lift banking secrecy laws after more charges that Luxembourg banks are involved in money laundering and fraudulent operations.

2002: Swiss career diplomat Peter Friederich charged with laundering drug money—proof that Luxembourg does know how to enforce her money-laundering laws; French government denounces Luxembourg as a haven for financial crime—alarming when such accusations come from the less-than-lily-white French.

2003: European Commission's statistical arm, Eurostat, headquartered in Luxembourg, is caught in numerous shady financial dealings, including bogus invoices from fake companies to fund an account for volleyball teams and expensive holidays.

> *Luxembourger Pierre Werner—twice the country's prime minister—is called the "father of the euro," but he called his 1960 idea for a common currency the "euror"—which, besides not exactly rolling off the tongue, sounds like a combination of "error" and "führer"—two words Europeans definitely didn't want connected with their cash. The idea he planted finally came to fruition in 2002, when the euro became the EU's common currency.*

History Review

It all began with a big rock—an outcropping, actually—in the middle of nowhere, looking out over some pretty woods and hills. Upon that rock, Siege-froid, the Count of Ardennes, began constructing a castle in AD 963 that would be so heavily fortified over the coming centuries that the triple-walled fortress was known as the Gibraltar of the North. Peering down over what is today the capital, Gibraltar Junior wasn't terribly effective in keeping Luxembourg safe from being invaded by the neighbors or from being handed over as a land bonus in treaties. Over the years, Luxembourg was yanked into the Austrian Empire, then Burgundy, then Napoleonic France, and later tossed to the king of the Netherlands.

In 1830, when politically part of the Netherlands, Belgium and Luxembourg rebelled against the ruling Dutch king. As a result, Belgium became indepen-dent and Luxembourg was ultimately split in two—the French-speaking half went with Belgium. Luxembourg gained a measure of autonomy with the little land she had left in 1839. The territory was dirt poor and so lacking in opportu-nity that a fifth of the population hightailed it over to the United States over the next sixty years. Full independence was at last achieved in 1867.

Although economically linked to Germany, with which she enjoyed warm re-lations in the early twentieth century, Luxembourg was twice overtaken by her neighbor—during the first and second world wars. The occupation was far worse the second time. The Nazis quickly launched a charm campaign, heavy on the propaganda, about how Luxembourgers were actually ethnic Germans and should embrace being part of Greater Germany. And then the Nazis held a referendum asking if Luxembourgers wished to join hands geographically as part of Anschluss. One imagines that the propaganda director was soon out of a job: 98 percent of Luxembourgers voted no, using the phrase that is now the national motto: *Mir wëlle bleiwe wat mir sin*—"We wish to stay as we are," i.e., independent. Furious, Nazis annexed Luxembourg anyway, rounding up the many dissidents and shooting them or sending them off to concentration camps. Luxembourgers were forced to speak only in German, and names that smacked faintly of French were Germanized. Even the name of their country was erased: it became *Gau Moselland*, or the district of Moselle country. The resistance grew stronger with general strikes and railway closures, particularly when the Nazis began calling up Luxembourg boys.[3] But Luxembourg was really hammered in the Battle of the Bulge—one of the bloodiest showdowns in European history.

BATTLE OF THE BULGE

By December 1944, the Allies had liberated Paris and Rome, chased the Nazis out of Belgium and Luxembourg, and were moving toward Germany. After months of heavy fighting, troops were fatigued, supplies were low, and the advancing front was thinning. Seeing a weakness in the formation as the Allies took a break, Hitler made a last-ditch effort to win the war. His plan: breach the front—forming a "bulge" where his tanks could break through—make a run for Antwerp in Belgium, and seize that port city and the land on the way to it. Three hundred thousand Nazis advanced on Allies starting on December 16, 1944, snatching back liberated territory. General Patton's troops, en route to Germany, quickly returned to engage in the war's fiercest fighting, worsened by the nasty winter—one of history's most frigid. Allied troops, poorly outfitted for the brutal cold, were blinded by snow that fell so thick that fighters could not see twenty feet away. In the agonizing battle that dragged on for six weeks, American deaths and casualties numbered over 75,000, and German casualties were nearly 68,000. Germany finally conceded defeat on January 27, 1945.

Invaded and occupied by Germany during both world wars despite claiming neutrality, Luxembourg ditched that apparently worthless concept after 1945, and signed on as a founding member of NATO. Now she is a partner in a controversial military coalition with Belgium, Germany, and France, called the European Security and Defense Union, which the United States sees as threatening to NATO (and to the American ability to manipulate Europe).

Luxembourg's major industrial moneymaker, Arbed, is Europe's biggest steel supplier.

Hot Spots

Luxembourg City: Stacked on a hill, the handsome capital city is brimming with everything needed by the wealthy: banks, fancy restaurants, wine stores, a medieval old town, and a modern urban center. But she gets plenty of beauty sleep, locking up early. Siegefroid's castle was dismantled in the 1800s, but parts of the casements—the labyrinthine escape routes that coil around under it—still remain, and the pedestrian way that winds down from the hill is called the most beautiful balcony in Europe.

Ardennes: Low mountains rise above thick woods in this northern region of rolling pastureland, meandering rivers, and such attractions as the Valley of the Seven Castles. Known for romantic inns and for her violent past: much of the Battle of the Bulge played out here.

> *Luxembourg's vineyards are mostly in the south, which is called "the good country."*

Hotshots

Courtesy of Luxembourg Office of the Prime Minister

PM Juncker, popular at home and in Brussels

Grand Duke Henri: Reigning monarch, 2000–present. Bourbon-blooded and handsome Henri has been unofficially running the place since 1998, but his dad, respectable Grand Duke Jean, officially abdicated and handed over the keys in 2000; Henri's likeness adorns the one-euro coin. With his wife, Cuban-born Maria Teresa, he is boosting the Catholic country's low birth rate. The royal couple's offspring number five thus far.

Jean-Claude Juncker: Prime Minister, 1995–present. Smart, kindly, and slightly nerdy Christian Democrat Juncker is pushing through banking changes and new financial laws that are yanking off the country's veil of secrecy. It's a delicate balancing act, since what makes Luxembourg rich is her banking attractiveness.

General George S. Patton (1885–1945): A national hero, the three-star American general helped liberate Luxembourg, and his quick actions in the last months of the war prevented the Nazis from prevailing at the Battle of the Bulge. In 1945, while in Hamm, Luxembourg, he was in a gruesome road accident that left him paralyzed; he died several days later. He's buried in Luxembourg, where a George Patton museum honors him.

Neo-Nazis: Yes, they are here too. At their only recorded "march" the participants numbered but four.

News you can understand: *352*, a weekly paper in English: www.352.lu

PART II

NEW EUROPE

INTRODUCTION

The ten countries that entered the European Union on May 1, 2004, aren't actually "new"—their histories and cultures go back for centuries, even millennia. To Western Europeans, however, they are all novel indeed, being mysterious places with names like "Ljubljana" and "Vilnius," that for much of the twentieth century lived in a dark parallel universe that the rest of Europe tried to ignore.

> *Most of "New Europe" was reborn in the 1990s: when the Soviet Union fell, the three Baltic States (Estonia, Latvia, and Lithuania), Poland, and Czechoslovakia reestablished independence, with Czechoslovakia going on to divide into two; Slovenia was born in 1991 when Yugoslavia broke up. Cyprus and Malta are the relative elders of the bunch—they've been independent since the 1960s.*

NEW EUROPE

Poland:	Most people
Hungary:	Most glum, most Roma
Estonia:	Most proud, best-behaved
Latvia:	Most vulnerable
Lithuania:	Most likely to be site of next Chernobyl
Czech Republic:	Most skeptical
Slovak Republic:	Most likely to be overlooked
Slovenia:	Most promising
Cyprus:	Most likely to be schizophrenic
Malta:	Most likely to bolt

Excluding the Mediterranean islands Cyprus and Malta—both former British colonies—the new EU countries came out of Communism, and, except for Slovenia, they were closely bound up with the Soviet Union, being either republics or satellites that spent almost five decades with Moscow panting down their necks. Becoming independent again only in the past decade and a half, these former Communist states are fledglings, filled with energy and hope but still bearing a few scars from their not-so-distant past. More than simply being repressed under the Soviets, who steamrolled their rebellions, these countries—most of them devastated during the Second World War—didn't have much of a chance to heal: under the Communists, those ugly days were simply swept under the rug. Unlike Western Europe, which had six decades to rebuild itself and forge friendships with former enemies, these countries are still confronting issues that go back to the 1940s—or sometimes even to the First World War.

These new EU members see the European Union as the great equalizer that can shell out the funds for agriculture and infrastructure that many need, and provide wider markets, and help attract more foreign investment. They also view the EU as the way to reconnect with the past that was ripped away. And plenty of them eye the EU rather warily, unsure that Brussels won't simply replace Moscow in dictating what they can and can't do.

> *Another feature that most of these countries share is that they are not as wealthy as those in the West, save for Slovenia and Cyprus, which have GDP levels around those of Spain and Portugal.*

While there's plenty of excitement about reconnecting with their European kin in the West, some of these countries are still peeved at Western Europe, for letting them fall to Communism and, despite encouraging them to rebel, not showing up to help when they defied Moscow. And the one thing that disappoints almost all is that the West seems utterly clueless about who they are, what they've been through, and the history that links them to the Continent. But for all the twitchiness of the moment, all across "New Europe" there's also a sense of exciting change and regeneration, and a joy at being brought back to the table with the European family.

17. POLAND
(Polska)
Split Personality

FAST FACTS

Country:	Republic of Poland; Rzeczpospolita Polska
Capital:	Warsaw
Government:	Republic
Independence:	November 11, 1918, independent republic proclaimed; 1989 independence from Soviet Union (Poland was a Soviet satellite)
Population:	38,537,000 (2006 estimate)
Head of State:	President Lech Kaczynski (2005)
Head of Government:	Prime Minister Jaroslaw Kaczynski (2006)
Elections:	President by direct public elections every five years; prime minister appointed by president, approved by Sejm
Name of Parliament:	National Assembly; Zgromadzenie Narodowe (Sejm and Senat)

Ethnicity:	97% Polish; 0.4% German; 2.6% Ukrainian, Belarussian, and other
Religion:	95% Roman Catholic; 5% Eastern Orthodox, Protestant
Language:	Polish
Literacy:	99% (2003 estimate); 25% may be functionally illiterate
Famous Exports:	Chopin, Copernicus, "the Polish Plumber"
Economic Big Boy:	PKN Orlen (oil and gas operations); 2004 total sales: $6.53 billion[1]
Per Capita GDP:	$12,700 (2005 estimate)
Unemployment:	17.2% (January 2006 Eurostat figure)
Percentage in Poverty:	17% (2003 official estimate); some figures say 40%
EU Status:	Joined May 2004
Currency:	Polish zloty

Quick Tour

From the mammoth bison that roam forests of ancient oaks to the snow-crusted Tatra Mountains peering over farms with oxen-pulled plows, Polska has always lived in a different world—or a few of them simultaneously. Straddling Russia and Germany—a lethal position for centuries—Poland was yanked back and forth between them for much of recent history, and she's now pulled between her own past and present: landscapes of medieval villages and Renaissance castles are broken by smokestacks of steel towns, the donkey-drawn carts on two-lane highways are swept aside by trucks and Mercedes, the farmlands that once fed most of Europe are now Europe's least productive, and Poland's former greatness is now captured mostly in history books that few outside Poland read.

CHEERING POLES

Few Americans (or Europeans, for that matter) are aware of Poland's many collective contributions. A few examples: Poles saved the city of Vienna from being pulled into the Ottoman Empire, pointed out that the sun is the center of our planetary system, made population growth possible in medieval Europe, deduced that air is a mixture of substances, created some of the world's most stirring piano concertos, discovered radioactivity, and were the most dynamic force in knocking down Soviet Communism. They also claim they invented vodka, but the Russians disagree.

The Big Gal of central Europe, Polska is by far the most significant of the ten countries that joined the European Union in 2004. Poland is weightiest in terms of size (nearly as large as Germany), people (more populous than the other nine together), and economic output (bigger than the next three countries' GDPs combined). More than any other Communist country, Poland won the world's heart in 1989, when, led by Lech Walesa and Solidarity, she broke out of her shackles and triggered the downfall of the Soviet Union. So moving was this country's heroic uprising, so promising was her newly opened economy, and so hopeful was the mood, that Poland alone was the impetus for the European Union to fling open its door and welcome in first Poland and then other countries from the East.

Since linking arms with the European Union, Poland is finding new muscle: she commands more EU funding than any other country. Over the next six years, some $110 billion in EU money will wing toward Polish coffers, much of it earmarked for modernizing the lost-in-the-dark-ages rural parts and helping out the millions of farmers who tend them. Additional moolah is flapping in from the World Bank and the United States.

After centuries of withering in the shadows of her neighbors, Poland now cuts a striking profile as a major European player—and not just in the European Union, where she is cozying up to the big babes on campus—France, Germany, Britain, Italy, and Spain. The country is also now a significant name in NATO and will take over NATO operations in Afghanistan in 2007.

DOES UNCLE SAM HAVE A DEAL FOR YOU!

Having been kicked around by Russia for centuries, post-Communist Poland was easily wooed by NATO, the U.S.-dominated security force created during the Cold War to keep the Soviet Union in check. Infuriating Moscow, Poland joined NATO in 1999, the first former Soviet satellite to do so. Poland promptly signed up for the biggest arms sale ever in central Europe, ordering forty-eight F-16 fighter planes from Lockheed Martin, the strongest lobbyist for NATO expansion. To sweeten the $3.5 billion deal, Lockheed Martin and the U.S. government promised to lure American companies to Poland as part of a $6.9 billion foreign investment package.

The fledgling republic is also President Bush's biggest fan. A 2005 attitude survey of Europeans, *Transatlantic Trends*, showed that 52 percent of Poles approved of Bush's foreign policies—the highest level of support in Europe, higher even than Bush's foreign policy approval rate in the U.S.[2] Poland was also Europe's most visible supporter of the 2003 invasion of Iraq; she sent troops for the reconstruction, and the Polish military stayed even when most other countries yanked their troops back. And with the right-wing Law and Justice Party heading the government, Poland is now waving her hand wildly in the air to be selected as a site for the American missile defense shield program.

POLAND AND THE U.S.

Poland isn't snuggling up to the U.S. simply because she is loyal. Money and security are two motivating factors: backing the U.S. in Iraq spelled billions of dollars for Poland. The government was compensated for sending the military to Iraq, and Polish defense contractors, wounded when the Soviet Union fell, raked in needed biz: munitions maker Bumar alone stood to make more than $500 million from what was viewed as the "Iraqi Opportunity." And Poland won't be paying anything to be part of the missile defense shield; it's more likely that the U.S. will be paying Poland to use the territory, which could become sovereign U.S. land. And there's a payback implied in Poland's pro-U.S. rah-rah-ing: Poland is very much expecting the United States, with or without NATO, to help fight Russia back if she moves on Poland. "The support for American military in Iraq," wrote the *Warsaw Voice* in 2004, ". . . is treated as nothing short of a guarantee of across-the-board help on the part of the U.S."[3]

And Poland is showing her clever side, devising novel ways to put herself on the map. In 2004, when the French and other Western Europeans began sniveling that Polish workers (symbolized by "the Polish Plumber") might take their jobs, the Polish Tourism Board initiated a brilliant campaign. The new poster featured a handsome "Polish Plumber" saying he'd rather stay in Polska, but inviting Europeans to visit. Even more effective in boosting tourism: a new Polish airline, Centralwings, is zipping passengers from Britain to Poland for some $30 round-trip.

So if everything is so darn peachy, why are Poles among the European Union's most unhappy people? Why is Poland causing the EU to fret, and why is the country gaining a global rep as a pain in the neck? The answer has to do with leadership—or lack thereof—and the pressing need for Poland to grow up. Here in the land where corruption runs rife (Poles, reports the *Economist*, are legendary cheats even on school exams), nearly 18 percent are jobless, more than anywhere else in the EU. And the employed are grossly underpaid. Doctors recently held a massive strike protesting their pay of $3 an hour; teachers make about $300 a month. Many Poles are fleeing in a brain drain that is diminishing the population by 0.5 percent yearly.

The national tourism board is trying to carve a new international image, but representatives in London apparently can't get around to answering repeated e-mails from travel writers or sending out newsletters to those who wish to

travel there. But the most inept people in the land may be those now warming
up the government power seats. Flaming nationalists, anti-Semites, and the extremely devout are all vying for power—and some say the Law and Justice
Party, which won in 2005, combines elements of all three.

MEET THE TWINS!

Imagine if Mary-Kate and Ashley Olsen turned into screaming nationalist
conservatives, went on a religious kick, and took to running the country.
That's the simplified take on Lech and Jaroslaw Kaczynski, the fervently
Catholic identical twins who campaigned on bringing a "Moral Revolution" to
Poland. Critics say their "revolution" consists of stripping gay rights, backing
the death penalty, and ensuring that abortion in Poland remains illegal—as
well as bringing Catholicism even more to the forefront, instilling nationalism,
and gunning for former Communists. The mischievous child stars of the famous Polish movie *The Two Who Took the Moon* starred in the 2005 parliamentary elections. Their Law and Justice Party was loudly supported by
controversial Catholic station Radio Maryja, which reportedly overstepped
Vatican rules by insisting that good Catholics would vote for the Law and Justice Party; reading between the lines, one might imply that those who didn't
would go to hell. Lech Kaczynski stepped in as president, and in 2006,
Jaroslaw became prime minister. The twins immediately teamed Law and
Justice up in a flimsy coalition with two of Poland's most outrageous parties:
Self Defense (an angry farmer's party known for hurling spuds at visiting dignitaries and worse) and the ultra-right League of Polish Families, whose virulent youth group includes neo-Nazi skinheads. The coalition partners
immediately raised eyebrows, but so have the actions of the twins' government. The EU and Human Rights Watch are so concerned about the government's attacks on homosexuals, whose gay pride marches are now often
prohibited, that they've both written warning letters underscoring the importance of human rights to all. With all the scandals, the heat is on for the twins
to call a new election—one which many hope they won't win.

*Run by Father Tadeusz Rydzyk, Radio Maryja claims to reach 3 million lis-
teners, many of them the rural poor. The Catholic station has triggered up-
roars for comments portraying Jews as extorting the government in trying
to get back lands lost during WWII; the station also referred to survivors'
compensation as part of "Holocaust, Inc." Radio Maryja defended accused
pedophile Father Henryk Jankowski, who'd shrugged off the sexual accusations as a "Judeo-Communist plot." The station, which regularly interviews the highest-ranking Law and Justice Party members, was recently*

rapped by the Vatican, which asked that Radio Maryja stop attacking Jews. The broadcast incidents speak to a far wider problem of anti-Semitism in Poland, where several political parties take a blatantly anti-Jew view, and where neo-Nazis are believed to number some 20,000.

Courtesy of Samoobrona Party of Poland

Poland does have some able leaders—Western European media support the higher-brow, probusiness candidates from Civic Platform—but skilled politicians in Poland seem to be outnumbered by venom-spewing clowns. And one of the more popular is Self Defense's Andrzej Lepper, currently vice speaker of Parliament.

Farmer's friend Andrzej Lepper. Watch out for flying spuds!

POLAND'S MOST FAMOUS CAMERA HOG

In a country marked by a shortage of strong leaders, Andrzej Lepper stands out. Then again, given his love of stunts, the square-jawed parliamentarian with slicked-back hair would stand out anywhere: the fancy-suited pig farmer is a bona fide ham. Forming Self Defense (*Samoobrona*) in 1993, Lepper first grabbed headlines for overturning rail wagons filled with imported wheat and organizing roadblocks of trucks hauling imported grain that competed with grain sold by Polish farmers; 20,000 and more began showing up for protests that often turned bloody. The former boxer sometimes plays Robin Hood, raiding corporate pork farms and making off with sausages to distribute to the poor, although sometimes he more closely resembles the Godfather—his minions at least once beat a civil servant, who had come to foreclose a farm, to an unrecognizable pulp. He's stormed the Ministry of Agriculture howling over trade policy; he's pushed hecklers into manure; and he's ordered mobs to toss eggs, potatoes, and even firecrackers at politicians supporting the sale of Polish industry and land—including visiting dignitaries from the EU. That his party could show up as Poland's most popular in 2004 (and third-most popular in the 2005 election) was a surprise to most Polish politicians, and a sign of how out of touch the establishment was with the nonurban masses. Lepper was laughed off as a loudmouthed nuisance when he ran for president in 2000—although, with over 1.3 percent of the vote, he fared better than former president Lech Walesa. But by 2001, Lepper and his Self Defense Party had secured enough votes to take fifty-three seats in the 460-seat Sejm, the lower chamber of Parliament. Then the fun really started, as parliamentary speakers were shoved from the podium by Self Defense ministers and Lepper's tirades began; if his microphone was shut off while he was blasting the government, he simply picked up a bullhorn and continued. Politicians from Brussels to Warsaw see Lepper as dangerous, but between his tirades that mix nationalism and the price of bacon, Lepper does make some valid points: he emphasizes the plight of small farmers who can't fight subsidized agribusiness, and gives voice to the rural poor, many of whom still plow with horses and harvest by hand, and whose small farms are expected to fold.

The reality is that Poland, historically divided by neighbors, is still split—economically, politically, and morally. Those divisions, combined with a defensive attitude born of years of being shoved around, often make the country that has so much potential a real headache on the international stage, instead of a country that is really getting ahead.

One final disappointment revolves around Poland's worship of the United States. It's not simply that the U.S. is dragging her feet on making good her promises on foreign investment, or that while Western Europeans are welcomed, Poles visiting the U.S. must buy visas and be fingerprinted—recent requirements that Poles see as a slap in the face. In her bid to forge a closer friendship and guarantee security from Uncle Sam, Poland sometimes appears to sell herself out. There is a bitter irony in reports that Poland—the country that loudly lamented the cruel treatment of civilians and political prisoners by Soviets and Nazis—was running torture camps and rendition centers of suspected terrorists, alongside the CIA.

History Review

If Poland acts defensive, it's understandable. Much of her recent history can be summed up in two words: Poor Poland. For the two centuries leading up to 1989, when she booted out the Communist regime, Polska stood out as the textbook victim of geography. Physically trapped between Russia and Germany, Poland was yanked continuously into the violent, horrifying exploits of her powerful neighbors. The surprise is that Poland ended up as the neighborhood weakling; for centuries, she was one of the most powerful kingdoms in Europe.

Filled with universities and splendid palaces, and headed by a religiously tolerant monarchy, historical Poland granted previously unknown rights to her subjects, including the right to a parliament that elected the king. After Poland coupled with Lithuania through royal marriage in 1386, the joint kingdom spread across Eastern Europe from the Baltic to the Black Sea. Europe's largest kingdom at the time, she was one of the Continent's mightiest powers for a few hundred years.

> *Source of power: The Federation of Poland and Lithuania, as the joint kingdom was later known, became wealthy from agriculture during the Middle Ages. Rich in grain, the Federation found a ready market in Europe's booming population. For centuries, Poland remained Europe's main bread basket.*

A literate land where education was valued, the kingdom became a publishing hotbed in the 1400s, but the 1500s were even more enlightened. During this "golden age" (influenced by Florentines and Venetians, with whom Polish royals were often cavorting and marrying), architects and mapmakers, poets and painters, scientists and philosophers filled the land that was also the home of Copernicus, whose heliocentric writings would spin the world in a whole new direction.

NEARLY FORGOTTEN COPERNICUS (1473–1543)

It was a scandalous, heretical idea at the time, so highly controversial that Renaissance astronomer/mathematician/teacher/doctor/lawyer/governor Nicolaj Kopernik, a devout Catholic, first broached his concept of a heliocentric universe in a small handwritten book (*Commentariolus*) given only to trusted friends. In fact, Copernicus's full-blown ideas, captured in *On the Revolutions of the Celestial Spheres* might never have seen the ink of the printing presses had not a copy of *Commentariolus* found its way into the hands of a German mathematician known as Rheticus. The German become so obsessed with Copernicus's idea that he traveled to Poland, moved in, and hounded the old man to let him take the scribblings of the second, more developed book to the printer, an act finally accomplished in 1543; it's said Copernicus died hours after seeing the book. Copernicus was actually a lawyer by training, and he did not have a deluxe observatory, often studying celestial movements through specially placed holes in the walls of his house. Although he kick-started the Scientific Revolution, Copernicus was not the first to postulate that the sun, not

Earth, was the center of our system; he was, however, the first to widely popularize that notion, and the one who definitely shoved aside Ptolemy's theory of a twisting geocentric universe. His book offered valuable theories, but no evidence. German astronomer Kepler later proved that Copernicus was right.

Poland's renaissance dried up by the late 1700s, after the country lost half her population to assorted wars, famine, and plagues. Seizing upon Poland's weaknesses, Russia, Prussia, Austria (and Sweden for a time) all began annexing Polish lands starting in 1772—a geographical gnawing called "The First Partition." Poles rebelled frequently, and after a particularly heated revolt, Poland's three occupiers ganged up and split all remaining Polish lands between themselves. What was once Poland was literally erased from the map in 1795, a devastating event known by Poles as "The Third Partition."

Violent uprisings, attempts on the czar's life, and assorted furtive acts by Poland's many secret societies didn't cease, nor did harsh reprisals. Nevertheless, Poland remained essentially "disappeared" until the First World War, a period even more traumatic for Poles. The three countries that had yanked apart Poland lined up on two different sides: Poles were forced to fight for countries they didn't support; worse, they often had to fight fellow Poles in battles that killed 1.5 million Polish troops and civilians.

From World War I, however, Poles finally regained independence. When dashing military marshal Jozef Pilsudski took Warsaw in November 1918, he declared Poland an independent, sovereign country; the world powers officially agreed the next year.

FATHER OF POLAND JOZEF PILSUDSKI (MARSHAL, 1918–1935)

After he was tossed into a Siberian prison as a young man for an assassination attempt on Russian czar Alexander III, Socialist Pilsudski went on to publish his own newspaper, *Robotnik* (*The Worker*). Obsessed with the idea of Poland as an independent country, he became a guerrilla fighter and bandit, robbing banks and trains to fund a private militia to fight Russia, which he saw as the Poles' greatest threat. Fighting in the First World War, he hailed all of Poland free and sovereign in 1918. The only problem was deciding where exactly Poland was anymore; Pilsudski tried to annex land from almost all of the neighbors. He finally settled for part of Russia and part of Germany—and most of Lithuania, where he had been born. Lithuanians don't like him at all.

Known for his handlebar mustache, brilliant military maneuvers, and hot temper, Pilsudski took over as head of state in 1918, leading Poland into half a dozen wars in the next two years. Four years later, he left to oversee the Polish armed forces—and Poland quickly blew through ten governments. Pilsudski returned in 1926, heading a military coup that killed hundreds and entrenched him as dictator.

> *"I shit on all of you,"* Pilsudski bellowed in 1926, when he burst into Parliament, which he called "The House of Whores." "The time has come to treat you like children, because you behave like children."[4]

Despite his bullish nature, Pilsudski is revered as the father of Polish independence, and to his credit he somewhat organized the ramshackle republic. Given her German/Austrian/Russian past, Poland was by then a highly messy state of assorted ethnicities who used half a dozen currencies and as many languages; the country was so mismatched that even trains couldn't travel easily, since different gauges of rail ran through different parts of the country.[5] When Pilsudski died in 1935, Poland disintegrated again, leaving her ripe for attacks by historical foes Russia and Germany.

> *During the late 1930s, the Soviets and Nazis schemed together on how to snatch Poland and the Baltic countries. (See "Dirty Words: Molotov-Ribbentrop Pact," page 320.)*

Poland had barely celebrated her twentieth anniversary of independence when her freedom did another vanishing act. The Nazis took western Poland in September 1939; the Soviets took eastern Poland two weeks later. For the next five and a half years, Poland suffered the war's longest continuous fighting, and trains rumbled through the countryside carrying millions of civilian prisoners to concentration camps. Nearly the entire Jewish Polish population of 2 million died in the camps, alongside 1.5 million gypsies, gays, Communists, and dissidents.

> *Due to her history of religious tolerance, more Jews lived in Poland than anywhere else in Europe—which is one reason Hitler pounced on the country and set up the most notorious concentration camps here, including Auschwitz, Birkenau, and Treblinka.*

THE WARSAW GHETTO UPRISING:
APRIL 19–MAY 16, 1943[6]

In October 1940, the Nazis forced Warsaw's 500,000 Jewish residents from their homes and shoved them into a ghetto located near a train station. Nearly 300,000 were hauled off to concentration camps over the next two years, and another 100,000 ghetto-dwellers starved to death or died from disease. In January 1943, when another 5,000 Jews were sent off on trains, a young band of Jews attacked the Nazis, a move that halted deportations for several months. When Nazis returned to continue deportations on April 19, 1943, several hundred young Jews fought back with homemade explosives. The resisters were overwhelmed within a few weeks, when the Germans torched every building and gassed the tunnels. Only a few hundred of the remaining 60,000 Jews in the ghetto escaped.

Germans demolished cities going in—nearly a quarter of Warsaw lay in ruin within two weeks—and they devastated them going out, leaving Warsaw a pile of bloodred rocks. But Russians weren't any kinder. During their occupation, the Soviets hauled off 1.5 million Poles to Siberia and systematically used Polish troops and officers as frontline human shields to absorb Nazi bullets. The Soviets even set up the Poles in the final Allied battle to reclaim Warsaw from the Nazis. Insisting that they would represent the Allies, the Russians didn't join in the battle; instead they watched from the other side of the Vistula River as the Nazis ravaged the outnumbered Poles. It was a deliberate move—Stalin had calculated that he would be ridding himself of many future Polish dissidents.

By the end of the war, 6 million Poles—over one-sixth of the population—were dead.

Relief didn't arrive when WWII ended. The Soviet Union, the Allies-approved supervisor during reconstruction, yanked Poland into her sphere of influence, putting in puppets as leaders and running the place from afar. Poland remained a Soviet satellite for four depressing, air-polluted decades, during which tens of thousands of intellectuals, writers, and dissidents were shipped off to Siberian gulags, locked up, or killed.

CLANDESTINE COMMUNICATION

Across the Soviet Union and her satellite states, underground political movements relied on small printing presses that cranked out thousands of pamphlets, broadsheets, and small books—some political essays and calls for reform, some works of poetry or fiction. The *Samizdat* self-publishing movement was particularly strong in Poland. So evolved was the subversive communication network in Poland—historically a haven for secret societies—that underground writings circulated via a clandestine postal system that operated with its own stamps.[7]

The Polish rebelled throughout the Communist era, most notably in 1956. The protest—the first major uprising in any Soviet-controlled country, except for East Germany in 1953—started during a food shortage. Workers in Poznan's locomotive factory wanted more than a 20 percent wage hike; they wanted bread. On June 28, 1956, their riot, during which protesters stormed the city jail, turned into a countrywide uprising involving some 100,000; it was ultimately quashed by the Polish army, which killed up to 100 workers. The riots had one positive consequence: reform-oriented Socialist Wladyslaw Gomulka was brought back to power. Gomulka pushed out Stalinists, cut the powers of secret police, gave more freedom to the press, dropped demands for collectivizing farms, tolerated Catholicism, and kept Moscow at more of a distance—for a time.

Gomulka later grew hard-line. When Czechoslovakians threw off the totalitarian yoke during 1968's Prague Spring (See "Former Czechoslovakia," page 348), Gomulka supported a Soviet crackdown and let Moscow borrow Polish troops to accomplish it. When Polish students demonstrated in protest, Gomulka rounded up their leaders, throwing hundreds in jail. Two years later, when dockworkers protested at Gdansk (foreshadowing the rise of Solidarity in 1980), Gomulka again tried to smother dissent with force; that time, thirty-five died in the showdown. Gomulka was pushed out of power as a result.

Poland's most memorable role as a satellite was triggering the fall of Soviet Communism—and the Catholic Church certainly helped. When Karol Wojtyla, the Bishop of Krakow, donned the papal robes in 1978 and took the name Pope John Paul II, he triggered a renewed call for independence that echoed across Poland and spurred dissent across Soviet bloc countries. The most powerful move out of Poland, however, came from the dock and shipyard workers in

Gdansk, a defiant group who'd staged its first major protest in 1970. When they rose up again in a 1980 protest, a spike was driven into Moscow's heart—one that would finally make it stop beating.

HUNGRY FOR CHANGE

The soaring cost of food started it. In July 1980, when the government responded to food shortages by increasing the price of meat, the country collapsed in strikes. Most destabilizing was the strike in the Lenin shipyard in Gdansk, where workers had organized an illegal union, *Solidarnosc* (Solidarity). The union chose feisty electrician Lech Walesa as its leader; even though he had been fired from his job, Walesa scaled the fence to join that summer's protests. Backed by workers from twenty other factories, Walesa negotiated an agreement with the Polish Communists. Fearing further rebellion, the Communists signed a twenty-one point agreement that August, giving workers the right to unionize and strike. Solidarity soon rose as a symbol for more rights to all, and before long a quarter of Poles in all professions rallied behind the banner of Solidarity, which transformed from trade union to political movement. Walesa instantly became a celebrity, but by the end of 1981, Walesa and other leaders were imprisoned and the country was cloaked in martial law. Curfews remained in effect for eighteen months—those long nights at home triggered a huge baby boom—but they were lifted in July 1983 under international pressure. Walesa, who won the Nobel Peace Prize that year, and hundreds of others were released. As the world looked on—and the Communist regime was continually condemned by Pope John Paul II and U.S. president Ronald Reagan, among others—Polish Communists were forced to open the country up little by little. Other factors, too, were at work: the brutal Soviet-Afghanistan war (1979–1989) was wearing down both the Soviet army and Soviet coffers. By the time Mikhail Gorbachev, who'd stepped in as premier in 1985, began promoting his ideas for opening up and restructuring the Soviet Union, strong independence movements were already well under way in Poland—and in Hungary, Czechoslovakia, East Germany, and Romania. In January 1990, the Polish Communist Party was dissolved (it was later reformed as the more open Democratic Left Alliance), and in May 1990, Solidarity candidates dominated the country's first free elections in four decades. Lech Walesa was sworn in as president that December.

After the regime had entirely crumbled and the country was an independent democratic republic yet again, Poland was slapped by uncomfortable political realities. Kindly Walesa was a charismatic protest leader, but he was clueless about running a government: he sacked prime ministers almost annually, and his administration was haunted by scandals.

> In 1995, running for a second presidential term, Lech Walesa lost to former Communist Aleksander Kwasniewski. That race was close, but when the two faced off again in 2000, Kwasniewski was reelected and Walesa picked up less than 1 percent of the vote.

Meanwhile, the Catholic Church wanted paybacks. Among other things, the Church demanded that religious education be taught in school and sex education be banned. More controversially, religious forces successfully pushed through a 1993 bill to outlaw abortion, which had been legal under the Communist regime.

The good news was that, on paper at least, Poland was vastly improving economically: in the decade between 1989 and 1999, when Poland was selling off many of her state-owned industries, the Polish economy grew by 25 percent[8] and the international media cooed about the Poles' increased wealth. Many people, however, weren't sharing the enthusiasm: a Polish government study showed that in 1995 a whopping 40 percent were living in poverty,[9] and even now plenty of houses in the countryside don't have running water.

THE BISON WITH WANDERLUST[10]

After the First World War, Polish bison were nearly extinct—a result of over-hunting by bison-happy Austrian archduke Franz Ferdinand and others, who shot them down with machine guns—but thanks to intervention by animal biologists, the beasts now roam the Carpathian Mountains and nearby forests, perhaps too freely in the case of the mammoth beast known as Pulpit, a bison said to stand nearly seven feet high. As a young bull, Pulpit and a pal wandered off the reserve, reportedly crossing southern Poland and making it to the Ukraine—where apparently there wasn't much action, since the two turned around and came back. Upon their return to the reserve, their friendship was poisoned—over females, as is so often the case. During the mating season, his traveling companion, not wanting competition, booted Pulpit out of the reserve. On his second trek, which lasted nearly a year, Pulpit's behavior was indeed beastly. He trampled over fences, destroyed crops, knocked over fruit carts, rammed down shacks, and, once, crashed into a funeral. His obnoxious behavior prompted the death wagon's horses to shoot off, knocking the corpse from the wooden hearse, while the bereaved scrambled up trees. A special committee tracked Pulpit down and successfully returned him to the reserve—but come the next mating season, he was pushed off again. This time, orders were to shoot him if he posed a threat, and, as if sensing the danger, Pulpit was on his best behavior, so gentle that children fed him sweets and biscuits as he revisited his former haunts. Apparently, he was eating far too much sugar; worried about his health (bison, too, have to watch out for tooth decay, obesity, and indigestion), the authorities had to intervene. Realizing that, like so many a wayward male, Pulpit needed a female to keep him in line, they brought him to a different reserve, where perhaps he found the love of his life. He never strolled off again. (The reserve was fenced in.)

Since she came galloping out of the gates in 1989, Polska has mostly been stuck: the great dreams that fueled independence have faded, Solidarity has sputtered, former leader Lech Walesa is out, the initially promising economic performance has stalled, and unemployment is spinning out of control. In short, Poland appears to be at her most painful moment in post-Communist history, but hopefully EU membership will eventually numb the pain. And a dash of decent leadership would certainly help.

Hot Spots

Warsaw: Hitler ordered the Polish capital demolished, ordering "Leave no stone standing atop another." The Nazis succeeded in the mission, demolishing 85 percent of Warsaw; it's said that only a few thousand people survived in the city that was formerly home to millions, a third of them Jewish. The Old Town was (surprisingly) rebuilt by the Soviets. With buildings painted in golds, pinks, and reds, and the clomping of horse-drawn carriages (now carrying tourists) across cobblestone squares, some say it's prettier than before. The Royal Way that stretches from the Royal Palace to the royal summer home is thick with culture—museums, galleries, churches, and palaces stretch out along this passageway that would still please a king—and the once-seedy nightlife is slowly giving way to slick clubs and chill-out lounges; there's even a growing fashion district.

> *The Big Screen: Warsaw is the setting for* The Pianist, *a movie about the April 1943 Ghetto Uprising. The film, which took the Cannes Film Festival's highest prize and garnered Roman Polanski a Best Director Oscar, is based on the true story of pianist Wladyslaw Szpilman (1911–2000), former musician for Polish state radio. Forced into the Warsaw Ghetto, he escaped to the Aryan part of the city and lived to write* Death of a City, *first published in 1949[11] and later republished as* The Pianist.

Krakow/Cracow: Hub of education, industry, and culture, Krakow holds Poland's regal and rebellious past: site of two 1790s uprisings against Russia and Prussia, which led to Poland's demise, she's now starring on the tourist

map as the setting of *Schindler's List*. Believed to have been founded after legendary Prince Krak slew the resident subterranean dragon, Krakow is one of
the prettiest cities of Europe. Nearby salt mines are dripping with elaborate
crystalline sculptures, including glimmering chandeliers and even a chapel of
salt; some say trolls used to live there.

Krakow: The setting for Schindler's List

Auschwitz: The most potent symbol of the horrors of the Second World War
and the Holocaust, this concentration camp's brick buildings and ovens still send
chills up the spines of the half million people who visit each year. In 1940, the
Nazi-occupied Polish village of Oswiecim had her name changed to Auschwitz
and her history altered forever when she became the site of a camp that held up
to 20,000, usually their last residence before death. First housing Poles, then
Russians, then gypsies, then Jews, the original Auschwitz was expanded to include several other sites, including Birkenau (Auschwitz II) a few miles away,
where the majority of Jews were sent. Here, in the complex of buildings with
room for 90,000, most were gassed and their bodies thrown into crematoria that
could incinerate more than 300 a day. The exact number of Jews, gypsies, gays,
and other Poles who died here isn't really known, but it was at least 1.5 million.
In 1996, plans to build a shopping center right outside its gates were halted.

SHINING UP THE RUST BELT

The smoke-belching factories in Poland that produce low-quality steel,
blacken buildings, and clog the air with brown clouds require major renovation

and are often shut down. In 2002, Poland put the bulk of her steel mills up for sale. U.S. Steel was interested in taking over 70 percent of Poland's steel production, but Anglo-Dutch firm LNM Holdings secured a deal. Poland is under the gun to clean up environmental damage lingering from the Communist years; European Union funding is helping the process along.

Gdansk: The port city where Solidarity first rose up in 1980, Gdansk was one of Europe's great cities when she was part of the fifteenth-century marine trading group the Hanseatic League; hard-hit during the Second World War, she was rebuilt and today is thick with domed churches, spires, and medieval design. Called Danzig by the Germans who held her until 1918, Gdansk was snatched by Poland during the post–First World War redesign of Europe. Reportedly a hotbed of neo-Nazis today.

Hotshots

Lech Walesa: President, 1990–1995. The former electrician led the union that snowballed into an independence movement. Incarcerated in 1981, he won the Nobel Peace Prize in 1983 (he wasn't allowed to leave to accept it) and donated his $200,000 Nobel Prize money to redeveloping the country. Out of politics for the moment, Walesa now heads his own foundation.

> *"In 1905, when Poland did not appear on the map of Europe, Henryk Sienkiewicz said when receiving the Nobel Prize for Literature: 'She was pronounced dead—yet here is a proof that She lives on; She was declared incapable to think and to work—and here is proof to the contrary; She was pronounced defeated—and here is proof that She is victorious.'" —From Lech Walesa's 1983 Nobel Peace Prize acceptance speech, delivered by his wife*

POPE JOHN PAUL II: KAROL WOJTYLA (1920–2005)

No pope was more visible than Polish Pope John Paul II, who came to holy power in 1978. While most popes spoke from the balcony, John Paul II made appearances in his papal chariot around St. Peter's Square in the Vatican. In 1981, the pope was shot four times during one of his Vatican spins. Didn't slow him down much, although his pope-mobile was soon covered in bulletproof glass.

Never has a pope accumulated so many frequent flyer miles. he personally spread his word, traveling all over the world from Cuba to Croatia, Mexico to

Canada—over 100 countries in all—speaking out against the Soviet Union, birth control, abortion, and the horrors of war. The first pope to be so loudly heard in the global arena, he helped bring down Communism, but wasn't so successful at stopping skyrocketing Western arms sales or preventing the U.S. from invading Iraq—both actions that he condemned. Controversially, he elevated the status of Opus Dei, and, after intensive lobbying from the U.S. Department of Agriculture in his last days when he could barely speak, he supposedly spoke out and approved genetically modified food. (During that time, he also supposedly endorsed nuclear energy.) As pope for nearly twenty-seven years, John Paul II launched more on their way to sainthood than any other—he canonized 476 and beatified 1,320—and is now on the road to sainthood himself. He was beatified mere months after his spring 2005 death.

Jerzy Kosinski (1933–1991): He put Polish literature on the English-speaking map, but isn't much loved by Poles. Born in Lodz, hawk-nosed Jerzy Kosinski, who moved to the U.S. after WWII, flapped to fame on the wings of *The Painted Bird*, a hard-hitting novel that casts Polish peasants unflatteringly as violent anti-Semites who, like hens in a chicken coop, attack those who stand out. A Polish Jew who escaped Nazi persecution with a birth certificate showing he was Catholic, Kosinski initially palmed off the novel as being based on his Second World War experience, but that claim was shot down by his many detractors. Dogged by accusations of plagiarism—among them a claim that his popular novel/screenplay *Being There* was a knockoff of a Polish novel—the man who won the National Book Award in 1969 responded to critics by penning a footnote-heavy novel, *The Hermit of 69th Street*, a parody of overfastidious citation. Brilliant but unstable, Kosinski pulled a plastic bag over his head and suffocated himself in the bathtub in May 1991, leaving a note. "I am going to put myself to sleep now for a bit longer than usual. Call the time Eternity."[12] Nobody accused him of plagiarizing that.

CULTURAL STANDOUT: CHOPIN (1810–1849)

"Poet of the piano" Chopin, considered the world's finest composer for that instrument, is a Polish national hero, despite spending nearly half his life in France. His parents met in the home of a Polish count, where his French father was tutor and his mother a housekeeper. Fryderyk (or Frédéric) was born outside Warsaw, when his father became French professor in the Warsaw Lyceum. Chopin began composing at seven, and was performing internationally at eighteen; by twenty-one, he was living in Paris, hobnobbing with painters and poets. At twenty-seven, he began a decadelong love affair with female novelist

George Sand. Weak from tuberculosis, worsened after a winter holiday in a damp monastery in Mallorca, Chopin composed some of his greatest works, including the *24 Preludes* and *Polonaise in C Minor* while deathly ill. The TB soon after killed him. "The world is suffocating . . ." he said, drawing his last breath, "swear to make them cut me open so that I won't be buried alive." Most of Chopin's body remained in Paris, but, as he'd requested, his heart went to Poland, the country he hadn't set foot in for eighteen years.

Roman Polanski: Son of a Polish Jew and a Russian émigrée, Polanski was born in France in 1933, but his parents brought the toddler to Krakow, an unfortunate move: during the war both were hauled off to concentration camps, where his mother died. Escaping the Jewish ghetto, young Polanski spent the war on the run, sleeping in barns. After the war, he studied at Lodz Film School, made several short films, and garnered international recognition for *Knife in the Water*, which was nominated for an Oscar. In 1968, he moved to California and horrified the world with psycho-thriller *Rosemary's Baby*; shortly thereafter, his life became something out of his films when minions of Charles Manson brutally murdered his pregnant wife, Sharon Tate. Polanski went on to make *Chinatown* and *Tess*, and returned to Poland to film *The Pianist*, which won numerous awards and is considered his finest work.

ESCAPING MEMORY: MICHEL SEDZIWOJ (AKA SENDIVOGIUS) (1556–1636)

The life of alchemist Michel Sendivogius is cloaked in legend: was he an escapologist (disappearing from flaming towers and dungeon chains), a form-changing wizard, or simply a man of medicine who tended to royals? What is certain is that in the late 1500s the scientist worked for the Polish king in launching Poland's metallurgical industry. Sendivogius's most important contributions were his books about science and alchemy. *On the Philosophers' Stone* (also called *A New Light on Alchemy*) went through dozens of printings in six languages and was devoured by the era's thinkers, including Sir Isaac Newton. Sendivogius is credited with first writing that air was a mixture of substances, although it wasn't until the eighteenth century that it was figured out what that mixture was.[13]

Marie Sklodowska Curie (1867–1934): The Polish-born scientist who discovered the nature of radioactivity—she coined the term—Madame Curie died of leukemia as a result. Before doing so, she became one of four people ever to win two Nobel Prizes: she shared the 1903 Nobel in Physics with her husband, Pierre Curie, and colleague Henri Becquerel, and took the 1911 Nobel in Chemistry for discovering two new elements, including polonium, named after her homeland. As her work was done in Paris, the French claim her too.

DRINKING MATTERS

Poles and Russians argue over who invented vodka, but Poles win in quality. Ultimat is the priciest, but Zubrowka is most beloved; each bottle's strand of bison grass, a turn-on to the beasts, imparts a vanilla-like taste; some say the secret is that it's coated in bison secretions. Gdansk's 300-year-old specialty: sweet 'n' spicy firewater Goldwasser, flecked with gold flakes. Also novel: pink rosewater liqueur Rosaline, prepared from an eighteenth-century secret recipe in a castle distillery.

Closing time? Many of Poland's vodka distilleries are doing badly and may soon fold.

News you can understand: There are plenty of interesting papers in Poland, but few in English. One exception: *The Warsaw Voice*: www .warsawvoice.pl

18. HUNGARY

(Magyarorszád)

Lost in the Past

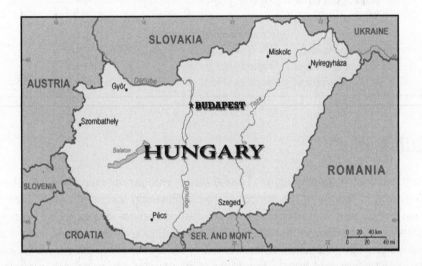

FAST FACTS

Country:	Republic of Hungary; Magyar Koztarsasag
Capital:	Budapest
Government:	Parliamentary democracy
Independence:	1001 (unified); 1920 modern Hungary formed; 1989 independence from Soviet Union, which had made it a satellite
Population:	9,982,000 (2006 estimate)
Head of State:	Laszlo Solyom (2005)
Head of Government:	Prime Minister Ferenc Gyurcsany (2004)
Elections:	President elected by parliament for five-year term; prime minister elected by parliament after public votes in parliamentary elections
Name of Parliament:	National Assembly; Orszaggyules

Ethnicity:	92% Hungarian; 6% unknown or other; 2% Roma (some say closer to 10%) (2001 census)
Religion:	52% Roman Catholic; 16% Calvinist; 14% unaffiliated; 11% other; 3% Lutheran; 2% Greek Catholic
Language:	94% Hungarian; 6% other
Literacy:	99% (2005) (dubious claim)
Famous Exports:	Medicinal liqueur Unicum, high-octane palinka, billionaire George Soros
Economic Big Boy:	MOL (oil and gas); 2004 total sales: $10.82 billion[1]
Per Capita GDP:	$16,100 (2005)
Unemployment:	7.3% (December 2005 Eurostat figure); Roma unemployment: 60%[2]
Percentage in Poverty:	10% (2003 estimate of UNDP/MTA)[3]
EU Status:	Entered May 2004
Currency:	Hungarian forint

Quick Tour

From sailboats whipping across Lake Balaton, Hungary's "inland sea," to rolling vineyards in Tokaj and the apricot orchards flowering across the great central plain—once loud with the clomping of warrior horses—the door is swinging open for Magyarország. Europe's airlines are bringing in hordes who marvel at domed and spired Budapest, the city along the Danube that glitters with imperial architecture and boasts hundreds of museums; others set off to soothe aches in castle-baths and island spas in this country, which has nearly 1,000 hot springs—more than anywhere except Iceland.

TAKING THE WATERS

Thanks to the thin crust of the Carpathian Basin, Hungary is rich in thermal waters that bubble up at around 90°F; Budapest alone has over 100 springs, and many are loaded with minerals and lauded for their therapeutic effects. Hungarians (and the millions of visitors who come for the spas) highly regard the ritual, claiming that "taking the waters" might cure everything from arthritis to neurological conditions. Not all thermal baths are the same—some contain iodine, fluoride, or sulphuric acid; others are radioactive or have a slight electric charge running through them. The settings are equally diverse, ranging from Roman baths and tiled Turkish baths to the cave spa at Tapolca. One of the most stunning environments: Budapest's

Hotel Gellert, which served as Nazi headquarters during World War II, and where one now soaks amid marble columns as sunlight streams through stained glass.

Glorious old-world cafés where revolutions brewed up are swinging open their doors yet again, the arts are celebrated in weeklong festivals, and music floats down the streets, escaping from opera houses and restaurants where gypsy bands play. Fish-rich rivers thread across this fertile land, where food is plentiful, soups are hearty, and everything is washed down with abundant, and tasty, Hungarian wine.

Hungary has twenty wine regions, and a wine industry that could boom. Tokaj wine, heralded by France's Louis XIV as "king of wines, and the wine of kings," questionably steals all the press (the white wine is an acquired taste), but many of the reds range from easy-drinking to elegant, and all can be tasted in Budapest's House of Hungarian Wines, in the castle complex. One sign of the potential: foreigners are buying up vineyards by the handful.

So why is the country known for cheerful fiddlers, fruit brandies, and zesty food the most melancholy in Europe, a land where the trademark posture is looking down at one's shoe and the national hobby is lamenting the past? Hungarians are haunted by history and a popular belief that they are cursed. What else but a hex (which they believe was put on them by retreating Turks) could explain Hungary's fall from greatness? What else could explain her chronic battles to hold on to her language, people, and land? What other European country is so jinxed, Hungarians will ask you, that it was invaded and occupied five times during the last century alone?[4]

"We know what it is to be losers. We have all been losers for centuries."
—Hungarian psychologist Margot Honti[5]

HUNGARY: SUICIDE EPICENTER

Is it the weather—the long winters and frequent gray skies? Is it something emitted from the ancient volcanoes in the west or the dreariness of the central terrain that's Ohio-like flat? Perhaps the culprit is a lard-happy diet or too much cream, or maybe it's a normal reaction to the sight of McDonald's overtaking the cities. Whatever the reason, Hungarians are a gloomy bunch whose leaders and writers have often done themselves in. Hungarian suicide rates are often the world's highest,[6] and they remain abnormally high. Among the middle-aged, for instance, only the Japanese kill themselves more. Sociologists attribute the self-destructiveness to pent-up rage; Hungarians say it's genetic—they just feel too much. And they always feel lousy when they think of their past.

Given that they ditched Communism, and the Soviets who once pummeled them down are long gone, and given that the standard of living is rising (or so the government claims) and more opportunity is on the horizon since Hungary joined the European Union, why are so many Hungarians utterly glum? The black hole of sadness, say many, stems from a feeling that their heritage was ripped away. Some point to 1526—often evoked as though it was yesterday—the year of the Battle of Mohács, when Turks from the Ottoman Empire captured two-thirds of the Hungarian Kingdom in two hours, a defeat that led to a 160-year occupation and dependence on the Austrian Empire to beat the Ottomans back. They finally did, in 1686, which ultimately led to Austrian domination. Five hundred years before the Turks took over, the Mongols invaded, an event that causes grumbles and loud sighs. But a much more recent event—having happened merely eighty-six years ago—was the Treaty of Trianon, the signing of a paper that for Hungarians was as significant as nailing Jesus to the cross. The Treaty of Trianon ended the Austro-Hungarian Empire and shredded Hungary's claim to greatness; that agreement, foisted upon the defeated Hungarians at the end of World War I, ripped Greater Hungary apart. She lost half of her people and two-thirds of her land; most of her timber, iron ore, and national wealth went with it.

Five million ethnic Hungarians—Magyars—now reside in neighboring countries.

GREATER HUNGARY

Never mind that the land in question was carved up at the end of World War I, and that most alive at the time are long dead. And never mind that Hungarians willingly went along with their corulers, the Austrians, in starting World War I, and that their shared empire was lost by defeat. The peace treaty the victorious Allies drew up on June 4, 1920, shrank Hungary's physical map—Romania, Slovakia, Ukraine, Croatia, Serbia, and Austria all picked up pieces—and millions of Hungarians ended up on the other side of the new borders. A gnawing sense of injustice still hangs in the air, and you can sense it in the hilltop bar

where Gabor, a college student, is drawing the outline of Old Hungary and saying he wants that land back; you notice it in the national museums that proudly
sell Treaty of Trianon badges and postcards, with the lost lands in black, chas-
tising "Don't Forget!" and you can feel it when tens of thousands march every
June 4 in loud protest. You can even see it on the TV weather map, which
shows the Hungarian Empire as she was in the days before being hacked up.
And the idea that Hungary deserves those lands back is not only a source of
chronic frustration to many Hungarians, including quite a few of the young, it's
a reason that the country is dividing between those who think the reunification
idea should be dropped, and those who think Hungary should pursue it. The
latter group typically supports Viktor Orbán, helping him rise as prime minister
of the country a few years ago, when he nearly drove Hungary back to her recent totalitarian past.

Master manipulator Viktor Orbán knew exactly what buttons to push, but he
didn't start his career as a politician with a promise to somehow unite ethnic
Hungarians. Ruggedly handsome, secretly wealthy, and obsessively driven,
brash Viktor Orbán rose to fame in the late 1980s by hitting yet another of Hungary's national quirks: the 1956 Revolution. Even Americans old enough to re-
member may not recall the ten days when Hungarians, urged by Americans to
rise up against Communists (and assured that the West would back them), did
just that—only to find themselves all alone. Tens of thousands were killed while
the West looked the other way, and Warsaw Pact forces—soldiers from Soviet
bloc countries—stormed in. Even if the event is just hazy history to
Americans—whose attention was diverted by a simultaneous crisis when
Britain, France, and Israel attacked Egpyt over the Suez Canal—it's still a lingering wound to Hungarians.

THE 1956 HUNGARIAN REVOLUTION

No period of the past fifty years better exemplified the Hungarian plight under Communism than the autumn of 1956, when Hungary—pushed by hunger,
stirred up by Radio Free Europe, and believing that Western powers would
come to her aid—stood up to the Soviet Union, alone as it turned out. Suffering
under Moscow's economic policies, which dictated life in the Communist state
that was a Soviet satellite, Hungarians were already unhappy that year, when
winter hit early along with drastic shortages of fuel and food. On October 23,
hundreds of thousands of students and workers revolted, toppling statues of
Stalin and Lenin, smashing out windows, and issuing a sixteen-point procla-
mation demanding that the Soviets cut loose their hold, end the secret police,
and send in more food. Moscow (in the form of Premier Khrushchev) answered

by rolling in tanks, and Warsaw Pact soldiers killed hundreds of demonstrators, inciting even more violence. Moscow finally caved in to one protest demand and allowed Imre Nagy, a Communist and former prime minister whom Moscow had previously forced out because of his reforms, to return to power. Nagy released political prisoners and ordered the Soviet troops out of Hungary—and they retreated. Emboldened, Nagy went further and announced that Hungary was pulling out of the Warsaw Pact and would become neutral on the world stage; Nagy also notified the United Nations of the desperate situation, but the UN, like the U.S. and the UK, did nothing. Panicked, Khrushchev unleashed more Warsaw Pact troops, who killed over 20,000 during ten savage days when tanks dragged corpses through the streets as a warning to protesters.[7] Brave Nagy lasted as prime minister only those ten days: he was kidnapped and hauled off to Romania, where he was imprisoned, found guilty in a secret trial, and executed in 1958. Buried in an unmarked grave, his remains were exhumed in 1989, and Hungarians reburied him as a hero. Hungarians are still upset that the U.S. and Western European powers so loudly opposed to Communism did not help in the 1956 Revolution; some believe that the West's lack of support was the result of a secret deal with the Soviet Union—that Moscow would not interfere in the 1956 Suez Canal crisis if the West ignored Hungary's plight.[8] They could be right.

"To every writer in the world, to all scientists, to all science academies and associations, to the intelligentsia of the world: HELP HUNGARY!"
—Message from the Hungarian Writers' Union to the free press during Hungary's 1956 Revolution.[9]

"To all those suffering under Communist slavery, let us say you can count on us."[10]*—U.S. Secretary of State J. F. Dulles in November 1956; his words rang hollow considering the U.S. had done nothing but watch while the Soviets regained control.*

Straight from law school, where he and other poli-sci students put together their own political party—the Federation of Young Democrats (Fidesz)—Orbán made his first dramatic display at the 1989 reburial of Hungarian hero Imre Nagy. The event was already rife with emotion, but Orbán made it more so with a dramatic speech demanding that Soviet troops leave Hungary, the first to be brazen enough to say so publicly since Nagy.

Orbán quickly commandeered Fidesz. Radically liberal and decidedly young—the party at first wouldn't allow members older than thirty-five—Fidesz swerved to the hard right when Orbán took over the wheel and began talking about uniting ethnic Hungarians wherever they lived. Within nine years, he'd climbed to the top of the political mountain—becoming prime minister in 1998 at age thirty-six. Orbán blocked opposition voices; he shut down newspapers and weakened public broadcasting, triggering outrage from international media watchdogs. The man who claimed to hate Communist totalitarianism—and who set up the House of Terror in the mansion that once served as an interrogation center and torture chamber for Soviet secret police—nevertheless did a fine imitation of autocratic leadership, continually stomping out dissent and trying to increase powers for himself. Orbán also stirred up the neighbors, passing a law that gave work, health care, and education benefits to the 5 million Hungarians living in surrounding countries. His

Victor Orbán wants to glue Old Hungary back together

moves were seen as an attempt to kick off a pan-Hungarian movement, fears not allayed when he spoke of the "spiritual and cultural reunification of the Hungarian people"[11] and referred to Transylvania—part of Romania—as "part of Hungary's living space."[12]

Throughout his term, he continued to cause a fiery split in Hungarians—most obvious in the days after the 2002 elections between Orbán and the Socialists, when the air was so charged that some feared Hungary was peering at civil war.

> *Seventy-one percent of Hungarians voted in the 2002 parliamentary election—the country's highest turnout—and the race was close, with Orbán's party actually winning more votes. However, due to a proportional voting system that weights votes from less populated areas, Socialists took the election. It was an emotional day: Orbán cried during his concession speech and so did his supporters. Fights broke out and street protests turned so violent that police teargassed the crowds. At least seven Hungarians missed the postelection fireworks; they'd died of heart attacks while casting their votes.[13]*

Many were surprised when Orbán was not reelected in 2002—and they were shocked again in May 2006, when Orbán lost again in another close race. Though he announced that he was stepping down from the party, it's hard to believe that Hungarians are done with him. Then again, maybe Hungary is changing. Recent polls indicate that she's no longer home to the saddest, most suicidal people in the EU. That role is now taken by Lithuania.[14]

But while many have been following Orbán's steps and missteps, they've been missing the background maneuvering of Russia, which hasn't fully receded from the Hungarian picture. Hungary became a NATO member in 1999, but she'd been the biggest purchaser of Russian arms throughout the 1990s. Known for her lax banking system, which all but encourages money laundering, Budapest is such a haven for the Russian mob that the FBI set up a bureau here. Moscow provides most of Hungary's natural gas, and kicks her a hefty wad from transit fees for a pipeline that runs under the country. What's more, Hungary needs an economic life—and Russian president Vladimir Putin in February 2006 dangled a multibillion-dollar package that entails Russia buying everything, from more Hungarian food to buying Hungarian energy companies, including petroleum and gas wholesaler MOL.[15] It's unclear whether Hungary's Socialist prime minister, millionaire Ferenc Gyurcsany, will bite.

> Many of Hungary's former Communist leaders are now politically active Socialists.

History Review

If Hungary's pessimistic streak shows through, it's understandable: in Hungary, change typically means a downturn in standards of living. Look what happened when the Mongols showed up in the twelfth century: they slaughtered half the Magyar population. Look what happened when the Turks showed up and won the 1526 Battle of Mohács: for a century and a half, Ottoman Turks ran most of the country, taking over beloved capital, Budapest, embarking on a depopulation plan, and requiring that non-Muslims pay steep taxes. And then when Austrians helped finally push the Turks out in 1699, the Habsburg clan frowned on Hungarian culture and suppressed the language that so defines the Hungarian people.

> During the Ottoman Occupation, many wealthy Hungarians fled to today's Slovakia, where they built up the capital Bratislava, attempting to create Budapest Jr.

LANGUAGE LESSON

The Hungarian (Magyar) language is a mystery with its forty-four letters, a dozen of them vowels. Officially, Hungarian is part of the Finno-Ugric group, which would make it similar to Finnish, but Hungarians point to the East as a more important influence, and indeed this land was routinely taken over from invaders coming from that direction, starting with Attila the Hun; even Hungary's official founder, Chief Arpad, rode in from Asia. Hungarians put surnames first—Orbán Viktor, for example—a custom shared with Asian cultures, and villagers in the Himalayan Mountains near Tibet are said to speak a language similar to Hungarian. Wherever it hails from, they love their language with a fierce pride; even in international Budapest, Hungarian often seems the only language spoken anywhere outside hotels, although some young people are fluent in English. If you don't speak Magyar (pronounced "Mawdyar"), you can often see ice come into a Hungarian's eyes as prices quickly rise. If you speak even a word or two, the price increases aren't quite as steep.

Despite Austrian disapproval, Hungarians clung to their language and revived it as the language of literature. The rebirth of Magyar, and an accompanying nationalistic spirit, fueled the Hungarian Revolution of 1848, led largely by writers who pushed independence from the Austrian Empire with demands called the Twelve Points—starting with freedom of the press and lifting of censorship, and going on to call for emancipation of serfs. That uprising against Habsburg rule did bring a brief taste of freedom—after concessions from Austria's emperor Ferdinand, Hungary ran independently for a whopping six months. However, the move was so unpopular in Vienna that Ferdinand was shoved off the throne; his nephew Franz Joseph succeeded him and unleashed Austrian wrath on Hungary. The plucky Hungarians fought fiercely, and Austrians had to bring in Croatians and Russian Cossacks to successfully return the wayward territory to Austrian rule. In 1867, however, the Magyars rose up against the Austrians again and demanded the eastern chunk of the weakening Habsburg Empire. This time they got it, and the Austrian Empire became the Austro-Hungarian Empire, with Magyars controlling lands to the north (today's Slovakia), to the east (today's Romania), and to the south (today's Serbia and Croatia).

The Hungarian spirit and landscape were remarkably transformed during the so-called Dual Monarchy. Much of the most spectacular architecture in Hungary—from the lacy towers of the parliament building to the ornately decorated town halls in small towns like Kecskemet—is a testimony to that opulent era, when Budapest rivaled Vienna as the grande dame of central Europe. With her hill-perched castle, thermal springs, and fabulous tile-wrapped buildings designed by the likes of Eiffel, the stunning metropolis on the Danube River was marked by fine music, high literature, provocative theater, and the many intellectual societies that met in grand cafés. The political machine was filled with visionaries: so thoroughly modern and avant-garde was the Budapest of the Belle Europe era, that one of Europe's first subway systems was unveiled here in 1896.

CAFÉ SOCIETY

Vienna may now have the reputation of being a café society, but coffee—or "black soup" as it was once known—first caught on here, introduced by the Turks who occupied Hungary starting in the 1500s. By the 1800s, the liquid fuel was exalted by Hungarians in hundreds of ornate cafés that were the official meeting spots for prestigious societies and weighty intellectuals. Revolutions were plotted and famous magazines born in the cafés, and the heavily wooded hangouts were magnets for writers of all sorts, since scribes were given free paper to capture their caffeine-powered thoughts. An integral part of Hungarian society, the idea breeding grounds were shut down by the Soviets who, for forty years, transformed the lovely establishments into warehouses. Since the 1990s, however, many of the history-steeped cafés have reopened and again serve whipped-cream-slathered coffee in antique china cups with cookies, glossy chocolate, and a glass of water—all on a silver tray.

Budapest's public transit system is exceptional; one rarely needs to walk more than two blocks to get on it. The escalators to the subway platforms, however, are so incredibly steep that the common reaction is vertigo.

Long kept down by their occupiers, Hungarians, when they ascended, were just as domineering as their former rulers; they forced other ethnic groups in the ceded territories (today's Slovakia, Romania, Croatia, and Serbia among them) to adopt the Magyar language and embrace Hungarian culture.

At the beginning of the twentieth century Hungary's future looked sweet, but that was apparently a *pálinka*-induced fantasy. Pulled into the First World War on the losing side, Hungary was left in a chaotic state in its aftermath. A 1918 revolution overthrew the king and formed a republic, but the country was soon overrun by outside forces. At the war's end, Czechs, Slovaks, and Romanians invaded and looted Hungarian cities, unleashing the pent-up rage that had built up under decades of heavy-handed Magyar rule. The Romanians were the most vicious: when they left after their 1919 occupation, they loaded up most of the country's remaining industrial riches—and even absconded with Hungary's trains.

The Allied victors' redrawing of post–First World War Europe shaved Hungary, leaving her one-third of her former size, creating a huge diaspora of ethnic Hungarians, and ushering in one of the lowest points of Hungary's rollercoaster history. Dictators assumed power over the demoralized Hungarian people in the shrunken land. Communist Béla Kun lasted only six months, but the next powermonger, Admiral Miklos Horthy, cracked the whip for twenty-four years. Under Horthy, Hungary became obsessed with the return of the territories. Starting in grade school, children learned about the necessity of stitching the land back together. Posters of the lost lands, shown in black on a map, hung from offices everywhere, with the caption "No, No, Never!"

Lured by the promise of regaining forested and resource-rich Transylvania, Horthy signed Hungary up with the Axis powers in World War II, another painful error. Horthy tried to pull out of the agreement in 1944, and the Nazis invaded; the Horthy regime was shoved out by the Fascist Arrow Cross movement, which deported and killed some 500,000 Jews in the last months of the war. When driven out by the Soviet army in April 1945, the Nazis blew up Budapest's beloved bridges and castle, leaving the city mostly a pile of boulders and dust.

Saddled with war reparations to Russia, Hungary was forced to turn over industry to the Soviets, and soon the Soviets simply took over, installing hardcore Stalinists in the Hungarian government who were quick to hang those who questioned their clout. Not only did Hungary lose any remaining wealth, the country was subjected to Moscow's planned economies, including collectivized farms and the accompanying frequent shortages of food. The weight of defeat, coupled with the apparatus of repression, was too much for Hungarians to bear; rebellions broke out, and the Soviets displayed their most ruthless side when Hungary tried to loosen their grip. After the 1956 Revolution, 200,000 Hungarians fled.

János Kádár, foreign minister under ten-day prime minister Imre Nagy during the 1956 Revolution, left the government in disgust after Nagy pulled Hungary out of the Warsaw Pact. Kádár landed in the power seat when the Soviets steamrolled the uprising—and he stayed there until 1988. Kádár initiated his tenure with a show of force, ordering 2,000 Hungarians executed and another 25,000 tossed in jail for their roles in the uprising. However, he soon lightened up. Riddled by guilt over Nagy's 1958 execution, Kádár went on to lead a relatively liberal Communist government.

Even after the 1956 slaughter, Hungary refused to play by all of Moscow's rules. Fearing another disaster, Moscow gave Hungary freer rein. The Catholic Church was allowed out of the closet, some political prisoners were released, and Hungary's government was allowed to pursue market reforms and loosen state control over the economy. By the 1980s, the economy was open to foreign investment, and Hungary launched a stock market as part of her "goulash Socialism" program—moves that made the country the wealthiest and economically healthiest of all the Soviet bloc countries, though, by the end, the economy was propped up by billions of dollars in IMF loans.

Starting in the 1970s, Hungarians could also travel to Western countries.

In the final years of the 1980s, when it was obvious the Soviet Union was sinking, Hungarians were quick to jump ship. By 1988, opposition groups had cobbled together the Hungarian Democratic Forum, which ushered in far-reaching political changes. In 1989, a new constitution was penned, allowing such freedoms as a multiparty system and the rights to demonstrate in protest and form trade unions. Sensing that there was little that exhausted Moscow could do, Hungary's reform-pushing Communists tore the first big rip in the Iron Curtain in 1989—literally snipping the barbed wire—and instructed border guards to stop enforcing the shoot-to-kill policy against those who fled into Austria. That summer, Hungary was *the* place for a holiday, as thousands of tourists from East Germany and Romania slipped out. By the end of the year, Hungary, too, had slipped out of the Soviet hold.

RADIO ROMA

Tourists love the festive Roma (gypsies), whose folk music greets them from street corners, but Hungarians haven't been too fond of them. Sixty percent of Roma are unemployed, and they're associated with crime, from pickpocketing to break-ins. Not represented in Hungary's parliament and harder-hit than any other group since the Communist safety net unraveled, at least they have their own radio station—which is funded by the EU. Broadcasting in their language, and playing Roma music, Radio Roma is a hit even with non-Roma; many say it's the best station in Budapest. (See "Slovak Republic," page 363.)

Even shaking free of the Soviets wasn't cause to bring out the plum brandy for long. Hungary was slammed in the early 1990s; the economy stalled, unemployment shot up to 14 percent, prices doubled and quadrupled, one-third of Hungarians sank into poverty, and depression slunk over the country. The fine freedom they had been anticipating for forty-four years seemed far worse than the Soviet days. Relationships suffered and divorce became commonplace; some 56 percent of young married couples split up.[16] Rapid cultural change also contributed to the collective malaise. Hungary quickly embraced all things Western, being the first former Soviet bloc country to open up a McDonald's, which became the most popular in the world. Burger Kings, KFCs, Irish pubs, sports bars, and British department stores popped up everywhere as the country began a fast-track program to reconnect with the West. One of the first Eastern countries to reach out to the European Union for membership, Hungary was also wooed by NATO; along with Poland and the Czech Republic, Hungary officially signed on with the mutually armed protection club in 1999.

Hot Spots

Budapest: The most attacked capital in Europe, and still bearing bullet holes from the 1956 Revolution, regal Budapest (pronounced "Booda-pesht") is actually a combo of two former cities—old world Buda, with wooded hills and seventeenth-century architecture, and more urban, modern, flatter Pest—which sit on opposite sides of the Danube River. She may rival Vienna again, if the old beauty ever gets that needed face-lift and businesses stop ripping off tourists.

The Danube: Forget the idea of it being blue, it's usually gray around here. Heavily polluted under the Soviet regime, the river that historically made Hun-

Geothermal hot spot Budapest, former belle of Eastern Europe

gary's capital an important trade city isn't as high, since Slovakia dammed it upstream.

Buda Castle: The hilltop castle that peered down over the Danube from the thirteenth century was supposed to protect Magyars, but over the years mostly helped out their enemies. Turks moved right in, making it their base during their stay; it took demolishing the castle to pry them out. The Nazis made themselves at home in the rebuilt structure, using it as a fortress and showing their thanks by blowing it up when they left. Rebuilt in the 1950s, the castle complex now houses plenty of stately monuments and assorted museums; a labyrinth winds around under it.

> It's said that Turks buried treasures in the castle labyrinths; during the Second World War, they held a subterranean Nazi town, complete with bomb shelters and hospital.

Pecs: Twenty miles from the field that changed Hungarian history with the Battle of Mohács, Pecs exemplifies Hungary's layered past in her main square. There one finds statues of Hungarian warriors, slain during the 1526 battle, and in the background a minaret looms, topped with a cross. The best showcase of the Ottoman occupation, and also rich in uranium.

Eger: The lovely Baroque town is known for the red wine called Bull's Blood, a name given after locals drank copious amounts of it, sloshing it on their shirts, and then beat back the Turks—who attributed their defeat to the alcohol-fueled fighters drinking bull's blood. The Turks returned a few decades later and took Eger with ease, but the name of the wine sticks. Outside town, in the Valley of the Nice Lady, wine-tasting cellars are built right into hills; the name of the valley comes from the lady who offered more than just Dionysian pleasures in her tasting room.

Refrigerators: In the typical Hungarian fridge, you'll find plenty of cream (the base for most soups), whipped cream (squirted on everything), and lard (squeezed out from a tube for that ubiquitous onion-garnished treat—lard sandwiches). No wonder at least 19 percent of Hungarians are obese.[17]

Taxicabs: Slimy unaffiliated cabbies bilk the foreigner, charging $20 or more for a five-minute ride. Alas, these scammers are just one form of Budapest's con artists, a group that also includes beautiful girls who invite the unsuspecting visitor for a round of drinks that rings up at $600 or more.

Borders: Sharing boundaries with seven countries, Hungary is a major corridor for drug-running, slave-smuggling, trafficking of arms and stolen cars, and any other activity deemed profitable for the Russian mob.

Hotshots

Ferenc Gyurcsany: Prime Minister, 2004–present. Young, rich, and charismatic, Gyurcsany, appointed as a fill-in in 2004, was elected two years later, making him the first Hungarian leader to last two terms. The smooth-talking tycoon urged fellow Socialists to "dare to be left again" and revamp their image from being dinosaurs left over from the Communist days. Purists scoff at his moneyed background and plans to raise taxes; they put quotes around "Socialist" when they use it to describe him.

Laszlo Solyom: President, 2005–present. Lawyer and professor Solyom is best known as head of the Constitution Court, where he helped kill capital punishment.

CULTURAL STANDOUT: BÉLA BARTÓK (1881–1945)

No musician strikes more of a chord with Hungarians than Béla Bartók, whose dramatic works were influenced by folk music. Ghostly pale with dark mystic eyes, Bartók's passion was ethnomusicology, a field he pioneered. After overhearing a Slovak peasant singing in 1907, he traveled across the countryside, convincing country-dwellers to allow him to record their traditional songs on wax cylinders. Pianist and composer Bartók's most scandalous composition was the sexually charged ballet *Miraculous Mandarin* that revolved around crime, prostitution, and murder. Upon its 1926 debut in Budapest, the shocked audience stormed out; future performances were banned. Bartók won favor shortly afterward, however, with two violin sonatas and his famous *Dance Suite*. Although his career was soaring, he loathed the interwar ship run by dictator Admiral Horthy, and ceased performing during the 1930s. When the Second World War broke out, he moved to New York—and composed for such VIPs as Benny Goodman.

Hungary has a rich history of literature and theater, though many works haven't been translated. Hungarian novelist and Auschwitz survivor Imre Kertész won the 2002 Nobel Prize in Literature for his works (including Fateless *and* Kaddish for a Child Not Born*), which capture characters lost under dictatorships.*

Franz Liszt (1811–1886): The Hungarian went down in history as one of the world's finest composers for such works as the *Hungarian Rhapsodies*, but during his life he was Europe's most gifted and passionate pianist who coaxed an orchestra's worth of sounds from the ivories. Deeply moved by St. Francis of

Assisi, Liszt became a priest at age fifty-five and wrote *St. Francis Preaches to the Birds*, a piece capturing the twittering of the swallows to whom Francis was said to address his homilies.

Hungarians claim movie producer Sir Alexander Korda (best known for The Third Man) *as their own, even though he worked mostly in England, where he was involved in propaganda and a spy network.*

Béla Kun: Self-proclaimed leader, 1918. Hothead Communist who grabbed the reins after the First World War, kicked off a 133-day second Bolshevik Revolution, and quickly became hated by everybody for prohibiting alcohol, requiring that children take baths and transforming churches into cinemas.[18] During his six-month regime, Kun seized lands from the rich—but forgot to turn them over to the peasants. The madman was the worst person to have heading the government when the mapmakers were redrawing Europe after 1918. His Communist policies won Hungary absolutely no favors with the Red-fearing Allies.

Hungarian Truth and Life Party (MIEP): The good news: they're not very popular. The bad news: the fact that this openly anti-Semitic, anti-Roma political party exists.

Scary: the rising forces of young skinheads in Hungary. Blood and Honor is one group known to stage demonstrations 400 strong in Heroes Square in Budapest.

DRINKING MATTERS

Apricots turn lethal in Hungarian brandy palinka, but even tougher to swallow is tarlike herbal swill Unicum, once claimed to be a royal favorite—they took it as a compliment when the emperor declared it "unique." Locals say it tasted even fouler when production was overtaken by Communists.

News you can understand: The *Budapest Times* gives the news in English: www.budapesttimes.hv

19. BALTIC STATES: ESTONIA, LATVIA, AND LITHUANIA
Humming Along

Overview

Covered in forests, dotted with castles, edged by spectacular coastline, and bursting with new energy, the gorgeous Baltic States—namely Estonia, Latvia, and Lithuania—are the most intriguing entries into the European Union. The allure is their mystery: these fetching countries could have fallen out of a distant galaxy, since few (even in Europe) know much about these parts that are thick with legend, knightly history, and virgin landscapes punctuated by windmills and tiny cottages. And most of the world simply ignored their turbulent past.

> *"If the rest of the world doesn't know we exist, it's for a simple reason: we were occupied [countries] forcibly incorporated in the Soviet Union. [The Baltic States were] kept behind the Iron Curtain with an iron fist—and that iron fist included not being allowed to travel and no people from abroad being allowed to land here. Our contact with the world was rudely cut off for half a century."[1] —Latvian president Vaira Vike-Freiberga, specifically speaking about Latvia, but spelling out the story of Estonia and Lithuania as well*

Say the names Estonia, Latvia, or Lithuania to most Americans and they'll meet you with a blank stare. Mention the Baltic States and they will probably think you're talking about the Balkans—the former Yugoslavia. Describe them as "former Soviet republics," which they were, and their residents have a fit, pointing out that they were independent countries before Moscow lassoed them into her Communist union. But these three long-forgotten Eastern countries are now rising globally. Low-cost European airlines are swooping into their capitals, connecting these far-yonder lands to Western Europe and bringing them into the tourism loop. Not only did the trio join the European Union in 2004—which is forking over money for agriculture and infrastructure—they also joined NATO, giving the rusty horse new life as it moved on to Russia's back door. The Baltic States hold key positions and territories in the post–Cold War reshuffle that's been under way since the Soviet Union fell in 1991, which is one reason Russia is so loathe to fully give them up.

> *Two leaders of Baltic countries spent many years in North America after escaping their homelands during World War II. Latvian president Vaira Vike-Freiberga used to be a psychology professor in Canada; Lithuanian president Valdus Adamkus worked for the U.S. Environmental Protection Agency.*

SOVIET SECRETS

The three eastern countries that hug the steely blue Baltic Sea were Russia's heavily guarded secret, marking the beginning of a figurative Iron Wall. The most westerly reaches of the Soviet Union for five decades, Latvia, Estonia, and Lithuania served as Moscow's eyes on the world; spying contraptions and military equipment littered their lush forests, and rockets pointed to the West from their shores. Their ice-free ports became Soviet shipping centers and military posts, and barbed wire blighted the stunning coasts of soft sands and bluffs, where nights were lit up by ominous searchlight beams patrolling shores to prevent escape.

Beyond mere strategic positioning, the unspoiled Baltic States were treasured by Moscow's VIPs as beachfront vacation getaways: high-ranking comrades built mansions, tucked away in woods along the sea, and Baltic capitals were adored as architectural gems and for the creativity and beauty locked within. Latvia, Estonia, and Lithuania brimmed with artists, dancers, fashion designers, and lovely women—many, including Latvian dancer Mikhail Baryshnikov, plucked by Soviets to showcase as their stars to the world.

The loss of Moscow's pearls is still a sore point for Russia, which mourns their absence with growls, economic backstabbing, and constant threats to yank them back. And that's one reason why Latvia, Estonia, and Lithuania, upon regaining their independence in 1991, all joined both the European Union and NATO: one provided economic stability, the other defense.

The recent appearance in these parts of Vice President Dick Cheney—who blasted Russia and (says the Russian media) rekindled the Cold War—is one show of the growing Baltic stature. With Russia at their border, these countries are now NATO's ears to the East—and Lockheed Martin is setting them up with fancy spying equipment. It's fitting that Latvia is flexing her muscle as host of the 2006 NATO summit, during which member countries are discussing NATO's extending reach. What's more, this trio is right in the heart of Russia's energy politics. Russia uses Latvia's port to ship oil and Lithuania's refinery to refine it—activities that provide billions to Baltic treasuries—and lately Russia has made moves to strangle these assets, apparently wanting to control them again. Russian natural gas company Gazprom is the sole supplier to the Baltic countries and prices for Russian energy are skyrocketing. Gasoline prices shot up 25 percent in 2006, which locals see as a deliberate move to hurt them. It was intentional when Russians excluded these countries when drawing up the deal with Germans to build a gas pipeline across the Baltic Sea—and now the Baltic countries and Poland are screaming that they deserve transit fees.

MEET THE BALTIC COUNTRIES

Lost in the blurry backwater dangling between Russia and Poland, the Baltic States are three distinct countries grouped together solely because of location and unfortunate history. They share a few similarities: stomping grounds for Teutonic knights and occupied by assorted rulers, they were first created as independent countries in 1920. Their independence, however, was yanked away after World War II, when they were marched into the Soviet Union. After rebelling for years—Lithuania most loudly—they regained independence in 1991, and all immediately flipped off Moscow and turned their gaze to the West, joining the two clubs that most matter (the EU and NATO). However, their ethnicities are as different as their languages—so dissimilar, in fact, that when an Estonian talks to a Latvian or Lithuanian, they have to speak English or Russian. The trio also have different "personalities." Generally speaking:

Estonia   is the least populous of the three with 1.6 million, a quiet beauty. Known for supermodels, well-educated ambassadors, and the fabulous medieval old town in capital Tallinn, Estonia is more closely linked to Finland than to any Baltic neighbors.

Latvia   is artistic and expressive: sizzling capital Riga is an art-nouveau paradise and the region's biggest tourist draw. Latvia has the biggest East Baltic port, and under the stable leadership of President Vaira Vike-Freiberga, Latvia is becoming the most prominent Baltic state.

Lithuania   is the wild child—she most daringly mouthed off to Moscow and kicked off the independence movement in the 1980s; Lithuania was the first Soviet republic to declare independence, triggering independence calls across the Soviet Union. Thanks to Soviets, she also holds perhaps the world's scariest nuclear plant

(currently being decommissioned). Historically linked to
Poland (and predominantly Catholic), Lithuania is
plagued with political scandals even though pretty
capital Vilnius is quiet—when Dick Cheney's not in town.

> "There's no Baltic identity with a common culture, common language, even
> a common religious tradition." —Former foreign minister of Estonia Toomas
> Ilves[2]

The Baltic States fell off the world's mental map for the second half of the twentieth century—and that wound still lingers. Estonians, Latvians, and Lithuanians are legitimately bummed. First they were ignored when they were ravaged during World War II—invaded first by Russia, then by Germany, then by Russia again. By the end of that ordeal, over one-half of the region's residents were dead or had fled. Worse, the Baltic States vanished from Western memory when the Soviet Union dragged them in. While the United States was preaching about the Evil Empire and Western Europe formed NATO (with the U.S. and Canada) to fight back against encroaching Communism, residents of Baltic States were waiting for the democracy-wavers to rescue them from Communist shackles. They waited, hiding in forests. They waited, slaving in Siberian gulags. They waited for someone to back up their frequent protests. But the West never came. "Nobody believed that [the Baltic States] would, for decades and decades, be left in the hands of the Soviets," says former Estonian prime minister Mart Laar. "That wasn't even a possibility. 'It's only a question of time,' everybody thought. But after decades went by, the idea about the West coming to their aid disappeared."[3]

THE FOREST BROTHERS

The dense stands of pine and birch that cover the Baltic countries are more than a lumber resource. Haunted by tales of witches and magic trees, these woods also served as home to a brave resistance community, when over 100,000 Estonians, Latvians, and Lithuanians fled the Soviets who returned near the end of the Second World War. Some preferred nature's hardships to those inflicted by Russians, but most of the "Forest Brothers" were guerrillas who slipped into cities to cut Soviets' power lines, sabotage their vehicles, and sometimes assassinate local Soviet leaders. Living in crude shacks during brutal winters, most Forest Brothers had been captured, killed, or had died by the time the Soviets made a final sweep in the mid-1950s. Those who remained were packed off to Siberian work camps; only a few returned in the 1970s to tell the story,[4] but you can still find their rusty weapons in the woods.

Now celebrating their independence and a sudden influx of European tourists, the Baltic countries are rebounding—recently, their economies are galloping, often growing by 10 percent a year—and they're awaiting the arrival of travelers from even more distant parts. Even though few Americans can find them on a map, at least some know one thing: the Balts can sing. In these countries, song signifies more than just the cheesy Eurovision contest, which both Latvia and Estonia recently won. Music was also the weapon of their revolt against the Soviet Union—the Singing Revolution. And for centuries, song was a vehicle to keep the language and cultures of these often-occupied countries alive.

History Review

The creation of Estonia, Latvia, and Lithuania as independent countries is a remarkable occurrence that for centuries just didn't seem to be in the cards. For 800 years, these northeastern coastal lands didn't have distinct political identities, being yanked back and forth between competing empires. First discovered by Vikings, the territories were later ruled by Teutonic and Livonian knights, whose castles still cover the countryside; Germanic merchants, who trailed the knights, made Baltic ports valuable trading posts in the Hanseatic League. The local people, mostly farmers who typically were treated as rightless serfs, just went along with the valuable property that changed owners every century or two, being handed off as war booty to ethnic Germans, Poles, Danes, Swedes, and Russians. The last group—the Russians—were always the most cruel, even back when they were led by czars.

THE BALTIC CONNECTION

Neither Europe's largest nor deepest aqueous body, the forked Baltic Sea that divides Scandinavia from Eastern Europe was once the steely wind-tossed waters upon which medieval trade flourished. The Hanseatic League—a profoundly important fourteenth- and fifteenth-century trading union of merchants that linked ports across northern Europe—made this region Europe's richest, as ships hauled grain from the Baltic States, wood and fish from the Nordic countries, and cloth and wool from Germany. After the mid-twentieth century, however, the Baltic Sea became a symbol of economic and political divide, cleaving the wealth and freedom of Scandinavia in the north from the poor, Soviet-occupied republics to the southeast.

> *Sweden, which ran Estonia and Latvia in the seventeenth century, launched education campaigns, opened schools, abolished serfdom, and even established peasant rights. By the time Swedes shoved off in 1721, handing the keys to Russia, most locals were literate and a printing trade had emerged, further shaping national identities. Russia, however, tried to "Russify" the locals, blotting out their languages and cultures.*

When Europe was remapped after the First World War, the Baltic countries politically forged their own separate identities. Baltic leaders slipped off to the 1919 Paris Peace Conference, where Europe was being reconfigured, and successfully lobbied the cartographers of the day. In 1920, the Baltic lands that had once been in Russia's empire were redrawn as three separate, independent countries—Estonia, Latvia, and Lithuania—carved from Russia's western frontiers.

Latvia and Estonia prospered from agriculture after independence, becoming richer than Sweden, the neighbor who had once been the overlord. Lithuania, however, was distracted after Poland snatched her capital away. (See "Poland," page 287). Freedom was brief. The trio, each puffed with national pride, refused to forge together as one regional military power, and were easy prey for the neighborhood vultures. By 1939, Russia and Germany were scheming to take back the strategic lands. Throughout the Second World War, the Baltic States were devastated in a violent tug-of-war between Russia and Germany, and were ultimately nabbed by Russia, which held them prisoner in the Soviet Union for the five decades that followed.

DIRTY WORDS: MOLOTOV-RIBBENTROP PACT

To Balts the three words "Molotov-Ribbentrop Pact" are synonymous with "ripped-away freedom." The 1939 "non-aggression pact," signed by emissaries of Hitler and Stalin, secretly divided the Baltic States and Poland into German and Russian "spheres of influence." Germany and Russia, then allied, divvied up the territories before sending in their armies to take over. Initally, Estonia, Latvia, and Lithuania were dished out to Russia, which invaded in the fall of 1939; Poland was attacked by both Germany and Russia, one from each side. The pact didn't hold up. Soon Germany and Russia were battling each other over control of the Baltic lands. Their territorial pissing matches and poor treatment of the residents killed a third of the population.

Poland was falling to Nazis, and the Allies had just declared war, when residents of the Baltic countries looked up in the fall of 1939 to see Russia's Red Army rolling in. The return of their historical tormentors horrified the Baltic peoples, all the more so when Soviets shoved millions—first intellectuals, aristocrats, and politicians, then commoners, farmers, and children—into trucks and trains and hauled them to Siberian work camps. Two years later, Hitler declared war on the Soviet Union, and Nazis marched in to cut the Baltic States loose from the Russian yoke. Nazis were initially greeted as liberators, but they too began shipping out dissidents and the region's many Jews. In 1944, the Soviets returned to push out the Germans. As the Red Army barreled in yet again, some 500,000 Balts escaped, the Russians bombing and torpedoing their ships as they fled. Another 100,000 Balts ran into the woods.

> *Nazis killed 300,000 Jews, almost the entire Jewish population living in Baltic countries. Nazis also killed non-Jewish Balts, but the majority of the 2 million Estonians, Latvians, and Lithuanians who died during World War II did so at the hands of the Russians.*

The next forty-six years were a tragic rerun. The Russians reoccupied the Baltic countries, this time transforming them into Soviet republics with centralized planned economies. Communal housing was the rule: six or more families were crammed into one house, where they shared one kitchen and bathroom, in a forced program of equality.

> *The United States government never recognized that the three countries were part of the Soviet Union, but that made little difference to the locals, who could be shot on the spot if they questioned it.*

Once-productive private farms were collectivized (production plummeted) and once-pristine waters were polluted by rapid industrialization as the Soviets transformed the Baltic States into the unglamorous egg, radio, and pharmaceutical centers of their Communist union. Farmers initially rebelled against collective farms, but after tens of thousands were shipped off in 1949, remaining agrarians caved in to the idea.

Due to emigration and war deaths, less than half of the original population was left. Ethnic Russians were hauled in to repopulate and industrialize the countries. Another reason Russians were sent: Soviets wanted to dilute the homogenous populations. Russian became the language of business and politics, and the only way to make headway in the Soviet world. The Balts rebelled, but quietly. They kept their languages and cultures alive, they formed secret societies, and they waited in vain for the West to release them.

In the 1980s, the second generation came of age and a defiant spirit rose up again. Simultaneously, the Soviet Union was falling apart. The war in Afghanistan was draining the military, and in 1986, Chernobyl spewed radioactive gases, creating an international furor. Soviet premier Mikhail Gorbachev unveiled his ideas for perestroika (economic restructuring) and glasnost (openness, or freedom of the press) in the 1980s, thinking that intellectuals would suggest subtle ways to reform. Not fully grasping the deep hatred of Russians who had long bulldozed the Baltic people and cultures, his ideas took a different course than intended. The younger generation wanted to open up and restructure the place, all right—by shoving the Soviet Union right out.

THE SINGING REVOLUTION

It started in 1987: first Lithuania's government, then Estonia's and Latvia's, declared that Soviet rule was invalid. Across the Baltic countries, calls for independence grew louder, and people marched in peaceful demonstrations a million strong. Music became a tool of defiance: Balts belted out their national songs, their native languages now voiced loudly and with nationalistic pride. Another symbolic act: in August 1989, Estonians, Latvians, and Lithuanians linked hands across three countries and 400 miles from Estonia to Lithuania on the fiftieth anniversary of the malevolent Molotov-Ribbentrop Pact. Lithuania first declared full independence from the Soviet Union in 1990—and underscored it again with a referendum in February 1991. The other two proclaimed independence in August 1991. Their announcements were met with handwringing by much of the world. Only Iceland immediately recognized them as independent and sovereign; almost every other country waited until the United States gave her official recognition in the autumn of 1991, shortly after the power regime in Moscow had collapsed.

Ever since the Baltic countries became independent, Russia has been huffing and puffing to get them back. Moscow lost not only her only ice-free ports—and the ones with the easiest access to Europe—she also lost her favorite playland, Latvia. Russian parliamentarian Vladimir Zhirinovsky threatened to pile Russia's nuclear waste at the borders and blow radioactive fumes across the Baltic countries with giant fans, and he made other far less laughable threats. Russia immediately began harping about the treatment of ethnic Russians, most of whom stayed in the Baltic States. Forgetting the centuries when Russia had forced those in her hold to learn Russian, Moscow had a conniption fit when the Latvian and Estonian governments turned the tables: they announced that to gain citizenship in their countries, Russians—one-third of the populations in Latvia and Estonia—would have to learn the local language. Many haven't—and thus aren't legal citizens. Meanwhile, their Soviet passports and citizenship are now invalid.

Over 1 million of the 8 million residents of the Baltic countries are now officially stateless.

But what's really eating Moscow is that the trio has joined the European Union and NATO. Entry into the EU promises greater economic stability for the Baltic countries, and means that Russia can no longer slap huge tariffs on goods from the countries or so easily yank their chains. And their entry into NATO—the club that symbolized everything that Cold War Russia loathed and feared—was an even harsher slap that hit the Russian paranoia button. Russia fears (correctly) that NATO will be spying on her, and meanwhile the Baltic States fear (also correctly) that Russia is sending in spies. In recent years, a slew of Russian diplomats, accused of being spooks snooping around about NATO, were deported from Estonia, Latvia, and Lithuania.

> "The fact that you can go to bed and not worry about somebody knocking on the door and putting you on a train for Siberia." —President Vaira Vike-Freiberga on why Latvia joined NATO[4]

NATO-BOUND: KA-CHING!

It's understandable that the Baltic countries wanted to enter NATO, the post–World War II arms club created to threaten the Soviet Union by mere presence alone. Russia is curled up next door, the Baltic armed forces are flimsy, and NATO membership carries a certain cachet. But why NATO invited the tiny Baltic States into the club is another matter. Granted, the Baltic States can provide intelligence about Russian activities, and no countries need NATO protection more. What the three incoming countries also offer: a bigger market for big-time arms sales, since NATO requires that 2 percent of a country's GDP be thrown at defense spending. Predictably, the largest arms manufacturer in the United States—Lockheed Martin—was the strongest lobbyist for NATO expansion. Before they'd even entered, the Baltic countries placed an order with Lockheed for a high-tech air surveillance system, Baltnet, with a price tag of $100 million.[5] That pretty much tapped their budgets; their air forces currently consist of borrowed planes.

News you can understand: The *City Paper* covers all three Baltic States in English: www.BalticsWorldwide.com

Also newsy: *The Baltic Times*: www.baltictimes.com

20. ESTONIA
(Eesti)
The Elder Sister

FAST FACTS

Country:	Republic of Estonia; Eesti Vabariik
Capital:	Tallinn
Government:	Parliamentary republic
Independence:	August 20, 1991 (from Soviet Union)
Population:	1,325,000 (2006)
Head of State:	President Arnold Rüütel (2001)
Head of Government:	Prime Minister Andrus Ansip (2005)
Elections:	President elected by parliament to five-year term; prime minister nominated by president, approved by parliament
Name of Parliament:	Riigikogu
Ethnicity:	65.3% Estonian; 28.1% Russian; 2.5% Ukrainian; 1.5% Belarussian; 1% Finn; 1.6% other
Religion:	65% unspecified or unaffiliated; 14% Evangelical Lutheran; 13% Russian Orthodox; 2% other Christian; 6% none

Language:	Estonian (official); also Russian, Ukrainian, Finnish
Literacy:	99% (2003)
Famous Exports:	Supermodel Carmen Kaas (best known for J'Adore)
Economic Big Boy:	Hansabank (banking); 2003 revenue: €360 million (about $450 million)[1]
Per Capita GDP:	$16,400 (2003)
Unemployment:	6.2% (January 2006 Eurostat figure)
EU Status:	Entered May 2004
Currency:	Estonian kroon

Quick Tour

Eesti seems to have shaken loose from a different century. With a skyline of green domes and orange tiled roofs, capital Tallinn holds a hauntingly beautiful medieval quarter of candlelit cafés and restaurants where menus of old style calligraphy are written on parchment, the staff dress in period clothes, and one downs medieval feasts at the slabs of wood tables—the fare includes bear. Tiny churches that comfortably hold about three dot the countryside, windblown islands beckon bicyclists and hikers, and witches are believed to inhabit the mist-tangled primordial bogs.

> *The pagan practices of Estonia's past are still celebrated. The dead are believed to return and wander about freely every August, and June 23 is a mystical night when Estonians prance through fields by moonlight, seeking out a rare fern believed to imbue magical powers upon those who pluck it.[2]*

A FEW QUIRKS

China she's not, but whatever you do, don't call Estonia "tiny," a description that really rankles Estonians. The country, they will point out, is bigger than Denmark, Iceland, or the Netherlands; she's downright gigantic when compared with fellow EU member Malta.[3] Estonians also get hot and bothered when the country is called "a former Soviet Republic." Sensitive former foreign minister Toomas Ilves suggested that a better description of Estonia before 2004 would be "Pre-EU."[4]

Land of fair maidens, rugged coast, and villages lost in dense forests, Estonia is the smallest, least populated, and most northerly of the Baltic States. Despite having a population of only 1.4 million, Estonia often boasts the region's flashiest politicians, who fluently spell out Estonia's charms in half a dozen languages. The country sparkles with a vibrant economy, and Estonians have the highest per capita income of the trio (well, that's not saying much).

> The late Lennart Meri, Estonia's brainy second president, spoke five languages, made documentary films, knew something about everything, and should have qualified for a Guinness world record when he outdrank Boris Yeltsin[5] while discussing the withdrawal of Soviet troops (which finally took place in 1994).

Now known as one of the most Internet-savvy places on the planet, with a third of the population online at home, Estonia was always the most tuned-in of the Soviet republics. Estonian TV could pick up Western channels—shows such as *Peyton Place* were popular in the 1960s—and Western music kept an underground spirit alive as clandestine bands smuggled in bootlegs of King Crimson and The Who, inspiring some to write their own rock operas.

FEISTY ESTONIANS

When the Soviet system was forced into place, Estonians were the Balts least likely to adopt Russian. When someone said something in Russian, Estonians often replied in their native tongue. Estonian dissidents also SOSed the Western world. In 1976, a group of Estonians sent a formal complaint about the Soviet occupation to the United States Congress, and, shortly thereafter, letters were flying to the Russian press and politicians. Before perestroika was even in effect, groups of intellectuals were defying Soviet law by forming secret societies and researching Estonian history. Mart Laar, a future prime minister, put together the Society of Estonian Heritage and headed off into farming villages to research the history of the Forest Brothers.

The Estonian government is a revolving door, where prime ministers blow out one year only to return the next; with her small population, say Estonians, anybody who wants to can probably have a chance ruling the country. Recently, leaders have been hammering Russia—the government considers Soviet "a terrorist regime"—to compensate Estonians for damages and loss of life under the Soviets. In the so-called White Book released in 2004, the Estonian government spells out the effects of Russian occupations, including the loss of 180,000 Estonian lives during the Second World War. Environmental damage inflicted by the Soviet army will cost about $4 billion to clean up, according to the White Book, the result of twelve years of research. The Estonian government demanded compensation of $250,000 for each person killed and $77,000 for each person who worked in the Soviet system. Given the huge total, the government added, Estonia would be happy to accept a timber-rich corner of Siberia instead of money. The reply from Russia's foreign ministry: no way.

> According to the Estonian government, 60,000 Estonians were killed or deported during the first month of Soviet occupation in 1940.

Estonia was the first Baltic state to put an intellectual face to the world—and the lobbying of Estonian politicians helped to pry open the EU door. But she isn't as goody-goody as it sounds. Intravenous drug use is rising; some point to young Russians as the reason. The United Nations shocked the country when it announced that Estonia's HIV rate is one of the world's highest—although it was unclear whether that was due to IV drug use or rampant prostitution. The government is starting up condom campaigns, but promoting protected sex runs counter to one of the country's new goals: boosting the birth rate.

Hot Spots

Tallinn: Like Estonians themselves, Tallinn is striking, her cityscape punctuated by ornate Russian Orthodox domes and by medieval buildings spilling down from atop the city's main hill. Spend a few hours in her romantic Old Town,

Old town Tallinn: Fall back into Hanseatic times

Courtesy of Tallinn City Tourist Office and Convention Bureau and you can really feel like you've fallen into the past. But modern problems pop up: never mind that Finland has helped Estonia with her border security—plenty of contraband still slips out from Tallinn to Helsinki, and Finland exports her rowdy "vodka tourists" here.

Estonian saying: There's really no summer, just three bad months for skiing.

HEAVENLY INFERNO

Estonia's dearest friend, Finland, whose capital Helsinki lies a mere forty miles from Tallinn, shares with Estonians the adoration of the sauna. Although Estonia is now nominally Lutheran, early attempts to Christianize the pagan masses flopped. Part of the reason: preachers kept threatening that the fires of hell awaited those who didn't convert. In that frosty part of the world, however, inferno-like temperatures sounded cozy. Estonians are known for their 120°F saunas, finished off by jumping through ice holes into glacially cold lakes.

Like the Finns, Estonians hold wife-carrying contests.

Saaremaa: Rugged bluffs, eagles, and thirteenth-century castles are part of the draw to Estonia's largest island, home to 40,000.

Pärnu: Bright cottages, mud baths, and white sand beaches await at Estonia's most popular summer resort.

Soomaa National Park: Pocked with peat bogs, which are believed to be mystical places and are traversed by canoe.

Tartu: Site of Tartu University, the Baltic States' first institution of higher learning when Sweden opened it in 1632.

Hotshots

Arnold Rüütel: President, 2001–present. Former Communist leader who helped push for Estonian independence in the late 1980s, he's an agronomist by formal training. Helped get Estonia into the EU, but at age seventy-eight, he's seen as a bit daft for the post.

Andrus Ansip: Prime Minister, 2005–present. Former chemist Ansip scored high in approval as mayor of Tartu, and is now preparing the country for the conversion to the euro.

Ken Marti, who became justice minister in 2003 at age twenty-eight, tried to resign soon thereafter. The reason: he'd been caught speeding in a residential neighborhood. The prime minister refused his resignation.[6]

Mart Laar: Prime Minister, 1992–1996 and 1999–2002; presently Estonian VIP-at-large in Brussels. Only thirty-two years old when he took over as prime minister, multilingual historian Laar bolstered Estonia's flimsy economy by easing business taxes and pushing through a flat 26 percent income tax. Has lots of ideas about how to promote Estonia, including selling ethnically pure Estonian genes to scientists studying disease. Wrote *War in the Woods* about the Forest Brothers.

Photo by Tiit Koha. Courtesy of Ismaalit Party of Estonia

Former PM Mart Laar publicized the Forest Brothers' lost history

Estonia was the world's first country to establish a flat tax—now 26 percent.

21. LATVIA
(Latvija)
The Middle Child

FAST FACTS

Country:	Republic of Latvia; Latvijas Republika
Capital:	Riga
Government:	Parliamentary democracy
Independence:	August 21, 1991 (from Soviet Union)
Population:	2,275,000 (2006 estimate)
Head of State:	President Vaira Vike-Freiberga (1999)
Head of Government:	Prime Minister Aigars Kalvitis (2004)
Elections:	President elected by parliament for four-year period; prime minister appointed by president, approved by parliament
Name of Parliament:	Saiema
Ethnicity:	57.7% Latvian; 29.6% Russian; 4.1% Belarussian; 2.7% Ukrainian; 2.5% Polish; 1.4% Lithuanian; 2% other (2002 estimate)

Religion:	Lutheran; Roman Catholic; Russian Orthodox
Language:	58% Latvian (official); 38% Russian; 4% Lithuanian
Literacy:	99% (2003 estimate)
Famous Exports:	Mikhail Baryshnikov, Minox spy radios, Laima chocolates
Economic Big Boy:	Latvenergo (energy generation); 2003 revenues: €312 million (about $380 million)[1]
Per Capita GDP:	$13,200 (2005)
Unemployment:	8.2% (January 2006 Eurostat figure)
EU Status:	Entered May 2004
Currency:	Latvian lat

Quick Tour

Amber tosses up on secluded shores like gifts from sea gods, and marshy fields where rockets once pointed at Europe are now nature preserves thick with storks. Wild horses still run through her valleys, sand caves wind around her coast, and Latvija loves historical exhibits, with everything from a museum of old bibles to one devoted just to bread. Latvia has always been the region's crown jewel to everyone who showed up here—including Teutonic knights, who believed that whoever held the capital Riga held the key to the Baltic Sea. Plenty vied for that key, and from German merchants to Scandinavian traders, they all left their mark, starting with the knights—whose rook-like castles litter this land thick with legends of wicked gnomes, caves with healing waters, and trees that turn those who chant magic words into werewolves during the full moon.

> Even well-educated Latvians say oak trees, worshipped by their pagan ancestors, have curative powers. Many Latvians keep "gray stones," found near oaks, in their homes and hold them when they want to feel grounded.

Wedged between Estonia to the north and Lithuania to the south, Latvia is the Baltic country most loudly blipping on world radar. That's partly a result of brainy polyglot president, Vaira Vike-Freiberga, who's become well known to the big boy heads of state during her seven-year presidency. In the country that blew through four currencies in fifteen years, and where prime ministers change annually, Vike-Freiberga is an anchor, helping Latvia cut a striking international presence.

But what is mostly making Latvia rise and shine is capital Riga, a beautiful jumble of architectural styles. Turrets rise next to S-shaped Dutch-style gables, shuttered fourteenth-century chalets nudge gilded sixteenth-century mansions, and the skyline of slender church towers, steeply pitched roofs, and domes in dusty pinks and daisy yellows tumbles down like a Picasso painting. Cut off from the West under Soviet rule, Riga was previously a travel magnet. Seventeenth-century writers lavished praise on this opulent trade city of operas, oyster restaurants, silk stores, and beautiful houses cascading with ornate baroque designs. The riches of the city, the third largest in the nineteenth-century Russian Empire, were most stylishly showcased in a flurry of construction from 1880 to 1910, when fantastical art-nouveau designs—here called by the German name *Jurgenstil*—made artwork of buildings: architects carved swirling-haired beauties and tumbling flowers into facades alongside busts of Zeus and space-age knights. With a third of the city decorated in *Jurgenstil*, Riga boasts the highest concentration of art-nouveau architecture in the world.

A NIGHT ON THE TOWN

In the Soviet days, Riga had only five restaurants, and most Latvians who went out spent the night waiting in lines. Now the hopping city of designer hotels is filled with chic restaurants (where you might order roe deer carpaccio, caviar-filled blini, ostrich steak, or kid goat) and cozy eateries, heavy with wooden barrels and iron pots, serve thick Latvian stews and chewy black bread with hemp butter. Strolling under brick arches and through medieval squares, you can find polka-dot-happy Zup Zup, (soup restaurant by day, dance club by night), upscale fish restaurant Skonto (where an indoor waterfall cascades into pools thick with swimming trout), the Eastern Front (a theater bar of Soviet cages, memorabilia, and busts of Stalin), and Balzams Bar (wrapped in oversize sepia photos of the eighteenth-century pharmacist who invented viscous liqueur Riga Black Balzams, served here dozens of ways). Music floats from all corners. At the stunning opera hall, *Demons*—a haunting opera in Russian—unfolds on three tiers; a few blocks away, hundreds sway to reggae at the Colonel, go-go girls prance on tables at Martini, and at Thank God It's Friday—a palm-tree-filled tropical watering hole—locals hop up on the bar to dance. "There's this wild energy here in Riga," says artist Andris Vitolins, a twenty-eight-year-old painter with tousled sandy brown hair. "Everything's growing and mixing so fast, you don't know what will happen next."[2] Reminders of the Soviet occupation, including bullet-riddled buildings and the solemn Museum of the Occupation of Latvia, are still scattered across the city. In Stabu, Riga's fashionable new quarter, where people lounge on tatami mats for Zen's tea ceremony or slouch in booths at red-glowing artists' bars, you'll find Corner House, a soulless concrete building marked with a plaque; it was a Soviet torture chamber that still gives Latvians the chills. The medieval quarter also holds powerful memories for Latvians; hundreds of thousands congregated here in January 1990 to prevent Soviet tanks from taking government buildings and the TV station.

> *"The whole country came to Old Town—some driving their tractors. Everybody made barricades of mattresses, garbage, cars—anything that would keep the tanks from entering—and people kept watch all night. And everybody was singing."[3] —Painter Andris Vitolins recalling January 1991, when Latvians feared that Soviet forces, after destroying the TV tower in Vilnius (see page 338), would also take over the communication center in Old Town*

Riga was the Soviets' darling, loved for her painters, sculptors, and clothes designers. Handed private apartments (a luxury) and studios, and kept stocked in supplies, Soviet-approved artists "were the golden eggs in the nest," says creamy-skinned Asnate Smeltere, a former top Soviet model, who once strode on West European runways (while KGB guards kept watch).[4] She now designs flowing painted silk skirts and beaded lace dresses that seem to float across her boutique, Salons A, where Scandinavians are snatching clothes off the racks. The city's many artists are now part of the free market whirlwind; chocolate factories and gypsum factories are being transformed into lofts, and nineteen galleries have recently thrown open doors: the city just started a citywide gallery walk. One hot spot: the five-story Artists' Union, where Soviet artists previously painted nationalist themes. Once a month, it's an open gallery where you can wander past odd installations (man suspended in cocoon, woman with lipstick-filled Mexican gun sling) and creative types working at looms or printing presses, while videos of horned dancers in balls flash on the walls.

Eat your heart out, Russia. The town that Soviets loved for her creativity now shows all signs of becoming the next Berlin.

> *Latvian joke: An American, a German, and a Latvian are in a field when an elephant runs out of the forest. The American thinks, "If I could harness that great animal's strength, I would be very powerful." The German thinks, "If I could sell the animal's meat, I would be very rich." The Latvian thinks, "I wonder what that elephant thinks of me?"*

Hot Spots

Riga: The liveliest and biggest of the Baltic capitals (population 800,000), riveting Riga rises along the Daugava River, a hodgepodge of styles, colors, and shapes—filled with artists, chic restaurants, and wild bars where the partying carries on late.

Art nouveau capital Riga is layered in architectural history

Jurmala: This stunning stretch of white-sand beach on the Baltic Sea is edged with thick pines. Peeking out from the trees are nineteenth-century wooden houses—some regal and towered, some tiny birdhouses—and a valued part of Riga's architectural legacy. Half of Riga moves here in the summer.

Cesis: History runs deep all around here, including in the recently excavated tenth-century village that's now an open-air architectural museum.

Latvian saying: We don't have four seasons here, just two winters: white winter and green winter.

Ventspils: Typically, about one-sixth of Russia's oil exports run out of this Baltic port; transit fees and related income sometimes contribute about one-sixth of Latvia's GDP.[5] Whenever Russia gets ticked, however, they shut off the pipeline, slamming the local economy.

Schools: Requirements that ethnic Russian students take several courses in Latvian is making schools a high-pressure zone. Russia recently donated history books to schools; they're in Russian, of course.

Hotshots

Vaira Vike-Freiberga: President, 1999–present. When she was a child, Vike-Freiberga's family fled incoming Soviets, but while she was a psychology professor in Montreal, she became intrigued with centuries-old Latvian folk songs, called *dainas*; Latvians have over a million and still sing them. "They're like a [musical] folk encyclopedia," she says—with topics ranging from ethics and aesthetics to "herding cattle and harvesting" and "what plants to pick for dying wool." Becoming a *daina* expert, she was invited back to Latvia in 1999 to open Riga's Latvian Institute. Stepping off the plane, she was greeting by the media asking, "We've heard you might be a presidential candidate—would you stand?" It was news to her—and she laughed off the rumors that swirled for six months; two days before the election, however, she was indeed asked to run. She won.

> Latvian legend holds that the country would become powerful and prosperous under the guidance of a woman leader. Recently, Latvia's economy has been expanding at around 10 percent.[6]

Aigars Kalvitis: Prime Minister, 2004–present. In the third change of the premier in 2004, the PM chair holds Kalvitis of the People's Party, whose name there is probably no point in memorizing.

Alina Lebedeva: Can we say "little troublemaker"? The ethnic Russian teen made Latvia front-page news in 2002, when she slapped British Prince Charles with a carnation—a protest against his pro–Iraq war stance. She made local news again in 2004, when she was suspected of torching the ministry of education for its policy of increasing the number of Latvian classes taught in schools.

President Vaira Vike-Freiberga: Smart, kind, beloved

Courtesy of Presidential Office, Latvia

Vladimir Zhirinovsky: Parliamentarian in Russia's Duma. Russia's radical right-winger typically wins over 13 percent of Russian votes and is the symbolic manifestation of Russia's obsession with Latvia. Wants Alaska back, too.

DRINKING MATTERS

Concocted since 1725 from a secret recipe of twenty-four herbs, flowers, and roots, black goo Riga Balsams cures even leprosy, Latvians claim; the caraway seed stars in bitter liqueur Kümmel, favored by golfers. Created for then-ruler Peter the Great, Latvians so highly regard their Kümmel that the government ships a case to Queen Elizabeth every year. Nobody knows whether she actually touches it.

22. LITHUANIA
(Lietuva)
The Wild Child

FAST FACTS

Country:	Republic of Lithuania; Lietuvos Respublika
Capital:	Vilnius
Government:	Parliamentary democracy
Independence:	March 11, 1990 (from Soviet Union)
Population:	3,586,000 (2006 estimate)
Head of State:	President Valdus Adamkus (2004)
Head of Government:	Prime Minister Algirdas Brazauskas (2001)
Elections:	President elected by popular vote for five-year term; prime minister appointed by president, approved by parliament
Name of Parliament:	Seima
Ethnicity:	83% Lithuanian; 6% Russian; 7% Polish; 4% other
Religion:	79% Roman Catholic; 10% none; 4% Russian Orthodox; 2% Protestant; 5% other

Language:	82% Lithuanian (official); 8% Russian; 6% Polish
Literacy:	99%
Famous Exports:	Fictional captain Marko Ramius (*Hunt for Red October*), Maury Povich's grandparents; assorted NBA players, including Darius Songaila (Chicago Bulls) and Arvydas Sabonis (ex–Portland Trail Blazer)
Economic Big Boy:	Mazeikiu Nafta (petrochemical); 2003 revenues: €1.54 billion (about $1.9 billion)[1]
Per Capita GDP:	$13,900 (2005)
Unemployment:	6.9% (January 2006 Eurostat figure)
EU Status:	Entered May 2004
Currency:	Lithuanian litas

Quick Tour

Lietuva looks deceptively sleepy—starting with mellow Vilnius and her pretty Baroque buildings and Catholic churches, where the religious line up for blessings with juniper twigs that sweep evil spirits away. Mud spas are set deep in pine forests, time ticks away slowly in Klaipeda's Clock Museum, the stunning castle complex on an island at Trakai looks as mighty as it did when built in the fifteenth century, and little happens along the curious Curonian Spit, a sixty-mile pine-dotted sand bar that stretches between lagoon and sea—except that it's slowly disappearing. Appearances to the contrary, Lithuanians are the most passionate—some might say headstrong—of the Balts. And they never get the credit they deserve for yanking on the thread that unwove the tapestry of the Soviet Union. Except, that is, from Russian parliamentarian Vladimir Zhirinovsky, who condemned Lithuania as "the republic from which comes the disease that destroyed."

THE REVOLUTIONARY LEADERS: SAJUDIS

Lithuanians were the nerviest dissenters this side of Solidarity—perhaps nervier. Unlike Poland's union, they had neither large numbers nor huge international support behind them—and their country wasn't a satellite, but a Soviet republic, whose supplies Moscow could turn off with a phone call. Early on, Lithuanians dramatically showed their disdain: in 1972, student Romas Kalanta registered his protest by setting himself ablaze. His dramatic death by fire led to a rebellion in the streets that took the army to quell. An underground current of dissidence carried on, encouraged by the Catholic Church. And when Gorbachev announced his reform ideas in 1985, Lithuanians saw a slender crack that they could rip apart.

Led by music professor Vytautas Landsbergis, the Lithuanian independence movement, Sajudis, first grew from writers, professors, and scholars who loudly condemned the repressive force of the Soviet Union. Sajudis demanded that Soviets admit to the mass deportations to gulags and to signing the secret Molotov-Ribbentrop Pact—both taboo topics. Sajudis denounced the Russian occupation during World War II and announced that Soviets had no claim to Lithuania since their forced annexation was illegal. The Lithuanian parliament proclaimed that Lithuania's laws took precedence over Moscow's, and in 1990 the local Communist Party severed itself from party headquarters in Moscow—allowing other political entities to run. Sajudis won in a landslide. In March 1990, Landsbergis, as parliament's chairman, did what no other leader of a Soviet republic dared: he declared Lithuania's independence from the Soviet Union. Furious, Gorbachev cut off oil supplies; even shipments of paper were banned—as if eliminating the press would eliminate Moscow's problem. It didn't: demands for independence grew louder. In January 1991, the Soviet army rolled in, targeting Vilnius's TV station and broadcasting tower. Tens of thousands of Lithuanians blocked the way; some were beaten back with rifle butts, some were crushed by tanks. The Soviet army killed thirteen and injured hundreds in the only violent confrontation of the Singing Revolution. Even when Soviets seized the communication tower, Lithuanians wouldn't give up: instead they went to the polls. In February 1991, Lithuanians voted for independence. Parliament again announced that Lithuania was a free sovereign independent country. Six months later, Moscow (and the rest of the world) came to the same conclusion.

Lithuanians are considered the friendliest Balts, Lithuanian men are the most dashing, and the landscapes—golden dunes swirling around fishing villages for instance—are the most dramatic, as are Lithuania's problems. The things that Lithuania most stands out for these days are the two that are most scary: her creepy Ignalina plant—a Soviet-made ticking time bomb of a nuclear reactor—and the organized crime that is always lurking about. Politically, too, the country is shaky: impeachments, bribery, and corruption—and presidents who refuse to step down after being ousted—are just part of the terrain.

NUCLEAR ALARM

The eerie Ignalina nuclear plant that provided nearly 80 percent of Lithuania's electricity and employs 5,000 workers was a Soviet idea—which is to say a bad one. The same gas-graphite design as Chernobyl, Ignalina is so shoddy that after the European Union spent a mountain of money trying to fix it, they concluded it was best just to seal it up—pronto. Terrorists also targeted Ignalina. In 1992, an employee intentionally introduced a computer virus, and the cooling system shut down. Two years later, a Lithuanian national demanded $8 million to prevent the plant from being attacked; shortly thereafter, the leader of the Vilnius Brigade—a notorious branch of the Russian-Polish-Lithuanian mob—threatened to bomb the plant if his son, facing the death penalty, was executed. The son was executed, and the plant was temporarily closed and kept under high security for several months, especially after German intelligence called up with info that the threat was quite real. Recently an unexploded grenade was found on the premises. The first reactor was shut down in 2005; the second will be sealed up in 2009. Decommissioning price tag: $2 billion, most of it picked up by the EU. Until then, tick, tick, tick.

Should you want to get the latest radiation levels, there's a Geiger counter displayed in the town center, a mile away from the Ignalina plant.

Latvia and Estonia aren't much alike, but Lithuania is really the Baltic oddball. Her history is wrapped up with Poland—with whom she once coruled much of Europe—and while Estonians and Latvians are usually Protestant (mostly nonpracticing), Lithuanians are devoutly Catholic. The other two are physically and mentally closer to the relatively wholesome Nordic countries, while Lithuania is in the thick of a black-market undercurrent, including trafficking of Lithuanian girls. With smuggling center Kaliningrad—a Russian enclave—and twisted Belarus as two of her borders, it's no wonder that, despite occasional crackdowns, the wheels of the country are just hard to scrub squeaky clean: they're being oiled by Mafia and local thugs who throw their weight around in politics and are known to warn off journalists who take a close look.

Vitas Lingys, a twenty-seven-year-old writer for Lithuanian paper Respublika, *was shot down outside his house in 1993, after publishing a piece about the Vilnius Brigade—and while researching another concerning the Brigade's arms smuggling. Boris Dekanidze, son of the Brigade's boss, was found guilty of ordering the hit and executed in 1994.*

Given that this is corruption-prone Lithuania and that the petroleum biz is notoriously dirty, one figures that all isn't lily-white at Lithuania's biggest moneymaker, the Mazeikiu oil refinery—which Russia seems intent on latching on to, one way or another.

STICKY POLITICS

U.S.-based Williams Holdings bought out the Mazeikiu oil refinery in 1999, fueling a huge flap. The prime minister stormed out of office in protest (the *Baltic News* reported that he was actually pushed out for alleged bribery) and Russia, which runs the pipelines to the refinery, halted crude oil supplies and effectively shut down the operation. After Williams hooked up with Russian oil company Yukos, the spigots were turned back on, and Yukos bought out Williams in 2002. However, Yukos declared bankruptcy in early 2006—and now Lithuania wants to sell off most of the company. Russia's state-controlled petrol company Lukoil is predicted to become a major stakeholder, which means that, in boardrooms at least, Russia will continue to run much of the Lithuanian show. Yukos, however, may throw a wrench in that. The company that has had so many problems with the Russian government wants to sell the operation to Poland major refiner Orlen—and keep Moscow out of the oil pot.

Despite modern woes, there's still something mysteriously compelling about Lithuania—the most undiscovered and some say the most fascinating of the Baltic States. And what makes her strange are her contrasts: the fervently Catholic country has a pagan foundation, and sites such as the Hill of Witches (filled with wooden sculptures) still dot the land alongside the chilling Hill of Crosses, a symbol of defiance against antireligious Communism. A statue of Frank Zappa—an inspiring voice to dissidents—rises up in Vilnius near the plaque commemorating a 2002 visit from President George W. Bush. And while the KGB Museum keeps memories of the Soviet occupation painfully vivid—former inmates give the tour past padded cells that not long ago muffled screams—Stalin World, Lithuania's warped amusement park, plays up the absurd. "Disney meets the Gulag" is how Stalin World's owner, a mushroom mogul, describes his theme park of wire fences and watchtowers, where propaganda blares from loudspeakers and actors dressed as Lenin and Stalin bark orders to comrades. At least Stalin World provides a home for six dozen toppled Soviet statues, now very passé, but some are concerned about the park's future plans to transport tourists here in cattle wagons to offer the full deportation experience.

History Review

Like the other Baltic States, Lithuania was originally an outpost for crusading Germanic knights. But unlike the other two, Lithuania was later a partner in an evolved kingdom that ruled much of Central Europe. She's since had a stormy relationship with Poland, her historical sibling and friend.

WELL, THANKS NEIGHBOR!

Lithuania and Poland were once ruled by the same family. The Lithuanian king wed the Polish princess in the fourteenth century, their union launching a three-centuries-long golden period for both: their lands stretched from the Baltic to the Black Sea, the place was thick with thinkers and creative types, and they had a powerful parliament that elected the king. Even after their kingdom fell apart, the Poles and Lithuanians remained close friends, living side by side in Vilnius, which in 1895 was grabbed by Russia. The Poles, however, forgot all about the warm gushy feelings at the Paris Peace Conference in 1919. When lobbying for Poland's new boundaries, Polish diplomats tried to snatch Lithuania back, explaining that Lithuanians were an insignificant little tribe that really belonged to Poland.[2] The cartographers didn't fully buy it, but Lithuanians were furious—all the more so when Polish leader Pilsudski militarily claimed the capital Vilnius and environs. (To be fair, Poles made up half of Vilnius's residents—and wanted to join with Poland.) Lithuanians did get their own country from the Paris cartographers—but it was a small patch of their original land. (They promptly snatched some of Germany.) For years they fumed over the matter, slamming shut the border between the two countries, severing all diplomatic relations, and naming Vilnius as their capital even if she wasn't in their borders; nevertheless, most Lithuanians refused to fight the Poles when ordered to do so by the Germans in the Second World War. For the Lithuanians, World War II had but one good result: it brought back Vilnius and environs. (Unfortunately, Russia, who returned the lost lands to Lithuania after taking Poland, was also included in the package.) Another sore point: Poland waited until the U.S. gave the okay before recognizing Lithuanian independence in 1991.

The religious tolerance of the former kingdom brought Jews from all corners to Vilnius, starting in the fourteenth century. So many arrived that Vilnius was dubbed "the Jerusalem of the North." Almost the entire group was killed or fled during the Nazi occupation, and Jews say that Lithuanians, many of whom were complicit with the Germans, turned them in—a source of lingering vitriol. While Nazis targeted Jews, the Lithuanians were hounded by Soviets, who didn't tolerate their authority-questioning attitude. Between 1940 and 1958, some 200,000 Lithuanians were imprisoned or sent to work camps—some run by Nazis, others by Soviets who pulled Lithuania into the Soviet Union after World War II.

*During the 1800s, when Russia imposed Russian as the sole language,
valiant Bishop Valancius kept the Lithuanian language alive by having
Lithuanian books printed in Germany and smuggling them in. He also
started secret schools, since nineteenth-century Russians weren't keen on
educating the masses.*

As in Poland, Lithuania's devotion to Catholicism helped offset Communistic
brainwashing. Lithuanians were spirited resisters against Soviet occupation in
the 1940s, but Russians shipped off most intellectuals and protesters to the gulag. Secret stashes of arms had mostly been uncovered by Soviets by the
1950s. But dissidence lived on, thanks to small printing presses that Soviets
could never completely root out. One publication that egged on resistance: the
secret journal of the local Catholic Church.

Hill of Crosses, a symbol of Lithuanian resistance

Courtesy of Lithuania State Department of Tourism

HILL OF CROSSES (KRYZIU KALNAS)

The spirit (and perhaps spirits) of feisty Lithuanians are embedded in this
holy hill covered by a thick jungle of crosses. Over 50,000 crosses stand
here—the earliest dating back to the 1300s. Many, however, appeared during
the Soviet era as metaphors of anti-Russian protest and anger. Soviets kept

steamrolling them down and they mysteriously kept popping back up. Even today the hill is surreal: it can induce shivers when the many crosses rattle about
in the wind.

---

*Lithuania was formerly the Soviets' ears to the West. Hidden in the thickly
forested countryside, Linksmakalnis—a Soviet snooping station—once
tapped into Western European communication systems, although the operation was so clandestine that details are still sketchy even now.*

Lithuanians collectively blew their top at Moscow much more loudly and in-
tensely than their neighbors, and their rebellion hammered some of the final
nails in the Soviet coffin. But when Communism fell, Lithuanian society fell apart
with it. Crime exploded in the 1990s after Soviet industry pulled out, and unemployment soared. Robberies and car theft were among the most frequent of the
200 or so crimes reported on an average day by the mid 1990s.[3] Banking scandals rocked the country—the two biggest banks folded in 1995—and corruption
ran almost unabated. But Lithuanians who lived abroad began coming back—
including a U.S. government policymaker called Valdus Adamkus, who'd left five
decades before; he became president in 1998. And amid a series of political
scandals, he was brought back in as president in 2004.

*Unlike Estonia and Latvia, Lithuania didn't put ethnic Russians through the
language hoops. While Lithuanian is the official language, Russians (and
pretty much anybody else who wanted it) were immediately granted citizenship in 1991.*

Hot Spots

Vilnius: Napoleon galloped through here on the way to and from Moscow,
and was so taken by the city's gothic church St. Anne that he longed to take it
back to France. Happily, he left the church behind; unhappily, many of his worn
troops were left behind too: they still find mass graves of their corpses. A fetching backdrop for movies—HBO filmed a miniseries about virginal British queen
Elizabeth I here—Vilnius may go down in history as the place where visiting
Vice President Cheney rekindled the Cold War, trashing Russia as a bully when
he stopped by in 2006.

Klaipeda: Lithuania's major seaport was once the haunt of Teutonic
Knights—and in 1939, Nazi Germany demanded it back, marking the first Nazi

move into Baltic territory. But that's old history. Now the lively city, with an intact old town that showcases architecture from the Hanseatic era, is home to jazz festivals and a sea museum where you can hear dolphins sing.

Curonian Spit: A finger of swirling sand that juts out into a lagoon, the Curonian Spit is a UNESCO World Heritage site, where ancient villages are buried underneath dunes. Formerly a magnet for writers, including Thomas Mann, who wrote *The Magic Mountain* while gazing out at the choppy waters, her fishing villages are now turned into laid-back resorts, but the place retains a magical feel—although you'd best come soon as the view may soon change. Lukoil is setting up offshore oil rigs.

Palang: The favored beach town along Lithuania's Amber Coast, it boasts white sands, a beautiful park, and of course an amber museum, now housed in a palace.

Borders: Plenty of illegal immigrants, arms, and radioactive materials are smuggled into and out of Lithuania from almost all sides.

Hotshots

Algirdas Brazauskas: President, 1993–1998; Prime Minister, 2001–present. The former Communist who dared cut ties with Moscow's Communist Party headquarters in 1989 doesn't seem to know what else to do but lead. Continuing as president after Lithuania's independence, he later jumped from the president's seat to the prime minister's.

Valdus Adamkus: President, 1998–2001 and 2004–present. A former underground resister, Adamkus left Lithuania for the U.S., where he worked for military intelligence and later became an Environmental Protection Agency policy analyst. Returned to Lithuania in the 1990s and was elected president in 1998. In his first meeting with President Putin, Adamkus demanded that Russia compensate Lithuania for five decades of occupation. The atmosphere quickly turned chilly, and Putin refused. Lithuanians voted Adamkus in again in 2004, ensuring a pro-U.S. stance.

Sajudis "The Movement": The dissident intellectuals revved up the Lithuanian independence movement, but didn't keep hold of the steering wheel for long.

Vytautas Landsbergis: De facto President, 1998–2000; head of parliament, 1996–2000. Round-faced, goateed Landsbergis—Lithuania's Lech Walesa—led the Sajudis independence movement, urging protesters to guard the TV tower and not to give up when Russia cut off energy supplies. De facto president after the country's first free election, when he headed parliament, he also served in that role again 1996–2000, but proved to be cantankerous and unbending; after he endorsed a TV censorship board and the practice of spying on journalists, public opinion turned against him.[4] The symbol of Lithuania's independence movement, he is still highly regarded—especially outside his country. Perhaps the gifted pianist and Condi can perform a duet if she too blows through town.

Viktor Uspaskich: Former Minister of Economy. Russian-born Uspaskich moved to Lithuania to build a gas pipeline, linked arms with Russia's Gazprom, and started a profitable food company. Now worth up to $200 million, Uspaskich renovates Russian Orthodox churches and funds facelifts for long-neglected towns. His good deeds paid off: the Labor Party he started in 2003 now holds nearly a third of parliament's seats. Uspaskich snagged a cabinet position as minister of the

Music professor Landsbergis struck a chord with calls for independence

economy, but an ethics committee booted him in 2005, saying he was making decisions based on private gain.

Vilnius Brigade: Syndicate troublemakers headquartered in the capital and linked to Russian and Polish Mafias, they smuggle pretty much anything from art and slaves to stolen cars, arms, and radioactive ingredients for dirty bombs.

M. K. Ciurlionis (1875–1911): Composer, painter, and amateur hypnotist, Lithuania's favorite creator was nothing if not intense: he excelled at mesmerizing the masses in both artistic fields, becoming best known for his symphony *In the Forest* and ethereal paintings before dying at the age of thirty-five.[5] A museum is devoted to him in second city Kaunas.

23. FORMER CZECHOSLOVAKIA
Czech Republic and Slovak Republic
Stirring up the 'Hood

Overview: The Shared History

Dead in the middle of Europe and thick with orchards, snowcapped mountains, and handsome cities brimming with dazzling architecture, the crossroads that became Czechoslovakia was key property throughout European history. Metal resources and abundant food made this region crucial to the Austrian Empire— at one point fetching Prague became the imperial capital—and her abundance of beer and liqueurs helped keep generations drunk. The eastern (Slovak) half of the country, home of castle-topped Bratislava, vineyards, and bubbling thermal waters, was so adored by Hungarians that it was once called High Hungary after millions moved in when sixteenth-century Turks invaded Budapest and stayed for 160 years.

HISTORICAL HOTSHOT: KING RUDY (1552–1612)

Holy Roman Emperor Rudolph II, an Austrian Habsburg who moved his kingdom from Vienna to Prague in 1577, wasn't content with material riches. He sought spiritual wealth as well, and hoped to unlock the keys to the universe. Rudolph kicked off a renaissance in Prague when he invited Europe's wisest men to move into his castle and uncover the true nature of Godliness and the mysteries of life. They arrived from all corners: magicians and musicians, artists and astrologers, alchemists and architects; respected scientific men— astronomers Tycho Brahe and Johannes Kepler, and Queen Elizabeth I of England's personal physician from London—were likewise drawn to the quest in Prague. Between boozy nights and long dinners with Rudy, they all toiled to explain the inexplicable: whether trying to transform lead into gold, calculate celestial movements, decipher ancient texts, or discover the restorative qualities of beer, they attempted to demystify the mysteries, find eternal life, and divine what lay ahead. Hundreds of spiritual seekers were lodged in Prague Castle; the corpses of those cast off as charlatans rotted in the dungeons below.

The land that held Czechs, Slovaks, Germans, and Ukrainians didn't actually become the country Czechoslovakia until 1919—and she was never the most stable of countries, since Slovaks and other ethnic minorities were hacked off that Czechs were always top dogs. Wealthy Germans in Sudetenland were also ticked: the Czechoslovak government hit them with a 20 percent start-up tax on all their riches, and huge tracts of their lands were given to peasants. Twenty years later, Czechoslovakia came unhinged, thanks to Nazi Germany; with the blessing of the Brits and the French (See "United Kingdom," page 75), Hitler annexed her northwest corner, Sudetenland—and soon invaded the whole country.

> In 1940, the government let the Germans roll in; Hitler threatened to pummel Prague with the Luftwaffe if they didn't. As promised, Nazis did not mar Prague's well-preserved beauty: they wanted Prague as the site for a museum dedicated to Jews—to be called the Museum of an Extinct Race. Slovak priest Jozef Tiso, however, quickly made a deal with Nazis: the Slovak-dominated eastern part of the country would become a Nazi-supporting independent country with Tiso in charge. Surprisingly, Sudetenlanders were Hitler's first foes, as they made clear in 1939: while marching through Sudetenland, Hitler experienced one of his first assassination attempts, when a German-Czech threw a knife at him. Some Sudetenlanders quickly organized resistance groups (and escape routes for Jews) and Count Joachim von Zedtwitz, a well-to-do German-Czech became a one-man resistance force, transporting Jews out of the country in his sports car; the Nazis assumed that with his Aryan looks and German ethnicity he was on their side.

Taking over after the war, Czechoslovakian President Edvard Beneš expelled 3 million ethnic Germans from Czechoslovakia and seized their lands, mostly in Sudetenland; 250,000 Hungarians were sent packing as well. The 1945–1946 exodus was as horrifying as the Nazi deportation: 300,000 died along the way, many killed in mass violence.

> The Beneš Decrees, approved by the Allies, are a growing point of contention in Austria, Germany, and Hungary, where former Sudetenlanders are demanding apologies and compensation for lost lands.

Moscow-backed Communists ejected Beneš from power and took control—installing a puppet government and transforming Czechoslovakia into a Soviet satellite, responsible for arms and munitions.

ARMS SALE! PRICES SLASHED! COME ON DOWN!

Under the Communist regime, Czechoslovakia was transformed into weapons-and-explosives central, best known for cheap rifles and Semtex, an explosive favored by guerrillas. (The product is so singularly Czech that Semtex is the name of a popular Czech energy drink.) Czechs and Slovaks had little say in the matter back then, but the arms industry (both legal and illegal) is still thriving today—and arms just have a way of walking out on their own. Czech and Slovak companies have supplied arms to China, Cuba, India, Iran, Vietnam, and Libya[1] among others (filling Soviet back orders), and they also produce weapons for assorted questionable governments and radical groups, including those in Yemen, Eritrea, and Sri Lanka.

Of all the countries locked behind the Iron Curtain, Czechoslovakia was always the most tantalizing to the West, giving just a wisp of an impression of the hidden Communist reality. The world first got a glimpse when grainy and intense Czechoslovak "New Wave" films trickled out in the 1960s—rating international attention and winning prestigious awards.

Czechoslovakia flickered across American TV screens in 1968 during "Prague Spring," when the Soviet satellite suddenly opened up. Then came the televised Soviet reprisals of August 1968 and images of crying Czechoslovakians throwing themselves onto incoming Russian tanks, followed by blackness as the communication system was unplugged.

PRAGUE SPRING

Czechoslovakia's economy slumped in 1968, and the Communist Party brought in fresh leadership to boost it. The party's new head, Alexander Dubcek, unveiled a radical reform plan that lifted more than the economy: Dubcek boosted the Czechoslovak mood. As part of a program dubbed "Socialism with a human face," he ripped away press censorship, allowed freedom of expression, and gave trade unions new rights. "We shall have to remove everything that strangles artistic and scientific creativeness," he told shocked Czechoslovakians. The Soviets in Moscow were also dumbfounded, but President Leonid Brezhnev liked Dubcek and did little except call him screaming every day. But Dubcek wasn't trying to make a break: to Brezhnev's relief, the reformer kept Czechoslovakia in the Soviet military collective—the Warsaw Pact—and toed most of the Communist Party line. But unlike in other Soviet satellites or republics, that spring—dubbed Prague Spring—Czechoslovakians listened to criticisms of the Soviet regime via radio and TV, read accurate news of the West, published uncensored novels, performed political plays, and said and did pretty much whatever they wished, wherever they wished. But when Dubcek allowed non-Communists into parliament, Brezhnev blew his stack. On August 20, 1968, Czechs awoke to the sight of their dreams being smashed. Tanks of Warsaw Pact troops—Poles, Hungarians, East Germans, Russians, and Bulgarians—rolled into Prague, the soldiers ignoring the pleas of those who climbed atop their tanks begging them to stop. An estimated 120 died over the next two days, including thirteen killed while trying to block troops from taking over the radio station that had become the symbol of freedom. By August 22, it was over. A Soviet-style blackout descended as the free press was shut down, Warsaw Pact troops permanently moved in, and Czechoslovakia transformed from the most open of satellite states to the most repressed. Dubcek, hauled off to Moscow, was soon fired as party head; he survived the ordeal, but spent the rest of his career tending to trees for the Slovak forestry service. More rigid Communists soon took power and ripped away the freedom he had given.

> "You may think Czechs behaved like cowards when they did not fight. But you can't go against tanks with empty hands . . . The only way you can help us is this: don't forget Czechoslovakia. Don't forget Czechoslovakia . . . even when Czechoslovakia ceases to be news in the paper." —Unidentified twenty-two-year-old Czech in a radio message to the world on August 23, 1968, as the Prague Spring experiment was collapsing[2]

For the next twenty years, Czechoslovakia pretty much dropped out of Western view, her memory kept alive only by writers such as Milan Kundera, who fled to France in 1975 and published *The Unbearable Lightness of Being* nine years later. Writers such as Vaclav Havel and Ivan Klima kept the questioning spirit alive with samizdat, an underground publishing movement born of typewriters and carbon paper; diplomats often smuggled out the writings to the West, where they were published as books. In general, though, the mood in Czechoslovakia turned gloomy as the new regime erased former rights, and 150,000 Czechs quickly fled the country. Dissidents, such as Havel, were forced to work as janitors and street sweepers, and the arts scene that blossomed during the Prague Spring withered under heavy censorship. In January 1969, student Jan Palach, livid that Czechoslovakia was again wrapped in Soviet chains, set himself on fire, dying in his protest against the Soviet occupation and blackening spirits further. One bright light glimmered on the scene, however, proving to be a source of huge inspiration; oddly enough, it was Frank Zappa.

FRANK ZAPPA (1940–1993)

Frank Zappa, the American musician whose experimental music—often long-winded, drugged-out rambles—lodged stinging social criticism and tackled every taboo, helped to launch Czechoslovakia's anti-Communist movement. The title of his song "Plastic People of the Universe" inspired a 1970s Czech rock band to take that name and write music that struck out at the totalitarian system. Refusing to take the test required of all performing artists— a propaganda quiz asking such trivia as Lenin's birthday—the group was banned from playing; they gigged around anyway. In 1977, when Plastic People of the Universe members were arrested and thrown into prison, local writers and artists formed a protest group, Charter 77, to fight censorship and promote human rights. Vaclav Havel, known for his biting plays about Communist bureaucrats (and for coining the name "Absurdistan" to describe life in that society), rose up as the dissidents' leader. Charter 77 became the voice of rebellion, frequently writing letters to Amnesty International and the *New York Times* publicizing the inhumane acts of the Communists and continually airing the government's dirty laundry in the Western press. They later became a symbol of the independence movement to shake free of Moscow-backed tyranny.

In November 1989, Czechoslovakia again blipped across our TV screens, this time with images of Vaclav Havel and Charter 77 leading Czechoslovakian protesters in the streets during the Velvet Revolution.

THE VELVET REVOLUTION

When the Berlin Wall fell in November 1989, a group of protesters took to the streets of Prague, calling for independence. The peaceful march might have been ignored, had not the police roughed up 100 or so: the next day, the country rose en masse and marched through the streets. During the next twenty-four days, hundreds of thousands showed up in Wenceslas Square, rattling key chains, chanting slogans, singing songs, and burning candles as they rallied around playwright Havel, demanding that the Communist government step down and the Soviet troops roll out. Their slogan was corny—"Truth and love will win over hatred and lies"—but it did the trick. In December, the Communist Party stepped down.

Vaclav Havel called the break with Communism "the Velvet Revolution" because it was soft; while hundreds were injured, nobody was killed.

In April 1990, Vaclav Havel stepped in as president of a free country. The new government flew in Frank Zappa and appointed the singer honorary consultant to the Ministry of Culture.

> "All I knew about Czechoslovakia before I got there was what I had seen on Cable News Network: people walking around in dingy, gray streets, and having a revolution. I had no idea how pretty and quiet it is . . . What they don't want [Czechoslovakia to become] can be summed up by the comment urgently made by one of the many kids who trailed me throughout my visit: 'Frankie, Frankie, please don't bring me Las Vegas.' "[3] —Frank Zappa in 1990

But Czechoslovakia disappeared yet again. In 1993, she vanished in an amicable split called the Velvet Divorce. Where once stood a united country now stands two: the Czech Republic and Slovakia, both recent entries into NATO and the European Union. The Czech Republic and Slovakia are a study in contrasts: the Czech Republic's capital is mysterious Prague, whose castled beauty lures 6 million tourists a year; Slovakia's capital is little Bratislava (where the Castle District is pretty), which has barely blipped on the tourist charts. The Czech Republic has a strong but cold leader, Prime Minister Vaclav Klaus, whose jaws are always flapping in criticism of the European Union; Slovakia has a kind but somewhat anemic leader, Prime Minister Mikulas Dzurinda, whose greatest achievement was convincing the European Union to take his country in.

> The Velvet Divorce of 1993 was partly about Czech dominance; neither Czechs nor Slovaks wanted the country to split, but the Czech and Slovak prime ministers had a blowout that decided the country's fate, and neither bothered to put the important matter to a vote. Even President Vaclav Havel was not consulted in the matter: he was so livid over the split that he quit as president. A few months later, however, he resumed the presidential post; now almost everybody, including Havel, believes the breakup was a good thing.

NOT IN MY BACKYARD

Even though they're now two separate countries, the Czech Republic and Slovakia do rile up the neighborhood (particularly Austria) with their nuclear power plants, which even plenty of Czechs and Slovaks oppose. Whether you're talking about the Czechs' Temelin plant (forty miles from Austria), which may be manned by Homer Simpson, since it breaks down every few months, or the Slovaks' Bohunice plant, an older Soviet design built to 1950s standards and lacking containment domes to trap leaking radioactive gases, the babies just aren't up to snuff, right down to their lack of safety features. They were only half-built when Soviet funding dried up, but American and Western European companies finished the jobs, admitting that they weren't up to Western standards. Austrians are so ticked that the plants were turned on that they occasionally block highways between the two countries, and the plants produce more electricity than their countries need. Which is why Western European countries helped finish the plants: Central Europe's nukes can unobtrusively—and profitably—deliver electricity to Western European countries where consumers often oppose nuclear plants.

24. CZECH REPUBLIC
(Česká Republika)
Jaded Loveliness

FAST FACTS

Country:	Czech Republic; Česká Republika
Capital:	Prague
Government:	Parliamentary democracy
Independence:	January 1, 1993 (separated from Czechoslovakia)
Population:	10,235,000 (2006 estimate)
Head of State:	President Vaclav Klaus (2003)
Head of Government:	Prime Minister Jiri Paroubek (2005)
Elections:	President elected by parliament, five-year term; prime minister appointed by president, five-year term
Name of Parliament:	Parliament or Senat
Ethnicity:	91% Czech; 4% Moravian; 2% Slovak; 4% other (2001 census)
Religion:	59% unaffiliated; 27% Roman Catholic; 9% unspecified; 3% Orthodox; 2% Protestant; 3% others (2001 census)

Language:	Czech; also Slovak, German, Polish, Hungarian spoken by minorities
Literacy:	99% (2003 estimate)
Famous Exports:	*Dvořák*, Milos Forman, Semtex
Economic Big Boy:	Cez (utilities); 2004 total sales: $3.3 billion[1]
Per Capita GDP:	$18,100 (2005)
Unemployment:	7.8% (January 2006 Eurostat figure)
EU Status:	Entered May 2004
Currency:	Czech koruna

Quick Tour

Hard to imagine a prettier place than this castled land, which has more royal structures per acre than anywhere else in the world; flowering orchards and lush vineyards carpet soft hills, and the heavily spired architecture is straight out of a fairy tale. From her fetching high-towered castles, where officials of yore oft tumbled out of windows, to Prague's elaborate astronomical clock, the Česká Republika that stitches together Moravia and Bohemia is stunning, surreal, and tinged with the macabre.

Prague's Charles Bridge: Fairy-tale pretty

Courtesy of Czech Tourism Board

> One of Prague's most beloved sights is the beautiful Apostle Clock on the
> main square. Every hour, elaborately sculpted saints and skeletons come
> out for a mechanical spin. Legend has it that when the work was created in
> the fifteenth century, Prague's Town Council so adored their unique time-
> telling marvel that they blinded the clockmaker to prevent him from ever
> making such a masterpiece for anyone else.

But Česká Republika has a dark, brooding side, and has long been a magnet for the strange and the sinister. In Prague, a sixteenth-century center for
alchemy, astrology, and magic, there's still an undercurrent of secrecy, and a
hint of malevolence that seeps out of the Vltava River—some say it holds evil
water sprites—as aptly captured in the eerie works of Kafka.

FRANZ KAFKA (1883–1924)

Born when Bohemia was still part of the Austrian Empire, coal-eyed, heavily
unibrowed Franz Kafka studied law, sold insurance, lived with his parents, and
regarded Prague as his curse. The combo created some of the strangest fiction
ever to see the ink of the printing presses—which they thankfully did since Max
Brod, the friend to whom Kafka bequeathed his writing, refused to destroy it as
directed. Although he lived long before Czechoslovakia became a Soviet satellite, Kafka painfully captured the terrible anonymity of being a powerless cog in
the machine. That sentiment of worthlessness is best expressed in *The Meta-
morphosis*, in which a worker wakes up as a giant insect—a state that also captured Kafka's chronic feeling of being a wimp in his overbearing father's eyes.
The insurance seller who spent his nights writing (and sometimes cavorting with
prostitutes) had few works published during his lifetime and never married, despite being engaged numerous times to several women. This problem, too, he
blamed on his father, to whom Kafka, upon learning he was dying of tuberculosis, wrote a forty-five-page tell-off letter that Dad never read. His disturbing fiction best captures the mysterious, malevolent part of Prague, but it is not without
humor. In *The Trial*, for instance, the judges who are perpetually reading thick
books, presumably about legal matters, are at last revealed to be delving deep
into porn. The writer, who is so tied to Prague that he is nearly a cliché, finally received public recognition in 2004, when a statue of his likeness was erected in
the square outside the Jewish Quarter apartment where he first scratched pen
across paper and brought his nightmares alive. His twisted writing endures, and
he's said to influence numerous creators from composer Philip Glass to novelist
Gabriel García Márquez. Can't say the same for his dad.

The once-common fear of Communism returning may have been conquered
(joining NATO helped), but corruption runs rampant and the place lives in

shadows: Russian and Ukrainian mobs have moved in, along with the Chinese, Yugoslavs, and Chechens; kidnapping is one means to recruit sex slaves for international rings, and one never knows what long-buried secret will next be unearthed in the woods.

> *One Soviet-era secret presented itself in the 2002 floods: the north's Spolana Neratovice chemical plant's hidden hoard of toxic chemicals came floating out and streamed into the Elbe river—source of drinking water downstream in Germany. The factory's ill-stored by-products, long kept hidden from the public, may be the reason for the mysteriously high number of miscarriages in the area.*

Some once-idealistic Czechs are disillusioned with the democracy that finally has materialized; cynicism has crept in since the innocent days when peace and truth could win over war and lies. Wages are now higher, but so is the price of everything from beer to rent; many Czechs can no longer afford living in housing-short Prague. The once dimly lit city flashes with neon, the arteries that were nearly void of cars are now clogged with traffic, and the stores that lacked variety are today crammed with slow-moving tourists. Nothing in this land has ever turned out as it was imagined, and even former president Vaclav Havel, like the neon heart he lit in the presidential headquarters, Prague Castle, was little more than a highly visible icon with limited power.

> *"Once I counted the changes of political regimes in my mother's life and there have been eight during her seventy-eight years. Britons have never experienced as many changes during their whole history, so no wonder we are a nation that doesn't show too much enthusiasm. We are skeptical optimists." —Former prime minister Vladimir Spidla in 2004[2]*

The Czechs' morose musings and the country's shady side are offset by her beauty which calls to the masses: so many stop by to see the fabled land that tourism now adds 6 percent of GDP to the national piggy bank and employs over 100,000. In fact, after Communism fell, Western travelers descended here first, wowed by the statue-lined Charles Bridge and the charming architecture that seemed to have dropped out of a seventeenth-century picture book. Prague became internationally chic as the world discovered her enchanting beauty—and silver-spooned American twenty-somethings swaggered in, buying up entire buildings; the printing presses that once cranked out underground writing began churning out hip weeklies for expats. Even if the sound of English is frighteningly common, Prague's allure endures.

Hot Spots

Prague: Gorgeous and vaguely creepy capital Prague is the most visited city in Central Europe. Best known for Kafka, revolts, beer, and the Charles Bridge—which survived six centuries of wars, but nearly washed away in the 2002 floods—the place is also getting a reputation for her prostitutes. Some 15,000 nocturnal ladies work here.[3]

Prague Castle: Built on a pagan sacrificial ground, spired Hradcany Castle looks more like a Gothic church and serves as the presidential palace.

Moravia: Thick with lavender hills and littered with hundreds of castles, the agricultural land in the south was once a powerful dynasty and still holds the Czech Republic's second biggest city, Brno. Pretty Moravia used to get ignored by the tourists, but now some are unlocking the secrets of this mist-wrapped region, which serves as the national vineyard. The treasure of Moravia, however, is slivovice, a potent plum brandy that everyone from peasant to duke made even during times when it was banned: at points, the valuable concoction even served as currency.

The skies: The Czech Republic joined NATO in 1999, but Czechs themselves say the current military equipment is not an asset. Czech-made helicopters frequently crash and a Czech-made trainer plane recently fell apart in midair. The Czech government plans to spend a few billion to buy Swedish fighter planes; other aggressive bidders for that juicy deal, such as Lockheed Martin, withdrew their offers over the government's alleged financial misdealings.

> Under EU requirements, bars now must have hot water and paper towels in the loo; many owners, says Radio Prague, are resisting the upgrade.

Bars: Tourists are typically the only ones who dare knock back the absinthe (complete with wormwood) that can be ordered in the bars here—the high-octane, mildly hallucinogenic "green fairy" is outlawed in most of Europe. It's said that Czechs drink more beer than anyone else in the world, and the country is home to the world's oldest working microbrewery, the world's first Pilsner, and the world's first "Budweiser" (the local manufacturer has been fighting with Anheuser-Busch over the name for more than a century, sometimes winning its cases).

Hotshots

Vaclav Havel: President of Czechoslovakia, 1990–1992; President of the Czech Republic, 1993–2003. Dissident writer whose incredulousness with the

Soviet situation helped to finally free Czechoslovakia from Moscow's hold, he led the Velvet Revolution of 1989. Havel—like Lech Walesa—was frustrated by his lack of real power; unlike the Pole, Havel lasted thirteen years. He wielded great clout with the masses, and was the unofficial diplomat of Central Europe to the West, but did make a few political U-turns. He said he wouldn't support NATO, but changed his mind and became a major NATO booster; mouths really dropped open when Havel backed the 2003 invasion of Iraq, for which President George W. Bush awarded him the Medal of Freedom as a supporter of U.S. policy. His wife, Olga, was as popular with Czechs as he was; within a year of her 1996 death from cancer, he married flirtatious actress Dagmar Veskrnova, who's twenty years his junior (she's in her late forties), causing a scandal and a drop in popularity. Many still love him anyway. Sick with cancer, the playwright who was a brewery caretaker during the Communist days (his punishment for lashing out at the system) lost half a lung in 1996 and has nearly died several times since. Havel is now working on his memoirs and lives part of the year in Portugal.

> Besides plays, Havel wrote essays, manifestos, and provocative letters. His 1978 essay "The Power of the Powerless," analyzing the Soviet brainwashing techniques employed to create a passive society, was one of his most influential works. Also notable were his critical letters to Communist leaders, factors that led to his three prison terms during their regime.

President Vaclav Klaus: The antithesis of Vaclav Havel

Photo by Petr Skvrne. Courtesy of Office of President of Czech Republic, Press Department

Vaclav Klaus: Prime Minister, 1993–1997; President, 2003–present. The EU's loudest and most articulate critic, the icy-eyed economist Klaus is driven and known to run over whoever or whatever is in his way. As finance minister, "the Professor" pushed Czechoslovakia onto the free-market fast track—leading the Czech Miracle. As prime minister, his fight with Slovak leader Vladimir Meciar led to the Velvet Divorce with Slovakia. He stepped down as prime minister in 1997, after being accused of misusing political funding for his Civic Democratic Party; when he did not secure the required votes for the prime ministerial position in 2002, he suffered a nervous breakdown. When Havel stepped down as president in 2003, it took three voting rounds in parliament for Klaus to nab the presidential seat. Some like him, and some really, really don't, and many are just plain shocked that Klaus still looms large on the political scene. His cocky, brusque style is legendary, prompting the joke, "What's the difference between God and Klaus? God doesn't think he's Klaus."[4]

Noteworthy: The divine works of Czech classical composer Antonín Dvořák might never have fallen on modern ears had he continued in his original line of work as a butcher.

News you can understand: Broadcasting for sixty-six years, Radio Prague has a story of its own, including being censored by the Soviets and airing broadcasts from hidden locations. Now it's the best one-stop source for history, culture, and news, and can be accessed in six languages on their remarkable Web site: www.radioprague.cz. Also notable: the weekly Prague Post.

25. SLOVAK REPUBLIC
(Slovakia, Slovensko)
The Forgotten Slav

FAST FACTS

Country:	Slovak Republic/Slovakia; Slovenská Republika/Slovensko
Capital:	Bratislava
Government:	Parliamentary democracy
Independence:	January 1, 1993 (created as separate state from Czechoslovakia)
Population:	5,439,000 (2006 estimate)
Head of State:	President Ivan Gasparovik (2004)
Head of Government:	Prime Minister Mikulas Dzurinda (1998)
Elections:	President elected by direct, popular vote, five-year term; prime minister appointed by president, five-year term
Name of Parliament:	National Council; Narodna Rada
Ethnicity:	86% Slovak; 10% Hungarian; 2% Roma; 1% Ruthenian/Ukrainian; 2% other

Religion:	69% Roman Catholic; 13% none; 11% Protestant;
	4% Orthodox; 3% others
Language:	84% Slovak (official); 11% Hungarian; 2% Roma;
	1% Ukrainian; 3% others
Literacy:	99% (2001 estimate)
Famous Exports:	absinthe, Andy Warhol's mother, the man who brought
	Prague her finest spring
Economic Big Boy:	Volkswagen Slovakia; 2003 total revenue: €4.43 billion
	(about $5.5 billion)[1]
Per Capita GDP:	$15,800 (2005)
Unemployment:	15.8%; under-25 rate: 30%
	(January 2006 Eurostat estimate)
EU status:	Entered May 2004
Currency:	Slovakian korun

Quick Tour

> *"The only thing I know about Slovakia is what I learned firsthand from your foreign minister, who came to Texas." —George W. Bush, then governor of Texas, to a Slovak journalist who asked what he thought of Slovakia. Bush had actually met the foreign minister of Slovenia, not Slovakia.*[2]

Cradled against the Tatra Mountains, where tranquil lakes are surrounded by pines, castle-happy Slovensko is crawling with 3,800 caves and twisting subterranean tunnels (and spelunkers crawling through them), bubbling with thermal waters, and dotted with pretty villages, some connected by a wine trail that passes through vineyards making lovely Chardonnay and Cabernet. But despite the opera, theater, and brainy young people in her capital city, despite the untouched medieval and renaissance architecture across the land, despite the skiing, health spas, and valleys that still are sites of harvest festivals, sweet little Slovakia is mostly undiscovered—and more often defined by what she was, than what she is. In fact, many Europeans still don't know that Slovakia is now an independent country—and not just the Czechs' "other half."

SLOVAKOCZECHIA

It might not have had the same ring, but if only they'd called the country "Slovakoczechia" maybe things would have been different. After all, the big gripe of the Slovaks was that Czechs, who made up less than half the country's

population, always came first in Czechoslovakia, starting with the name. Slovaks never even wanted to be roped in a country with the Czechs from the
start. Unfortunately, Slovaks arrived a bit late for the 1919 mapmaking
marathon during the Paris Peace Talks—the Czechs had held them back—and
by the time they showed up in France, Czech leader Beneš had already convinced the powers-that-be that the two regions should be combined. Despite
the Slovaks' intense lobbying to make Slovakia separate, Czechoslovakia was
a done deal. It's no surprise they fell apart in 1993; Czechs and Slovaks had
never exactly been good mates: even in 1918, as the First World War drew to a
close, the two kept battling with each other, despite fighting on the same side.[3]

Although it all seems for the best now, initially the split looked like it would
lead Slovakia right back to where she had come from: namely a menacing totalitarian society. That her heavy-fisted prime minister Vladimir Meciar, who negotiated the breakup, was toppled (or rather blocked) from power was less a
show of democracy (he'd received most of the vote in the 2002 general election) than a result of background maneuvering by the EU and the U.S. and in
this case one has to applaud their involvement.

VLADIMIR "DON'T MESS WITH ME" MECIAR

Nationalist Vladimir Meciar, who became Slovakia's first prime minister after he sawed the country off from Czechoslovakia, made a shambles of the
country, starting with the economy; he handed huge low-interest loans to his
chums, while ignoring unemployment rising into the high double digits and
the screaming need to reform. During his six years as prime minister, he
turned at least one TV station into a Meciar-controlled vanity channel and
tried to fine others who weren't rah-rah-ing his questionable moves; he
threatened to raise the newspaper tax and cut supplies of newsprint to jour-
nals that lodged criticism of his wacky leadership—and he punched a reporter who asked about the recent million-dollar renovation to his home. The
former Communist stayed buddy-buddy with Russia's power elite and thugs
and negotiated cheap energy deals. His foreign relations were a mess—he
offended Hungary's leaders by making a joke about the expulsion of Hungarians after the Second World War—and his domestic politics were shadowy:
head of the secret service, he may have been linked to a political kidnapping,
but the witness, who was about to spill the beans, mysteriously died. In short,
Meciar appeared to be marching the country into a dictatorship when the European Union and the United States noticed and began having a fit. Letting it
be known that if Meciar returned to power, the doors to NATO and the EU
would slam shut, the U.S. government was so worried about Meciar returning

in the 1998 elections that it funded an ad campaign urging people to vote. Slovak voters brought Meciar back anyway, but his bid for power was blocked from within. Although his party actually garnered the most votes—20 percent—none of the other parties would join his to form a coalition, so he was barred from the prime minister's chair.

With Meciar out of the picture, the new government of Mikulas Dzurinda had to sprint to get the country into the EU. That they pulled it off is remarkable. Then Dzurinda successfully song-and-danced to lure foreign investment to Slovakia. Slovakia's economy, despite high unemployment, is now stable—like Slovenia, Slovakia looks likely to soon be invited to adopt the euro.

Problems remain, including one that haunts the neighbors as well: gypsies, known these days by the more politically correct "Roma." They can be found all over Central Europe, but Roma are a particularly hairy issue in Slovakia, where they often live in trashy villages where the shacks have holes in the roofs. With near universal unemployment—few are willing to hire them—they were the group most affected when the government cut welfare payments in 2004; Roma responded by looting supermarkets. Numerous organizations are trying to address this ongoing social problem, but few have made much progress. One sign of hope: Roma music is all the rage across Central Europe, and Roma literature, sometimes published with EU funds, is increasingly popular too.

THE BAND FORMERLY KNOWN AS THE GYPSIES

Their culture is rich, their history tragic, and Roma have never been embraced by any European society. With their large families (women often have six children or more) and scanty education (the government often sent all Roma to schools for the retarded), the group that long ago hiked over from India has usually been left out in the cold; burglar rings of men and pickpocketing bands of mothers and children—who toss babies toward victims as a distraction while they grab wallets—have done little to polish their image. The situation is worse since the fall of Communism, leaving Roma without any socialized safety net, and with few employment opportunities. Some Romanies have headed west; a band of them made headline news by camping in a Viennese park and eating the resident swans. Now some Western European countries require special visas from Slovaks, believed to be a method to keep Roma out. The EU is funding cultural awareness projects all over the place, but the truth is Roma are Europe's great unloved, and efforts to integrate them successfully are daunting. Roma have a harder time of it in Slovakia, where more than two-thirds are unemployed, the worst rate in Europe. In this country of high overall unemployment, Roma are increasingly targets of violence—a gang of Slovak teenagers recently broke into the house of a fifty-year-old Romany woman and beat her to death.

Slovakia also has all kinds of touchy issues from the past, including Hungary. In the 1870s, Slovakia fell under Hungarian (Magyar) rule when the Austrian Empire added "Hungary" to her name. Slovaks, forced to learn German under Austrian rule, were now forced to learn Hungarian, and the Magyars, on a nationalistic roll, were heavy-handed about Magyarization. Hungary's attempt to stamp out Slovakian culture has never been forgiven; Czechoslovakia's expulsion of Hungarians after the Second World War only increased the tension between the two. And the recent Slovak damming of the Danube River has Hungarians damning Slovaks from downstream.

Another tricky historical issue is the role Catholicism played in Slovakia's past. Many Slovaks would rather forget that during World War II their country, led by Monsignor Tiso, supported Nazis and allowed them to build arms plants and work camps. Initially, many Slovaks were unaware of the priest's collusion with the Germans, but resistance groups eventually grew from a "whispering campaign." In 1944, the angry Slovaks rebelled against Tiso in the Slovak National Uprising, which Germans easily crushed—although that too didn't make it into a recent history book written by a Slovak priest.

PASS THE WHITE-OUT

The Catholic Church, horribly persecuted under the Communist regime, has traditionally had a strong hand in politics in this religious country: the first calls for an independent Slovakia came from a priest (Andrej Hlinka, who put together Slovakia's first powerful political party in 1918), and the Second World War government was led by another priest (Jozef Tiso, who cooperated with the Nazis). More recently, a priest wrote the official Slovak history textbook for schools—and kicked off a huge scandal. *History of Slovakia and the Slovaks*, written by Father Milan Durica, is riddled with errors and thick with whitewashing: he made Tiso's work camps sound like health spas, even praising the fine dentists on hand and their use of gold fillings, and skipping over such facts as that some 65,000 Slovakian Jews perished after being "resettled" to other parts of Europe. Also missing from his happy-go-lucky rendition: that Tiso's government was charging Jews for their transport to death camps. Although the Catholic Church reportedly stood by the book when it was released in 1997, the Jewish community was furious, as were others, though no group was more red-faced than the EU: they had commissioned the book, paying a reported €69,000 (about $90,000) for the historical mistake.[4]

Despite all the challenges, Slovakia appears to be coming into her own. Tourists are finally arriving, and after meeting with Russian President Putin in Bratislava, perhaps President George W. Bush now knows the difference between Slovakia and Slovenia. Well, maybe.

Hot Spots

Bratislava: Okay, so it's not Prague, but the tourist board is sure trying. Mostly built by Hungarians when they moved here en masse to escape the sixteenth-century rule of Turks in their country, the old town surrounding the hilltop castle is very lively, and students who crowd into the bars have plenty of ideas about how to turn Slovakia around, including PR to announce she exists.

Donovaly: Slovaks' fave ski resort.

Banska Bystrica: Made rich by her silver mines, this castle town is still rich with gothic and renaissance architecture.

Rohancska Vahay: Tucked into deeply folded mountains, this area boasts six alpine lakes complete with waterfalls.

Castle Hill in Bratislava: Where
Bush and Putin met

Slovakian border with Hungary: Tension here runs particularly high between Slovaks and Hungarians, who make up about 10 percent of the Slovakian population.

Hotshots

Mikulas Dzurinda: Prime Minister, 1998–present. Who knows how he did it, but earnest Dzurinda definitely wasn't dawdling when he started reforming the place, whipping it into shape, or close enough, to earn an EU invitation for 2004 entry. Although he is of center-right Christian Democrat inclinations himself, he has liberalized the country greatly. Plenty of hurdles lie ahead, including making his people like him. Admired by the international community, Dzurinda was slapped by results from a late 2003 confidence poll: Slovaks gave him an approval rating of—ouch!—a mere 5 percent. By January 2006, he was up to 49 pecent on the approval charts.

Courtesy of the Slovak Republic Government Office

PM Dzurinda: EU loves him, people not so sure

Alexander Dubcek: Head of Czechoslovakian Communist Party, 1968. The reform-minded Communist from the east initiated the Prague Spring in 1968, and the only change he made that stuck was to give Slovakia more autonomy. Died in a 1992 car crash (some suspect foul play), which is tragic, since Dubcek, the most beloved Slovak, might have successfully filled the necessary role of strong, likeable leader.

Ivan Gasparovik: President, 2004–present. The good news: the lawyer is not Meciar, who had been predicted to win the 2004 presidential election. The bad news: since he used to be Meciar's right-hand man, he may turn out to be essentially a Meciar clone. Meciar, however, didn't see it that way when he was defeated that spring; he refused to shake his former mate's hand. No doubt Meciar feels doubly betrayed: not only did Gasparovik win, he defected to SMER, Slovakia's new populist party, which is also the country's most popular.

HISTORICAL HOTSHOT: JOZEF TISO (1887–1947)

Opponent of the 1919 linking of the Czech part of the region with the land held by Slovaks, Monsignor Tiso was quick to convince the Nazis he'd support them if they gave him the keys and granted Slovakia independence from Czechs. Tens of thousands of Slovak Jews were deported from Slovakia during his regime, with Auschwitz as their destination, but the man of the cloth told his people they were bound for a special homeland for Jews. The priest was tried by the Czechoslovak government in 1947, after it had returned to power and pulled Slovakia back into its loop. Tiso was found guilty of treason and collaboration with the Nazis; he was executed by hanging that same year. Some Slovaks still regard him as the true father of their country, since he first put Slovakia on the map without the "Czecho" before it, but others find his memory repulsive. A move to erect a public statue in his likeness in 2000 blew up; thus far the man stands in storage without his pedestal.

News you can read: *Slovak Spectator*, slovakspectator.slc, Slovakia.org

26. SLOVENIA
(Slovenija)
Most Likely to Succeed

FAST FACTS

Country:	Republic of Slovenia; Republika Slovenija
Capital:	Ljubljana
Government:	Parliamentary democracy
Independence:	1991 (from Yugoslavia)
Population:	2,010,000 (2006 estimate)
Head of State:	President Janez Drnovsek (2002)
Head of Government:	Prime Minister Janez Jansa (2004)
Elections:	President elected by popular vote, five-year term; prime minister elected by parliament
Name of Parliament:	National Assembly; Državni Zbor
Ethnicity:	83% Slovene; 2% Croat; 2% Serb; 1% Bosniak; 12% other (2002 census)
Religion:	58% Catholic; 23% unspecified; 10% none; 4% unaffiliated; 2% Orthodox; 2% Muslim; 1 % Christian

Language:	91% Slovenian; 6% Serbo-Croatian; 3% other
Literacy:	99%
Famous Exports:	Strange artists, the Polka King, Laibach
Economic Big Boy:	Petrol (Petrochemical); 2003 revenue: €1.211 billion (about $151 billion)[1]
Per Capita GDP:	$21,000 (2005)
Unemployment:	6.3% (January 2006 Eurostat figure)
EU Status:	Entered May 2004
Currency:	Slovenian tolar
Known for:	Not being Slovakia

Quick Tour

Slovenija—the thickly forested land that spills down from the Alps and snuggles up between Italy, Austria, Croatia, and Hungary—has a little bit of everything: there's skiing in the mountains, hiking in the woods, and plenty of traditional festivals in the villages that spring up between wheat fields and vineyards. The place is crawling with subterranean caves that lead to thermal springs, gorges, and underground rivers filled with strange creatures, and the Adriatic washes her shore. But what is putting Slovenia on the world map in bold colors is capital Ljubljana, where beyond the pretty domed buildings and steeply angled red-tiled roofs lies one of Europe's most creative scenes.

> *Language lesson: In Slovenian,* j *has the sound of a* y—*so the capital is pronounced "lyoo-blya-na."*

SLOVENIA VS. SLOVAKIA

The two Central European countries do have a few things in common besides identical starting letters. Both Slovenia and Slovakia entered the EU and NATO in 2004, and both their languages have the same Slavic roots. Both are very young countries. Slovenia was born in 1991, Slovakia in 1993. Beyond that, Slovenia and Slovakia have as much in common as do España and Estonia—which is to say not much. Slovenia was part of Communist Yugoslavia, which was relatively relaxed and stayed out of the Soviet Union, and Slovenia was always a prosperous state—the richest of Yugoslavia—and usually got on well with the neighbors. Slovakia, on the other hand, was one half of the former Czechoslovakia, a Soviet satellite that suffered harsh Moscow-dictated Communism. Highly agricultural, Slovakia is still relatively poor and has plenty of problems, including relations with neighboring Austria and Hungary. Slovenia, with a stable government, strong economy, and low unemployment, was the ideal candidate for EU admission; Slovakia, with her wavering government, iffy economy, and high unemployment rate, was a big EU gamble.

Easy on the eye, Slovenia has an international identity problem. Chronically confused with Slovakia, Slovenia has for centuries been plenty hard to find on the map. Prior to 1991, the country didn't exist. Part of Yugoslavia (1945–1991), before that (1918–1945), she finished last in the Kingdom of Serbs, Croats, and Slovenes. Before that, everyone from Austrians to Romans, Germans to Turks, and Venetians to Hungarians called Slovenia their territory. That's the price Slovenia paid for being a resource-rich land straddling the Adriatic and the Alps, the Balkans and the West. For most of her existence she was dragged off with the neighborhood toughs.

THE BALKANS VS. YUGOSLAVIA VS. SLOVENIA

Slovenes cringe when their country is referred to as one of the Balkans, which geographically is debatable: she lies at the northwestern edge of the Balkan peninsula, which swells between the Adriatic and Black seas and contains Greece, Albania, Macedonia, Romania, and Bulgaria as well as the other countries of the former Yugoslavia. Mellow Slovenes never had much in common with fellow Yugoslavs, except for language similarities: geographically, Slovenia is closer to Venice than to Belgrade or Sarajevo. Nevertheless, along with the other five republics in the former Yugoslavia, she was governed by Communist Josip Broz Tito, who kept her bound to Yugoslavia even if she didn't really fit in.

Independent from Yugoslavia since 1991—and escaping that country's civil war—Slovenia is the shining star of the new EU. Her economy is stable and taking off, and she'll adopt the euro in 2007. Overnight one of Europe's most popular holiday destinations, Slovenia is the wealthiest of new EU countries, and by every measuring stick the healthiest. With few historical hang-ups, a well-oiled economic machine, and a contented society, technologically savvy Slovenia is the most likely to soar. Here creativity is regarded as a national treasure: after all, Slovenia's creative types, by pushing the envelope, pushed open the doors to independence.

ARTY SLOVENIA

Ljubljana is awash with art, artists, and politically driven art collectives, such as Alkatraz—a former army barracks converted into a village of artists' studios, galleries, newspaper offices, and performance spaces. Here science meets creativity with, say, twirling robotized bugs programmed with electrical neural-like systems that respond to touch, or multimedia installations broadcasting the dangers of the media and advertising the crassness of commercialization.[2] The Slovenian art scene is supported by the national government, which spends nearly 1 percent of GDP on the arts, commissioning and subsidizing projects and even sending artists to New York and across Europe to open their exhibitions—one indication of how much the country embraces those types who splash colors and sculpt words. Another show: nineteenth-century poet France Preseren and twentieth-century architect Joze Plecnik adorn Slovenian paper money.

History Review

Lassoed to the Austrian Empire since the fourteenth century, Slovenia made a geographical departure when that German-speaking kingdom was shattered after the First World War.

> Napoleon conquered this area, calling it the Illyrian Provinces, and planned to run it as a naval base on the Adriatic. Even after she was returned to the Austrian Empire, Slovenia continued many of the practices Napoleon initiated, including free schools for the masses.

Hoping they'd have more in common with groups who spoke similar languages, in 1920 Slovenians sign up in a new country with Serbs and Croats. In name alone, the Kingdom of Serbs, Croats, and Slovenes illustrated the power structure in the newly mapped land, and the groups' enthusiasm about being part of it. Even the Slovenian language—different from Serbo-Croat—wasn't officially recognized, and Slovenes were seen as third-class citizens in the country ruled by a Serbian king. Some Slovenes wanted to secede from the start, but a small country is a vulnerable country, and by the time the Second World War broke out it was too late: their land was seized first by Fascist Italy, then by the Nazis, with tens of thousands of Slovenes deported to concentration camps. Leading the resistance movement that rose up to lash back at the Fascists was locksmith-turned-military man Josip Broz Tito; after the war ended, he nailed the former kingdom of Serbs, Croats, and Slovenes back together again (with a few additions) as the Socialist Federal Republic of Yugoslavia, which he ruled first as prime minister, then as "president for life." An avowed Communist, he nevertheless disliked Stalin and kept Moscow at arm's length.

ISTRIAN PENINSULA

The toe of land dangling off Slovenia's southwest and dipping into the bay of Venice is heartbreakingly beautiful, which is why this land and her many nearby islands have been fought over for centuries, being snatched by Austrians, Venetians, and Napoleon. Now divided into Slovenian, Italian, and Croatian sections, all of Istria was claimed by Italy after the First World War. In 1946, Tito annexed part of the area, driving out 300,000 Italians and killing 20,000 more in his anti-Fascist sweeps. During the postwar years there was so much hatred between Italians and Slovenians in the border city of Nova Gorica (known as Gorizia on the Italian side) that a wall was erected cutting right through it. Part of the divider came down in 2004, when Slovenia entered the EU, but resentment still lingers on both sides. Ongoing issue: the return of houses to Italians who fled after the Second World War.

Yugoslavia, or the Socialist Federal Republic of Yugoslavia as she was formally known, was a real mix: under Tito she pulled together six republics, three religions, two alphabets, and a dozen ethnic minorities. There wasn't much chance to break from the country when Tito was alive—while the dictator looked warm and cuddly compared to Stalin, he nevertheless ruled with an iron fist and the frequent help of his secret police. He wasn't about to bid farewell to resource-laden Slovenia, Yugoslavia's industrial motor: with 8 percent of Yugoslavia's population, Slovenia contributed 20 percent of the country's national income. After he died in 1980, the Communist machine likewise kept wealthy Slovenia locked in its hold, although dissent was simmering. Calls for autonomy grew into a movement for independence, which the Yugoslav government successfully resisted. Until, that is, a group of smart-aleck Slovenes hacked away at their handcuffs in an innovative way: by mocking the Communist machine.

YANKING THE CHAINS[3]

Shortly after Marshal Josip Tito finally loosened his thirty-five-year-long grasp on Yugoslavia by dying, a group of young Slovenes in tiny mining town Trbovlje devised a powerful way to illustrate the absurdity of living under Communism. Instead of protesting, they parodied the totalitarian system, saying it just wasn't totalitarian enough. Called *Neuer Kollektivismus* (New Collectivism), the group began their subversive attack with art that captured nationalistic leadership in its absurdity. In 1987, NK entered a prestigious Yugoslavian poster contest—a serious annual competition for a design to commemorate National Youth Day. NK's submission: an old Nazi poster of a patriotic-looking youth—with the Yugoslav flag waving where the swastika used to be. Their submission won, and the judges lavished praise on the design for "expressing the highest ideals of the Yugoslav State." Just before the poster was to be plastered across the country, its Fascist origins were revealed. The government was so horrified that Youth Day—one of the most important holidays of the Tito era—was quickly erased from the calendar and never celebrated again. Taking advantage of "the Poster Affair," NK formed a band. Well, sort of—it was more a politicized, musical, experimental theater group with an industrial beat. Taking the German name for Ljubljana—Laibach (a pointedly sensitive move considering Slovenia was Nazi-occupied in WWII and Tito hated Fascists)—the four-man group goose-stepped across the stage in black uniforms and blasted speeches from Tito, Mussolini, and Hitler mixed with covers of "Let It Be" and "Maggie May" with their lyrics barked like orders. Censors quickly shut down Laibach's performances and banned NK's art shows, which made the group so infamous—a TV commentator implored the public to kill them—that even out-of-touch peasants knew who they were and the grave threat that they posed. Laibach moved to Ljubljana, where they continued pushing the censors' buttons by staging art shows of political posters calling for the death of political posters (while distributing propaganda about the propaganda machine), which infuriated the government more. Tens of thousands poured in to see their edgy exhibits and performances. The controversial group was charged with disseminating propaganda; the charges were dismissed, and, realizing that the more they condemned NK and Laibach the more power they gave them, the Slovenian censorship board gave up and let them do pretty much whatever they wished. With the general lifting of censorship, the whole country opened up, and calls for independence grew louder.

With Slovenian censorship turned on its ear, the media became more brazen. In spring 1998, so many politically provocative publications were flying around, and there was such a new spark of discussion and hope in the air, that the season was dubbed "Slovenian Spring"—although the Yugoslavian national government wasn't as open as the Slovenian state government. When a Slovenian magazine devoted an entire issue to the idea of an independent Slovenia, the national government became apoplectic as it debated how to fight against this new Slovenian "secret war." Another publication went further. *Mladina*, formerly the propagandistic magazine for Socialist youth, suddenly turned into a Slovenian version of magazines like *Spy*. Part investigative, part humor, the ballsy publication began targeting the national government in general and skewering Defense Minister Branko Mamula in particular. Publicizing his arms sales to Libya and famine-ridden Ethiopia—for which Mamula was dubbed a "salesman of death"—*Mladina* humiliated him further describing how the defense minister had used Yugoslav soldiers as slaves to build his grand villa on the Adriatic coast.

The article didn't play well: Mamula was forced to resign, and the military decided the magazine's writers should pay. Further infuriating the military, one of

Mladina's star journalists, Janez Jansa, got his hands on a document showing that federal Yugoslavia was planning to militarily suppress Slovenia's move toward independence. In 1988, Jansa, along with another *Mladina* journalist, the editor in chief, and the soldier who had leaked the information, was hauled off to a military trial. The trial of the "Ljubljana Four" was so serious that it was closed to the public and the media, and was conducted in Serbo-Croat. Its effect was to solidify the independence movement.

Of all the writers, Jansa was targeted most fiercely, and the public rallied around the twenty-nine-year-old, demanding he be found innocent. When Jansa, along with the other journalist and the army man, was found guilty and sentenced to prison, Slovenians erupted in anger and demanded independence in demonstrations of 30,000 and more. Petitions were signed, more articles written, the Slovenian legislature passed laws affirming the right to determine Slovenia's future, and Slovenia held her first multiparty elections, which pro-independence parties won. After a few weeks in prison, the writers and the army man were released. In December 1990, Slovenians voted in a referendum about whether their country should break away from Yugoslavia and become her own sovereign state; 88 percent voted yes.

In 1991, Slovenes took over manning their borders, and the Slovenian government declared Slovenia independent. The Yugoslav armed forces briefly disagreed, showering Ljubljana with bombs from above and then

Courtesy of Social Democratic Party of Slovenia

Janez Jansa: Left-wing journalist turned right-wing populist

marching in. Sixty-six died in the resulting ten-day War of Independence, but Slovenian leader Drnovsek, voted in to continue running the country after independence, quickly negotiated their (generally) peaceful retreat.

> "For more than a thousand years we were waiting to have our own independence, and we have had it now for ten years. People see it as very precious." —Ernest Petric, Slovenian representative to the United Nations[3]

The Slovenian departure from Yugoslavia first inspired Croatia, then Bosnia, to try the same, and before long, the secessionist mood and Serbia's attempt at domination had kicked off an ugly Balkan war. Slovenia didn't enter into the fighting, which never crossed over her borders, although plenty of fleeing Yugoslavs did.

The United States blamed Germany for helping to spark off the Bosnian War. Why? Germany was quick to recognize Slovenia's 1991 independence, which inspired Croatia and Bosnia to secede from Yugoslavia. The U.S. didn't recognize Slovenia as a sovereign state until 1992, much to Slovenian chagrin.

Slovenia could afford to secede: oil, steel, iron, coal, and mercury are but a few of her natural treasures, and agriculturally she can hold her own. The country also has a fine wine industry, harking back millennia to the days when she was run by the Romans. Nevertheless, the post-independence economy initially went into shock after losing Yugoslav markets, but Slovenia gracefully changed gears. Western Europe quickly picked up the slack, buying two-thirds of Slovenia's exports; many Slovenian workers became co-owners of the firms that employed them under Communism. The computer industry boomed; over 200 software companies operate in Slovenia, and Ljubljana, with her university population of 35,000, has plenty of young, educated entrepreneurs.

There have been a few snags in recent years as well. Janez Jansa, who was rabidly antimilitary as a reporter, was appointed the country's first minister of defense and became a power-crazed arms nut. He was booted out as defense minister in 1994, amid allegations of roughing up citizens, tapping phones, and tailing journalists. A first bid for NATO membership was rejected in 1997, causing such a furor that the foreign minister was forced to resign. (Slovenia joined NATO in 2002, but to do so she had to change her maritime law that had prevented nuclear-powered vessels from traveling through Slovenian waters.) Slovenia's initial stab at entering the EU was blocked in 1996 by Italy, which was still furious about the status of Italians' homes in the Slovenian part of Istria. And the status of the "erased"—those 130,000 refugees who came to newly independent Slovenia to avoid Slobodan Milosevic's ethnic cleansing—is still an issue hanging heavy in the air. In 2004, Slovenes—led by Janez Jansa, who by then had gone very right-wing—voted against giving the erased Slovenians citizenship, a question mark on Slovenia's generally shining record.

Despite his political yo-yo-ing, Jansa is still hugely popular: he was elected prime minister in 2005.

NEIGHBORLY RELATIONS

Slovenes generally get on well with the neighbors, although there is occasional squawking. Austria, which once lorded over the area, is now a major trading partner, but there's friction in southern Carinthia, where Slovenes are the majority of the population and want the government to put up street signs in Slovenian too—an issue which makes right-wing nationalist leader Jörg Haider, governor of those parts, go ballistic. Relations with Croats, with whom Slovenes always had more in common than with Serbs, are sometimes problematic and tinged with competition: they get into territorial pissing matches over fishing waters, which are poorly defined between the two countries. Italians are huge supporters of the local tourism industry, and dealings with sometimes-prickly Hungary are generally smooth.

> *Future issue: Slovenia co-owns a nuclear power plant with Croatia. Built in the 1980s, the plant is located in Krsko, Slovenia, but Croatia is responsible for dealing with the radioactive wastes. Lately Croatia has been grumbling loudly about the arrangement.*

Hot Spots

Ljubljana: Many hadn't heard of the Slovenian capital before U.S. president George W. Bush and Russian president Vladimir Putin met here to discuss arms in June 2001, and most still can't spell it, but this beautiful capital shines with culture and is a magnet for those searching for neo-bohemia. Some liken it

Courtesy of Ljubljana Tourism Board

Artist haven Ljubljana: Tourists can now find it

to Paris of the 1920s, Prague in the 1980s, or Seattle in the 1990s. Just don't start a chain restaurant or buy up their land.

Italian border: Italians flood into the region of Istria at weekends, drawn by the casinos and the prostitutes. The bridge between Italy and the Balkans, this boundary is crossed by smugglers carrying everything from tobacco to slaves.

Piran Bay: Croat and Slovene fishermen sometimes snipe at each other in this disputed zone, Slovenia's only maritime access to the Adriatic Sea.

Bohinj: Slovenia may be a thoroughly modern and Internet-connected country, but they still celebrate the *Kravji Bal* (Cow's Ball), a festive, old-time bash in the alpine meadows, that marks the annual change of cattle pastures.[4]

Hotshots

Janez Drnovsek: Prime Minister, 1992–2002; President, 2002–present. He's been leading Slovenia since the 1980s. Never a hard-core comrade—he was said to cut out of Communist policy meetings to head to the slopes—the economist is a well-traveled polyglot who got Slovenia into the clubs that matter. Definitely a left-leaning humanist, he demanded that Western leaders apologize to Muslims over Denmark's cartoon controversy, and he was so upset about the crisis in Darfur that he signed Slovenia up to fund housing for 10,000 refugees.

Janez Jansa: Defense Minister, 1990–1994; Prime Minister, 2005–present. Parliamentarian and leader of Social Democrat Party; his investigative reporting about Yugoslavia's defense minister—and the trial that followed—spurred Slovenia to independence. As defense minister himself, Jansa was accused of illegal arms sales, using his position for political influence, tailing journalists, and being linked to nefarious activities. Jansa turned ultraconservative after he stepped up as leader of the Social Democrats in the mid-1990s and introduced legislation barring citizenship for refugees. Definitely has a fan club.

Josip Broz Tito (1892–1980): Yugoslavia Prime Minister, 1945 onward; President for life, 1953–1980. Tito went down as the world's most beloved dictator: he reduced ethnic tensions to a dull roar and kept Yugoslavia out of the Soviet Union. His dislike of Stalin was good for Yugoslavia's economic health, since the Communist country was forced to trade in Western markets. Tito also unleashed his secret police, carted political prisoners off to an Adriatic island, and gagged the press. Some still mourn his 1980 death.

Laibach: Musical offshoot of artists' collective Neue Slowenische Kunst (NSK)/Neuer Kollektivismus (NK), they helped kick-start independence with their totalitarian-swiping industrial band. Though they're now targeting NATO and the EU, they played a concert at the EU Accession festivities in Dublin, and they are so respected that even the official website of the Slovenian government describes Laibach as "absolutely pivotal in the field of music." Propelled to cult status, they gig everywhere these days.

> *Laibach also formed its own republic—complete with real passports. The documents reportedly work, and those friends of Laibach with the VIP versions are said to have received VIP treatment from passport controllers who aren't quite sure just where the country is.*

Other creative hotshots: Architect Joze Plecnik (1872–1957) left his unique mark and mix of styles on Ljubljana, Vienna, and Prague. Besides the Alkatraz bunch and architect-sculptor Marjetica Potrč—who had a solo show at New York City's Guggenheim—another big name is Irwin, a collective of anonymous artists. In theater, the playwright Ivan Cankar is most influential, but let us not forget perhaps the world's most famous Slovenian-American, the late Frankie Yankovic, best known for his fancy footwork as "the Polka King."

CREATIVE STANDOUT

Of all the Slovenes who ever picked up a pen (or quill as the case may be), none is more revered than France Preseren (1800–1849), whose lyric poems held high lofty ideals, and were often quoted during the independence struggle. Writing in the mid-1800s, when nationalism was on the rise and Austria was trying to suppress all non-German languages, he used poetry as a vehicle for politics, demanding freedom and more rights for the Slovenian people. Like Laibach, he raised the censors' hackles; one collection was withdrawn from sale in 1847. Like Laibach, censorship only made him more famous; his works were published in a newspaper the following year. His words have been quoted in Slovenians' most trying times, including during the "Slovenian Spring." In 1989, his poem "Zdraylijica" ("The Toast") was set to music as the country's national anthem.

The Toast
God's blessings on all nations,
Who long and work for that bright day,
When o'er earth's habitations
No war, no strife shall hold sway;
Who long to see
That all men free
No more shall foes, but neighbors be.[5]

News you can understand: *Slovenian News,* http://slonews.sta.si

27. CYPRUS

(Kýpros)

Adding Division

FAST FACTS

Country: Republic of Cyprus (aka Greek Cyprus); The Turkish Republic of Northern Cyprus (aka Turkish Cyprus) only recognized by Turkey

Capital: Nicosia (divided between Republic of Cyprus and TRNC)

Government: Republic

Independence: August 16, 1960 (from United Kingdom); TRNC formed separate "republic" in 1983

Population: 784,000 (2006, including about 170,000 in TRNC)

Head of State and Head of Government: President Tassos Papadopoulos (2003); TRNC: President Mehmet Ali Talat

Elections: President elected by popular vote for five-year term

Name of Parliament: House of Representatives/Vouli Antiprosopon; TRNC: Assembly

Ethnicity:	77% Greek; 18% Turkish; 5% other
Religion:	78% Greek Orthodox; 18% Muslim; 4% other (2004 estimate)
Language:	Greek, English, Turkish
Literacy:	99% male, 97% female (2003 estimate)
Famous Exports:	Lace, wine, political headaches
Per Capita GDP:	Greek Cyprus: $21,600 (2005); TRNC: $7,200 (2004)
Unemployment:	5.3% (2005 Eurostat figure, Republic of Cyprus)
EU Status:	Member since 2004
Currency:	Cypriot pound; Turkish lira

Quick Tour

A rocky outpost of jagged mountains surrounded by crystal waters, enticing Kýpros beckoned everybody who set an eye on her in the last 9,000 years to come on over. Cleopatra and Alexander the Great, Phoenicians and Persians, Greek and Romans, Crusaders and Turkish Ottomans are but a few who claimed this island adored for her beauty and valued for her strategic location. And they all left their architectural touches from ancient Roman villas to Venetian city walls, and from knights' fortresses to miniature churches thick with Greek frescoes.

YOU CALL THIS EUROPE?

Much fought-over Cyprus is puny—about half the size of Connecticut—and it's rather a stretch to even call her part of Europe. Given that she lazes in the very northeast corner of the Mediterranean—a mere forty-seven miles from Turkey and sixty miles from Syria—she's much closer to the Middle East, and has long been considered part of Asia. So how did far-flung Cyprus, a problematic and divided island, become part of Europe and get into the European Union in 2004? Greece insisted on it, threatening to veto nominations for all the other new EU countries if Cyprus wasn't on the list.

Cyprus is literally layered with history: ancient amphitheaters rise up along lavish Orthodox churches, Apollonian temples nudge medieval monasteries, Crusader castles stand guard over citrus groves, slender minarets peer over hills blanketed in vineyards, and mosaic masterpieces glisten in the sun against a backdrop of deep blue sea.

> Legend holds that love goddess Aphrodite washed up in seafoam, spreading cheeriness and amour across the island as she flitted through woods and plunged into cool pools, with laughing Adonis (and hundreds of others) hot on her trail. It's fitting to recall that Cyprus was also stomping ground of battle-prone Greek god Ares.

The striking contrasts are obvious in more than her relics: in winter you can ski atop Mount Olympus, and then sun at the beach. Urban tensions in the capital city are forgotten in tiny mountain villages, where wine is served straight from the barrel and the mule serves as transportation. In the midst of the flower festival, the medieval festival, or the kataklysmo flood festival—when cities erupt in rollicking water wars—you'd never know there's ever been the slightest turmoil on this island, and that blood soaked this land. If you can ignore the barbed-wire fences that divide the capital, or fail to notice the tens of thousands of troops on patrol, then you can happily sit in a taverna sipping the retsina with a hint of pine and delving into plates of tender lamb. Lapped by cobalt waters, Cyprus is a festive land of folk dances and boisterous wine festivals, where you can lounge at seaside resorts, explore medieval villages, scuba dive in Coral Bay, or hunt for turtles, and it can all appear utterly peaceful if you stay crocked and keep your eyes and mouth shut.

> Cyprus is so steeped in the past that developers, farmers, and archaeologists turn up lost cities and palaces every few years. The Cyprus tourist board claims that the missing continent of Atlantis might be lodged under the island—yet another draw to the "the island of love."

But the truth is that fun-filled vacation getaway Cyprus is patrolled by some 50,000 troops (from Turkey, Greece, and the UN), making her the most militarized place on the planet—outside of the line that divides North and South Korea. When you peel away the travel posters and postcard images, Cyprus is a fractured mess—geographically split, ethnically divided, economically unbalanced, and politically separated. Not that you can tell that from looking at an atlas: on maps, the island in the very eastern Mediterranean appears to be one country. But look more closely and you can see the 110-mile UN buffer zone—the Green Line—that runs through capital Nicosia and cleaves the island, creating two Cypruses that pretty much hate each other's guts.

Tranquil Kyrenia Harbor: Is Atlantis hiding underneath?

CYPRUS: THE SPLIT

The southern two-thirds of Cyprus—Greek Cyprus—holds ethnic Greeks, the northern third—Turkish Cyprus—holds ethnic Turks, and the two regions now run as separate countries, with separate governments and little overlap in economies. One hitch: nobody recognizes Turkish Cyprus as a legitimate country—except Turkey, which makes sense since Turkey had a major hand in creating her. The conflict that has raged here for decades has brought a strange division into Europe: even though the whole island theoretically came into the European Union in 2004, only the Greek part is practically in it: only Greek Cyprus can officially trade with the EU and access most EU funding—the two biggest draws for joining that club; only residents of Greek Cyprus can travel freely in Europe as EU citizens. And while the Greek part of Cyprus is growing relatively wealthy, with per capita incomes of $21,000, Turkish Cyprus remains undeveloped and poor, with per capita incomes of $7,000 a year. And Cyprus is now the only country in the world where the capital is divided.

You can blame Cyprus's division on geography—her location in the far East Mediterranean makes the island a strategic military post. Blame it on British control freaks who, back when Cyprus was a British colony, refused the islanders' wishes and foisted their own plan on them; blame it on the U.S., Russia, and Israel, who profit from selling arms. Blame it on the hysterical grudge between Greeks and Turks, which goes back for centuries. And blame it on

Cypriots themselves for not seeing how their chains were being yanked historically, and for being stubborn mules in solving the problems today. Or simply
blame it on the human tendency to turn disagreements and power struggles
into battles and massacres, and grudges into wars. But despite numerous attempts to glue the island back together again since 1974—when Turkey invaded the island to stomp out a Greece-sponsored coup—the split remains.
Neither part of the island thinks the other one is legit—and the international
community persists in recognizing only one Cyprus, the Greek one.

THE CYPRIOT SOAP OPERA: MEET THE CAST

Greeks and Turks had managed to live together on Cyprus for centuries—
albeit not always happily—but the events of the last fifty years really ripped the
island apart. What triggered that division: outside forces—namely Greece,
Turkey, Britain, and the U.S.—just couldn't keep their fingers out of the Cypriot
pot, which they've continuously stirred and heated up until it reached a furious
boil that spread across the island in a violent wrath.

In this soap opera, the players include:

Greek Cyprus aka the Republic of Cyprus: The tourist honeypot and the
only Cypriot government that's internationally recognized, Greek Cyprus is relatively wealthy, organized, and happy to keep Turkish Cyprus out of the EU;
Greek Cypriots (who regard one-third of their island as occupied by Turkish
Cypriots) are often downright haughty—and led by a president apparently determined to prevent reunion. Some 12,000 Greek troops are deployed here; in
the south, two British military bases are now their own sovereign countries.

Turkish Cyprus aka the Turkish Republic of Northern Cyprus (TRNC):
The Turkish Cypriot leader stormed out of the newly created government in
1963 and never came back. Turkish Cypriots were shoved north when Turkey
invaded in 1974, and in 1983, T-Cypriot leaders declared the north an independent sovereign country. Recognized solely by Turkey, she's ostracized, abandoned, and derided by Greek Cypriots as a "pseudo-state" with her own
"president" and "prime minister." Also a haven for criminals and base for 30,000
Turkish troops. Greek Cypriots are ticked that with 18 percent of the population,
Turkish Cypriots control over a third of the Island, and say Turks have damaged
many historical sites. Turkish Cypriots are ticked that now Greek Cypriots won't
let them back into the government.

Greece: Never mind that her enemy Turkey is physically closer: Greece,
which ruled Cyprus in ancient times, planted the seeds for today's problems in
the 1950s (and before) by inviting Cyprus (with her ethnic Greek majority) to
join up with Greece—a nationalistic notion that also would have allowed
Greece to expand her hold on the Mediterranean and establish military posts
close to Turkey. Blocked in the attempt, Greece sent in guerrilla fighters—and

later supported a 1974 coup to lasso Cyprus, which led to the island being divided.

Turkey: The defunct Turkish Ottoman Empire ruled this island for the better part of 300 years, but the Brits (who took over in the nineteenth century) ensured they were never fully out of the picture. Turkey, along with Turkish Cypriots, was violently opposed to the Greek Cypriot wish to join Greece: Turkey lobbied the Brits, who blocked that union. Turkey almost invaded a few times: when Greece sponsored a coup on Cyprus in 1974, Turkey sent in her armed forces and split the island.

Britain: Britain, which ran Cyprus as a colony from 1925 until 1960, refused to let Cyprus unite with Greece (because Brits would have risked their dominance in the Mediterranean and because they need Turkey's aid as a NATO partner) and created Turkish guerrilla groups to battle Greek Cypriot guerrilla groups. Cyprus is alarmingly dysfunctional because most Cypriots never wanted the independence that the British foisted upon them.

U.S.: Arms, anyone?

The most recent attempt to shove the country together as one was a hard-peddled UN peace plan—called the Annan Plan—which aimed to remap the island, rearrange people, and, most importantly, bring the two governments back together in one confederation. In April 2004, just before Cyprus entered the EU, Greek Cypriots in the south and Turkish Cypriots in the north were asked in separate votes whether they would accept the Annan Plan to reunite Cypriots. The Turkish north—which wanted the benefits of EU membership—voted yes, overwhelmingly. The Greek south—which did not want to share EU funds with Turkish Cypriots—voted no, overwhelmingly. Thus, the island stayed divided. When Cyprus came into the EU, the Turkish north was locked out. (However, the international community was so hacked off at the Greek Cypriots that the U.S. lifted a trade restriction on Turkish Cyprus, and special EU funding is going to the north.) And that's only one illustration of the tension that lingers on this island where time does not heal wounds. This Siamese twin of a country is the problem child of the EU, bringing drama and confusion not witnessed anywhere else in today's European Union. Until reunification, the northern third of Cyprus remains pretty much out in the cold.

History Review

The Greeks who settled on Cyprus back in 333 BC did more than introduce pagan gods, mosaic-covered walls, and statue-lined temples to the island of peaceful bays, dusty mountains, and cypress trees. They also introduced the bloodline that is still the most dominant on Cyprus; for all of the island's existence since, most

Cypriots have been ethnically Greek and have spoken the Greek language. Romans ejected ancient Greeks in AD 58, but the Greeks' descendants saw a flurry of governments as everyone from Byzantines, Franks, and Venetians to Richard the Lionheart and the Knights Templar took turns running the place.

> Richard the Lionheart, on his way to the Crusades, conquered the island in 1191, quickly taking a bride. His honeymoon wasn't blissful. Villagers killed his prized hawks, so he knocked down a few villages in response,[1] then hastily left, handing the island to the Knights Templar, whose pigheaded rule made them hated: they'd barely unpacked their bags when the Cypriot masses revolted, driving them out in 1192.

Besides the ancient Greeks, the most influential group ever to shore up were Ottoman Turks, who conquered Cyprus in 1571. In some ways extraordinarily advanced, the Muslim rulers tolerated the religions of whatever lands they took, and recognized the church's highest leaders as shepherds of the local flock.

> By acknowledging the Eastern Orthodox Church, which was then losing power, the Ottomans established it as the powerful leading religion of Cyprus—and also relegitimized the Church internationally.

There was a price to pay, literally, for the Ottomans' religious tolerance: non-Muslims paid high taxes, and the taxes soared during the three centuries of Ottoman rule, while the actual level of tolerance plummeted. Some Christians converted to Islam to avoid the annual dues; some dressed as Muslims by day, but practiced as Christians by night. Those who didn't convert struggled to pay the taxman, who began using any method necessary to extract payment. Violence, desecration of churches, and rape became increasingly common, and by the 1800s the situation was intolerable. Greece fought off the Ottomans and won independence in 1829—and even back then some Cypriots longed to join up with Greece.

Russia inadvertently brought freedom for Cyprus. As a result of losing a war to Russia in 1878, the Ottoman Empire had to give up most of her territories. Not wanting Russia to gain a foothold in the Mediterranean, Brits pushed in and ended up controlling the island, with a nod from the Ottoman Empire, which retained background power—and most Turks who had lived on Cyprus simply stayed. Cyprus in the eastern Mediterranean was a fetching complement to another British colony, Gibraltar in the western Mediterranean; together, they gave the British navy dominance over the entire sea.

*   *   *

When the Ottoman Empire fell in 1925, Britain took complete control of the island—and many Turks remained, making up about one-sixth of the population. The British presence kicked off an independence movement and guerrilla war: many Greek Cypriots wanted enosis—to become part of Greece—and militants wanted Brits off their island, even if it required shipping them off as corpses.

By the end of World War II, the signs were everywhere: across the island, posters demanded "Enosis, and only enosis!" The Greek Orthodox Church, headed by Archbishop Makarios in Cyprus, loudly supported the enosis idea, and priests passed out petitions, which were duly signed by the devout. The Church organized a referendum: most Cypriots voted yes on unifying with Greece. In 1954, Greece asked the United Nations General Assembly to endorse the union of Cyprus with Greece. After Turks and British had weighed in on the matter, the UN decided not to take a formal stand. At that news, Cypriots blew up, calling a general strike. Britain responded by essentially banning the idea, threatening that supporters could be jailed for five years, and in 1956 deporting Archbishop Makarios, while sending in 40,000 troops. But still most Brits on Cyprus didn't grasp how the grassroots enosis movement was snowballing.

The enosis movement was not homegrown. Most Cypriots knew little about Greece, and seemed blissfully ignorant of the poverty in the Hellenic state that was usually run by a dictator. The calls to join Greece—and re-create the ancient Greek Empire—were actually planted and orchestrated by Greece, which also shipped over guerrillas to help the cause. Greece's Radio Athens (picked up on Cyprus) blared propaganda extolling the joys of being back together, but Greece's motives were as much militaristic as nationalistic. Greece wanted a foot in the waters off Turkey, long their mortal enemy. Manipulated by powers in Athens, Cypriots saw reunion with Greece as a step into the great promised land.

The British who taught in Cypriot schools—including writer Lawrence Durrell—laughed off the proenosis petitions their pupils passed out. Few took note of the increasingly passionate masses given by Archbishop Makarios. So on April 1, 1955, Brits were shocked when the typically sleepy island erupted in violence. Granted, the bombs that exploded a police station mailbox and a radio station were crude; the enosis flyers that blew down the streets were almost comical, having been signed by Dighenic, the Cypriot mythological superhero who could bound across whole islands. Some Brits brushed off that first attack as an isolated incident. It wasn't.

EOKA: THE FIGHT FOR UNION

In the mid-1950s, Greece shipped over her WWII resistance hero Colonel George Grivas, a former guerrilla leader. His goal: to cause enosis through civil uprising. His method: molding minds through EOKA, or the National Organization of Cypriot Fighters. Grivas recruited from schools where the entire student body frequently signed up with the secret society. At first, EOKA members peacefully collected signatures on petitions and attended rallies. But by summer 1955 they began attacking Brits, Turkish Cypriots, and Greek Cypriots who didn't support enosis. Twelve-year-old girls assaulted police with soda bottles; groups of laughing boys on bikes tossed bombs into crowds; students beat up teachers believed to be against union with Greece. The flags of EOKA and Greece soon fluttered over schools; Brits demanded they be taken down. Petrified, the school board instead shut down the schools, and thousands of school kids followed Grivas, the pied piper of EOKA, into the woods, where the group ran paramilitary training camps. EOKA had secret members everywhere—at newspapers, in the government. And EOKA's attacks over the next four years became bloodier. EOKA torched Turkish Cypriots' homes and ran Turks out of Greek Cypriot villages. Murders were everyday events: a British officer was shot down in downtown Nicosia while holding his toddler's hand, Turkish Cypriot women and children were slaughtered, Greek Cypriots who didn't make enosis their life cause had their work places bombed. Nicosia's main drag, Ledra Street, was so frequently coated in blood that it was dubbed "Murder Mile."

The British refused to bow to terrorism. Instead, they created more by helping Turkish Cypriots form a Turkish resistance/guerrilla fighter group. Headed by Rauf Denktash, TMT (Türk Mukauemet Teskilati) was every bit as brutal as EOKA—and more violence was the result.

Nearly 80 percent of Cypriots wanted to unite with Greece, but nearly 20 percent did not—the Turkish Cypriots, who feared living in an even more Hellenized state, preferred *taksim*, a partitioned island with Brits running the place. Turkey, like Greece a new NATO member, was adamant. Turkey didn't want Greece in the backyard at all. Assessing the options—allow Cyprus to be united with Greece (a move that would infuriate Turkish Cypriots and Turkey), or divide the island and keep her as a crown colony (which would infuriate Greek Cypriots)—the British authorities came up with a daft solution: make Cyprus free. Colonies worldwide were crying out for freedom, but Cyprus had to be forced to declare herself an independent country. Predictably, Britain was allowed to keep two military bases on the island as part of the deal. And enosis with Greece was outlawed.

* * *

On August 16, 1960, Cyprus dejectedly proclaimed independence. Archbishop Makarios became president and Turkish Cypriot Rauf Denktash became VP as part of an elaborate power-sharing agreement. In 1963, President Makarios killed Turkish Cypriots' veto power. Infuriated, Denktash led Turkish Cypriots out of government. Turkish Cypriots haven't had a say in the running of the republic of Cyprus since.

EOKA attacked a Turkish Cypriot village in 1964, massacring dozens, and Turkey nearly sent in her air force. President Lyndon Johnson talked Turkey out of striking, threatening to stop providing Turkey with arms if she attacked. UN peacekeepers came in, but violence continued—in fact, thanks to Greece, it grew worse. In 1974, Greece was being run by an unpopular military junta. Trying to gain popular support by hitting the enosis chord, the junta backed a coup in Cyprus to forcefully unite Cyprus with Greece. EOKA briefly took over the government, and 3,000 Cypriots died in a bloody rampage. Five days later, 30,000 Turkish troops dropped out of the skies and marched in from the coast to stomp out the coup and avenge previous atrocities. Turkish soldiers ran nearly 200,000 Greek Cypriots out of the north, killing some 5,000. The Turks pushed all Turkish Cypriots to the north, and Turkish forces occupied the area, splitting the island into two ethnic parts. The fragmentation endures. Until 2003, neither group could cross the Green Line into the other section. Now, Greek Cypriots can enter Turkish Cyprus for day trips—and vice versa—but the two societies remain estranged.

In 2003, when both governments lifted the ban on crossing the Green Line, a total of 17,000 from both sides made the trip in the first three days.

In this land, where the common language appears to be disagreement, more and more Cypriots agree on one thing: they are sick of the schizophrenic lifestyle. Who knows when both sides will agree to a unification plan? But the sooner the better: this island is an overarmed powder keg, just waiting for another spark.

Hot Spots

Pafos: The famous Greek Cyprus harbor isn't the biggest draw: the region's real riches lay in her hinterland. Nea Pafos holds a treasure trove of Roman mosaics, discovered when a farmer plowed over them in 1962; and beyond medieval churches you'll find Petra Tou Romiou, legendary birthplace of Aphrodite.

Aphrodite's Love Rock: Temples to Aphrodite are scattered across Cyprus (and the Mediterranean), but the huge black rock found not far from Pafos must have been supercharged. Excavated in the 1950s, it revealed the existence of a love cult who had moved there and dedicated their lives to the goddess, imitating her wanton ways before the coal black boulder. Local Cypriots flocked there when the rock's role was uncovered, leaving shreds of their knickers in front of it as a modern sex sacrifice, apparently hoping for an aphrodisiacal effect.

Limassol: This southern coastal area powers the tourism economy and is famous for her colorful Carnival celebration and raucous wine festivals. A bit into the countryside of cherry trees and monasteries, you'll find Krassohoria— the old wine villages, where the dry red is made the old way.

Famagusta: Turkish Cypriots now occupy it, and Greek Cypriots call it "a ghost town"—but the G-Cypriots still hold outlying sandy beaches, including Ayia Napa, a fishing village turned tourist trap, and Protaras, a sailor's paradise.

> In recent years, many of the icon-rich Greek Orthodox churches in Turkish Cyprus have been demolished, ransacked, looted, and otherwise stripped of their treasures. While some is vandalism, smugglers are also at work: they've even peeled frescoes from the walls.

Mass graves: Their locations are secret, but Cypriot leaders sometimes mumble about revealing the whereabouts of the skeletons from 1974 battles, including at least some of the 2,000 or more Cypriots who have been missing (and presumed dead) for three decades.

Hotshots

Tassos Papadopoulos: President of the Republic of Cyprus, 2003–present. Many thought he was the perfect man to stitch Cyprus back together, but many were apparently dreaming. Instead, he encouraged Greek Cypriots to vote against reunification in the April 2004 referendum. That move tarnished his reputation internationally, and now the world is much more sympathetic to Turkish Cyprus than previously. That he's still popular with Greek Cypriots doesn't bode well for reunification.

Glafcos Clerides: President of Greek Cyprus, 1993–2003. He nearly provoked an ugly showdown in 1998 when he signed on for an antiaircraft defense system, but under international pressure—and threats of an attack from Turkey in response—opted not to deploy it.

Rauf Denktash: Vice President of (Unified) Cyprus, 1960–1963; president of Turkish Federated State, 1974–1983; founder and President of Turkish Republic of Northern Cyprus; 1983–2005. The Turkish Cypriot lawyer launched the antienosis resistance in the 1950s, loudly publicized the plight of Turkish Cypriots in the 1960s, walked out of the united government, and formed the republic in Northern Cyprus; he hasn't done Turkish Cyprus any favors lately by dragging his feet on reunification, and letting international criminal fugitives and drug traffickers move in without fear of extradition. Sidelined in the 2004 election that brought pro-EU Mehmet Ali Talat to power.

Mehmet Ali Talat: Prime Minister, 2004–2005; President, 2005–present. Theoretical leader of the Turkish Cypriot government—which Greek Cypriots will remind you doesn't really exist—Talat has tried to unify the island. But like everybody else in this scenario, he's a pain in the neck: when the EU gave his government $300 million in aid, even though the Turkish north wasn't even really part of the EU, Talat sniffed that it just wasn't enough.

Archbishop Makarios: President of (unified) Cyprus, 1960–1977. Born in 1913, Makarios—as head of church and state—was a walking conflict of interest, as well as the most powerful man on Cyprus and in the Greek Orthodox world. A major supporter of enosis, he later dropped the idea—EOKA tried to assassinate him for that—and the man who was the Church's most holy was rumored to be quite a ladies' man as well. Always clad in black robes, his chest heaving with so many pendants that he looked like a walking jewelry display, charismatic Makarios kept Cyprus from entirely disintegrating in her most troubling times.

News you can understand: Lots of top-notch press here, including *Cyprus Mail*, www.cyprus-mail.com/news and *Cyprus Weekly*, www.cyprusweekly.com.cy

Makarios: Led church and state in troubled times

28. MALTA
Most Likely to Secede

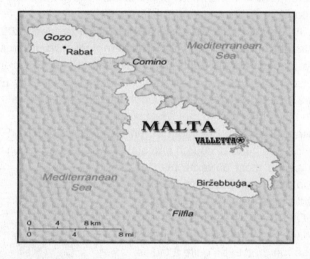

FAST FACTS

Country:	Republic of Malta; Repubblika ta' Malta
Capital:	Valletta
Government:	Republic
Independence:	September 21, 1964 (from UK)
Population:	400,300 (2004 estimate)
Head of State:	President Eddie Fenech Adami (2004)
Head of Government:	Prime Minister Lawrence Gonzi (2004)
Elections:	President appointed by house of representatives, five-year term; prime minister appointed by president, five-year term
Name of Parliament:	House of Representatives
Ethnicity:	Maltese (descendants of ancient Carthaginians, Phoenicians)
Religion:	98% Roman Catholic
Language:	Maltese and English (both official)
Literacy:	93% (2003)

Famous Exports:	Knights and falcons
Per Capita GDP:	$19,700 (2005)
Unemployment:	7.8% (January 2006 Eurostat figure)
EU Status:	Entered May 2004
Currency:	Maltese lira

Quick Tour

Gold-glowing palaces and square-shouldered forts peer down over glistening water, brightly colored buses bounce along cliff-hugging roads, restaurants serve up fish caught mere minutes before, and nearly half the year is a religious holiday: Malta's festive nature, honey-hued beauty, and balmy weather are just a few of the reasons that so many crowd onto such a small rock, known as the historical home of the Knights of Malta and formerly as "the most heavily bombed place on earth."

> Most of Malta's friendly inhabitants, all of whom speak English, are related.

MALTA VS. MALTA

Best to have a microscope handy if you want to find Malta on a world map: the five sun-drenched islets, together known as Malta, stretch out for a total of a mere 150 miles between Africa and Europe, making the archipelago appear to be a speck in the Mediterranean with a star. Malta is also the name of the largest island, which holds capital Valletta. The other islands are Gozo and Comino; Comminotto and Filfla are virtually uninhabited pebbles.

> Maltese, an Arabic-derived language peppered with Italian, is a remnant of the Phoenician settlers who arrived here from Lebanon. Almost every village in Malta has her own dialect.

Granted, apart from exploring ancient temples, strolling through courtyards where songbirds twitter, touring palaces, and flopping around on the beach, there's not much to do on sleepy Malta, where "Empty Wasp Nest Found in Attic" is literally headline news. Of course, you could go to mass here—she's one of the world's most devout Catholic countries, where over 70 percent regularly attend church and women still don black shawls; some Maltese still ritualistically kiss loaves of bread before slicing them. If there in spring or fall, you could always go hunting—a favored island activity, even more thrilling from speedboats.

BIRD CRAZY

There are about three trees on the islands, hence Malta has few native birds. Twice a year, however, the sky is thick with huge flocks of thrushes, turtle doves, quail, and woodcock winging from Africa to Europe and back six months later. You'd think the birds might have figured out an alternate route, because every time they pass over Malta, hunters are waiting; thousands of the feathered creatures drop out of the sky hourly becoming that night's dinner or next week's mounted wall piece. Some 3 million birds are shot or captured while flying over Malta each year, a practice that has environmentalists cawing about the fate of the migratory birds. Hunting, however, is a time-honored activity on the food-short island, and they ain't stopping it now.

Fears that the EU might clamp down on hunting caused a huge flap, and islanders nearly shot down the idea of joining up with the European Union. The prospect of becoming an EU member was a highly charged issue that brought back memories of when Malta—a British colony during World War II—was little more than a dispensable island. An attractive target, since she was dotted with British bases, Malta was pummeled by German bombs for two and a half years.

THE ATTACK ON MALTA

Britain ran it, Italy wanted it, and Germany knew that if Allied forces continued to use Malta as a naval base, North Africa could never be taken. The attacks on the Mediterranean islands started in June 1940, but the most vicious siege began on January 16, 1941, after Hitler ordered that Malta be "neutralized." For the next five months, air-raid sirens blared nonstop and the sky rained bombs, in the longest continuous daily bombardment of the war. With Nazis soaring down to drop their payload in half a dozen sorties a day, the red flag that alerted islanders to another incoming enemy plane was constantly flying over the Governor's Palace and the skyline of domed churches soon crumbled. The pitifully armed Maltese tried to fight back using the island's three decrepit biplanes—locals named them Faith, Hope, and Charity. Shelters were hastily created in the colony, which had been taken by surprise. Moats were transformed into ditches, caves became homes, and hundreds of bomb shelters were chiseled out of the limestone hills. Thousands died in the bombings. Food supplies ran out, and many of the islanders nearly starved to death, since food-carrying convoys were routinely sunk en route to Malta. British forces took months to show up and take their place next to the fighting Maltese. The Allies, whose bases had made the island a target, did not initially consider Malta worth saving.

In 1943, both King George VI and President Roosevelt arrived on "Siren Island" to personally honor the Maltese whom they'd mostly abandoned during the siege. The British king presented the George Cross for Heroism to Malta— "the most heavily bombed place on earth"[1]—marking the first time the medal was ever presented to a nation; Roosevelt gave the Maltese a plaque. But despite all the hoopla and kind words, Malta—wiped out physically and economically—didn't get a penny of aid then or after the war. Britain refused to turn Marshall Aid funding over to her colony Malta despite the heavy damage. Being cut off from money she needed for reconstruction—and that the feisty Maltese deserved—ultimately led to Malta declaring independence. The archipelago has bounced along a bumpy road ever since.

> The fierce debate over EU entry did beg the question of why the European Union wanted to include far-flung Malta in the first place. Is the EU interested in the oil that might lie off Malta's coast? Did they want to extend official European borders closer to Africa? Do they feel guilty for Malta being ravaged during the Second World War? Or is it again really a matter of military and transport: are the EU planners thinking that sometime in the future it might be handy to use her as a fortress again—or at least as a strategic site to guard western Mediterranean sea lanes? Why would the EU care so much about bringing in Malta, a far-yonder rock with scanty natural resources, that Brussels offered her more exemptions than anywhere else? One thing you can be sure of: they don't plan on tapping Malta for her lumber. There's barely enough to construct a toothpick.

History Review

Never mind that she has scarce water and poor soil, and that the only bountiful resource is limestone: with her boulder-strewn beauty, Malta—the only pit stop between today's Libya and Sicily—has lured in just about everybody who sailed by over the past 7,000 years. Neolithic peoples who worshipped fertility goddesses were among the first inhabitants who climbed up and began rearranging the rocks; some of the dozens of temples they left are crude, Stonehenge-like assemblages; others, such as the Hypogeum, are elaborate subterranean affairs that have archaeologists baffled about how they could have been created with crude tools.

> Excavated with obsidian and flint, the subterranean 500-square-meter Hypogeum—discovered in 1902—was a place of worship and burial ground, which may have taken centuries to construct. Few clues are left about exactly who created the multistory temple of echo chambers, statuettes, and caves but whoever it was, they mysteriously disappeared around 2500 BC.

Home to Phoenicians, Carthaginians, Romans, Vandals, Goths, Sicilians, Normans, Arabs, and Genoese over the next few thousand years, Malta was also the site where St. Paul was shipwrecked in AD 60—another reason why some regard the land as divine. Spiritual seekers and religious pilgrims say that Malta is one of the world's centers of cosmic power.

Winding up in the hands of Spaniards in the fourteenth century, geographical hand-me-down Malta was passed on to Holy Roman Emperor Charles V, then running Spain. He changed Malta's history when he gave the island to Knights Hospitallers in 1530 with a mandate that they calm the pirate-plagued waters that were proving treacherous to Spain's gold-filled ships. The sixteenth-century Knights Hospitallers (aka Knights of Malta) left the most indelible mark on the land: the capital, Valletta, is dense with their Renaissance and Baroque palaces, and they spread the faith around just as thickly. All of Malta is heaving with churches—over 320 of them, some lavishly decorated, others hidden in caves.

> The knights were Catholic, but were none too happy to find that Malta had an Inquisition Board on the island. Inquisitors looked askance at the Knights' possession of banned books and general amnesia about their vows of poverty and chastity. Nevertheless, the Inquisition typically took aim at the locals: Muslim slaves were among those accused of invoking Satan with magical spells, but even the villager who ate meat on Fridays might be hauled before the board and flogged.

THE DAYS OF THE KNIGHTS OF MALTA

The Knights Hospitallers became legendary for battles with Arabs, but the original charge of the chivalrous group—most of them European aristocrats—was to tend to pilgrims who fell ill while trekking to the Holy Land. Running hospitals in Jerusalem for seventy-four years, the Knights were ousted in 1187, when Saladin's Arabs took the city. The Knights then sailed to the island of Rhodes, which they fortified so heavily that they remained there safely for two centuries. In 1522, however, Suleyman the Magnificent unleashed 200,000 of his Ottoman fighters, who so ravaged the Knights' population that the few survivors were given free passage in exchange for a promise they'd stopped attacking Muslims—a false promise, as it turned out. The homeless knights wandered about the Mediterranean until 1530, when Holy Roman Emperor Charles V waved a tempting offer under their noses: if they battled pirates, particularly the Berbers who plundered ships nearing North African waters, they could have Malta. The Knights held their ground well on the island—too well, thought Suleyman, who sent out his warriors again in 1565. This time the Knights, with the help of the locals and the limestone caves that served as shelters from cannonballs, fought back the invaders; when the Ottoman warriors tried to break into villages, they were greeted with swords and vats of hot grease. Ottoman ships sailed back to Turkey after four months, and the Knights rebuilt and refortified the islands splendidly, thanks to their aristocratic tastes and the bags of gold that Charles's successor, Philip II, paid as reward. The pope sent over his chief engineer, who designed a grid system for Valletta, and Europe's finest architects and artisans were shipped in to create the most sumptuous palaces of the day. Poets, artists, musicians, and thousands of courtesans turned up as well, as Malta launched its rollicking golden age. Before long, however, the brave Knights had degenerated: famous for battling pirates, the Knights became pirates themselves, not only plucking riches from passing ships, but running a slave trade of the passengers taken captive. By the late eighteenth century, the sodden, bloated Knights couldn't even hold down their fort. So worthless were the island's defenders that when Napoleon arrived in 1798, his forces captured Malta without firing a shot.

Napoleon booted out the Knights and the Inquisitors in 1798, but his fondness for looting gold- and silver-laden churches ensured the French wouldn't last long. The religious Maltese were so distraught at the theft of the holy riches that they called for British help. Brits sent the French packing in 1800, and kept control of the island—a key Mediterranean port. Officially British territory by 1814, Malta remained a crown colony for a century and a half. And it might have stayed longer had not Dom Mintoff (rightly) had a fit when Britain refused to fork over any Marshall Plan money.

Bombed during the Second World War, Valletta's opera house still hasn't been repaired.

Despite an outward appearance of happy homogeneity, the Maltese are a deeply divided people. And much of that division stems from the land's most infamous politician, Dom Mintoff, whom some Maltese worship and some out-and-out despise. Beak-nosed and bespectacled, Rhodes scholar Mintoff flew to fame in the 1950s, grabbing control of the Labor Party and becoming prime minister in 1955. Upset when Britain denied reconstruction funds to Malta—devastated solely because of her association with the British—Mintoff flew another idea: change Malta's status to more than a colony, but an actual part of Britain, and get Marshall funding that way. The Maltese people backed his idea in a vote; but the British scoffed at the idea. Mintoff stormed out of office—the prime minister's seat remained vacant for the next five years—and hatched a new plan: independence.

And that's when the Catholic Church came into the picture—dividing the island as never before, and so recklessly abusing power that even the pope told local church authorities to back off.

A DIFFERENT SORT OF INQUISITION

Civil marriage—marriage outside the Church—is not such a fiery issue today, but in 1960s Malta it was on par with signing your soul to the devil. When Dom Mintoff ran for prime minister in 1962, promising to allow civil marriage on the islands, he might as well have sprouted horns in the view of Malta's archbishop Sir Michael Gonzi. The archbishop took the extreme step of excommunicating not just Mintoff but his whole Labor Party. Soon called the Iron Archbishop, Gonzi declared that voting Labor—even reading the party's newspaper—was a mortal sin. The archbishop forced priests to devote entire masses to lecturing about the evils of Labor—and, more outrageously, to use the confessional as a spying tool to discover how parishioners planned to vote. Sinners voting Labor were not absolved—and were told they would be damned to eternal hell if they dared cast a vote for Mintoff's party. Even children were pushed by priests to grass on their parents and confess the adults' political affiliations. Whenever Mintoff gave a public speech, the Church drowned it out with the ringing of bells. Priests distributed whistles to the devout Catholic—they were to blow them at Labor gatherings, and were directed to chant, throw stones, or do whatever was required (murder was hinted at) to ensure Labor did not win the election. The archbishop won that round at least. The Labor Party finished second, and Mintoff came into parliament as opposition leader only to see the Nationalists lead the country to the independence he'd campaigned for. But the archbishop's actions had raised plenty of eyebrows in Rome; the pope finally shipped over a replacement in 1969.

Mintoff finally snatched back the premiership in 1971, and went on a rampage. He upped fees to the British to use Malta for bases, charging an exorbitant $40 million annually, which was initially used to fund education. Several years later, he pushed the British out of port, along with NATO. Disgusted by the supposed white knights of the Cold War, he befriended Libya's Muammar

Qaddafi (who gave him great prices on oil) and North Korea's Kim il-Sung, the slightly less nutty father of current leader Kim Jong-il. Mintoff invited Soviet ships to refuel at the facilities NATO had built, signed a multimillion-dollar trade agreement with Russia, and nearly derailed a 1975 U.S.-Soviet global arms agreement because he wouldn't sign. Increasingly autocratic, Mintoff took on the Church—seizing property, barring priests from visiting prisons, and outlawing religious schools—and his alleged henchmen made high-profile appearances on Malta's streets. Many of Mintoff's political foes soon disappeared; some fled, and at least one turned up dead. The Mintoff administration began talking of making Malta a one-party country, and there was little dissent in parliament, at least in 1981. That year, the Nationalist Party won the majority of votes, but Labor took the most seats—and the Nationalists walked out in protest. By 1984, Malta was a mess. Tourism was down, foreign investors had pulled out, and unemployment shot up to 20 percent. Mintoff, under pressure, finally pushed back his chair from the prime minister's desk.

Mintoff made Malta stand out for all the wrong reasons, and when he stood down as prime minister in 1984, many heaved a sigh of relief. (However, he wasn't done with politics: he simply took a place in Malta's House of Representatives.) When the Nationalists, with Eddie Fenech Adami at the helm, took over running the country in 1987, they sought to undo almost all that Mintoff had done. Adami welcomed NATO ships back into port and signed Malta up for NATO's Partnership for Peace program. The prime minister also reached out to Europe, and in the early 1990s began negotiating for Malta's entry into the EU. That move blew up in his face; in 1996, voters threw the Nationalists out of power. The new Labor government pulled Malta out of the NATO group and ditched plans to enter the EU. The appearance of Malta in the 2004 enlargement looked most unlikely—until, that is, Mintoff rattled the country again.

By then seventy-two years of age, Mintoff, who was rabidly against joining the EU, apparently didn't see what he was doing that tumultuous day in 1998, when he ripped the carpet from under his own party. Mintoff had made no secret that he had little respect for Labor's new leader, Prime Minister Alfred Sant, who was Harvard-educated and modern. When parliament was voting on giving the Knights of Malta their own sovereign state on a Maltese fort, Mintoff snapped. Not only did he not like the idea, he didn't like Sant, and he so ripped the prime minister over the next hour that the House of Representatives fell apart. Sant was forced to call early elections when he lost a no-confidence vote, and Labor lost. Nationalist prime minister Adami was soon on the phone to Brussels putting Malta back on the road for EU entry, assuring the enlargement commissioner that yes, this time, Malta's application would stick.

Hot Spots

Valletta: The sixteenth-century palaces shimmer as the sun drops into the red bay in this fortress city, built up by Malta's Knights. Renowned as one of the world's finest showcases of Baroque, capital Valletta was also one of the first European cities designed on a grid. Space is getting tight in Grand Harbor, where cruise ships vie for moorage with NATO warships.

Mdina: The walled city on the island of Gozo is a tumble of garden-wrapped squares, sixteenth-century cathedrals and palaces (still owned by nobles) housing valuable Renaissance paintings, including the famous *Beheading of St. John* by Caravaggio.

Valletta: Famous for her wild knights

Courtesy of Malta Tourist Office

Malta's second-largest island Gozo claims that she was made famous by Homer's Odyssey: *it was here, Gozans claim, that the sea nymph Calypso nursed Ulysses back to health, keeping him captive for seven years, but never convincing him to marry. Homer called the island Ogygia.*

Birds' balconies: Back in the 1500s, when respectable women were forced to stay at home (making lace, one supposes) while the menfolk went out cavorting, the gals could watch the movements of their guys from balconies with far-reaching views—and potential consequences, considering the place was chockablock with courtesans.

Summer homes: With Malta already one of the most densely populated chunks of land in the world, the Maltese government negotiated EU waivers to prevent Europeans from buying second homes on their island. After Malta became independent in 1964, the British kept hanging around for another decade, until the Maltese pressured many out of their summer cottages.

The media: Both major parties own their own newspapers, TV, and radio stations—in which they air the dirty laundry of the other party's politicians.

Freemason lodges: Never mind that none is officially registered with the police, freemasons and secret societies are rumored to run rampant on the islands.

> Although it's part of Malta mythology—February 10 is the Feast of St. Paul's Shipwreck—some religious scholars say Paul's ship did not hit the rocks here, but in Greece.[2]

Maltese territorial waters: When the Maltese government recently sent out a team to survey the coastal shelf for petroleum, the Libyan navy blocked the move and sent the ship packing back to Malta. Now Libya is muscling into Malta's oil exploration.

Hotshots

Eddie Fenech Adami: President, 2004–present; Prime Minister, 1987–1995 and 1998–2004. Devout Catholic and Nationalist Adami is a man of his word. He vowed to get Malta into the EU (succeeding in 2004), and vowed to resign from the premiership when he turned seventy in 2003; he did, simply walking into the presidential role instead.

Lawrence Gonzi: Prime Minister, 2004–present. Nationalist Gonzi is also devout. It may be in his genes: his uncle Sir Michael Gonzi was the "Iron Archbishop" who led the anti-Labor movement of the 1960s.

Birdlife Malta: The organization that tends to wounded winged creatures and campaigns for bird rights, is often under fire from hunters. Some active members have received death threats.

Knights of Malta: They once brought

Courtesy of Government of Malta

Adami led the Maltese flock into the EU

hospitals, churches, and palaces to Malta, along with plenty of prostitutes. Now supposedly a do-gooder group, they number in the tens of thousands and are considering starting their own mini-country—complete with passports, stamps, and postal system—in the same Maltese fort where they fought off Ottoman invaders in 1565. The organization also plays a starring role in numerous conspiracy theories.

Notes

Unless otherwise noted, all information in "Fast Facts" boxes is from the handy 2006 edition of the CIA's *World Factbook*.

Chapter 1: France

1. Forbes Global 2000 for 2005.
2. Source: EU: Financial Report of European Agricultural Guidance and Guarantee Fund, Annexe 11, Évolution des Dépenses du Feoga—garantie par état membre.
3. Paul Gallis, "France: Factors Shaping Foreign Policy and Issues in U.S.-French Relations," CRS Report for Congress, Congressional Research Service, Jan. 3, 2006.
4. Source: BBC.
5. Bruce Crumley and Adam Smith, "Sisters in Hell," *Time International*, Dec. 2, 2002.
6. Ibid.
7. Lowell Ponte, "France's Rising Right," *FrontPage Magazine* (www.frontpagemag.com), Apr. 23, 2002.
8. So sniffed U.S. State Department spokesman Richard Boucher.
9. So admonished Christopher Hitchens in the *Wall Street Journal*, "The Rat That Tried to Roar," Feb. 6, 2003.
10. "In Pursuit of Genius: Jean-Antoine Houdon and the Sculpted Portraits of Benjamin Franklin," Philadelphia Museum of Art (http://www.philamuseum.org/exhibitions/special/97.html).
11. So estimates Napoleon expert Paul Johnson, as noted in Stephen Goode's "Napoleon's Legacy leads to Gulag . . . ," *Insight Magazine*, Sept. 12, 2003.
12. Dan Bloch, "Bonaparte Founded G-Men," *Washington Star*, Aug. 18, 1935 (http://www.fbi.gov/libref/historic/history/historic_doc/docstar.htm).
13. Rashid Tlemcani, "Islam in France: The French Have Themselves to Blame," *Middle East Quarterly*, Mar. 1997.
14. Source: *Library of Congress Country Studies: Algeria*, "France in Algeria, 1830–1862."
15. Robert Hughes, "Sublime Windbag: Writer, Lover, National Hero, Victor Hugo . . . ," *Time*, Apr. 27, 1998.
16. "Franco-Prussian War," Microsoft Encarta Online Encyclopedia, 2004.
17. Figure according to Globalsecurity.org.

18. "Pétain's Crimes Still Split French," *Jerusalem Post*–AP, Aug. 2, 1995.

19. Richard Cavendish, "Months Past: Death of Marshal Pétain," *History Today*, July 1, 2001.

20. Sources: *Wikipedia, The Free Encyclopedia* (en.wikipedia.org); *New Statesman & Society*; *The Economist.*

21. Information drawn from numerous sources, including *Library of Congress Country Studies: Algeria* and Robert Rinehart, *Countries of the World: Algeria.*

22. Source: EU: Financial Report of European Agricultural Guidance and Guarantee Fund, Annexe 11, Évolution des Dépenses du Feoga—garantie par état membre.

23. "Cometh the Hour, Cometh the Ghost," *The Economist*, Oct. 20, 2005.

24. As noted on "About France" (www.ambafrance-au.org/aboutfrance/home.en .htm).

25. Dominique Pobel and Jean-Francois Viel, "Case-Control Study of Leukaemia Among Young People Near La Hague Nuclear Reprocessing Plant . . . ," *British Medical Journal*, Jan. 11, 1997.

26. Paul Webster, "Le Pen: Populist Who Rose from Ashes," *The Guardian* (London), Apr. 22, 2002.

Chapter 2: Germany

1. Forbes Global 2000 for 2005.

2. See: "Background Notes," Germany-info.org.

3. Christopher Booker and Richard North, *The Great Deception: The Secret History of the European Union.* London: Continuum, 2003.

4. Source: CIA World Factbook (www.cia.gov/cia/publications/factbook/).

5. Margaret MacMillan, *Paris 1919: Six Months That Changed the World.* New York: Random House, 2001: p. 161.

6. Source: "Weimar Republic," *Wikipedia, The Free Encyclopedia* (en.wikipedia.org).

7. Ibid.

8. Source: "Adolf Hitler," *Wikipedia, The Free Enyclopedia* (en.wikipedia.org).

9. Dorothea von Schwanenfluegel Lawson, "World War Memories," Germanculture .com.

10. Matthew White's war-death statistics Web site (http://users.erols.com/mwhite28/ warstat1.htm).

11. "Germany's Deadly Legacy," *German Life*, July 31, 1997.

12. Jacob Hellbrunn, "Springtime: Germany's Newfound Strength," *The New Republic*, Oct. 16, 1995.

13. "History of the Federal Republic of Germany," *Wikipedia, The Free Encylcopedia* (en.wikipedia.org).

Chapter 3: United Kingdom

1. Forbes Global 2000 for 2005.

2. Source: WTO.

3. "United Kingdom: Unemployment," European Foundation for the Improvement of Living and Working Conditions (www.eurofound.eu.int).

4. The 2001 report by Professor David Warburton of the University of Reading is discussed by Richard Alleyne, "Celebrity Chefs Dish Up Dinner Party Neurosis," *The Daily Telegraph* (UK), Dec.4, 2001.

5. Alan Travis, Richard Norton-Taylor, and Rosie Cowan, "July 7 Reports Fail to Silence Inquiry Calls," *The Guardian* (London), May 11, 2006 (http://www.guardian.co.uk/attackonlondon/story/0,,1772161,00.html).

6. "Hamza's Sermons," *The Telegraph* (London), Feb. 8, 2006, (http://www.telegraph.co.uk/news/main.jhtml?xml=/news/2006/02/08/nhamz408.xml&sSheet=/news/2006/02/08/ixnewstop.html).

7. Kevin Sullivan, "Foes of Foreigners grow vocal in Britain," *The Washington Post*, May 4, 2006.

8. "British National Party," *Wikipedia, The Free Encyclopedia* (en.wikipedia.org).

9. Jamie David, "Expelled BNP Founder Plans Court Battle," Aug. 24, 2003 (http://politics.guardian.co.uk/farright/story/0,11375,1028498,00.html).

10. Nick Cohen, "Bigots, Racists, and Worthless Buffoons . . ." *The Observer* (London), May 7, 2006 (http://www.guardian.co.uk/commentisfree/story/0,,1769485,00.html?gusrc=rss).

11. "Life of Crime: Yob Culture," BBC News, (http://news.bbc.co.uk/hi/english/static/in_depth/uk/2001/life_of_crime/yob_culture.stm).

12. Assorted organizations, including UN Development Program, International Adult Literacy Survey, and Organization for Economic Cooperation and Development.

13. Source: Literacy Trust, using information from Book Marketing Ltd., which conducted surveys in 2001.

14. Kevin Sullivan, "Blair Reshuffles Cabinet after Elections," *The Washington Post*, May 6, 2006 (http://www.washingtonpost.com/wp-dyn/content/article/2006/05/05/AR2006050500456.html).

15. Some information drawn from EnchantedLearning.com, Explorers series. See also "Hot Shots" below.

16. Source on Galton: Nicholas W. Gillham, "Sir Francis Galton and the Birth of Eugenics," *Annual Review of Genetics*, Jan. 1, 2001.

17. Victorian Station, "The Great Exhibition at the Crystal Palace" (http://www.victorianstation.com/palace.html).

18. As noted in "The Rhodes Scholarships: A Giant Step for White World Domination," *The Conscious Observer Newsletter*, October 1995.

19. Matthew Sweet, "A Bad Man in Africa," *The Independent*, March 16, 2002.

20. Sources include: Matthew Sweet, "A Bad Man in Africa," *The Independent*, Mar. 16, 2002; and James North, "The Randlords," *The New Republic*, May 19, 1986.

21. Long laughed off as a conspiracy theory, Echelon does exist: Australia recently admitted to be part of it, former CIA director James Woolsey copped to it in a *Wall Street Journal* editorial that he wrote (see: James Woolsey, "Why We Spy on Our Allies," *The Wall Street Journal*, March 17, 2000), and the European parliament

wrote a report on it: "Report on the Existence of a Global System for the Interception of Private and Commercial Communications—Echelon," European Parliament, July 11, 2001 (http://fas.org/irp/program/process/rapport_echelon_en.pdf).

22. Information derived from reports from think tank Bellano, the University of Bremen, Greenpeace, and *The Guardian* (London), among other sources.
23. Peter Oborne, "The End of the Affair," *The Spectator*, 2002.
24. Some information here derived from an article written by Prince Michael of Greece, "To Be Young and Royal," *Vanity Fair*, September 2003.
25. Ibid.

Chapter 4: Italy

1. Forbes Global 2000 for 2005.
2. Jeff Israely, "The Berlusconi Channel," *Time*, Mar. 3, 2003.
3. Sophie Arie, "Toxics Scandal in Mozzarella Country," *The Guardian* (London), Oct. 14, 2004; Gail Edmondson and Kate Carlisle, "Italy and the Eco-Mafia," *BusinessWeek*, Jan. 27, 2003.
4. Some information draws from Norman Davies, *Europe, A History*, 1997, and H. A. L. Fisher, *A History of Europe*, 1970.
5. James Hardy, "Fury Over PM Muslim Slur," *Mirror*, Sept. 28, 2001.
6. Author Margherita Marchione is the source of some info.
7. Robert P. Libbon, *Instant European History: From the French Revolution to the Cold War*, New York: Ballantine Books, 1996: pp. 76–77.
8. Benito Mussolini, *The Cardinal's Mistress*, English translation: Hiram Motherwell, 1929, as noted on Oddbooks.co.uk.
9. Margaret MacMillan, *Paris 1919: Six Months That Changed the World*. New York: Random House, 2001: p. 280.
10. Statistic from Datamonitor: "Young Cannot Afford to Leave Home," BBC, Mar. 12, 2003.
11. Source: William T. Grant Foundation, "Adolescence Not Just for Kids," *The Washington Post*, Jan. 2, 2002.

Chapter 5: Belgium

1. Forbes Global 2000 for 2005.
2. So claims Belgian businessman Jean-Michel Nihoul, a defendant in the case of Marc Dutroux, the pedophile and murderer. Dutroux keeps insisting he was securing his victims as part of a ring, and that the government is not investigating his leads.
4. Barry James, "Belgium Pedophilia Scandal . . ." *International Herald Tribune*, Dec. 16, 1999.
5. Rosemary Bechler, "Everyone Is Afraid: The World According to Abou Jahjah," Opendemocracy.com interview, May 20, 2004.
6. "New Government to Amend War Crimes Legislation in Attempt to Avert Crisis Within NATO," AP Worldstream, July 8, 2003.

7. Glenn Frankel, "Belgian War Crimes Law Undone by Its Global Reach . . ." *The Washington Post*, Sept. 30, 2003. Additional information derived from AP and *The Economist*.

8. Some information in this section is derived from the fascinating and beautifully written book by Thomas Pakenham, *The Scramble for Africa*. New York: Random House, 1991. Another source: Adam Hochschild, *King Leopold's Ghost*. New York: Mariner Books, 1999.

9. Ambrose Evans-Pritchard, "Belgian Fury at Film on Leopold's Congo terror," *The Daily Telegraph* (London), July 4, 2004.

10. Information in this section derived from interviews, the Belgian Tourism Board, *The Economist*, and *Lonely Planet World Guide: Belgium*.

11. Barry James, "Eurocapital in Search of a Human Dimension," *International Herald Tribune*, Oct. 23, 1998.

12. Sebastian Lapaque, "Simenon the Myth in Seven Legends," *Le Figaro Littéraire*, Jan. 9, 2003.

Chapter 6: Ireland

1. Forbes Global 2000 for 2005.
2. According to the *Economist*'s "World in 2005" survey.
3. Source: *Wikipedia, The Free Encyclopedia* (en.wikipedia.org).

Chapter 7: Spain

1. Forbes Global 2000 for 2005.

2. Source: World Tourism Organization, June 2004.

3. Source: BBC.

4. "Spanish Reporters: Government Silenced the Truth About the Attacks," Inter Press Service, Mar. 18, 2004 (www.commondreams.org/headlines04/318-10 .htm).

5. Source: *El País*.

6. "11 March 2004 Madrid Attacks," *Wikipedia, The Free Encyclopedia* (en.wikipedia.org).

7. Elaine Sciolino, "Spain Is Firm: Troops Won't Return," *The New York Times*, May 7, 2004.

8. Some information from David Gilmour, *Cities of Spain*, Chicago: Ivan R. Dee, 1992; and John A. Crow, *Spain: The Root and the Flower*, Berkeley: University of California Press, 1985.

9. James Townsend, "Tracking Spain's Gold to Moscow," *The Wall Street Journal*, Aug. 4, 1994.

10. *Newsweek*, March 2, 1970. See: http://hitlerstoppebyfranco.com/franco_jews .htm.

11. John Hopper, *The New Spaniards*. London: Penguin Group, 1995.

12. Dale Fuchs, "Spain Labors to Bring Home Baby—and the Bacon," *The Christian Science Monitor*, June 26, 2003.

13. T. D. Allman, "The King Who Saved His Country," *Vanity Fair*, August 1992. (Interesting article, although Allman is out to lunch to claim that siestas are a thing of the past, and that Spaniards often holiday in Switzerland because it's cheaper.)

Chapter 8: Portugal

1. Forbes Global 2000 for 2005.
2. Source: UK Trade and Investment: "Portugal: Setting Up."
3. Based on interviews with Portuguese.
4. Source: *The World Factbook*; International Planned Parenthood Federation; some studies say closer to 20 percent of the women can't read.
5. Between 1991 and 2001, 38 percent of Portuguese finished mandatory nine years of schooling, according to an April 2, 2003, statement by Portuguese UN Ambassador Gonçalo de Santa Clara Gomes to the Commission on Population and Development.
6. "Victory in Portugal Lifts European Right," *International Herald Tribune*, Mar. 19, 2002.
7. Barry Hatton, "After Shaky Start, Portugal's New prime minister still looking for chance to prove himself," Associated Press, Aug. 8, 2004.
8. Ibid.
9. Source: *Wikipedia, The Free Encyclopedia* (en.wikipedia.org).
10. Source: *Library of Congress Country Studies: Portugal*.
11. Ibid.
12. Source: "Portugal—The Treaty of Windsor," Manorhouses.com.
13. Source: Daniel J. Boorstin, *The Discoverers: A History of Man's Search to Know His World and Himself*, New York: Random House, 1983—using a journal of one of da Gama's crew as the source.
14. Ibid.
15. Ibid.
16. According to the M2 Wine Education Center (http://www.intowine.com/port.html).
17. Some information from *Wine Spectation* as well as from the M2 Wine Education Center.
18. Source: "History of Portugal," *Wikipedia, The Free Encylclopedia* (en.wikipedia.org).
19. "Europe: Those big boys next door; Portugal and Spain," *The Economist*, Jan. 25, 2003.
20. Source for all above information: Fatima.org.
21. "Links Between Europeans Living Abroad and Their Countries of Origin," Council of Europe Parliamentary Assembly, Mar. 5, 1999.
22. Isabel Romão, "Country Report: Portugal," European Database (http://www.db-decision.de/CoRe/Portugal.htm).

Chapter 9: The Netherlands

1. Forbes Global 2000 for 2005.
2. Many immigrants and foreign-born workers are well-integrated in Dutch society; however, the proportion of those leaning on the welfare system is far higher

among immigrants, and the rate of unemployment and crime is often linked to not learning the language. The problem is at a peak in Rotterdam.

3. Interview with *Rotterdams Dagblad*, as noted by *Wikipedia, The Free Encyclopedia* (en.wikipedia.org).
4. Andrew Osborn, "Rotterdam plans to ban poor immigrants . . . ," *The Guardian* (London), Dec. 2, 2003.
5. Giles Milton, *Nathaniel's Nutmeg.* New York: Farrar, Straus and Giroux, 1999.
6. "Aceh backgrounder," Indonesia Alert (www.indonesiaalert.org); "The Dark Side of Power," Radio Netherlands (www2.rnw.nl/rnw/en).
7. "Matters of Taste: Foodways of the Dutch Golden Age," Albany Institute (www.albanyinstitute.org).
8. Zbigniew Szydio and Richard Brzezinki, "A New Light on Alchemy," *History Today*, Jan. 1, 1997.
9. Paul Doolan, "Time for Dutch Courage in Indonesia," *History Today*, Mar. 1, 1997.
10. Ibid.
11. Source: "Royal Flush," *Forbes*, March 4, 2002.
12. Some say it was the French who bungled the name; some say the Brits.
13. Van Gogh lived with the prostitute Sien Hoornik in 1882–1883.
14. As noted by John McEwen, "The Odd Couple with an Ear for Painting," *The Sunday Telegraph* (London), Apr. 14, 2002.
15. Richard Edmonds, "Van Gogh, the Good Dr.," *Birmingham Post*, Oct. 23, 1999.
16. Forbes Global 2000 for 2005.
17. According to Friends of the Earth.
18. So alleged former Nigerian oil minister Dauzia Loya Etete as reported by *Forbes*: Silvia Sansoni, "Dirty Oil," *Forbes*, Apr. 28, 2003.
19. Excerpts from *The Praise of Folly*, noted on www.historyguide.org/intellect/erasmus.html.

Chapter 10: Austria
1. Forbes Global 2000 for 2005.
2. "History, Part 2," the Austrian Embassy, Washington, D.C., Austrian Press and Information Service (http://www.austria.org/index.php?option=com_content&task=view&id=23&Itemid=68&limit=1&limitstart=1).
3. Michael Jandl and Albert Kraler, "Austria: A Country of Immigration?" Migration Policy Institute, March 2003 (http://www.migrationinformation.org).
4. This section draws on information from *Newsweek International*; *The Economist*; AP; Reuters; and the BBC.
5. Thomas Fields-Meyer, "Alpine Uproar," *Time*, Feb. 2000.
6. Joshua Hammer, "Austria's Power Player," *Newsweek International*, Feb. 14, 2000.
7. Ibid.
8. Source: Statistics Austria (www.statistik.at).
9. "Joint Settlement on Holocaust Restitution," Agreement of Austrian and U.S. governments, Jan. 17, 2001. See: http://vienna.usembassy.gov/en/policy/final.htm.

10. Gyles Brandreth, "Everything You Wanted to Know About Freud but Were Afraid to Ask . . . ," *The Sunday Telegraph* (London), May 12, 2002.
11. "Sigmund Freud," Internet Encyclopedia of Philosophy (http://www.iep.utm.edu/f/freud/htm).
12. J. Masson, *The Assault on Truth: Freud's Suppression of the Seduction Theory.* London: Faber & Faber, 1984; A. C. MacIntyre, *The Unconscious: A Conceptual Analysis.* London: Routledge & Kegan Paul, 1958.
13. Adolf Hitler's speech at Königsberg, Mar. 25, 1938 (from http://www.spartacus.schoolnet.co.uk/2WWanschluss.htm).
14. Letter of Mexican envoy Isidro Fabela to League of Nations Secretary-General Joseph Avenol, dated Mar. 19, 1938; *Library of Congress Country Studies: Austria*, Appendix, Jan. 1, 1991, Federal Press Service.
15. Source: *Library of Congress Country Studies: Austria*.
16. "Austria: Nazi Terror in the Wake of the 'Anschluss,'" *Library of Congress Country Studies: Austria*, Jan. 1, 1991, Federal Press Service.
17. Johannes Pflegerl, "Living in Migration in Austria," *Journal of Comparative Family Studies*, Sept. 22, 2001.
18. Ibid.
19. Source: www.nationmaster.com.
20. Ibid.
21. "Wolfgang Amadeus Mozart," *Wikipedia, The Free Encyclopedia* (en.wikipedia.org).

Chapter 11: Greece

1. Forbes Global 2000 for 2005.
2. "Poverty and Social Exclusion: Population at Risk of Poverty . . . ," Eurostat press release, Apr. 7, 2003.
3. Source: *The Guardian* (London).
4. Patrick Quinn, Associated Press, Aug. 29, 1998.
5. Source: "Democritus," *Wikipedia, The Free Encyclopedia* (en.wikipedia.org).
6. Donald Nicol, *Last Centuries of Byzantium* (Cambridge: Cambridge University Press, 1993.)
7. So says William St. Clair in his book *Lord Elgin and the Marbles* (New York: Oxford University Press, 1998).
8. Eurostat Unemployment Report for January 2006.
9. Patrick Quinn, Associated Press, Aug. 29, 1998.
10. Source: *Forbes*.
11. Some information from "Very Happy Birthday," ABC News, Jan. 29, 2003.

Chapter 12: Scandinavia: Denmark, Sweden, Finland, and Norway

1. H. A. L. Fisher, *A History of Europe*, Vol. 1. London: Fontana, 1970: p. 191.
2. Ibid. p. 193.
3. Insights provided by Anne Katarine Paulsen in a November 2003 interview.

Chapter 13: Denmark
1. Forbes Global 2000 for 2005.
2. "UN Criticizes National Immigration Policy," *The Copenhagen Post*, May 29, 2001.
3. Dan Damon, "Lessons from Danish prisons," July 2, 2003, BBC (http://news.bbc.co.uk/2/hi/europe/3036450.stm).
4. Peter Stalker, *Oxford Handbook of the World*, New York: Oxford University Press, 2000.
5. "Karen Blixen," *Library of Congress Countries of the World: Denmark*, Jan. 1, 1991.

Chapter 14: Sweden
1. Forbes Global 2000 for 2005.
2. "Mix and Match," *The Economist*, June 24, 2003.
3. "Danish Far-Right Leader Pia Kjaersgaard," Agence France Presse, May 23, 2002.
4. Sarah Gold, "Letters to His Mistress Shed Light on Nobel" (review of *Alfred Nobel* by Kenne Fant), *Publishers Weekly*, July 19, 1993.
5. Some information drawn from "Alfred Nobel: The Man Behind the Prizes," *Los Angeles Business Journal*, Oct. 8, 2001.
6. David Wiles, "The Road to Sweden's Oil Free Future," *Sweden Today/Sweden.SE* (http://www.sweden.se/templates/cs/Article_14363.aspx).
7. Professor Åke Daun, "The Swedish Myth," The Swedish Institute, Sept. 9, 2005 (http://www.sweden.se/templates/cs/Article_12355.aspx).
8. Source: OECD Social Cohesion Data.
9. According to Sveriges Riksbank.
10. According to European Foundation of the Improvement of Living and Working Conditions, EMIRE.
11. "Sweden: Dark Shadows," *The Economist*, Nov. 13, 1999.
12. Lofthus, "Swedish Biz Decries Racist Music," *Billboard*, Jan. 24, 1998.
13. Paul Gallagher, "The Man Who Told the Secret," *The Columbia Journalism Review*, Jan/Feb 1998.
14. "Nordic Eugenics: Here, of All Places," *The Economist*, Aug. 30, 1997.
15. J. M. Roberts, *Twentieth Century: History of the World 1901 to 2000.* New York: Penguin, 1999: p. 388.
16. "Too Good to Be True," *The Economist*, Jan. 21, 1999.
17. "The Swedish Way of Laundering," Ian Taylor, *Contemporary Review*, 1997.
18. Information drawn from Taylor, "The Swedish Way of Laundering."
19. Source: Scandinavian Studies.
20. "A Nordic and European Tragedy," *The Economist*, Sept. 13, 2003.
21. Sources: *Billboard* and *Wikipedia, The Free Encyclopedia* (en.wikipedia.org).

Chapter 15: Finland
1. Fortes Global 2000 for 2005.
2. "Shouting Men of Finland Perform Ice Break," BBC News, Mar. 2, 2004.

3. Peter Stalker, *Oxford Handbook of the World*, Oxford: Oxford University Press, 2000.

4. Paija Ali-Yrkkö and Ylä-Anttila Reilly, "Nokia: A Big Company in a Small Country," ETLA Series B 162, Taloustieto Oy, Helsinki, as noted in "Finnfacts."

5. Tomi T. Ahonen, "In Search of the Killer Applications of 3G" (http://www.conted .ox.ac.uk/cpd/electronics/links/killer_applications_for_3g.asp).

6. According to the 2003 PISA survey conducted by the OECD.

7. Source: Finnish Sauna Society (www.sauna.fin).

8. Source: "Finland Battles High Suicide Rate," Reuters, Dec.8, 2003.

9. Saska Snellman, "The Pies Have It," *Helsingin Sanomat*, Apr. 10, 2001.

10. Source: Mario De Biasi, *Meet the Finns*, as noted by Finnish Foreign Ministry's Virtual Finland Web site (http://formin.finland.fi/).

11. Source: *Wikipedia, The Free Encyclopedia* (en.wikipedia.org).

Chapter 16: Luxembourg

1. Forbes Global 2000 for 2005

2. "Alcohol Consumption," *The Economist*, July 1, 2004.

3. Much information in this section draws upon "Brief Historical Survey of the War Years in Luxembourg" by Roland Gaul, published on the Luxembourg tourism Web site (www.luxembourg.co.uk).

Chapter 17: Poland

1. Forbes Global 2000 for 2005.

2. "Transatlantic Trends 2005—Topline Data 2005," published by German Marshall Fund of the United States.

3. Michale Jeziorski, "The State of Arms," *Warsaw Voice*, May 26, 2004.

4. Robert Pearce, "Josef Klemenis Pilsudski: Robert Pearce Introduces the Man Who Has Been Called the 'George Washington of Poland.'" *History Review*, Sept. 1, 2003.

5. Ibid.

6. Source: Holocaust Learning Center.

7. Jan Stopasal, "Creative Bloc," *Time International*, May 20, 2002.

8. Peter Stalker, *Oxford Handbook of the World*. Oxford: Oxford University Press, 2000: p. 255.

9. The report, the PAN "Committee of Prognosis—Poland in the 21st Century," is discussed in depth by Czeslaw Mojsiewicz, "Fears and Doubts in Poland: Internal Obstacles to European Integration," *World Affairs*, Vol.158, Sept. 1, 1995.

10. Source: *Kaleidoscope* magazine, Sept. 1994; also see: www.polishvodka.com .pl/bisons.htm.

11. Source: United States Holocaust Memorial Center.

12. "Death of a mythmaker," *Newsweek*, May 13, 1991.

13. Information mostly derived from the article by Szydlo Zbigniew and Richard Brzezinski, "A New Light on Alchemy," *History Today*, Vol.47, Jan. 1, 1997.

Chapter 18: Hungary

1. Forbes Global 2000 for 2005.
2. See: Kristen Schweitzer, "Shadows of Poverty, Business Hungary," publication of American Chamber of Commerce in Hungary, September 2003 (http://www.am-cham.hu/BusinessHUngary/17-08/articles/17-08_34.asp).
3. See: Kristen Schweitzer, "Shadows of Poverty, Business Hungary," publication of American Chamber of Commerce in Hungary, September 2003 (http://www.amcham.hu/BusinessHUngary/17-08/articles/17-08_34.asp). Some say closer to 30%.
4. Allies invaded in 1918 at the close of World War I; Czech, Slovaks, and Romanians invaded in 1919; Nazis invaded in 1944 when Hungary tried to change teams; Soviets invaded in 1945 to chase Nazis out; and Soviets invaded again in 1956 to put down a revolution.
5. F. Branfman, "In Search of the Hungarian Soul," *Budapest Week*, June 2, 1992.
6. American Foundation for Suicide Prevention.
7. "Hungary 1956," History Learning Site (www.historylearningsite.co.uk/hungary_1956.htm).
8. So believe some Hungarian journalists who prefer to remain unnamed.
9. "Those Heroic Days . . . ," *Facts About Hungary*, ed. Imre Kovacs (New York, Hungarian Committee, 1958), pp. 83–68. See: Richard Lettis, "The Hungarian Revolt," Hungarian-history.com (http://www.hungarian-history.hu/lib/revolt/rev03.htm).
10. As quoted on http://historylearningsite.co.uk/hungary_1956.htm.
11. "Viktor Orbán, an Assertive Hungarian," *The Economist*, Feb.28, 2002.
12. Ibid.
13. Helen Connolly, "Hungary for New Leadership," *The Guardian* (London), Apr. 10, 2002.
14. Peter Sanfey and Utku Teksoz, "Does Transition Make You Happy?" European Bank for Reconstruction and Development, June 2005; suicide rates source: WHO.
15. Simon Araloff, "Russia to Pay for Hungary's Reform," Axis Information and Analysis, May 10, 2006.
16. Michael Kovrig, "Splitsville in Old Hungary," *U.S. News and World Report*, Aug. 7, 2000.
17. OECD figures for 2000; OECD notes that the percentage of obesity might be even higher.
18. Margaret McMillan, *Paris 1919: Six Months That Changed the World*. New York: Random House, 2001: p. 265.

Chapter 19: Baltic States: Estonia, Latvia, and Lithuania

1. Interview with author, April 2004.
2. "Estonia Minister Rails Against the West's Arrogance," Reuters, Dec. 14, 1999.
3. Michael Tarm, "The Forgotten War," *City Paper* (The Baltic States), 1996 (http://www.balticsww.com/forgotten.htm).

4. Ibid.
5. Interview with author, April 2004.
6. Susan B. Glasser, "Tensions with Russia Propel Baltic States Toward NATO," *The Washington Post*, Oct. 7, 2002.
7. "The Baltic States: Knocking at the Clubhouse Door," *The Economist*, Aug. 30, 2001.

Chapter 20: Estonia

1. "The Top 1,000 Companies of Central Europe 2005," Central European Capital Ltd., 2005.
2. Lonely Planet World Guide: Destination Estonia (www.lonelyplanet.com/destinations/europe/estonia/htm).
3. "The Top Ten Misconceptions about Estonia," *City Paper* (The Baltic States).
4. Estonia Guide, *City Paper* (The Baltic States).
5. "The Baltic Bobsleigh," *The Economist*, Feb. 5, 1998.
6. Source: *Helsingin Sanomat*.

Chapter 21: Latvia

1. "The Top 1,000 Companies of Central Europe 2005," Central European Capital Ltd., 2005.
2. Interview with the author, March 2004.
3. Interview with author, March 2004.
4. Interview with author, March 2004.
5. So says Frank Brown, *Newsweek International*, Nov. 3, 2003.
6. "Latvia History: A Brief Chronology," *City Paper* (The Baltic States) (www.balticsww.com/tourist/latvia/history.htm).

Chapter 22: Lithuania

1. "The Top 1,000 Companies of Central Europe 2005," Central European Capital Ltd., 2005.
2. Margaret MacMillan, *Paris 1919: Six Months That Changed the World*. New York: Random House, 2001.
3. "Lithuanian Government Declares War Against Rampaging Crime," *Itar-Tass*, Jan. 18, 1997.
4. Liudas Dapkas, "Lithuanians Are Tired of Outspoken Leader . . . ," Associated Press, July 26, 1998.
5. Lithuania Guide, *City Paper* (The Baltic States).

Chapter 23: Former Czechoslovakia: Czech Republic and Slovak Republic

1. Kenneth Banta, "In a secluded wood 55 miles east of Prague . . . ," *Time International*, Mar. 26, 1990.
2. BBC: "On this Day—1968: Russia Brings Winter to Prague Spring."
3. David Corn, "Frank Zappa: Trading Partner," *The Nation*, Mar. 19, 1990.

Chapter 24: Czech Republic

1. Forbes Global 2000 for 2005.
2. Gareth Harding, "Proud Czechs Refuse to Be EU Pawns," United Press International, Apr. 22, 2004.
3. Francis Harris, "Czech Gangs Kidnap Women as Sex Slaves," *The Sunday Telegraph* (London), Mar. 8, 1998.
4. Jan Stojaspal, "In Winning Form? . . . ," *Time International*, June 17, 2002.

Chapter 25: Slovak Republic

1. "The Top 1,000 Companies of Central Europe 2005," Central European Capital Ltd., 2005.
2. Knight Ridder News Service, June 22, 1999.
3. Peter Green, "School Text Glorifies Slovakia's Role as Nazi Puppet," *International Herald Tribune*, Aug. 13, 1997; "Skewed Book on Holocaust to Remain in Slovak Schools," *Jewish Telegraphic Agency*, July 11, 1997.
4. Peter Green, "School Text Glorifies Slovakia's Role as Nazi Puppet," *International Herald Tribune*, Aug. 13, 1997.

Chapter 26: Slovenia

1. "The Top 1,000 Companies in Central Europe 2005," Central European Capital Ltd., 2005.
2. Samantha Henry, "The Art of the Possible," *Newsday*, Feb.17, 2002.
3. Ibid.
4. Source: *Lonely Planet World Guide: Destination Slovenia* (www.lonelyplanet.com/destinations/europe/slovenia/).
5. Thanks to Jaka Bartolj.

Chapter 27: Cyprus

1. Source: *Lonely Planet World Guide: Destination Cyprus* (www.lonelyplanet.com/destinations/europe/cyprus/).

Chapter 28: Malta

1. So called by the George Cross Data collection board.
2. Some information in this section drawn from *Lonely Planet World Guide: Destination Malta* (www.lonelyplanet.com/destinations/europe/malta.htm).

Bibliography

Books

Blainey, Geoffrey. *A Very Short History of the World*. London: Penguin Allen Lane, 2004.

Booker, Christopher, and Richard North. *The Great Deception: Can the European Union Survive?* London: Continuum International, 2005.

Boorstin, Daniel J. *The Discoverers: A History of Man's Search to Know His World and Himself*. New York: Random House, 1985.

Cirlot, Juan Eduardo. *Gaudí: An Introduction to His Architecture*. New York: Triangle Postals, 2002.

Crow, John A. *Spain: The Root and the Flower*, 3rd ed. Berkeley: University of California Press, 1985.

Davies, Norman. *Europe: A History*. London: Pimlico, 1997.

Evans, Graham, and Jeffrey Newnham. *The Penguin Dictionary of International Relations*. London: Penguin Books, 1998.

Ferguson, Niall. *Empire: How Britain Made the World*. London: Penguin, 2004.

Fisher, H. A. L. *A History of Europe, Vols. I and II*. London: Fontana, 1970.

Fox, Kate. *Watching the English: The Hidden Rules of English Behaviour*. London: Hodder and Stoughton, Ltd., 2005.

Gilmour, David. *Cities of Spain*. Chicago: Ivan R. Dee, 1992.

Hochschild, Adam. *King Leopold's Ghost: A Story of Greed, Terror, and Heroism in Colonial Africa*. New York: Mariner Books, 1999.

Hooper, John. *The New Spaniards*. London: Penguin, 1995.

Libbon, Robert P. *Instant European History: From the French Revolution to the Cold War*. New York: Fawcett, 1996.

Library of Congress Country Studies for all countries.

Martin, Russell. *Picasso's War: The Destruction of Guernica and the Masterpiece That Changed the World*. New York: Plume, 2003.

McCauley, Lucy, ed. *Travelers' Tales: Spain*. San Francisco: Travelers' Tales, 1998.

McEvedy, Colin. *The Penguin Atlas of Recent History: Europe Since 1815*. New York: Penguin, 2002.

MacMillan, Margaret. *Paris 1919: Six Months that Changed the World*. New York: Random House, 2003.

Nadeau, Jean-Benoit, and Julie Barlow. *Sixty Million Frenchmen Can't Be Wrong: What Makes the French So French*. London: Robson Books, 2004.

Norman, Peter. *The Accidental Constitution: The Making of Europe's Constitutional Treaty*. Brussels: EuroComment, 2003.

Orwell, George. *Orwell in Spain*. London: Penguin, 2001.

Reid, T. R. *The United States of Europe: The New Superpower and the End of American Supremacy*. London: Penguin, 2004.

Roberts, J. M. *The Penguin History of Europe*. New York: Penguin, 1999.

Stalker, Peter. *Oxford Handbook of the World*. New York: Oxford University Press, 2001.

Viault, Birdsall S. *Modern European History*. New York: McGraw-Hill, 1990.

Newspapers, Magazines, Broadcast Media, and Online Resources

The Baltic Times
Budapest Week
The Christian Science Monitor
City Paper—The Baltic States
Columbia Journalism Review
Contemporary Review
The Daily Telegraph
Der Spiegel
Economist
El País
EUbusiness.com
EUobserver.com
The European
Forbes
The Guardian (London)
Helsingin Sanomat
History Review
The Independent
International Herald Tribune
The Jakarta Post
The Jerusalem Post
Le Monde Diplomatique
Lonely Planet Country Guides
The Nation
National Geographic
The New Republic
New Statesman
New Scotsman
Newsweek
The New York Times
The New Yorker
The Observer (London)

Searchlight
Time
US News & World Report
The Wall Street Journal
The Washington Post

ABC News
Associated Press
BBC
CBS News: *60 Minutes*
CNN
National Public Radio
PBS
Radio Free Europe
Radio Netherlands
Radio Prague
Reuters

Columbia Encyclopedia
Common Dreams (www.commondreams.org)
Enchanted Learning (www.enchantedlearning.com)
The European Union Online (http://europa.eu.int)
Europe Direct (http://europa.eu.int/europedirect)
Lonely Planet (www.lonelyplanet.com)
Microsoft Encarta
Wikipedia, the Free Encyclopedia (http://en.wikipedia.org)
Government Web Sites for all countries
Tourism sites for all countries

Index